BRUCE DORSEY

Reforming

GENDER IN THE

Men and

ANTEBELLUM CITY

Women

Cornell University Press

Ithaca and London

First published 2002 by Cornell University Press
First printing, Cornell Paperbacks, 2006

Printed in the United States of America

Library of Congress Cataloging-in-Publication Data

Dorsey, Bruce, 1960–
 Reforming men and women : gender in the antebellum city / Bruce
Dorsey.
   p. cm.
 ISBN-13: 978-0-8014-3897-4 (cloth: alk. paper)
 ISBN-10: 0-8014-3897-7 (cloth: alk. paper)
 ISBN-13: 978-0-8014-7288-6 (pbk.: alk. paper)
 ISBN-10: 0-8014-7288-1 (pbk.: alk. paper)
  1. Sex role—United States—History—18th century.   2. Sex
role—United States—History—19th century.   3. Social reformers—United
States—History—18th century.   4. Social reformers—United
States—History—19th century.   5. Social problems—United
States—History—18th century.   6. Social problems—United
States—History—19th century.   I. Title.
  HQ1075.5.U6 D67 2002
  305.3'0973—dc21   2001008380

Cornell University Press strives to use environmentally
responsible suppliers and materials to the fullest extent
possible in the publishing of its books. Such materials
include vegetable-based, low-VOC inks and acid-free papers
that are recycled, totally chlorine-free, or partly composed
of nonwood fibers. For further information, visit our website at
www.cornellpress.cornell.edu.

Cloth printing   10 9 8 7 6 5 4 3 2 1
Paperback printing   10 9 8 7 6 5 4 3 2 1

Reforming

Men and

Women

For Tim

Contents

Acknowledgments

A different kind of benevolence of spirit and resources made this book possible. I am grateful to the Pew Program in Religion and American History at Yale University, the Center for the Study of American Religion at Princeton University, the McNeil Center for Early American Studies at the University of Pennsylvania, the Library Company of Philadelphia, and the Historical Society of Pennsylvania for their generous support of my research and writing. I also thank the remarkable archivists and librarians of the Library Company of Philadelphia, the Historical Society of Pennsylvania, the American Philosophical Society, the Presbyterian Historical Society, the Philadelphia City Archives, the American Antiquarian Society, the National Archives, the Library of Congress, the Princeton University Library, the Rare Book Collection in the Van Pelt Library at the University of Pennsylvania, the John Hay Library at Brown University, the Quaker Collection at Haverford College, and the Friends Historical Library at Swarthmore College for guiding me through their collections.

It has been my good fortune to be associated with Swarthmore College, a unique place of intellectual excellence and collegial learning, where the ideas and spirit of this book and its author have been nurtured. I thank the college for its financial support through faculty research funds, Joel Dean Student-Faculty Research Grants, and the James A. Michener Faculty Fellowship, all of which made possible invaluable time for research and reflection. For countless conversations and scholarly good fellowship, I thank Tim Burke, Robert Bannister, Yvonne Chireau, Leslie Delauter, Allison Dorsey, Robert DuPlessis, J. William Frost, Michel Gobat, Laura Gotkowitz, Nora

Johnson, Pieter Judson, Jason McGill, Marjorie Murphy, and Carol Nackenoff. I also extend my appreciation to all former students who have inspired me with their dedication to learning and unknowingly helped me to refine the ideas for this book; and I offer special thanks to my capable research assistants: Joshua Silver, Tim Stewart-Winter, Sarah Yahm, and especially Cecilia Tsu.

Numerous scholars have given liberally of their time and deliberation to assist me with this book. William McLoughlin was an early inspiration for this project and an extraordinary dissertation advisor. Mari Jo Buhle has been a wonderful guide into the history of gender, and she has graciously read countless versions of papers, articles, and chapters since I began this project. I am indebted to many people for reading portions of this manuscript or for helpful discussions of its content: Nancy Ammerman, Mia Bay, Gail Bederman, Mari Jo Buhle, Tim Burke, Mark Carnes, Jim Cullen, Konstantin Dierks, Toby Ditz, Richard Dunn, J. William Frost, David Hackett, Dallett Hemphill, Susan Juster, Sarah Knott, Naomi Lamoreaux, John Landry, David Lehman, Jan Lewis, Carol Nackenoff, Gary Nash, Louise Newman, Tony Rotundo, Leigh Schmidt, Lyde Sizer, Jean Soderlund, Michael Topp, Deborah Gray White, Donald Yacovone, and Michael Zuckerman. I also thank the participants in the seminars at the McNeil Center for Early American Studies, the Black Atlantic Project at Rutgers University, the Fellows Conference of the Pew Program in Religion and American History, and the Center for the Study of American Religion at Princeton University. Their thoughtful questions challenged me to write and interpret with greater passion and nuance. It has been a pleasure to work with Peter Agree, John Ackerman, and Sheri Englund at Cornell University Press, and I wish to thank them for their unwavering confidence. I also thank the *Journal of Social History* for permission to reprint portions of my previously published article, "A Gendered History of African Colonization in the Antebellum United States" (vol. 34, fall 2000).

Martha Hodes read every word of this manuscript and offered her brilliant insights at every turn. There is no idea in this book that was not first tried out in conversations with her or in drafts that she painstakingly read. My vision as a historian and a writer has expanded with every one of our discussions. Her impassioned desire that our writing about the past make a difference in the present has inspired me. Woody Register generously read the entire manuscript. His demands for conceptual and narrative clarity have made this a better book. I want also to thank the readers for Cornell University Press for their careful reading and discerning commentary.

Friends and family have sustained me and enriched my life while I was writing this book. I thank my parents, David Dorsey and Betty Dorsey, for teaching me to believe in myself and to place no limits on what I can accomplish. I am grateful for the love and good fellowship I continually receive from Connie Cashman, Ruth Purcell, Chris Purcell, Jon Dorsey, and Joanne Dorsey, and their families. Carol Manson, Karen Howell, and John Howell have given me their enduring friendship and heartfelt support. Peter Littman and Becky Blythe opened their home and their lives to me, introduced me to surfing, and joined me in thoroughly engaging dinner conversations that only occasionally drifted into the history of masculinity. Konstanin Dierks has been a steady and loving friend, a trusted confidante, and a generous scholar with whom I look forward to many more years of shared interests and political passions. Sarah Knott has recently become a dear friend and generous colleague. Woody Register has been a devoted friend, a never-ending source of encouragement, and a trusted companion on the difficult journeys of an academic life. I owe him my deep gratitude. I want also to thank Shelley Jodoin, for her support during this book's beginnings, for her great courage, and for being an extraordinary mother to my son.

My love for two other people transcends the process of writing this book. I wish to thank my son, Timothy Dorsey, for his boundless enthusiasm for life, for the patient ways he teaches me, for the loving life we share together, and for his promising future as a man who always questions the injustices in this world. It is only fitting that I dedicate this book to him. Martha Hodes is a gift from God to me. I am a better person and historian for knowing her. She is my inspiration, my soul-mate, my muse, and my partner in love and life. I owe her my gratitude and my love in ways that are too deep to capture fully in words.

Reforming

Men and

Women

Prologue

In the manuscript room at the Historical Society of Pennsylvania, turning
back and forth through the pages of two fraying leather volumes, I
double-checked the dates to make sure. Someone had suggested to me
just days before that nineteenth-century reformers were a wordy and musing
bunch. But I had not expected to see those musings so similarly rendered by
men and women. Those dusty volumes were the diaries of Mary and Lewis
Ashhurst, who both began to keep personal journals in January 1834. Both
twenty-seven years old and married for three years, the Ashhursts had one in-
fant son and had recently experienced the death of another. They were a
prosperous white couple who had lived all their years in Philadelphia. Lewis
was an aspiring entrepreneur, expecting soon to become a junior partner in
a center-city mercantile firm. They attended the "thoroughly evangelical" St.
Paul's Episcopal Church and found an outlet for their evangelical zeal in numerous benevolent societies and charities. Both also found a space for their
spiritual introspection in their respective journals.[1]

On exactly the same day, February 5, 1834, perhaps inspired by a recent
sermon, Mary and Lewis wrote remarkably similar entries, each expressing
anxieties about their abilities to exert an "influence" on family and friends.
Lewis wrote: "How little influence in religious views, am I able to exercise on
my own family. O Lord help me to amend defects in my character, and to be
faithful to their souls." Mary's entry sounded the same theme: "Fear that instead of exerting any religious influence among my friends I am only becoming too much interested in their worldly concerns."[2] That this white
middle-class husband and wife chose to think and write about "influence"

1

reveals a great deal about the history of gender and reform in the antebellum United States. No other term possessed a deeper set of gendered meanings in that culture. "Influence," when used in a positive way, signified the private regenerative quality of womanhood that mobilized both conservative and radical defenses of women's activism and defined benevolent work as essentially feminine. However, it also exposed the ambivalent place that reform-minded men occupied in that feminized culture of reform. And when used in a negative way, "influence" connoted the corrupting masculine temptations and deceptions that young men faced in the city. In all cases, its meanings were shaped by evolving notions of gender. For Lewis, this proved to be the first and only mention of familial influence in his diary. While he remained introspective, Lewis focused his anxieties instead on his own character and his public usefulness in church and reform work. But Mary repeated her concern for a domestic influence throughout the subsequent pages of her journal as she endeavored to lead various relatives and household servants toward an evangelical conversion. She also carried that concern for influence into her activism outside the home. When visiting city neighborhoods for her tract society, she attempted "to influence a woman to give up keeping a dram shop," just as on another occasion, she tried to influence a female beggar to live a more temperate life.[3]

The significance of this snapshot of two lives rests in the totality of their experience together, as man and woman—and all that those categories meant to them. Simply to view this as a reflection of how Mary and Lewis inhabited distinctly "separate spheres"—a public life for him and a private retreat for her—distorts the shared experiences of these two young evangelicals. Both were benevolent activists and reformers; both participated actively in Sunday school, tract, missionary, temperance, and colonization societies. And yet, even as we glimpse a moment when that shared conception of religious activism might have been a means of bridging their differences, we can see that they encountered that moment—and the gendered meanings embedded in it—in distinctly different ways.[4] To understand more fully the lives of northern reformers in the years between the Revolution and the Civil War, it is imperative to examine gender as a whole, not only to investigate the experiences of both men and women reformers, but also to interrogate the ideological processes by which reformers invoked concepts and symbols of the masculine and the feminine to fashion and advance their reform agendas, and how those imaginings of gender shaped the ways reformers marked the boundaries of race, nation, and class in the early years of nation-building in the United States.

Historians have passed through two distinct phases in their interpretations of antebellum reformers during the second half of the twentieth century. From World War II until well into the 1970s, historians explained benevolent societies as part of evangelical revivals and a perceived hegemonic Protestant national culture during the early republic. Two seminal books published in 1960 by Clifford Griffin and Charles Foster established this conceptual framework, and coined phrases such as "united evangelical front" and "evangelical benevolent empire" that shaped a generation's language about pre–Civil War reformers. This first wave of historical writing concentrated on the major national organizations—the American Bible Society, American Sunday School Union, American Temperance Society, American Anti-Slavery Society, and others—and on the men who ran them: wealthy merchants, businessmen, and enterprising clergymen. During this period, historians' interpretations centered on issues of status anxiety, positing the thesis that these reformers desired and exerted some measure of social control over the objects of their benevolence or over the laboring classes in general.[5] This focus on male reformers and issues of social control continued through the 1970s. By then, practitioners of the new social history exposed the profound transformations within local communities resulting from industrialization, thereby giving a more sophisticated expression to the social control thesis; yet the first wave of social history scholarship did not contest a narrative that assumed reformers to be elite white men.[6]

A second phase in the historiography of antebellum reformers coincided with the growth of women's history, which challenged for the first time the preoccupation of antebellum historians with male reformers. Historians of women asserted not only that women were present in grassroots benevolent and reform societies, but also that women frequently surpassed men in their zeal and commitment to this form of activism. Beginning with the work of Nancy Cott, Mary Ryan, and Carroll Smith-Rosenberg in the late 1970s, and continuing with the contributions of Nancy Hewitt, Suzanne Lebsock, and Lori Ginzberg in the 1980s, women's historians resurrected reform activism as a space where American women (by which they typically meant middle-class white women) expanded the boundaries of a constrictive gender ideology and created for themselves a visible public presence in antebellum communities. The primary agenda of this history involved discovering a women's culture within reform activities, determining whether a sisterhood of women transcended race or class divisions and exploring the social functions that reform played in white middle-class women's lives.[7] I am deeply indebted to this scholarship. It provides the proverbial shoulders on which this book stands. And yet I wish to push its conceptual boundaries farther and offer a broader history of pre–Civil War reformers.

This book expands the analytical framework for writing the history of gender and reform in antebellum America. It advances the premise that categories of both manhood and womanhood are critical for understanding antebellum reformers and that those categories were inextricably bound together in the reforming work that men and women shared. The book portrays a holistic history of gender and reform by documenting and exploring the life experiences of both men and women reformers, and the contested meanings of manhood and womanhood among urban Americans, both black and white, working class and middle class, in the antebellum North. More than simply bridging the gap between two phases of the historical literature on reform, I offer a different perspective on the history of topics— antislavery, temperance, poor relief, and nativism—that have produced a trail of historical interpretations. The newness of the interpretation rests not in its use of gender as a category of analysis, but in how it portrays both men and women as gendered beings.

This quest for a holistic history of gender has been informed by the direction that gender studies has taken over the past decade or more. Prophetic voices, such as those of Gerda Lerner and Natalie Zemon Davis, insisted as early as the mid-1970s that the history of gender must encompass more than merely an analysis of the lives of women. In Davis's words: "It seems to me that we should be interested in the history of both women and men, that we should not be working only on the subjected sex any more than an historian of class can focus exclusively on peasants. Our goal is to understand the significance of the *sexes*, of gender groups in the historical past."[8] This book shares that objective. It is part of an intellectual quest to engender all of American history, a quest in which my work does not stand alone. I have been influenced by feminist scholarship whose premise is that gender is a historical, ideological process and that gender has been a principal signifier of power throughout history.[9]

Historians of gender are keenly aware that what people in the past designate as gender—the meanings they attribute to "man" and "woman"—has depended on how those historical actors constructed concepts of difference and developed a language for distinct groups of others. Most commonly, gender has functioned so that "man" is constituted as the binary opposite of "woman," and "woman" as the opposite of "man." In other words, what proves that a man is definitely a man is that he is not a woman. Gender has also been a way for historical actors to naturalize inequalities by positing corresponding references to the presumed naturalness of men and women's bodies. But constructing gender on the foundation of difference has never been limited exclusively to the conceptual opposites of male or female. Over time, gender has been constituted against a backdrop of many other contrary images. As Caroline Walker Bynum has noted, "Gender-related symbols, in their full complexity, may refer to gender in ways that affirm or reverse it, support or question it; or they may, in their basic meaning, have little at all to do with male and female roles."[10] Recently, historians of gender in America have disclosed the ways in which class and racial difference in-

formed dominant gender conventions, shaping the meanings of both masculinity and femininity. Whether this manifested itself in working-class men
linking whiteness to manhood or turn-of-the-century bourgeois men and
women employing gendered and racial discourses of civilization, ideologies
about class and race shaped the meaning of gender for Americans in the
past. To say this in another way, in different historical contexts, some men
have attempted to prove that a man was truly a man because he was not, for
example, a boy, a slave, a savage, a primitive, an American Indian, a Mexican,
or a Chinese.[11] Gender history exposes the patterns of exclusion that define
equality and inequality in a society and the relationships of power that maintain those boundaries.

The history of gender needs to disclose, then, the indistinct lines that de-
lineated public and private, or the visible and invisible, in a society. Scholars
in eighteenth-century studies and feminist critics of Jürgen Habermas's theory of the public sphere have highlighted the unstable boundaries between
public and private in the late eighteenth century.[12] A deeper understanding
of public actions in that age requires an examination of the discursive interplay of notions of patriotism, religious duty, and the passions, as well as contemporary meanings of "public" and "private." The historical development
of visibility is equally complex. Part of the irony of gender construction is
that men and women, and the categories of man and woman, can be both
extremely visible and yet wholly invisible at exactly the same moment. This
was certainly true in the early American republic. For example, when white
women were assuming an undeniably visible economic presence as northern communities made the transition to market capitalism following the
Revolution, they were also made invisible ideologically by a discourse that
defined production and commerce as exclusively masculine attributes. At
the same time that all women were consciously excluded from full citizenship and participation in the body politic, white women were made conspicuous as the symbols of Columbia, liberty, and virtue on the one hand and
the symbols of public danger—irrationality, seduction, prostitution, and
luxury—on the other. Although men remained overly visible in the public
realm of politics and commerce in the new republic, they remained
strangely invisible to themselves (and to later historians) as gendered subjects. Women were considered "the sex," while men spoke a language that
positioned themselves as the universal. This is perhaps what Joan Scott
means when she writes "that 'man' and 'woman' are at once empty and
overflowing categories."[13] The historian's challenge, then, lies in emptying
the full vessels and filling the empty ones; this entails reading the silences as
well as listening to the prominent voices that surrounded the construction
of gender in American culture.

Religion and reform offer ideal sites for exploring this type of analytically complex gender history. Both gender and religion have commonly been constituted as moral systems, employing language and performance rituals that both embody and prescribe values. Religious reform, therefore, can illustrate well the blurred boundaries between public and private in early America.[14] Moreover, religious activism stands among the rare arenas of nineteenth-century life where men's and women's lives and identities very closely intersected. Hardly any instances of benevolent or reform work were the exclusive province of men or women. Women created and administered societies, made policy decisions, influenced public officials and institutions, raised money, visited the needy, and distributed spiritual or temporal assistance, just as men did. Both single and married women performed economic and political actions as reformers that otherwise might have been closed to them in a patriarchal legal system, often paralleling and even competing with their husbands, fathers, and brothers. Reform activism, therefore, became a space in which men and women debated, disagreed, and at times reconciled their shifting understandings of gender with their own actions and experiences.[15]

Because this is also a book about the history of masculinity in America, I hope to suggest a set of directions for the historical interpretation of early American manhood while this field is yet in its formative stages. One part of this effort involves exposing and analyzing the rival images of manhood that developed within northern communities between the Revolution and the Civil War. While much of the initial writing on the history of early American manhood has concentrated on white middle-class men and the symbols of manhood that they engendered, this book expands the canvas of gender history by also exploring the multiple constructions of working-class, immigrant, and black manhood in this era. White manhood in the antebellum United States cannot be fully understood without examining how white men forged their identities in response to the masculine identity and classification of, say, black men or Irish immigrant men. Yet more important, the manliness enacted by African American and Irish men themselves reveals the creative performances of masculine identity by marginalized men in America that were neither entirely nor exclusively a reaction to dominant ideals of manhood that white men promoted.

Northern communities experienced an immense social transformation during the first half-century of the new republic, an often bewildering array of changes in social relationships, political expressions, print technologies, and spatial organizations. If a Rip Van Winkle had slept through Washington Irving's own adult lifetime, he would have witnessed a world starkly different from the one he knew before his long slumber. Three interrelated developments, in particular, altered the features of society in the northern states between the American Revolution and the Civil War. Each of these developments was pivotal to the maturing sectional identity of the North, and each posed a specific set of problems that troubled reform-minded individuals and influenced the reform solutions they proposed during the antebellum years.

First, in the years after the Revolution, Americans in the North were forced to confront the demise of a system of bound labor and then to adjust to a different configuration of labor that affected the lives of both workers and those who built their livelihoods upon the labor of others. Historians have devoted surprisingly little attention to the consequences stemming from the end of unfree labor (both white servitude and black slavery) in the North, despite the fact that northern cities had previously relied heavily on bound labor, at least until the Revolution. In New York City, for instance, slaves made up 20 percent of the population and between one-third and one-half of the labor force in 1750, and white indentured servants accounted for an equal proportion of laborers. In Philadelphia, on the eve of the Revolution, more than one-third of the city's laborers were bound in service to someone else. After the Revolution, however, the use of bound labor decreased rapidly. White indentured servitude quickly fell into disuse; and black bondage had completely disappeared in Philadelphia by 1800, thanks to black and white efforts alike.[16] In the wake of bound labor's demise, the concepts of *slave, servant,* and *dependent* still retained powerful symbolic meanings; white laborers actively resisted using the label "master" for their employers or "servant" for themselves. The poor found themselves disengaged from a traditional system where support had rested in paternalism and the household, and now confronted the perilous whims of a wage-labor economy and the frayed public safety net of poor relief. Finally, the end of bound labor meant a blossoming of communities of former slaves who created a collective life as free men and women, despite glaring reminders that their freedom was constrained and limited in a white republic.[17]

A second major transformation corresponded to a cluster of events that historians now commonly refer to as "the market revolution." Expanding export trade during the European wars between 1790 and 1815, combined with expansive transportation technologies in the years after 1815, produced an economic landscape in which Northerners, both in cities and in the countryside, increasingly encountered international and domestic markets for foodstuffs and manufactured goods. Traditional household economies began to wither under the assault of land and population pressures, the pervasive increase in outwork, and the concomitant rise of industrialization during the antebellum years. Northern cities remained at the forefront of this transformation. Urban working men and women experienced this change most directly as the commodification of numerous facets of their lives and, most important, as a dependence on wage labor for their sustenance and livelihood.[18] For the new urban middle class, the market revolution meant a justification for personal ambition, an increasing identity with nonmanual occupations, and a paradoxical attachment to and detachment from a rising consumer society. The rise of wage labor and a new market economy combined to confirm a separate bourgeois class identity.[19]

A third major development that shaped northern society was the making of American nationalism and the expansion of a U.S. empire in the antebellum years. At its core, this involved the ideological project of determining who constituted the nation (or "the people," in the republican language of the era). Urban dwellers in the Northeast did not have to migrate to western territories or fight Indians or Mexicans for additional land to participate in the fashioning of nationalism in the United States. They helped to delineate the boundaries of the nation every time they debated or fought over who should be included among the citizens of the republic. Those issues certainly arose in the reactions to American Indian removal in the 1830s and the Mexican War in the 1840s. But they also emerged as Northerners responded to the problem of slavery and the position of free African Americans in the nation; they arose as well when native-born residents and Irish-born immigrants fought over the citizenship rights of education and suffrage in the cities of Boston, Philadelphia, and New York. Colonizationist, abolitionist, and nativist movements were intimately connected to the controversies surrounding American nationalism, as were the violent riots that ensued in the wake of each of these reforms.[20]

Few historians have associated antebellum reform movements with the project of empire- and nation-building in the nineteenth century, but antebellum Americans clearly did. Catharine Beecher certainly recognized the connection. In the opening chapter of her *Treatise on Domestic Economy* (1847), entitled "The Peculiar Responsibilities of American Women," she not only linked the subordination of women to these three transformations in northern society, but she also asserted that women's domesticity could be an active agent in conquering the "barbarous" and the "foreign," both within and outside the geographical boundaries of the United States.[21]

These three developments—the end of bound labor, the rise of a market-driven and wage-labor economy, and conflicts over the nature of the citizenry—provide the backdrop for nearly all the reform movements that appeared in the North before the Civil War. They constitute themes that course through a gendered narrative of antebellum reform like streams flowing toward the ocean. A few brief illustrations will make this clear. The meaning of *dependence*—a concept with obvious gendered import—remained inextricably tied to the demise of bound labor and the rise of a liberal market economy in the new republic. Poverty, and its relationship to the population of newly freed slaves, thus evoked concerns about shoring up the boundaries between independence and dependence. Reformers likewise cast the problem of excessive drinking as dependence and its solution as independence. Little wonder, then, that temperance activists became obsessed with the rhetoric and symbolism of the American Revolution and its ubiquitous references to independence. Images of wage labor (or, as white antebellum Northerners called it, "free labor") and slavery were likewise woven into the controversies surrounding colonization and abolitionism. Yet it is important to remember that concepts of slavery and dependence appeared just as commonly during disputes over increased Irish Catholic immigration to northern cities, proving how crucial they were to defining citizenship rights for black and white Americans alike.

To illustrate these themes, this book is organized around several specific sets of problems that northern reformers wished to redress in the years between the American Revolution and the Civil War.[22] Chapter 1 explores the ways in which the stage was set for the gendering of reform activism in the nineteenth century. It examines the question of why the post-revolutionary age produced a particular climate of gender ambiguity that linked notions of manhood with activism in a masculine public sphere and yet, for the first time, also created a space for a new and expanding public presence for reforming women. After exposing the contestability of gender in the revolutionary age and the ways in which women activists exploited those ambiguities to assert a visible role in reform, the next four chapters address four particular problems that inspired numerous and often competing reform societies and movements in the early nineteenth century. This book cannot hope to be a study of all reform movements in the antebellum era, for as Ralph Waldo Emerson once quipped, "What a fertility of projects for the salvation of the world!"[23] Centering each chapter around a particular problem, rather than around a reform movement, allows me to develop a gendered history of the full range of organizations and strategies that emerged in response to that issue. My objective in these chapters is not so much to advance a single narrative. Rather, I present in each of these four chapters a comprehensive analysis of the gendered construction of that major social problem and the ways in which gender shaped the reforms generated in response to it. Chapter 2 addresses the problem of poverty; chapter 3, the problem of drink; chapter 4, the problem of slavery; and chapter 5, the problem of Irish Catholic immigration.

The competing perspectives of male reformers and female activists, working-class and middle-class reforms, and white and black organizations can be juxtaposed in the same way that categories of manhood and womanhood must be in a holistic history of gender. Black and working-class activists have too often been ignored in a literature that has privileged white and middle-class voices. As a result, the myriad ways in which class, ethnicity, and race have fashioned the meanings of gender have been overlooked, and voices outside the white middle classes have been silenced or relegated to their own historical literatures. I have tried to redress that imbalance. Achieving a balance of the voices and perspectives of working-class, immigrant, and African American communities and their institutions, however, is much more difficult for the eighteenth century. Immediately after the Revolution, for instance, northern free black communities struggled against poverty and sought to create social institutions that could remedy their disproportionate hardships; but under these conditions they left behind only a smattering of written sources, with much less introspection for the historian to interpret. Within a few decades these circumstances changed considerably. By 1830, African Americans in the North were publishing their own newspapers, organizing their own national conventions, and creating networks of voluntary associations and other venues for the leadership of black reformers.

I have chosen to focus my analysis on the city of Philadelphia, but always within the larger context of similar developments throughout the urban North. This approach allows me to transcend the problem of typicality and uniqueness that plagued the earliest case studies of the new social history. Although Philadelphia was the republic's largest city during its first thirty years and a leading industrial center until well after the Civil War, to date no book on the history of religion or reform has been written on antebellum Philadelphia. This is particularly surprising since almost every kind of benevolent and reform society (prison, Bible, Sunday school, antislavery, and charity societies) appeared for the first time in this city. Philadelphia thus offers distinct advantages for an examination of the ways northern reformers responded to perceived social problems. After all, Philadelphia was at the forefront of the rapid transition from a bound-labor to a wage-labor economy after the Revolution. The community also exhibited nearly all of the characteristics and new measures of that era's religious awakening. Most important, as the southernmost northern city, Philadelphia possessed the nation's most vibrant free black community, allowing a comparison of black and white reformers and an exploration of the racial dynamic at the core of antebellum reform projects.

The book's first chapter explores the beginnings of reform activism in the United States, focusing an intense gaze on developments in Philadelphia immediately following the American Revolution. From that moment, the regional distinctiveness of the religious culture of colonial Philadelphia, rooted in the cultural prominence of Quakers, gave way to patterns of behavior that nearly all northern cities shared by the beginning of the nineteenth century. By then, Philadelphia's experiences closely mirrored those of Boston, New York, and other northern towns and cities, all of which were transformed in similar ways by the social changes associated with industrialization and the new market economy. Hence, this book tells a story of northern reformers that is set, more often than not, in the city of brotherly love.

CHAPTER 1

Gender and Reformers
in the New Republic

Let woman share the rights, and she will emulate the virtues of
man; for she must grow more perfect when emancipated.

MARY WOLLSTONECRAFT, *A Vindication of the Rights of Woman*
(1792)

I n December 1795, three weeks after a group of young white Quaker
women led by Anne Parrish created the nation's first female charitable
society in Philadelphia, John Marsillac, a Quaker physician, delivered to
them a cautionary letter. Marsillac envisioned a limited realm of action for
these women. He veiled his support for the new Female Society for the Relief
of the Distressed with fears that it might expose itself, as well as the Society of
Friends, to "slander and calumnies" if the women promised to assist more
poor persons than they reasonably could. Perhaps Marsillac's concerns also
arose because these benevolent women dispensed poor relief to people who
were not Friends, or, more likely, because the women visited and relieved
the poor of both sexes. He cautioned them to "consider whether it would
not be more beneficial to your estimable Labours if you limit yourselves to
distressed Women, particularly Widows and Orphans." For the sake of propriety,
these women assumed a deferential pose and copied Marsillac's letter directly into the Female Society's minutes. Their deference, however, extended only so far, and not far enough to alter significantly the scope of their
benevolence. The Female Society continued to aid impoverished women,
since they constituted a preponderance of Philadelphia's poor. They also
persisted in visiting and assisting a broad spectrum of the city's poor during
the 1790s—widows with or without children, entire families distressed by illness or injury, elderly men and women, free black men and women, and recent immigrants to the city.[1]

11

In this brief episode, the novelty of women organizing independent benevolent societies becomes apparent, as do the uncertain responses of men (especially those with benevolent aspirations of their own) to this novelty. Voluntary associations had existed for only a few decades in America's largest city, but in that short time they had already emerged as assemblies of men. At no previous time had a group of women staked such a claim as public women in this area, although it would certainly not be the last time they did so. Voluntary associations organized and operated exclusively by women grew exponentially in the early republic.[2] A group of African American women had, in fact, organized the Female Benevolent Society of St. Thomas, a mutual benefit society, at the African Church two years before these Quaker women began, but the Female Society was the first female charity organized independent of a church and providing general assistance to the poor rather than to dues-paying members. Within a year after founding the Female Society, women Friends also established separate charity school societies for black women and for poor white girls. Following their example over the next two decades, other white Protestant women created as many as a dozen new benevolent associations, including the Female Association for the Relief of Women and Children in Reduced Circumstances (1800), the Union Society for the Education of Poor Female Children (1804), and the Female Hospitable Society (1808). Confusion reigned, however, with respect to the boundaries of women's benevolence. Some men immediately criticized these actions, others expressed their favor, and still others waited and voiced a conflicted and equivocal attitude toward women's new societies.

This episode also reveals the first instance of conflict between men and women over the presence of women in the voluntary sector of public life.[3] It is likely that John Marsillac had begun to sense the disruption that these unmarried Quaker women could produce in the gendered arrangement of religious activism among eighteenth-century Friends. He might have also sensed the new challenge that these women's public actions posed for the masculine domain of voluntary associations and social welfare in the city. When white Protestant women began organizing benevolent societies in the 1790s, they stepped into an arena that was at once a customarily masculine space and also a newly formed stage of public activism. The complicated interaction of men and women reformers emanated from these circumstances, as well as from their responses to late-eighteenth-century discourses regarding religious activism and public service.

This chapter exposes the alternative paths by which women sanctioned a role as "public women" in their own minds and within prevailing religious and political discourses, despite misogynist associations with sexual disorder and prostitution bestowed on the notion of a "public woman" in the late eighteenth century. An ambiguously gendered discourse surrounding women's and men's civic actions during the revolutionary era opened a door for an empowered women's activism, and it produced a unique moment wherein men and women reformers negotiated a shared space for benevolent activity in the urban landscape. The republican revolutions in the eighteenth-century Atlantic world witnessed the emergence of a public sphere of ideas, print culture, sociability, and politics that developed in conjunction with a private sphere of civil society expressed through market exchange, property, virtues, and the family. Rather than being sharply defined and fundamentally opposed, notions of public and private were unstable and ambiguous in revolutionary America. In that uncertain gender milieu, men and women together created the public sphere of social and civic action out of the private sphere of individual conscience, before "public" and "private" came to mean a rigid dichotomy between the political and economic realm of men and the domestic realm of women in the nineteenth century.[4]

Historians have not yet adequately connected the debates regarding women and the public sphere during the American Revolution with developing gendered notions of religious activism. Previous studies have assumed that a nineteenth-century gendered ideology that conflated religious reform with femininity and moral motherhood flowed directly out of the eighteenth century. But the gender conventions of these two eras were not the same, nor should we assume that the ideology of domesticity was the uncomplicated and legitimate daughter of "republican motherhood." Rather, if we examine the ambiguities inherent in prevailing notions of white masculinity in the eighteenth century, we can see how they contributed greatly to the uncertainty of gender conventions in revolutionary America. When white and black men began organizing benevolent societies, masculine ideals based on independence and civic virtue became complicated by cultural discourses that emphasized feelings and sympathy. At this beginning moment of organized benevolence, African American men and women found they needed to act both collectively and individually to create their own institutions for education and poor relief, thereby exposing a charitable environment that promised them freedom, yet offered only white paternalism in its stead. Former slaves knew very well the promises and disappointments of the American Revolution, that the boundaries of citizenship and emancipation were tied to the meanings attached to established and evolving categories of men and manliness in the new nation.

This gender uncertainty created a juncture wherein independent women appeared more visibly, not only in an emerging market economy and new republican politics, but also in new female voluntary associations and benevolent societies. No fixed ideology had yet developed to interpret women's benevolent activism as the supposedly natural expression of a woman's different gender identity, rooted in maternity, domesticity, or nurturing compassion. Instead, reformers initially viewed women's humanitarian activism, in part, through the lens of civic virtue that was applied to both men and women. At the same time, the African American women and young unmarried Quaker women who created the first women's benevolent organizations in Philadelphia also found that they needed to exploit available models of spiritual authority—despite inherent implications of feminine disorder— to justify their presence in the public arenas of voluntary charity and reform. The new Quaker women's benevolent societies in fact opened a middle ground for young white women reformers between these two gender poles of masculine virtue and feminine spiritual authority.

It was the far-reaching ambiguities about men and masculine identity during the revolutionary era, then, that set the stage for an expanded presence of benevolent women in the public sphere. To see this gender system as a whole, we need to begin with an exploration of the historical construction of manhood in eighteenth-century America.

A Manly Independence

The language of public action and civic community during the era of the American Revolution was imbued with gendered meanings and symbols, with the prized values of independence, virtue, and citizenship carrying explicitly masculine associations. From the opening lines of Thomas Paine's *Common Sense* in 1776 through the debates over the federal Constitution in 1787, revolutionary discourse remained a gendered one. As Paine wrote in 1777, "To know whether it be the interest of the continent to be independent, we need only ask this easy, simple question: Is it the interest of a man to be a boy all his life?"[5] That he chose "man" and "boy" rather than "adult" and "child" illustrates the pervasive sense that the body politic implied a specific kind of body, a masculine one.

Popular literature—sentimental fiction and drama—also contributed to the gendering of revolutionary political discourse and revealed the reciprocal interplay of white bourgeois notions of manhood with the ideological edifice of a masculine public sphere. In 1787, in the shadow of Shays's Rebellion and the Constitutional Convention, Royall Tyler's play *The Contrast* was performed for theater-goers in New York, Philadelphia, and Baltimore.[6] *The Contrast* parodied the staple of sentimental novels consumed in Britain and America in the late eighteenth century, while invoking a particular message for the new republic. Tyler presented his hero as representative of an ideal gentleman's manliness, and named him, without a trace of subtlety, Colonel

Manly. Although intended to be both fictional and comical, *The Contrast* illustrates nearly all of the common features of male self-representation and
the configuration of white masculinity during the revolutionary age (figure
1).[7] Manly's masculinity was defined against a series of negative others,
hence the play's title. For Tyler, Manly's patriotism, military honors, chivalry,
and good-natured compassion could be contrasted principally against the
foppish attachment to European fashions and deceitful and rakish abuse of
women evident in other male characters.[8] Like Crèvecoeur's American
Farmer, American men asserted their superior manliness to their British or
French counterparts, despite a derivative reliance on European models for
conceiving masculine prowess. Manliness was measured, in part, against the
standards of other (non-American) men. "The American is a new man,"
wrote Crèvecoeur; "here they are become [*sic*] men," in Europe they were
like "so many useless plants."[9]

Eighteenth-century ideals of white manhood remained inseparably tied to
the hierarchical structure of society. In British society, a conspicuous division
existed between a gentleman, with his freedom from the toils of labor, and
the masses of ordinary men who could never escape working for their subsistence. According to the ideal, an English gentleman lived independent from
money-making and could be expected to put aside his self-interest and exert
his virtue through civic service, martial glory, or philanthropic largesse.[10] The
ideology of republicanism inscribed virtue as an essentially masculine attribute. Derived from the Latin words for "man" and "manliness," the word
"virtue" implied heroic, self-denying, and disinterested exertions for the
public good, like military courage or civic responsibility. Virtue's opposites
were those "effeminate" traits sure to plague a republic—cowardice, idleness, and especially luxury.[11]

Few eighteenth-century urban Americans could pass for an English gentleman of this ideal type because few ever truly rid themselves of the tinge of
money-making and labor. The urban elite had risen to their heights in the
social hierarchy precisely because of the great wealth they had accumulated
as international merchants.[12] Men who aspired to a manliness modeled on
the virtuous gentleman continually had to negotiate between that ideal and
the vagaries of economic risks and relationships of credit, reputation, and
patronage they knew in their daily lives. As the eighteenth century pro-
gressed, the outward markings of gentility (manners and civic virtue) assumed greater importance in marking an Anglo-American gentleman, so
that, as one historian has phrased it, "one was a gentleman if one looked and
acted the part." Class and gender, in other words, entailed a measure of performance in eighteenth-century society. As did their counterparts in the
South, northern urban elites hoped to portray themselves as disinterested
gentlemen. George Washington's success in cultivating that image through-

FIGURE 1. The first play written and performed in the United States, *The Contrast* illustrated revolutionary-era conceptions of masculinity. In this frontispiece, Colonel's Manly's servant Jonathan deflects an assault, declaring: "I feel chock full of fight." Royall Tyler, *The Contrast: A Comedy in Five Acts* (Philadelphia, 1790). Courtesy of the Brown University Library.

out his public life provided them with a model. Thus, at one point in Tyler's play, Colonel Manly declares his intention to refrain from profiting from his government securities, choosing instead to follow Washington's example to serve his country while reaping no reward other than glory.[13]

Real-life aspiring gentlemen found the risks of performing manly gentility fraught with difficulty. Philadelphia's wealthiest merchant and financier, Robert Morris, after being dogged for years with accusations of using his public service for private gain, decided by the late 1780s to dissociate himself completely from mercantile pursuits and make himself into a landed and leisured gentleman. His opulent marble palace, appointed with the finest furnishings, as well as other efforts to make himself into an English aristocrat, were a short-lived reality. Morris's land speculations went bust, the marble palace on Chestnut Street remained unfinished, and Morris spent three and a half years in debtor's prison before dying in a humble Philadelphia apartment in 1806.[14] Urban merchant elites lived in a world of failure and risk, and they frequently resorted to gendered language and imagery to represent their personal narratives of ruin as threats to their own masculinity.[15]

Philadelphia's most famous citizen devised perhaps the most successful (and most brazenly transparent) strategy for negotiating a masculine identity between the conflicting forces of ideals and experience, and in the process represented himself as a primary model of American manliness. Whether in his *Autobiography* or his advice from "Poor Richard," Benjamin Franklin self-consciously portrayed his life as both text and performance, creating a persona designed for emulation. Franklin portrayed his early life as a consummate example of an industrious and frugal artisan:

> In order to secure my credit and character as a tradesmen, I took care not only to be in *reality* industrious and frugal, but to avoid all *appearances* of the contrary. I dressed plain and was seen at no places of idle diversion. I never went out a fishing or shooting; . . . and to show that I was not above my business, I sometimes brought home the paper I purchased at the stores, thro' the streets on a wheelbarrow. Thus being esteemed an industrious, thriving, young man.[16]

For Franklin, manliness entailed acting the part. He championed the twin virtues of industry and frugality as the best method for economic success in his 1758 essay, "The Way to Wealth," a compendium of *Poor Richard's Almanacks*. According to Franklin, idleness, luxury, and debt simply rendered "to another, Power over your Liberty." "The Borrower is a Slave to the Lender," Franklin preached, "disdain the Chain, preserve your Freedom; and maintain your Independency: Be industrious and free; be frugal and free." His own industry, along with the generous patronage of government printing contracts, allowed Franklin to retire from his printing business at age forty-two. At that moment, he deliberately set out to live as a free and disinterested gentleman. This status gave Franklin a vehicle for his numerous projects for civic improvement and public good. Franklin the statesman, and Franklin the founder of civic institutions, were by-products of this new manly persona he assumed. Franklin drew no clear distinction between private interest and personal happiness on the one hand, and civic virtue and public good on the other. They were part and parcel of the same quest for masculine identity.[17]

Correspondingly, Franklin's obsession with the masculine pursuit of virtue and success led him to express a set of ambiguous and conflicting ideas about women. For him, women always seemed perched somewhere between the industrious helpmate and the luxury-addicted spendthrift. Franklin's writings, as one scholar notes, frequently "juxtaposed the symbols of tea tables and spinning wheels." He praised the frugality of his own wife in print, but kept a miserly watch over her expenditures in private. Evidently knowing that his male quest for success was not entirely self-made, Franklin depicted women as both assistants and hindrances.[18]

Whether a man considered himself a gentleman, an artisan, or a farmer in the late eighteenth century, he measured manliness in terms of independence. Navigating the various chains of dependencies reinforced this notion for men in an elaborate dance of male self-representation. Middling folk in the revolutionary era found themselves surrounded by ubiquitous references to dependence and independence, whether in their own personal and family relationships or in the political and literary works they read. Personal and business debts, political patronage, parent-child relations, and servitude and slavery came to be understood within the context of dependence, so that what seemed like "common sense" in Tom Paine's pamphlet was the manner in which he situated independence in familiar and familial terms.[19]

For the vast majority of urban craftsmen, a gentleman's status remained an unattainable goal. Achieving a respectable "competency," becoming master of his trade, and controlling independently the means of his livelihood constituted a more realistic expression of a craftsman's manly success. Anne Parrish's father, Isaac Parrish, wished as a young man to become a physician, but financial misfortunes and the death of his father left his family landless. So Isaac entered an apprenticeship as a hatmaker and worked at that trade for over half a century. During the Revolution, Parrish owned a home with a building behind it that served as both his hatmaking shop and shelter for a cow and several pigs. Still, Parrish retired from his business, as the later memoirs of his sons recalled, with a "respectable competence."[20] A successful artisan prized hard work and thrift, although perhaps never to the extreme of Franklin's Poor Richard. Tradesmen knew that even in good times they could rarely experience full employment; only in flush times could male heads of households earn enough to pay for life's basic necessities. Most other times, they could be driven into poverty by seasonal unemployment, epidemics, or workplace accidents. In the face of these conditions, urban laboring men created a masculine culture of their own, centered around both work and leisure.[21]

Laboring men turned to traditional plebeian leisure activities to forge a masculine identity that contrasted sharply with men aspiring to gentility. Taverns, dance halls, city fairs, and crowds offered laboring men a site for a street culture that distanced them from their dependent and precarious work lives. Similarly, laboring men, including newly freed black men, often employed extravagant dress, along with music and dance, as forms of independent self-expression, creating an intermingling of white and black laborers in working-class male spaces that provoked anxieties among urban elites. In one revealing incident, a free black man encountered the wrath of local authorities for keeping just the type of "disorderly house" that incited elite fears of racial and class defiance. He was charged with keeping "a place of resort for all the loose and idle characters of the city, whether whites, blacks or mulattoes; and that frequently in the night gentlemen's servants would arrive there, mounted on their masters' horses . . . and indulge in riotous mirth and dancing till the dawn." Masters also noted in advertisements for runaways that both their white servants and black slaves were similarly enticed by frolics and dances.[22] In addition, Philadelphia's artisans and laborers mobilized politically for the first time during the revolutionary years, assuming leadership and power through radical committees and the militia and projecting a radical democratic ethos into the masculine realm of politics. Artisans and laborers, through political action in the republic, discovered their own independent manly expression of civic virtue.[23]

As it spread throughout the middling ranks of white men, this language of independence implied that true manliness could always be counterposed against various manifestations of dependence, thereby situating class, racial, and sexual difference at the very core of the Revolution's ideology. The racial implications were perhaps most explicit. White workers discerned the pervasive cultural power of social independence at the same moment that bound labor and servitude were undergoing an important transformation. The colonial seaport economy had relied extensively on the work of bound laborers, white and black. As late as 1750, nearly 40 percent of Philadelphia's workers were slaves or servants. By 1800, however, bound labor had nearly disappeared, accounting for less than 2 percent of the work force.[24] Colonel Manly's white attendant, Jonathan, took umbrage when addressed as a "servant" by a man of similar employ, illustrating by his response the shifting attitudes about servitude: "Servant!" he declares, "Sir, do you take me for a neger,—I am Colonel Manly's waiter." Although confessing that he performed all the tasks a servant would, including blackening the Colonel's boots, Jonathan insisted he was "a true blue son of liberty," and that "no man shall master me."[25] For the revolutionary generation of white men, where slave imagery permeated the ideology of independence, servitude became intertwined with dependence, slavery, and blackness. White workers clung to the label "freemen," and associated manliness with whiteness and freedom from dependence. By the turn of the century, crowds of white workers violently turned away black men from public celebrations of the Fourth of July in Philadelphia, thereby reserving the "independence" in Independence Day and Independence Hall for white men only.[26]

Dependence had become the opposite of manliness; it is small wonder, then, that manhood in revolutionary America was also frequently measured against another negative other—the image of white bourgeois women. Popular urban magazines that flowed off the presses during the nation's early years portrayed the antithesis of the virtuous republican citizen as irrational, seductive, foppish, luxury-ridden, and effeminate. The idea of woman as citizen ("citizeness") was so rare precisely because women served as the symbol of what independent republican political actors should not be.[27] Tyler contrasted Colonel Manly's character with his sister Charlotte, depicted as flirtatious, coquettish, and obsessed with fashion and conspicuous consumption. Tyler employed Charlotte's own voice to juxtapose the masculine against his critical (misogynist) images of the feminine: "My brother is the very counterpart and reverse of me," Charlotte states. "I am gay, he is grave; I am airy, he is solid; I am ever selecting the most pleasing objects for my laughter, he has a tear for every pitiful one." Manliness implied not being feminine. White men's fears concerning personal failure, business reversals, or the plight of the republic were most frequently figured as a problem of effeminacy. Yet in Tyler's play, women are not depicted as the naturally and innately compassionate ones. Instead, Manly is the one who "spoke the language of sentiment, and his eyes looked tenderness and honour."[28]

Hence, another ideal—the "man of feeling"—also shaped white middle-class manliness in late-eighteenth-century America, heightening the ambiguity in this era's gender discourse. Both evangelical religion and literary sentimentalism (although each in different ways) called for a reformation in male behavior to emphasize tenderness, emotion, and passion. A masculine persona based on sentiment came to be inseparably woven together with middle-class attachments to politeness, consumerism, and commerce. Whether in the plots of Samuel Richardson's or Henry Fielding's novels, the rules of civility in courtesy books, the treatises of Scottish moral philosophers, or the evangelical message of revivalist sects, eighteenth-century readers found themselves inundated by appeals for reforming men's manners.[29]

Meanwhile, moralists and philosophers since mid-century had regularly been suggesting that men possessed a set of feelings—an irresistible part of their human nature—that could be awakened by the sufferings of others, what they commonly called "sympathy" or "humanity."[30] Sympathy implied one's "fellow feeling," a passion that could imagine the sufferings of another, creating an essential bond of sociability. The good-natured man or the man of feelings, nevertheless, directly subverted long-established associations of masculinity with rationality and femininity with passion. Although medical writers continued to describe women's bodies as more delicate and there-fore possessing greater sensibility, sentimental writers and evangelical preachers countered by endorsing an ideal manliness in which emotions and passion rivaled reason.

Confusion and contradiction abound in this jerry-built ideology of sexual difference. By characterizing benevolent sentiments with gender-neutral terms such as "humane" and "humanity," sentimental writers perhaps tried to distance men's feelings from too close associations with effeminacy and softness, which might jeopardize the firmness of men's resolve in the world of commerce. As Adam Smith strained to emphasize, one's "sensibility to the feelings of others" did not have to be "inconsistent with the manhood of self-command." The key for men of refinement and gentility was to be feeling and sympathetic without falling into the trap of effeminacy—a never-ending twisting and refashioning of themselves that offered little hope for success. That manliness could mean independence, toughness, and self-command, while also connoting feeling, sympathy, and humaneness, was one of many contradictions inherent in eighteenth-century gender conventions. It was this uncertainty about manliness and the new goals of humanitarianism—was ideal manliness defined by feelings or independent actions?—that cre-ated a climate that opened a door for women's activism in a masculine arena of voluntary associations.[31]

This language of sympathy was an essential feature of eighteenth-century humanitarianism, and it interfused itself throughout the earliest expressions of men's benevolent activism in post-revolutionary American cities. With no-table frequency, men's benevolent societies spoke of "humanity," "friends of humanity," and "noble feelings" of compassion when writing letters, society minutes, or addresses to the public. Tench Coxe recounted the origins of Philadelphia's abolition society as a narrative of the "many persons of nice feelings & humane sentiments" who rallied to promote the gradual abolition of slavery. This man of sympathy and feeling echoed in a contemporary de-scription of Elliston Perot, a Quaker active in the Philadelphia Dispensary, First Day School Society, and Prison Society. Perot was portrayed as "a person of the kindest feeling and most affectionate manner," who was "in every sense of the word a really *Good Man*." By contrast, reformers depicted their

opponents as hard-hearted men, who, in the words of Pennsylvania Abolition Society president James Pemberton, had allowed their hearts to become
"callous to the feelings of humanity." Of course, sympathy was as unstable
and uncertain as the gender meanings attached to it. Misplaced or excessive
sympathy not only threatened a man with effeminacy, but also jeopardized
the connecting bonds of society.[32]

Nowhere was this better illustrated than in the debates over public pun-
ishments in Philadelphia in the 1780s that prompted the formation of the
Philadelphia Society for Alleviating the Miseries of Public Prisons (the
Philadelphia Prison Society) in 1787. Philadelphia's most ubiquitous reformer in those years, Dr. Benjamin Rush, exploited fears of an overwrought
sympathy in his essay entitled *An Enquiry Into the Effects of Public Punishments
Upon Criminals, and Upon Society* (1787), which spurred a full-scale reform of
Pennsylvania's criminal punishment system following the Revolution. Dissat-
isfied with the infamous "wheelbarrow law" that allowed judges to sentence
convicted criminals to public labor while chained together in the city streets,
Rush turned the justification for public punishment on its head. Public punishments not only hardened the sensibilities of criminals, Rush contended,
but they also impaired the feelings of sympathy that bound communities together. Because sympathy was the root of the humanitarian spirit, men of
feeling would naturally be moved to sympathize with the distress of publicly
punished criminals. But when they perceived that the law of the state caused
that distress, they would be forced to suppress those feelings. This frustrated
sympathy, Rush argued, eventually weakened those sensibilities in the
human breast until they "cease to act altogether," destroying the very source
of men's benevolent actions. Rush saw no alternative but private punishments, removed from the view of the populace, and he proceeded to articulate a "penitential ideal" in which criminal punishment would be a source of
moral reformation rather than public shame. He outlined a proposal for
houses of repentance ("penitentiaries") where criminals could be segregated
from society and offered the opportunity to be restored to the path of
virtue.[33]

Like-minded white male reformers established the Philadelphia Prison Society just two months after Rush published his essay. Prison society activists
professed that they were moved by humanitarian feelings to relieve the woes
of the incarcerated, boldly declaring that benevolent obligations were "not
cancelled by the follies or crimes of our fellow Creatures." Yet they also
wished to move beyond charity, to secure changes in public policy that removed punishment from the arena of public spectacle and placed it within
the realm of benevolent reformation. The immediate impact of their reforming zeal was phenomenal. Between 1787 and 1790, Philadelphia reformers took these abstract ideas and refashioned the entire system of crimi-

nal punishment in Pennsylvania. By 1790 the state legislature had replaced the practice of public punishments with a new system of private punishment and established a Penitentiary House designed to introduce solitary confinement as the method for reforming a prisoner. Philadelphia reformers created a system of reformative incarceration that culminated in the construction of Eastern State Penitentiary in 1829 as a rival to the Auburn and Sing-Sing penitentiaries in New York. In less than five years during the 1780s, one benevolent society transformed the nature of criminal punishment and set in motion a vision of penology whose legacy remains today.[34]

Voluntary associations such as the Prison Society constituted a nearly exclusive masculine domain in American cities before 1790, although still a relatively new phenomenon even for men. Although scholars have exposed the informal associations of women at tea tables, gossip circles, and early salons, formal organizations of women were nearly nonexistent before the 1790s.[35] White men, by contrast, could choose from a spate of embryonic voluntary associations where they could join with other men for cultural, political, or economic benefit. Fraternal organizations; trade associations; ethnic and immigrant societies; political clubs; veterans' associations; scientific, professional, and philanthropic institutions; fire companies; and militias offered conspicuous public membership to white men in the city. And free African American men, despite their recent transition from slavery to freedom, created their first voluntary association during the 1780s.

Meeting commonly in coffeehouses and taverns, these multifarious occasions for assembling together reinforced ties of association and exclusion that characterized the male political world during the revolutionary decades. Thus when ten white Quaker men decided in April 1775 to form the Society for the Relief of Free Negroes Unlawfully Held in Bondage (later renamed the Pennsylvania Abolition Society), it made perfect sense to meet for the first time at the Rising Sun Tavern. It was perhaps an unthinking decision to place men's benevolent activism into both a masculine public sphere and a definitively masculine space. By that act alone, they dispelled any doubts that women might join them in their antislavery reform. Taverns had come to be defined in eighteenth-century America as spaces where only white men entered as equals. Women who visited taverns were commonly regarded as "public women" in the most pejorative meaning of the phrase—as prostitutes or madams. At the same time, these male reformers never felt exactly comfortable with this choice of meeting place and recorded after their second meeting that it was the "desire of most or all of the Members of this Society to meet in some Private House."[36] Perhaps they wished to distance themselves from the associations with drink, radical politics, or masculine leisure that working-class taverns connoted, or perhaps they desired to connect humanitarian reform with a privatized realm of sensibility and feeling.

In either case, the new venue was a tacit reminder that religious benevolence might be a space for shared benevolent activism among bourgeois men and women. Situating their reform actions in a private house placed them within the shared space of an eighteenth-century household, where both men and women could be productive laborers as well as affectionate caretakers, further illustrating the gender ambiguities surrounding the reforming man of feelings.

Constituting the public sphere as masculine did not necessarily exclude women, nor should one assume that no women appeared in the public sphere that male reformers were creating. Women emerged as living persons with real-life experiences in that otherwise masculine domain of male reformers during the 1770s and 1780s. From the earliest records of the abolition society, for example, women appeared as either slaveholders, slaves, or anonymous financial contributors. The abolition society's first case involved a formerly enslaved woman named Dinah Nevill, of mixed American Indian and African ancestry, who along with her three children faced the threat of being sold back into slavery. Another early case involved an obdurate slaveholding widow named Ann Humphreys, who met the visiting antislavery reformers with "a Very Unpleasant Reception," while insisting on retaining her slave named Harry. And in 1784 a Quaker woman donated twelve pounds to the abolition society (more than ten times the annual contribution of each society member), with the stipulation that her money not be spent on attorney fees or court costs. Although she acknowledged men's control of this reform, perhaps by excluding her contribution from the masculine realm of the courts, she hoped to support the society's other benevolent objectives—relieving the poverty and unemployment of former slaves—goals that more closely resembled the benevolent work performed by Quaker women. Missing from all these instances of women's presence, however, were autonomous or authoritative roles for white or black women activists, positions that recognized women as equals or co-partners in the cause. Women most frequently entered the public sphere of reform in the 1770s and 1780s as dependents, deviants, or as problems to be solved. While the abolition society was meeting in the male-only space of a tavern, these male activists conducted their benevolence surrounded by groups whose status they considered to be dependents—slaves, children, and women.[37]

African Americans knew firsthand the limitations as well as the advantages of the new expressions of late-eighteenth-century humanitarianism. Their lives were touched by the actions of the Pennsylvania Abolition Society far more than by any of the other newly formed white benevolent societies. Abolition society members, mostly Quakers, proved to be the sole white advocates for black freedom rights under Pennsylvania's 1780 gradual abolition law.[38] By retaining a committee of Philadelphia's finest lawyers, the abolition society tirelessly brought freedom suits on behalf of slaves whose masters failed to register them or brought them into the state for longer than six months—either action could legally produce their freedom. Reorganized in 1787, with a new name (the Pennsylvania Abolition Society) and an influx of wealthier and non-Quaker white male members, the abolition society enlarged its benevolent objectives over the next three years. They focused on improving the condition of free blacks, by creating four additional subcommittees to offer moral advice and employment to former slaves and to find apprenticeships and create schools for educating their children. The new goals of improving the conditions of free blacks proved more vexing and difficult to achieve than the legal battles that the society had waged in the early 1780s. These goals also revealed that the moral advice and piecemeal efforts of white reformers (even when operating from the best motives) could not keep up with the needs of an ever-increasing free black population.[39]

As the eighteenth century came to a close, more and more African Americans chose to rely on the often meager resources of their own self-governed institutions rather than the inconsistencies and condescension of white paternalism. Free black men and women assembled their own benevolent and education societies to authenticate a life of freedom that was hard-earned rather than a gift.

While northern state legislatures debated the merits and logistics of gradual emancipation laws after the Revolution, African Americans created thriving free black communities in northern cities, which made their own organizations possible. Free blacks outnumbered the few slaves residing in Philadelphia, New York, Boston, Providence, and Newport within a decade after the Revolution. New York's free black population alone increased from one hundred people on the eve of the Revolution to over seven thousand by 1810. Philadelphia's free black community grew even more dramatically. Free African Americans numbered over one thousand when the Revolutionary War ended in 1783; that number increased to six thousand by the close of the century and then climbed to over twelve thousand by 1820, making Philadelphia home to one of the largest urban concentrations of free black people in North America.[40] A burgeoning community of former slaves made it both possible and necessary for them to join together for collective assistance.

Free African Americans in the Northeast had few resources for charity toward people outside their homes or neighborhoods; and yet black women and men established a handful of their own voluntary benevolent associations during the 1780s and 1790s. Self-governing organizations were so important in the urban black community that African Americans accorded their societies places of honor at any public celebrations or parades. The first of these was created as early as 1780 in Newport, Rhode Island. By 1787, free black men in Philadelphia had organized their own mutual assistance society known as the Free African Society. Because black mutual benefit societies possessed much more limited financial resources than white benevolent associations, they had to limit their relief to their own members' hardships. The Free African Society in Philadelphia amassed a treasury of £12 after its first nine months; two years later in 1790, the treasury was slightly more than £42. By contrast, the Pennsylvania Abolition Society's annual revenues during the 1790s averaged almost £200 per year, and the Quaker women in the Female Society for the Relief of the Distressed amassed a treasury of close to £1,000 in their first year and averaged nearly £60 in annual donations over the next ten years.[41] It is not difficult to see why charity resources were so scarce among newly freed blacks, especially when half of the black population in 1790 still lived in white households. Many of these newly emancipated slaves, both men and women, waged a continual struggle for economic survival that accompanied their freedom in what one historian has described as "a world filled with both barriers and opportunities." Former slaves found work as common day laborers, dock workers, seamen, or domestic laborers, but a significant number also exploited self-employment opportunities as artisans, retailers, or small-scale proprietors.[42] Successful black entrepreneurs, together with semiskilled and unskilled laborers, turned to a familiar strategy of mutualism that had been commonly adopted by men's trade or ethnic associations. They pooled their funds to assist members who became ill, injured, unemployed, or in need of burial expenses. The Free African Society was the first of several fraternal and mutual benefit societies established by Philadelphia's growing community of African Americans. Before the turn of the eighteenth century, a Female Benevolent Society (1793) and a male Friendly Society (1795) were established at St. Thomas's African Episcopal Church, and several black Masonic lodges emerged in the city, each providing sickness and burial benefits for dues-paying members.[43]

When black men and women sought to enhance the education of their children, they exposed the deficiencies of white benevolence. The abolition society's Committee on Education tried to establish several schools for free blacks to supplement Quaker charity schools, but the results were inconsistent and disheartening for black families. The school they constructed on Cherry Street in 1793 to accommodate one hundred students repeatedly suffered from falling enrollments. Too many free black families were forced to indenture their children at young ages, and antislavery activists failed to convince white masters that school attendance was valuable. Eventually black leaders realized that they had little choice but to create schools of their own. Richard Allen organized the first black Sunday school at Bethel Church as early as 1795, and several other former slaves, including Absalom Jones, opened schools in their homes. When the abolition society withdrew its support in 1799 from schools that employed black teachers, because the society thought they were too lenient with the children, Jones and the other black teachers continued to instruct the children at their own expense. By 1804, Absalom Jones had enlarged his school at St. Thomas's Church, and, three years later, Richard Allen organized a black charity school association called the Society of Free People of Color for Promoting the Instruction and School Education of Children of African Descent. The free black community in Philadelphia discovered that voluntary associations, intimately tied to the African Church, were the best hope for creating an independent and self-reliant black community in Philadelphia.[44]

Such independence allotted members of black men's benevolent societies a measure of manliness according to late-eighteenth-century gender ideals.[45] Black mutual assistance, independent of white oversight and benevolent white reformers, reflected African American men's efforts to establish a distinctive black masculinity that accompanied their hard-won freedom. Even their practice of disciplining wayward members and criticizing extravagant leisure, often portrayed by historians as the prudish and class concerns of black eiltes, can be seen as examples of a rhetoric of manly virtue that depicted luxury and conspicuous consumption as signs of effeminacy and ruin. The Free African Society's appeal to its Boston counterpart to discourage feasts and dances stated, "While we are feasting and dancing, many of our complexion are starving under cruel bondage; and it is this practice of ours that enables our enemies to declare that we are not fit for freedom." Hence the men chosen to be overseers of fellow members' moral behavior were expected to be "sober and exemplary members, and men of good report."[46] These examples of manliness could not develop while the black community remained dependent on white patronage and assistance.

In the era of American Independence, men perceived the greatest threats to their own manliness as coming not from women, but from other men. Rising political aspirations and power for craftsmen and laborers, the blurring of traditional social rankings, and vices associated with a street culture of formerly dependent men, all contributed to elite and middling men's growing anxieties about manly behavior and the masculine self-definition of the reforming man. Meanwhile, as philanthropic men hailed a new humanitarian sensibility, whether as a product of the Enlightenment or the fruit of a new millennialism, they also sought to maintain a complicated balance between a manhood of reason and feeling. They consistently constituted these differences in gendered terms. Effeminate and foppish men, republican help-meets, and seductive coquettes dominated the social and political rhetoric of republican America. These various constitutions of difference, and the ambiguities they aroused about gender, created a unique moment in which white women's public presence in the realm of religious reform emerged for the first time.

"'Tis Virtue's Work"

Despite historians' all too frequent use of the paradigm when describing women in revolutionary America, Philadelphia's first female benevolent societies were not created by "republican mothers."[47] They were not formed by the wives or daughters of revolutionary patriots nor by women claiming the same fervent support for the Revolution as the men in their families (although some later societies were). In fact, former slave women organized the first independent women's association two years before white Philadelphia women, when they formed the Female Benevolent Society of St. Thomas in 1793. This black women's mutual assistance society offered relief benefits to dues-paying members, but lacked the resources to direct its charity toward the general population of the city's poor.[48] The earliest white women's benevolent societies were not even established by the one group of women who possessed the greatest measure of autonomy in eighteenth-century America for establishing their own institutions, asserting their spiritual equality, and speaking with acknowledged authority to both men and women: the married women active in the leadership of the Quaker women's meetings. Instead, the first white women's charity societies in Philadelphia emanated from the labors of young, unmarried Quaker women: women without sons to raise up as good republican citizens or husbands to soften and influence toward compassion and sympathy; women who had been pacifists or loyalists during the Revolutionary War and who had been unofficially excluded from positions of authority in the Friends women's meetings.[49]

The point here is not to suggest that historians abandon the concept of the "republican mother" in a gendered history of the revolutionary era, only that we need to move beyond it as an all-encompassing paradigm for white middle-class women during this period. White and black women in both the laboring and middling classes found myriad ways to legitimize their public actions in an unreceptive environment during the early republic. How can historians explain the newly freed African American women, the unmarried Quaker women, and the mixture of patriots, loyalists, and neutrals who constituted the earliest religious activists and produced the first female benevolent societies in the new nation? By advancing benevolent causes, white women activists chose to maneuver among alternative paths that could sanction a public role for themselves. Along the way, they effectively exploited, and in turn challenged, prevailing discourses that associated the "public woman" with sexual disorder. But first they had to convince themselves and others that one did not have to occupy a male body to affect public opinion in the new American republic.

John Marsillac's encounter with the women of the Female Society illustrates an emerging conflict over the nature of the public sphere in the new republic. According to Jürgen Habermas, a bourgeois public sphere emerged in the eighteenth century as a realm that mediated between the state and society. It constituted a space where public opinion was formed, contingent upon a print culture and a reasoning populace. Habermas describes the associative dimension of the public sphere in this way:

> A portion of the public sphere comes into being in every conversation in which private individuals assemble to form a public body. . . . Citizens behave as a public body when they confer in an unrestricted fashion—that is, with the guarantee of freedom of assembly and association and the freedom to express and publish their opinions—about matters of general interest."[50]

By creating female charitable societies, white bourgeois women participated in the formation of public opinion regarding a central feature of urban public life—poverty and poor relief. Poverty and poor relief would eventually become an issue of first importance in urban political discourse during the two decades following 1815. But at this moment in post-revolutionary America, these young white women entered into debates of public opinion concerning an issue in urban life that reverberated into many others, including social welfare, family, labor, and education. Charitable women in the post-revolutionary era thus created what one scholar has described as "an institutional location for practical reason in public affairs."[51]

Critics of Habermas have aptly observed that the uncritical treatment of gender is a crucial flaw in his theory of the public sphere. One of the initial attractions of this theory for feminist scholars was its divorcing of the public from the state, conceptualizing a space for public action for those groups (such as women and African Americans) who were systemically denied the franchise and officeholding. Yet Habermas fails to recognize that his categories of citizen, worker, and consumer are not merely political or economic concepts, but gendered concepts as well. As critics have noted, the universal citizen that Habermas depicts as genderless, is in fact male.[52] Only by addressing the gendered categories embedded in notions of public and private, can we begin to expose the evanescent and often contradictory nature of a public/private dichotomy in the revolutionary era.[53] In divergent ways, benevolent-minded religious women in Philadelphia exerted a public presence—by appropriating strategies of activism that at times exploited masculine gender imagery and at other times employed feminine gender imagery available in the early republic.

Recall that gender language and imagery permeated political discourse during the revolutionary decades and that central concepts of public service such as virtue and independence carried with them decidedly masculine meanings. Still, a prevailing ambiguity shaped the gendered definitions of men's behavior and masculine identity. Thus, when white women wished to assume a legitimate and respected presence in the public sphere in the United States during the post-revolutionary years, they found it useful (even necessary) at times to appropriate a set of widely accepted masculine symbols, masculine language, and in some cases a masculine persona, to assert an authoritative public role.[54]

During the American Revolution, white women of all classes became visibly present in the revolutionary struggle, despite these essentially masculine assumptions about the public sphere. They rioted in the streets, mourned their dead, and supported their military men.[55] Urban women's most prominent expression of virtuous patriotism emerged in their role as boycotters of British imports and as manufacturers of American substitutes. Women proved essential to the colonists' nonimportation initiatives in their rebellion against the British Empire. The boycott of tea became the most visible vehicle for women's display of public virtue and patriotism. Even the nine-year-old daughter of a prominent patriot created quite a stir when offered a cup of tea at the home of New Jersey's Tory Governor William Franklin. She politely took the cup, raised it to her lips, curtsied, and then threw the contents out the window. In December 1773, a crowd of eight thousand Philadelphians of all ranks, some of whom might have been women, prevented a shipload of tea from unloading at the custom house and intimidated the ship's captain into returning with his cargo to England.[56] Light verse and poems penned in the commonplace books of white women expressed a prevalent sentiment that women could make a firm patriotic commitment and could act as virtuously as men.[57]

The place of white women in public reveals yet another instance of the two-faced nature of the republican ideology that inspired the Revolution—its ability to promise an inclusive equality while simultaneously being the agent of exclusion and inequality. That this ideology served both to inspire the noblest critique of slavery while also justifying its perpetual expansion merely confirms the two faces of republicanism that surfaced when women asserted a public presence.[58] During the 1770s and 1780s, men and women writers expressed ambivalent attitudes toward female patriotism and public virtue. On the one hand, they attested to the necessity of women's patriotism, expecting women to exercise public virtue. New Jersey's constitution, after all, briefly left the franchise open to women during the 1780s. Yet, on the other hand, while female symbols commonly appeared as Liberty and Columbia, women's patriotism (or the lack thereof) was just as commonly associated with imagery of women as disorderly, passionate, and irrational. Luxury, effeminacy, and corruption became the feminine counterparts to the masculine triad of the Revolution—virtue, independence, and the public good. Numerous writers, both men and women, questioned whether women possessed the wherewithal to fulfill their essential role or whether it was possible for women to perform public virtue. Broadsides, such as "The Female Patriot" printed in New York in 1770, mockingly pondered whether women could sacrifice luxury for the virtue of patriotism.[59] For every voice like Judith Sargent Murray and Benjamin Rush calling for the intellectual equality of women, there were many others berating women as irrational creatures and linking the woman in public with sexual disorder and prostitution. Political discussions in newspapers frequently conflated a female citizen ("citoyenne" or "citizeness") with a "woman of the town."[60]

This ambivalence about women's political activism is critical for understanding the attitudes about women's benevolence that developed after the Revolution. Although men's and women's actions were viewed through the same lens of public virtue during the revolutionary decades, for women the emphasis was usually placed on their incapacity to achieve that standard. Not surprisingly then, some women found they could best assert their public virtue by appropriating symbols and language not associated with the feminine, by acting in ways that paralleled men in public.

Women activists after 1790 did not legitimize their spiritual authority or their benevolent duty, then, based on a call to universal attributes of motherhood. Rarely did the writings of women themselves in their annual reports, or the numerous sermons by male ministers on their behalf, resort to maternal imagery prior to 1815. Post-revolutionary conceptions of benevolence lacked the conflation of femininity and compassion that would become so common in the nineteenth century. In part, this was because the first female benevolent societies in Philadelphia worked out their conception of women's activism within the framework of public virtue, with its meanings inherited from a mix of republican and Christian ideals. Virtue, after all, was the most prized value in the civic imagination of republicanism. Benevolent actions matched the spirit of self-sacrifice that defined virtue. Benjamin Rush referred to benevolence as that "virtue which must not be constrained," while Thomas Branagan suggested that "*republicanism* and *benevolence*" were "synonimous [*sic*] terms."[61] The trouble with conflating benevolence and virtue was that this form of virtue could be ascribed to the actions of both men and women. A poem "To the Benevolent Band" praising the work of the Female Society also framed the work of women's benevolence around the idea of public virtue.

> 'Tis virtue's work, beyond the vain parade
> Of rambling folly's gay fantastic plume,
> Whose transient glare of vanity must fade
> Beneath the blasting winter of the tomb.
> But you, dear girls, despise the empty show,
> The call of duty claims your nobler powers.[62]

Isabella Graham, who pioneered white female benevolent societies in New York City, also exploited masculine imagery of public service and civic virtue when she compared the actions of a new women's benevolent society with a general landing his troops on a hostile coast during wartime. In the minds of post-revolutionary reformers, acts of benevolence could be understood as a demonstration of a woman's public virtue.[63]

The antithesis of benevolence in this post-revolutionary discourse on public activism was not inhumanity or cruelty, but rather luxury and fashion. Eighteenth-century writers on both sides of the Atlantic married luxury and effeminacy together as part of a two-headed union—concepts inseparable to the point of being synonymous. Luxury was at once the cause and the symbolic expression of effeminacy. Whenever proponents of reform contrasted benevolent action with its opposite, they pointed to luxuriant and fashionable persons, juxtaposing the benevolent woman against the woman of vanity. This contrast is apparent in "To the Benevolent Band," as well as in statements by many other benevolent spokespersons. Thomas Branagan, a Methodist essayist and ardent republican, noted the "peculiar dissimilarity" between "the pious and prudent female, who takes a supreme delight in relieving others' woe," and that proud and conceited "votary of fashion; whose physiognomy and attitudes while strutting the streets, beggars description."[64] Jacob Janeway of Philadelphia's Second Presbyterian Church proclaimed the women of the Female Hospitable Society as shining examples of virtue for nonvirtuous women to emulate: "Ye gay, ye thoughtless females, who flutter through our streets—who sparkle in the ball-room—who agitate your bosoms with debasing passions at the card-table— . . . who wear away life in doing *nothing*—come hither, and learn, from these benevolent females, how to *live*,—learn the *luxury* of doing good."[65]

This conception of benevolence as the antithesis of luxury was also employed to encourage donations and gifts to benevolent societies. Charity sermons by laymen and ministers often repeated the contrast between benevolence and luxury, suggesting the proper way to dispose of wealth. "How many donations," Episcopal Bishop William White wondered, would have been consigned to "self-indulgence," "dissipation," or "excess," but instead became the instruments for making possible "a mass of good."[66] This appeal was not restricted to women alone; both men and women were encouraged to funnel their energies and their monetary resources into the cause of benevolence. When women's organizations made financial appeals, they frequently reminded their audiences of the contrasting nonvirtuous behavior— none more clearly than the managers of a female charity in Providence, Rhode Island, who after explaining the financial needs of their organization asked the other women, "Who would not relinquish a frivolous amusement, or a useless ornament, to enjoy that most estimable of all pleasures, an approving conscience."[67] Philadelphia's benevolent women understood personally the connections among luxury, uncharitable behavior, and public virtue. Susan Boudinot Bradford, founding member and treasurer of Philadelphia's Female Association for the Relief of Women and Children knew that connection well; she was that same nine-year-old girl who first expressed her public virtue two decades earlier by dramatically tossing the hated tea out of the governor's mansion. By politicizing purchasing decisions, women's public activity through benevolence modeled itself on a notion of public virtue. Yet, like the language inherited from the Revolution's nonimportation efforts, this discourse still evoked doubts about women's capacities for performing that model of virtue, with its masculine meanings. Benevolent women once again found themselves bounded by the gendered associations between luxury and effeminacy, even as they opened a door into a masculine realm of public action.[68]

Activist women found themselves engaging in all the business tasks of benevolent work, particularly the economic concerns surrounding fundraising, which brought them repeatedly into an arena primarily inhabited by men. Reformers insisted that collecting donations and other fundraising methods constituted as true an act of benevolence as the gift itself. White middle-class women accounted for a substantial share of the money raised by benevolent societies; one minister once described them as the "honoured collectors for the *'poor and needy.'*" These women's financial endeavors differed very little from benevolent men's. Critics and supporters alike attested that women competed with and frequently outperformed their male counterparts in raising money.[69] The Female Association demonstrated benevolent women's resourcefulness by producing revenues from member donations, investments in stocks, sales of manufactured goods, fundraising dinners for visiting dignitaries and military heroes, a cotillion party, a concert by the Handelian Society, and fees donated by judges and inspectors of elections. They also hired a professional fundraising orator who delivered charity sermons in towns from Salem, Massachusetts, to Philadelphia. These business ventures signified independent economic actions during an era that saw little change in patriarchal control of married women's property and that increasingly defined middle-class women's lives as unproductive.[70]

Heightened concern about luxury and women's prominence in religious fundraising also coincided with a new consumer culture in the late eighteenth century, illuminating the intimate connections between consumerism and benevolent activism in the new nation. British habits of consumption had begun to change earlier in the century. Consumer goods—dress, tablewares, furniture, tea, and other wares—became readily available and demanded by ever larger portions of the population. A budding middle class transformed what once had been luxuries, accessible only to the rich, into necessities for everyday life. Urban centers in America began witnessing similar changes by the 1770s, and before long, the rural North found itself in the midst of a new consumer culture. The process accelerated after the Revolutionary War. Cheap British manufactured goods weighed down the shelves of shopkeepers, and signs of fashion and expansive consumption could be seen everywhere in American cities.[71]

Appeals directed to men and women to refrain from luxury and to be stewards of their wealth assume greater meaning when viewed in light of evolving gendered expectations for purchasing and control of family income. Historians have begun to speculate about the historical circumstances that eventually made women the principal purchasers of household goods. During the colonial era, husbands typically shopped for household items. But in late-eighteenth-century cities, when the separation of work from the home left many middle-class families with men's diminished role in household labor and women's declining productive contributions to the family income, wives more frequently assumed responsibility for household purchases. As one scholar has theorized, the new consumer culture of shops and shopping became imagined spaces inhabited by masculine sellers and feminine buyers, regardless of the sex of either party in that transaction. Whether women gained greater control over decisions of family expenses as a result of this change remains to be proved.[72] The evidence drawn from benevolent-society sources, however, is suggestive. Money was indispensable to the system of voluntary benevolent societies, and women performed a substantial amount of the fundraising for both men's and women's charitable and missionary societies. That Presbyterian minister Ashbel Green felt compelled to remind a group of benevolent women of their duty to consult their husbands before giving to a charity suggests that some middle-class women may have been usurping that authority over the family income.[73]

This fixation on luxury was also part of a larger cultural phenomenon— the initial formation of a middle-class identity in America—a process in which white Protestant women played a significant part. The middle class constructed a paradoxical attitude toward the new consumerism—depen-

dent on it for economic power and social status, but critical of the vice of luxury when expressed by the rich above them and the poor below them. This
simultaneous attachment to and detachment from a market economy
helped to define the Anglo-American middle class and produced the anti-
materialist critique that dominated nearly every reform movement in antebellum America.[74] Embedded in these discussions of luxury and benevolence
was a not-so-muted critique of the consumer behavior of the "lower sort."
Middle-class reformers expressed growing anxieties about white laborers and
free blacks who resorted to "stylin'"—extravagant dress, hairstyles, and body
movements—to contrast their marginality with the ideals of republican
equality.[75]

The strategies that benevolent women employed for sanctioning their
public role in the city become more apparent when we return to a gendered
analysis of the concept of "independence" (recall that notions of dependence and independence carried strongly gendered connotations during this
era). Independence, like virtue, was attained by a process of negative refer-
encing; it was a trait acquired by exclusion, by a person not embodying its opposite—dependence or servitude. But for much of the eighteenth century,
independence could also be realized by establishing relationships of dependence. A gentleman was by definition a man not only independent of
employer and landlord, but also a man who possessed dependents. The
greater the number of those dependent on him, of course, the greater the
independence, and hence manliness, of the man. This engendering of independence as a primary feature of eighteenth-century white manhood was
inseparable from its corollary association of women with dependence, thus
making both independence and its opposite sex-specific attributes. White
men proved that they were men by asserting that they were not boys, slaves,
or women, all of whom they considered to be dependents.[76]

The independence that young women experienced through new benevolent societies corresponded with a greater independence and visibility for
women in the northern urban economy during the 1790s. With the transition to capitalism and the early stages of a market revolution, cities such as
Philadelphia witnessed a significant increase in women who were, in the
words of one historian, "everywhere visible as aggressive and ostensibly independent economic agents." Women's labor made possible the adaptation
of many urban households to a market economy. Just when Philadelphia
women were creating the first women's benevolent societies in the mid-
1790s, Americans were at the height of a twenty-year-long commercial
boom. The Napoleonic Wars expanded European markets for U.S. foodstuffs and other exports and produced substantial wealth for merchants and
proprietors in port towns such as Philadelphia. This boom also corresponded to a time when the participation of women in the labor force was at

an all-time high. Widows, female heads of households, and unmarried women could be found working as ironmongers, shopkeepers, glass engravers, shoemakers, coopers, tavernkeepers, seamstresses, and milliners. Although women remained central to the new market capitalism, prevailing discourses insisted on a woman's dependence and invisibility by associating market activity and economic independence with masculinity. This difference between the material conditions of urban households and the ideological edifice that framed market participation further contributed to the ambiguities of gender in the post-revolutionary years.[77]

Activist women, then, asserted a measure of independence in forming women's benevolent societies. For benevolent women to assume a clearly independent public role, it was essential for them to establish relationships in which others were dependent on them. Unmarried Quaker women in the first women's societies knew few direct relationships of others' dependence in their own experiences. In fact, it is difficult to measure the degree to which independence was a conscious aspiration of white women during this era. Women's desire for independence could be hidden within a maze of conflicting aspirations, especially considering the prevailing constraints against expressions of economic and political independence. Wealthy Quaker matron Elizabeth Drinker voiced one perspective in her diary, when after reading Mary Wollstonecraft, she wrote, "I am not for quite so much independance." But the increasing numbers of white women who chose not to marry, expressed greater inclination to sue for divorce, or cast ballots in political elections in New Jersey also reveal nascent aspirations for women's independence after the Revolution.[78] From the moment women engaged in benevolent work (whether poor relief or charity schools), they situated themselves in positions where poor men, women, and children, white and black, native-born and recent immigrants, became their dependents. For young and single women this was novel; for all benevolent white women it was a means of distinguishing class and racial differences between themselves and the chosen objects of their care. White women activists adopted a language of exclusion based on class and race in order to be included in the public sphere in the revolutionary age, revealing another instance of how they could appropriate masculine imagery to establish a public presence.

White middle-class women discharged an important community service through female charity societies in post-revolutionary Philadelphia—disbursing outdoor relief and assuming part of the responsibility for leading the poor "into the path of virtue." Frequently, male city officials turned to women's organizations to disburse aid to the poor, acknowledging their own incapacities. In 1814, a city committee appointed to distribute firewood asked that the Female Association accept the task since "this committee feel themselves inadequate to the trust, from want of knowledge of those poor who are the fittest objects of this charity." The treasurer's books of the Female Society indicate substantial payments from Philadelphia poor officials to the society for services rendered between 1798 and 1805. Unchaperoned members of women's benevolent societies visited the homes of poor families, evaluating their needs, instructing them about industry and frugality, and assisting with supplies of food, clothing, and fuel. These actions of white benevolent women demonstrated that neither public welfare nor charity, as understood in the late eighteenth century, could be considered a male-only prerogative.[79]

Participation in voluntary benevolent societies provided activist white women an opportunity to engage in behavior with a political—and hence masculine—cast to it. This political behavior can easily be overstated, yet to some degree benevolent women developed a distinctly female culture of politics. Within their societies, women established constitutions, held regular elections, drafted reports and handbills for publication, debated public policy, and developed throughout that process a sense of their own usefulness and leadership skills. They engaged in a kind of partnership with local public officials, lobbying for funds, providing necessary social services, and articulating their own views concerning poverty and relief. By seeking and securing an act of incorporation from the state legislature, women in voluntary associations were able to engage in activities otherwise prohibited for married women in early America. They could collectively buy and sell property, bring lawsuits in court, invest their resources in stocks and bonds, and assume legal guardianship of children—rights and privileges legally denied to married women. Before incorporation, some women's societies insisted on electing an unmarried woman as treasurer to prevent the society's funds from being submerged, like a married woman's identity, into the property of a husband.[80]

White women's public political presence in benevolent reforms accorded with the overall uncertainty that characterized women's politics during the 1790s. Much like the new market economy, the rancorous political culture of that decade witnessed a growing visibility of white women coupled with an ideological façade that endeavored to keep them invisible. Although denied full citizenship and suffrage rights, white women appeared conspicuously in the street culture and festive celebrations of the new national political life. Both Federalists and Democratic Republicans relied on the organization of women and on the public displays of women's political loyalties during Independence Day and during Washington's birthday and funeral festivities. White women of all classes participated in a politics of the street, square, or commons; black women, by contrast, found safe opportunities for political action more limited. Festivals celebrating the French Revolution, such as the "Feast of Reason" that thousands of Philadelphians attended in August 1794,

gained widespread support among working-class women and men and offered opportunities for women to develop a political consciousness of their
own. A growing number of women discussed the political controversies of
the era. Their presence in a previously male-only arena was enough to make
William Cobbett bemoan the "whole tribe of female scribblers and politicians" he had observed in Philadelphia during the 1790s, who "began to talk
about liberty and equality in a good masculine style." Many educated women
became familiar with Mary Wollstonecraft's *Vindication of the Rights of Woman.*
Perhaps they stopped themselves when they read, "Let woman share the
rights, and she will emulate the virtues of man; for she must grow more perfect when emancipated." Or perhaps they glanced at Charles Brockden
Brown's *Ladies Magazine* and noticed the favorable review of the *Vindication*
placed alongside a song entitled "Female Extravagance." This suggestion
that virtue was not exclusively a male attribute echoed in the discourse surrounding female benevolence during the same time and place, just as did the
nagging conflation of femininity with irrationality and a lack of restraint.[81]

Ultimately, this manner of conceptualizing women's benevolence in the
language and symbols of virtue was short-lived. The conception of women's
benevolence changed in the nineteenth century, as did the gendered meaning of virtue. By the early nineteenth century, a feminine and private meaning of virtue superseded its masculine and public predecessor, establishing
virtue as a term for female chastity rather than civic action or martial
courage.[82] In part, the rise of evangelical benevolent societies solidified a new
conception of women's public activity. Rather than virtue, men and women
writers after 1820 most frequently used the concept of "influence" to explain
women's benevolence. Influence unlike virtue, did not have centuries of in-
vested meaning in republican or Protestant thought. It implied an inward,
quiet, and less visible behavior. It was a much more passive idea than virtue
and less overtly politicized. Most significant, it implied a more rigid difference between men and women, depicting women as more naturally suited
for benevolent work.[83]

Historians of women and benevolence have suggested that this nineteenth-century discourse that conflated benevolence with female influence
obscured the various political and economic actions performed by activist
women. Why such obvious conflicts between ideology and actions went unchallenged has puzzled these scholars; in other words, when prevailing gender conventions by the 1820s depicted women's actions as private and domestic, why did not contemporaries object to the presence of white women
in the masculine realms of economics and public policy?[84]

Perhaps the changing gendered language of benevolence introduced
here—from virtue to influence—can unravel this puzzle. The precedents for
these masculine-coded economic and political actions by women activists

had been firmly established long before a new feminized discourse regarding women's benevolence became entrenched in the antebellum era. Women reformers created a female culture of political behavior, affected public policy, and engaged in a variety of market and property actions while their benevolence was still understood within a framework of public virtue embedded with masculine meanings. They did this before changes in gendered discourse began to define all white bourgeois women's activities as entirely within the world of the nonproductive, nonpolitical, privatized home. Urban Americans, then, may not have ignored behavior that conflicted with their understanding of feminine propriety. Instead, the activities of women activists went unchallenged because they did not conflict with the ambiguously gendered understanding of benevolence in the post-revolutionary era, which associated both men's and women's actions with a discourse of public virtue. Only when more rigidly defined differences emerged within a class and gender ideology that reified maternity, domesticity, and innate female piety, did a disparity exist between the public actions and the prescriptive ideals of womanhood.

Between Mothers and Prophets

While some women confirmed their place in a masculine public arena through the rhetoric of virtue, other benevolent women activists sanctioned their presence in the public sphere by appropriating discourses that employed feminine, rather than masculine, imagery and language. After all, republicanism was not the only source of ideas regarding public duty during this era. White women activists who founded the first women's voluntary associations also searched for spiritual authorization for their benevolent actions. If we are to understand how women could justify their public presence as benevolent reformers in the new republic, we need to investigate the varieties of spiritual power that women could embrace. In the case of the women activists who formed Philadelphia's first female societies, they navigated a path through the prevailing models of women's spiritual authority in the eighteenth century. In particular, single Quaker women developed their own middle ground between the authority resting in the actions of their women's meeting and the self-representations of visionary prophets.

The earliest Quaker female benevolent societies in the new nation, such as the Female Society and the Aimwell Association, established themselves separately from the Friends meeting, with a membership comprised entirely of young unmarried women. A typical activist had just entered her twenties when she joined one of those societies. These young women were attempting to map out a place for themselves in a community that offered few outlets for single women to express their religious duty.[85] Friends in the American colonies had embraced the elaborate system of monthly, quarterly, and yearly meetings devised by English Friends to divide their religious business between separate men's and women's meetings; but despite its promise of sexual equality and a prominent role for women, this system effectively excluded young and unmarried women. The preponderance of women's responsibilities and duties among Quakers resided in the local women's monthly meeting, which was dominated by older married women (whom the earliest Friends referred to as "mothers of Israel"). This was not merely a sign of age or maturity, but reflected the privileges that marriage and maternity brought to Quaker women's work.[86]

Quaker women assumed two major responsibilities through the women's meeting: oversight of marriages and the disbursement of charity within the sect. Usually women Friends gained positions of authority not based on wealth or class but rather on the success of a mother in ensuring that her children married other Friends within the meeting's rules.[87] Monitoring marriages gave them a special role in preserving the integrity of the sect and offered a measure of authority over certain Quaker men. Both the prospective groom and bride had to appear before the women's monthly meeting, giving these women supervision not only over their daughters, but over the lives of young men as well. Older and married women also controlled the dispensing of charity to poor Friends. Age and marriage did not make a Quaker woman more compassionate, but they gave her the authority to supervise poor families that always accompanied the distribution of charity. Because it was not considered appropriate for unmarried women to inspect their own contemporaries' marriages or to oversee poor Quaker men and their families, they were effectively excluded from the main business of the women's meeting. Anne Parrish's experience confirms this. Her mother, Sarah Parrish, appeared regularly in the women's meeting minutes, assigned to various ad hoc committees to inspect the soundness of marriages or the moral behavior of women Friends; but as a young unmarried woman, Anne was nearly absent from those meeting records.[88]

These functions of the women's meetings assumed even greater significance during the mid-eighteenth-century Quaker sectarian reforms. Women Friends contributed appreciably to the success of that movement, which sought to achieve greater solidarity among Friends by more stridently disciplining members for marrying contrary to their traditions and by discouraging slave ownership and political officeholding among pacifist Friends during British colonial wars.[89] Inspired by prophetic voices of reformers such as John Woolman and Anthony Benezet, these measures eventually eliminated slaveholding within the Society of Friends. Yet the movement also brought a gender balance to Quaker religiosity at mid-century, narrowing the differ-

ences between men's and women's Quaker identity. Men relinquished political power, public office, and the commercial benefits of slaveholding, while
women defended the sect against the encroachment of the world by inspecting marriages and ensuring the charitable care for poor members. The exclusive domain of men's politics and commerce, then, was sacrificed for a
shared endeavor by both men and women to ensure the purity and discipline of the sect. The result was a familial-based insularity that guaranteed
the survival of the sect's first principles of peace and simplicity, yet, in the
long run, weakened its power in the religious culture of the city.[90]

Where, then, could single Quaker women fulfill their desires for religious
activism? One opportunity ensued when a woman became recognized as a
minister and traveled with the approval of her local meeting. Some young
women chose this alternative path for establishing their spiritual authority by
personifying religious visionaries or prophets—asserting that they possessed
special gifts of revelation, that God spoke directly to and through them.[91]
Quaker women ministers had figured prominently in the Society of Friends
since its beginnings. Spurning a professional in favor of a lay ministry, Quakers saw the essential qualification for ministry not in university training but
rather in a spiritual gift that God could bestow equally on any receptive person, man or woman. This was the basis (along with the doctrine of the Inner
Light) for the spiritual equality advocated by the earliest Friends. Those who
migrated to the American colonies brought the practice of women lay ministers with them, and women made up roughly 30–40 percent of the sect's
traveling ministers well into the eighteenth century.[92]

All Quakers accepted the fact that a minister spoke the words of God
rather than his or her own. In the earliest years, female Friends prophesied
in public, experienced and interpreted dreams and visions, and worshipped
with emotional and bodily ecstasy (the "quaking" that gave them their
name). During the dramatic era of the English Civil War and Interregnum,
visionary prophets interrupted church services, shouted down parish priests,
and denounced the authority of archbishops and kings, all the while exploiting the symbols of feminine spirituality and disorder. In the process, Quaker
prophetesses entered "a highly public arena—in streets, marketplaces,
churches, fields, and prisons"—where they helped establish a new spiritual
community.[93] During the eighteenth century, Quaker women preachers still
considered themselves divinely inspired voices of God, but the times as well
as the Quaker community had changed. By then American Friends had developed both an insular quietism centered on the silence and discipline of
the meeting house and urban wealth and respectability derived from the
counting house.

Quietism never fully replaced the spiritual gifts of visions and prophecy
that empowered some Quaker women's ministry and that allowed them to

assume public personas uncommon among the majority of white women in America.[94] Ann Moore, for example, although adopted as an orphan by a Pennsylvania Quaker family, was recognized by her local meeting as possessing the spiritual gifts of a minister when she was in her twenties. Moore's journal recorded the thoughts and actions of a spirit-driven and empowered minister of God. During one itinerant ministry, as she was preparing to leave New York City for Long Island, she wrote, "the divine power seized me, and made my flesh and bones to tremble and a voice passed through me, saying, 'The poor servants have not been favoured with the crumbs which fall from their master's table.'" So she remained with the families she was visiting, and in her words, "handed forth the crumbs which were committed to my trust."[95]

The infusing of the spirit authorized a new public role for young unmarried Quaker women. Rebecca Jones recorded the exact moment, July 9, 1758, at age nineteen, when she entered upon the public stage as a minister. On that summer evening, she recounted, "I stood up in great fear and trembling, and expressed a few sentences very brokenly," marking that as "my first public appearance." Susanna Hudson became a minister (a "public Friend," in the parlance of Quakers) at age seventeen, Jane Fenn at sixteen, and at twenty-two Elizabeth Hudson set out on her first ministerial travels.[96] Some female Friends used their spiritual authority as ministers to invert prevailing gender conventions, escape intolerable marriages, or challenge male dominance in a variety of its guises. Although most Quaker women waited until their children were grown before traveling as ministers, some left their children in the care of their husbands while they traveled on lengthy journeys to Europe or other parts of America.[97]

Other Quaker women exploited the role of visionary woman to assume a public political voice. Ann Moore twice traveled over a thousand miles during the Seven Years' War to preach to British Army commanders in Albany. Along the way, she debated a Presbyterian minister over whether the Bible gave women the authority to preach. During this time she experienced numerous dreams, which she called "visions of the night season." The vivid imagery of her dreams, and the events in her life, corresponded to the religious and political crisis that Quakers encountered during the war. In one vision Moore saw a giant woman draped in black clouds with a blood-red face (and a blood-red cloud hovering above) waving a large sword at her. Although Moore interpreted the woman as a sign of her own weakness and the sword as the spirit of melancholy and fear, she also might have been thinking about her own stepson ("my poor captive son") who had shunned Quaker pacifist principles and joined the army. Moore's dream merged her maternal concerns with fears that fellow Friends had not embraced the sect's mid-century reform movement, which urged them to conform more closely to Quaker testimonies against war, luxury, and slaveholding. In another dream, Moore saw "a yellow woman" who "had been in captivity" and a man who jumped out violently at her, projections again of slavery and violence. Moore's own anguish, as she recorded in her journal, that "I could not rule my own family, nor persuade my Friends at home to walk orderly" had induced her dreams and emboldened her desire for a traveling ministry.[98]

Although Moore never recorded whether she ever exhorted Quakers to free their slaves, narrating her dreams may have offered one way for a Quaker woman at that time to declare that message publicly. None of the four women's meetings in New Jersey and Pennsylvania studied by one historian recorded any discussion of slavery during the years before 1760. After the Revolution, the success of the Quaker reform of slavery within the Yearly Meeting perhaps made an antislavery message from a woman minister more palatable. Sarah Harrison, a Philadelphia minister, visited Friends throughout the South in 1788 and urged them to free their slaves. She is credited with freeing two hundred slaves, including nearly fifty at one meeting in Virginia, where she prayed with their owners and convinced them to manumit their bond people. Like Moore's, Harrison's ministry also joined visionary experience and a woman's prophetic voice; she apparently possessed the gift of interpreting dreams, a talent of which many friends and neighbors frequently availed themselves.[99]

Divinely inspired women, then, could assert a public presence in the late eighteenth century in ways that bypassed the masculine legitimacy of civic virtue; hence the few African American women who labored as itinerant preachers during the early republic also relied on visionary experiences to sanction their authority to preach the gospel in an inhospitable religious climate. Black women preachers encountered opposition on all fronts: from white churchgoers, who scoffed at the notion of poorly educated black women preachers; from black clergymen, whose leadership roles within black churches were threatened; and from their own husbands and families, who resisted these women's challenges to conventional gender roles. It comes as no surprise, then, considering the hostility these women encountered both within and outside their various denominations, that black women preachers relied on extraordinary spiritual gifts or experiences to authorize their unique calling to preach in public. A former slave named Elizabeth, who declared that she had been "called to be [a] mouth-piece for the Lord," recounted the numerous ways that visions influenced her conversion, her calling, and her assurance that she "was sustained by some invisible power." When "asked by what authority I spake? and if I had been ordained?" she recalled on one occasion, "I answered, not by the commission of men's hands: if the Lord had ordained me, I needed nothing better." Zilpha Elaw related in her *Memoirs* that a vision of light and a voice from God spoke directly to her that "thou must preach the gospel."[100]

Jarena Lee experienced frequent dreams and visions that guided her life choices and undergirded her difficult ministry. She was born in Cape May, New Jersey, in 1783 to free black parents, who were forced by economic difficulties to bind her out as a domestic servant at the age of seven. By 1804, Lee had moved to Philadelphia and experienced a conversion under the preaching of Richard Allen in the African Methodist church. Lee recounted the events leading to her conversion in a language of passivity, noting an internal struggle with her hatred toward one particular individual, a temptation to suicide, and the transforming power of a scriptural text.[101] Yet she described her call to be a preacher with words that were anything but passive, declaring that a visionary experience empowered her commission. Sometime around 1810, Lee heard a voice telling her directly, "Go preach the Gospel!" She immediately replied, "No one will believe me," only to hear the voice tell her again, "Preach the Gospel; I will put words in your mouth, and will turn your enemies to become your friends." Fearing that it might be Satan deceiving her, Lee cried out, asking God to confirm what she had just heard. At that moment, she saw a vision in "the form and figure of a pulpit, with a Bible lying thereon, the back of which was presented to me as plainly as if it had been a literal fact." That night, she wrote, she was so excited she preached in her sleep, and two days later boldly approached Richard Allen "to tell him that I felt it my duty to preach the gospel." As bishop of the African Methodist Episcopal (A.M.E.) Church, Allen never granted Lee the same status as ordained male preachers, yet Lee eventually attained recognition and acceptance as an "exhorter" in the A.M.E. church.[102]

Extraordinary spiritual experiences emboldened these women to challenge their opponents directly and to spurn the gender conventions regarding women in public. Elizabeth recalled that the Methodist elders "came out with indignation for my holding meetings contrary to discipline—being a woman." Prior to this, she described how "the Spirit came upon me with life," and "as for myself, I was so full I hardly knew whether I was in the body, or out of the body." Visionary experiences offset the limited educational training that these free black or former slave women possessed. It gave them a stronger sense of independence, freed them from the constraints of male-dominated denominational requirements for ministry, and provided them with self-worth derived from direct contact with God rather than through literacy or formal education.[103] Yet visionary women, whether Quaker or evangelical (white or black), also willingly defied any associations their spiritual authority evoked with the negative imagery of a "public woman." After all, the conflation of enthusiastic religion and visionary experiences with disorder and illicit sexuality was ubiquitous in the early republic.[104]

What was the relationship, then, of these various modes of performing women's public religious activism to the experiences of the white women who founded the earliest benevolent societies in Philadelphia in the 1790s? With the alternatives ranging between mothers of Israel on the one hand and visionary prophetic women on the other, these young white women reformers negotiated a middle ground between these extremes. Their benevolent activism relied on both the ideological context of women's public service within republican and Quaker contexts and their self-presentation in the likeness of visionary women to legitimize their authority for the novel task of establishing an independent charity.

Perhaps if the records of black women's mutual benefit societies during the 1790s had survived, we might be able to discern and compare the ways in which African American women's spiritual authority from visionary experiences translated into action for the black women who first experimented with voluntary associations. Without substantive records for these societies, we are left only to speculate. Still, African American women in late-eighteenth-century northern cities were likely familiar with the spiritual authority asserted by women preachers who had been inspired by visionary experiences. The reform career of Isabella Van Wagenen (later self-named Sojourner Truth), although certainly in a different era than post-revolutionary America, illustrates that remarkable encounters with the supernatural often corresponded with a woman's reforming activism.[105]

Anne Parrish, the founding force behind Philadelphia's first women's societies, illustrates this middle ground between the visionary woman and the sectarian guardian that Quaker women could assume. In 1793, at age thirty-three, Anne Parrish faced a crisis of social, political, and religious importance. Her parents contracted yellow fever during the epidemic that forced half of Philadelphia's population to flee the city and killed over five thousand residents, more than one-tenth of the population. According to accounts of her friends and her own letters, Parrish apparently "supplicated and covenanted with her God" that if God would be pleased to allow her parents to survive this plague, she "should be dedicated to Him in any allotment He might be pleased to call her to labor in." Her parents recovered, although two of her younger brothers died. Parrish then proceeded from "a secret sense of Duty" to devote her short life to the work of religious benevolence, founding along with several younger Friends the Female Society for the Relief of the Distressed and the Aimwell School for poor white girls, which initially met in her own home. This new benevolent activist's life story, then, exhibited remarkable parallels with the imagery of the visionary woman.[106]

A familiar motif in narratives of the prophetess is her identification with physical weakness, illness, or near-death experience, followed by her overcoming these limitations to proclaim a powerful message from God. The infirmity merely highlights the image of the female prophet as an empty vessel to be filled by God. Visionary women commonly enhanced that condition by abstaining from sleep, fasting, or otherwise pushing themselves to exhaustion, after which followed a dream, a vision, or some other extraordinary spiritual experience. Although Anne Parrish never suffered from yellow fever, she vicariously experienced a near-death experience through her parents and brothers, after which she proceeded to declare (in words and actions) a moral lesson for the Quaker faithful. Parrish did not consider herself a prophet, preacher, or minister. She did, however, express a message that challenged the prevailing sectarian conventions of benevolence among Quakers.[107]

The poor-relief society founded by Anne Parrish and her friends marked a significant break from the charity administered by married Quaker women because they directed their benevolence for the first time toward non-Friends in the city. The Female Society's goals mirrored those of many Quaker men who began to redefine benevolence in the 1780s, wishing "to do good" for all humanity rather than for Quakers alone. By joining the prison, abolition, or First Day (Sunday) school societies, these men considered benevolent activism as more than tribalistic safeguarding of their own sect.[108] Parrish's ideas of religious piety combined new evangelical sentiments introduced into late-eighteenth-century Quakerism with biblical imperatives and the language of sympathy. Her co-workers in the Female Society desired not only to express the truth of the Inner Light within all humanity, but also to respond to Christ's example and to "adopt the precepts He taught, to visit the Sick, feed the Hungry, and clothe the Naked."[109] Parrish reported in her letters that several older Friends were uneasy about the forms of her new benevolent activity. "Could I walk on in the *beaten path* without daring to think for myself, but relying entirely upon the judgment of those advanced in life," she pondered, "I might perhaps find an *easier way*." But her choice, she recalled, was a more difficult and trying path; she hoped that "the time will come when I shall be better understood." With striking introspection, she unveiled the challenge that her benevolent actions made to her inward-directed Quaker elders:

> None seem to understand my language. Some I meet with seem to be as insensible to my meaning as though I spoke in a foreign tongue. Even some I dearly love, cannot altogether unite with me. I believe they are afraid I shall be singular, and . . . led astray. I know some of them are religiously inclined, and would rejoice to see me so too, but my ideas of religion differ a little from theirs.

Parrish perceived her benevolent actions as emanating directly from the Divine, as "a stream of sympathy" flowing "so powerfully to the oppressed and suffering" that she felt "insensible to almost everything else." The source for this impulse, she explained, lay in an inspiration outside herself: *"I neither taught this stream of sympathy to flow, nor directed its course."*[110] It is entirely possible, then, that Parrish's prophetic message generated a cool reception from the leading wives and mothers in the Friends' Women's Meeting in Philadelphia. This new activism posed an alternative path to the definition of pious femininity and the role of a public woman. Parrish legitimated and sustained her new public persona by cleaving to a spiritual authority, not to ideas of motherhood or to symbols of masculine civic action.

Dorothy Ripley, an Englishwoman who traveled to the United States at the turn of the century to engage in religious reform, illustrates a more extreme example of the interrelationship between the prophetic woman and a new public role in benevolent activism. Ripley was raised in a Methodist family, but drifted toward Quakerism as a result of a dramatic bodily conversion experience (family and friends thought she was dead for nearly an hour, during which time she experienced a vision of the crucified Christ). Although no Quaker meeting accepted her, she felt that God had implanted in her a sympathy for the African race and had directed her to travel to Washington, D.C., to create a school for young black girls. By the time she arrived in the United States, Ripley's mission, and the visionary source of her calling, were already well known by Philadelphia Quakers. Thomas Cope noted in his diary that Ann Mifflin, a Quaker minister and activist in both the Female Society and Aimwell School, had approached him seeking financial support for Ripley's efforts. (Mifflin had herself criticized a Methodist meeting in the 1780s for refusing to allow a young woman to speak, when as Mifflin believed, "Male & Female are declared to be one in Christ.") Although Cope refused to help Ripley, he found "something extremely novel & interesting" in her mission, calling it "a spectacle rare & wonderful indeed," and benevolence worthy of admiration. But Cope was put off by the extraordinary spiritual empowerment that Ripley claimed. "I am told that in all her movements, even on trivial subjects," he wrote, "she professes to be directed by revelation from Heaven; truly then, she professes much."[111]

Ripley also approached the leaders of Philadelphia's black churches, Richard Allen and Absalom Jones, requesting permission to preach before their congregations, feeling that God had so commanded her. Jones allowed Ripley to preach on a Sunday evening in May 1803, but Allen refused her request on much the same grounds as he had denied Jarena Lee (that women preaching "was diametrically opposite to the letter and spirit" of the A.M.E. discipline). Perhaps Allen also sensed Ripley's condescending attitude toward black ministers. Her memoirs recorded her pleasure at discovering that Allen "although a coloured man" appeared "to have a knowledge of divine

things." Nonetheless, two influential members of Allen's Bethel Church
arranged for Ripley to speak on a Monday evening. When she was heckled by
a drunken white soldier, black church members noted the similarities between the persecutions that both they and Ripley faced.[112] Yet, like many
other independent women in the early republic, Ripley continually had to
fend off sexual advances from men and accusations that she was "a lewd
woman," because she traveled alone and dared to subvert the religious and
gender boundaries that declared a woman should not preach. Despite all
that, Ripley was the first woman ever invited to preach in the Hall of the
House of Representatives in Washington, D.C.[113] Anne Parrish's and Dorothy
Ripley's experiences were not typical; prophetic women never have been.
Still their self-representations marked them off from other public women in
the post-revolutionary era, suggesting the close affinity between some
women's benevolent actions and the role of the religious visionary.

But the religious visionary was only part of the middle ground constituted
by the benevolent activism of young Quaker women. Despite their exclusion
from the Friends women's meetings, and the definitive differences in their
benevolent objectives, the Female Society, Aimwell School, and the Society
for the Free Instruction of African Females still relied on the methods of religious activism established by the matrons of the women's meeting. Although their vision of benevolence expanded to encompass non-Quakers, all
three women's societies borrowed many of their organizational techniques
from the women's meetings. Female societies chose a clerk and a treasurer,
the principal officers of the women's meeting. The Female Society also immediately established a "visiting committee" to visit the homes of the poor in
their neighborhoods and throughout the city. They called on the homes of
those they relieved and monitored the schools and institutions where the
poor were assisted. Visiting committees adapted the practice of social visits
that Quaker women had developed in the women's meeting and transformed it into a popular tool of voluntary benevolent societies. Visiting committees became the frontline instruments of religious benevolent work.[114]

Almost immediately, the activities of these young Quaker women rivaled
the established religious labors of the Friends women's meeting. After 1795,
the Female Society raised and spent more money each year than the
Philadelphia Women's Monthly Meeting did for relieving poor Friends.
They raised and spent between four and six times as much as the women's
monthly meeting during their first three years of operation.[115] When other
benevolent women wished to begin a charitable society, they too observed
and borrowed from the actions of these young Quaker women. Several evangelical women—Rebecca Smith, Sarah Stille, Sarah Bayard, and Susan Bradford—who organized a charitable society in 1800, attended the meetings of
the Female Society to observe their operations.[116]

As the nineteenth century opened, the prominence of Quakers in Philadelphia's benevolent culture was soon eclipsed by other Protestants, especially men and women inspired by evangelicalism. A declining Quaker presence can, in part, be attributed to demographics. For more than a century Quakers had been increasingly outnumbered by new Protestant immigrants, diminishing their proportion of the city's population. Wealth and social prestige helped them maintain a measure of influence that extended beyond their numbers. Several other factors combined at the end of the eighteenth century to create a culture of religious benevolence dominated by evangelicals rather than Quakers. The mid-century reform movement that enforced a sectarian unity among Friends around the issues of marriage, slavery, and war also resulted in decreasing membership with each passing year. After the Revolution, two competing impulses—a tribalistic insularity rooted in that reform and a sympathy with evangelical enterprises among a new generation of Friends—produced rival visions of Quaker religiosity that eventually produced a bitter schism among Philadelphia's Friends. However, the models of voluntarism that Quakers established with such efforts as the Female Society and the Pennsylvania Abolition Society shaped the work of benevolent and reform enterprises in the nineteenth-century city.[117]

In the revolutionary decades, Americans commonly employed gendered language and symbols to delineate public service in the republic. Yet the ambiguity inherent in that discourse, the confusing lines between public and private, and flexibility of notions of virtue, independence, and humanity opened a door for a shared religious activism among benevolent men and women. In that moment, activist women negotiated a new public presence between the Scylla of public virtue and the Charybdis of the visionary woman. Neither path was achieved without costs, and neither produced complete autonomy for religious women. Still, these paths—and these women—did shape the dynamic of gender and religious activism in the new nation.

Poverty

My world is dead;
A new world rises, and new manners reign.
. . . the strangers gaze,
And I at them, my neighbor is unknown.

    EDWARD YOUNG, "Night Thoughts; or The Complaint" (1742)

In autumn 1799, Mary Wright received word that her husband Dominick would soon set sail as a seaman on board the ship *Jane Brown*, from Philadelphia to London. In all likelihood, no romantic or tearful farewells passed between Mary and Dominick. She probably never saw him leave. Perhaps somewhere among her deepest fears she knew something was amiss. What she did not know at that moment was that Dominick had no plans for returning and even less intention of sharing his hard-earned wages with his young bride. He left without granting her power of attorney or ordering that she could receive a portion of his monthly wage. At age nineteen, Mary suddenly found herself thrust into a state of penury, faced with supporting herself by whatever means she could find. All too soon she learned the extreme perils confronting any woman who became poor in a seaport city during the early republic. If she did not succumb to the epidemics of yellow fever that periodically laid waste to the city, she might still catch one of the many deadly diseases that took her neighbors' lives. Winter would assault her in far too many ways, as temperatures dropped precipitously, ice obstructed the rivers, work became scarce, food and firewood became even scarcer, and rents continued to escalate. She might have sold sexual favors to transient men at the wharves and markets to obtain some necessary income, while carefully avoiding the watchful eye of local authorities. If she bound herself out as an indentured servant or domestic help, she faced the possibility of physical, emotional, or sexual abuse from a master or mistress. It is hard to say that any of these circumstances would have been worse than what actually happened to Mary Wright. Only twelve months after Dominick abandoned her, she "was taken with a Fit" (from either mental or physical illness) and, being too close to a fireplace, fell into the flames and "got burnt in a most distressing manner." She was brought to the Philadelphia almshouse, a remedy for poverty designed by the city's male leaders, and was admitted there on October 7, 1800.[1]

At the opening of the nineteenth century, Mary Wright's neighbors and those who administered charity in the city would hardly have thought about censuring Mary for her impoverishment. When describing hardships like hers and other dependent poor, they invoked words such as "distressed" or "misfortune," and phrases such as "reduced in circumstances" or "fallen into poverty." Mary Wright knew firsthand that poverty produced problems, but she experienced them while much of her community looked on with sympathy. Nearly a decade of yellow fever epidemics had made these stories all too common. Yet less than two decades later, residents of Philadelphia had begun to change their perspective concerning the poor. By that time, people like Mary would constitute the problem itself in the minds of a growing number of Philadelphia residents, including those who were most active in bestowing charity.

In the midst of a market revolution, middle-class Protestants in northern cities embraced a new working definition of benevolence that quickly superseded eighteenth-century models of humanitarianism. Philadelphia's activists experienced that change most dramatically during the 1820s. In that decade, a hostile attitude toward poverty developed from mounting dissatisfaction with poor relief, commingled with skepticism about the moral culpability of the poor. Under the pressure of economic distress and rising public tax burdens, the city's affluent white middle classes shifted their loyalties away from private efforts to relieve and educate the indigent. Pious Protestants, who had balanced both humanitarian and missionary objectives since the 1780s, now dedicated their energy and resources more freely toward evangelistic enterprises. As an evangelical vision of benevolence gained ascendancy among religious activists, the material needs of the poor became redefined as spiritual ones. Conversion and moral reformation—the forging of character—were thought to be the best gifts that could be bestowed on impoverished folks in the back alleys and suburbs of the city. Through this process, evangelicals reshaped the meanings of brotherly love and duty to God in an urban community.

Mary Wright's adversity, like that of thousands of other women who lived precariously in search of adequate wages in industrializing northern cities, should alert us to the ways in which gender influenced her plight, illustrating that antebellum controversies surrounding poverty and benevolence emanated directly from a failure to address the issue of women's economic dependence. A growing feminization of poverty in the early nineteenth century complicated the responses of benevolent activists in American cities. Laboring women (and their children) constituted the largest sector of the poor requiring public and private assistance, yet many activists failed to address the gendered reality of poverty. Male-operated private charities responded to the poor as if solutions to their poverty could be achieved through presumed manly virtues such as independence and industry, overlooking the unique dilemmas caused by a woman's dependence.

Some middle-class benevolent women, in contrast, assumed leading roles during the 1820s as defenders of the character of the poor and the legitimacy of private charities. Despite their defiance of mounting public hostility, which blamed the indigent for their own poverty and condemned benevolent societies for encouraging pauperism rather than resolving it, in the end a cluster of cultural currents proved too strong for these women to withstand. Popular opposition to poor relief rooted in the principles of economic liberalism combined with an ascendancy of evangelical Protestantism to push northern benevolent activists toward spiritual solutions to social problems. This, in turn, led them to develop a new gendered conception of reform, one that placed greater emphasis on the sexual differences between men and women and characterized benevolence as a decidedly feminine action. All of these currents set the stage for the late antebellum era when white middle-class concerns about poverty became manifest in sentimental fiction. In this literature, the plight of poor working women captured the attention of middle-class audiences only as they represented a vehicle to express their class anxieties about sustaining the gender privileges of domesticity and women's dependence.

Poverty and Benevolence in the New Republic

For most Americans in the early republic, the state remained an insignificant feature of public life; thus urban residents frequently turned to private societies to address the numerous social problems they encountered. For some, voluntary associations offered a means of asserting class and racial dominance, but for others the choice to organize together entailed a strategy to stave off those efforts at domination and control. Following the American Revolution, urban activists launched the first great era of benevolence in America. By 1800, Philadelphians had organized the nation's first abolition society, prison society, free medical clinic, female charitable society, and Sunday school. Dozens of other associations followed these early leaders, providing food, clothing, and shelter for the poor, charity schools for indigent children and adults, schools for enslaved and free blacks, homes for orphans and widows, and reformation for city prostitutes.[2] Although influenced by Enlightenment and republican ideals, most benevolent Philadelphians saw their activism as a religious endeavor, as an expression of Christian piety in doing good for one's fellow human beings, especially those perceived as poor or needy.

Almost all benevolent societies shared a similar organizational structure. They usually began by adopting a constitution that established the association's objectives and operating rules. Societies relied on a membership of individuals who subscribed an annual donation of between one and three dollars. Money truly greased the wheels of charitable efforts, and nearly all post-revolutionary religious benevolent societies remained critically dependent on member subscriptions. Very rarely did the largesse of a few wealthy patrons finance a benevolent society. These organizations operated, as one historian has suggested, as a "subscriber democracy." Members then elected officers and managers who assumed the bulk of the responsibility for operating the society; managers dispensed the relief, operated the schools, drafted the annual reports, spent the money, and made the policy decisions. Both managers and members often rotated in service on visiting committees, which provided the backbone for urban benevolent work.[3]

It did not require a great deal of ingenuity to transform these kinds of associative actions designed for ameliorating social problems into organizations for accomplishing primarily religious objectives. The preeminent religious event of the first half of the nineteenth century—the Second Great Awakening—took root slowly in the cities of the North. Whereas frenzied revival meetings erupted on the southern and western frontiers between 1790 and 1810, evangelical pietism awakened with a less dramatic missionary sensibility in urban areas of the mid-Atlantic. Soon after 1800, religious activists founded benevolent societies with more expressly evangelistic objectives. Inspired by foreign missionary efforts begun in the 1790s, Philadelphians founded the nation's first Bible society in 1808, the Bible Society of Philadelphia. Tract and missionary societies soon joined with Bible societies and evangelical Sunday schools to introduce a new type of benevolence that aspired to convert unbelievers, reform sinners, and spread the knowledge of the Christian gospel. These evangelical voluntary associations, not open-air revival meetings, marked the first stage of this religious awakening in northern cities.[4]

Even with the emergence of evangelistic societies, urban religious benevolence prior to 1820 still shared both humanitarian and missionary objectives. Christian activists (including evangelicals) supported poor-relief and charitable societies while also laboring on behalf of the city's new Bible, tract, and Sunday school societies. Lay men and women and their clergy saw little contradiction between these two types of benevolent activism; both were biblical duties for all Christians.

The same individuals organized and operated both charity and evangelistic societies, offering perhaps the strongest evidence that Protestant activists made few distinctions between these two strains of Christian service.[5] The benevolent careers of Robert and Sarah Ralston illustrate this mergence. The activities of these two white evangelical Presbyterian activists, although perhaps more prodigious than the average reformer, mirrored the behavior of countless other benevolent men and women between 1790 and 1820. Robert Ralston was one of a new breed of elite merchants in the early republic. He was born in Chester County, Pennsylvania in 1761, arrived in Philadelphia as the Revolutionary War concluded, and proceeded to build his mercantile fortune from very little starting capital. His deep-felt evangelical piety found expression in numerous religious and charitable societies. No one, except perhaps Benjamin Rush, was as ubiquitous in Philadelphia benevolent enterprises at this time. Ralston seemed to have his hand in every benevolent activity that emerged in the new republic, and he fashioned a balance between the missionary and charitable associations that he supported. While serving as a manager of the Philadelphia Dispensary, the Fuel Savings Society, and the Magdalen Society, Ralston also figured prominently in the creation of the Philadelphia Bible Society, Missionary Society, Tract Society, and the First Day (Sunday) School Society. His activism spilled out in a variety of directions; he served both as the secretary of the committee for relieving St. Domingue refugees and as treasurer for the group that helped finance the first independent African American church during the 1790s.[6]

Sarah Ralston's activism likewise balanced humanitarian and missionary objectives. The daughter of Philadelphia mayor Matthew Clarkson, she married Robert in 1785 and gave birth to twelve children over the next twenty-one years. Despite such a large family, she was one of the original managers of the Female Association for the Relief of Women and Children in Reduced Circumstances in 1800, and, until her death in 1820, she participated in most of the major women's societies in Philadelphia, founding the Orphan Society, the Single Women and Widows' Society, and the Female Bible Society. Many contemporaries hailed Ralston as a model of female religious benevolence in the early republic. Publisher Mathew Carey, who himself had no sympathy for missionary societies, described her as "a mirror of goodness" and "a model for imitation" for every woman who desired to attain the highest honors of her sex.[7]

The Ralstons were certainly extraordinary in the breadth of their benevolent activities, although not in their shared focus on both humanitarian and missionary objectives. Divie and Joanna Bethune crafted nearly identical benevolent careers in New York City, and countless other men and women in cities throughout the North followed a similar pattern during the same decades. In the new nation, men's and women's activism continued to converge as expressions of public virtue.[8]

Before 1820, then, it is not possible to draw a sharp line between charity and evangelism. Benevolent women simply crossed over and labored in both poor-relief and evangelistic societies. Whereas two out of every three poor-relief activists in charities such as the Female Association also joined evangelistic societies such as the Female Bible Society or the Female Domestic Missionary Society, a majority of Female Bible Society managers in turn worked for societies that relieved the poor, widows, or orphans.[9] Benevolent evangelicals thus struck a happy medium between humanitarian and missionary sensibilities during the first two decades of the nineteenth century. They believed the anticipated millennium would be faithfully ushered in by the expansion of benevolence in all its forms.

From the founding of the republic until sometime after 1815, Protestant benevolent activists voiced a palpable sympathy for the condition of their poorer neighbors. Benevolent society spokespersons expressed neither a condescending nor an overtly critical attitude when commenting on destitute individuals. Their reports and speeches echoed a common refrain that poor people were not vicious merely on account of their poverty. Customary distinctions between the worthy and unworthy poor certainly existed, but the poor were not universally characterized as having an inherently inferior moral character. The difference between them and us, Jacob Brodhead told an audience of female charity supporters, "is owing, neither to their greater crimes, nor our superior merit." Despite their distressed circumstances, he reminded his listeners, "they are your brethren, and your sisters." Jacob Janeway took this attitude a step farther, venerating the poor as individuals who were especially blessed by God. After all, Jesus himself was "a poor man, dependent for his subsistence on charity."[10] Even when they acknowledged that poverty at times could be attributed to misconduct, religious charities resolutely censured this excuse for refusing to assist the needy. Thomas Branagan vigorously warned his readers not to "use the mean, pitiful reflection, that their misery is the offspring of their own imprudence!" "Away with such paltry subterfuges," Branagan concluded, "obey the first impulse of your melting heart," and let compassion lead to generosity. Benevolent activists remained convinced that improprieties among a few of the poor should not lead to a condemnation of countless others whose poverty was a product of circumstances beyond their control. Baptist minister William Staughton hoped that he might never see the day when "the poor is separated from his neighbour" or when "the poor is hated even by his own neighbour."[11]

Ministers and benevolent laypersons in the early republic thought they had a clear understanding of what they meant by "the poor" and saw no need for sophisticated studies to determine their composition or character. Benevolent activists defined poverty in a manner that permitted them to conceive of the poor as neighbors. Poverty, they surmised, was a fate which could, and often did, befall people of all stations and circumstances. It was a product of economic or other misfortunes, and they interpreted it as the work of God's providence. An individual or family might be reduced to penury by a variety of unforeseen forces, especially epidemics, injuries, and the capricious forces of commercial life.[12] Hence the earliest reformers employed a language that spoke generically of "the poor," an abstract term describing a fairly homogeneous group, not differentiated by class, gender, or race. Their own social experiences in the turn-of-the-century city further substantiated that definition of the poor. The working poor actually were their neighbors. At the beginning of the nineteenth century, northern cities such as New York, Boston, and Philadelphia still resembled small walking cities. Some residential segregation by class had begun to take shape, with wealthy residents tending to cluster in the city's commercial core, but most neighborhoods sheltered a mixture of social and economic groups. The working poor resided in alleys and lanes throughout the heart of the city.[13] When the 1790 census was taken in Philadelphia, such wealthy luminaries as William Bingham (Speaker of the Pennsylvania Assembly), Thomas Willing (president of the Bank of North America), William Lewis (attorney for the United States), and the renowned physician Benjamin Rush all resided on Third Street, south of Chestnut. Just around the corner, on Elbow Lane, lived a barkeeper, a bank teller, a cooper, a tin man, two white laborers, one free black laborer, and their families.[14] If these working families were thrust into poverty, their plight was within sight and sound of their wealthier neighbors. Thus the first scholar Anne Parrish admitted to the Aimwell School, operated by the Society for the Free Instruction of Female Children, was a peddler's daughter residing in Pewter Platter Alley where Parrish also lived. Benevolent activists did not always know intimately the objects of their care, but they felt that somehow they understood the reasons for their plight, whether it was a death in the family, devastating illness, French and Irish immigrants' fleeing political turmoil, or African Americans' seeking refuge from slavery.[15]

A crisis in confidence in the very idea of poor relief during the 1820s profoundly shattered this subtle balance in benevolent activism. And in the process, the meaning of benevolence itself for nineteenth-century Americans was forever transformed. The "poor in heart" would replace the actual poor as the objects of religious reformers' zeal and activism, as middle-class Northerners grew intolerant of an expanding class of dependent poor in its cities.

From Neighbors to Strangers

During the early nineteenth century, Americans' economic optimism often rivaled their religious expectancy. Soon after the news arrived that the

Treaty of Ghent had ended the war with Britain in 1815, many Americans voiced a buoyant confidence about the economic opportunities awaiting the young nation. They hoped for a new era of prosperity now that the inhibiting chains of an embargo and war had been severed. Newspaper editor Hezekiah Niles proclaimed that all that remained for Americans was to "march steadily on to the high destinies that await our country." Theirs was not a case of blind optimism. The conclusion of the War of 1812 did indeed coincide with a brief economic boom. Robert Ralston commented that a "flood of prosperity has undoubtedly attended the Country since the restoration of peace. A prosperous time I think may also be calculated upon for some months to come."[16]

A harsher truth, however, rested below the surface of this economic expectancy. An end to wartime hostilities opened the floodgates to inexpensive European goods entering American markets. While some merchants and consumers experienced a boom, fledgling industries and craftsmen in the cities were hit hard by the influx of cheap imports. Robert Ralston anxiously reconsidered his optimistic prediction for a prosperous future: "When the Country comes to feel the effects of the large importations in the present year . . . I should not be surprized if a very great reverse was to be the Consequence." Families of working Philadelphians, already disrupted by the war, did not bounce back so quickly when hostilities ceased. Hard times for the city's manufacturing establishments meant even harder times for the working poor who lived from hand-to-mouth even in the best of times. The number of poor residents seeking assistance from public and private relief institutions began a gradual climb after 1815.[17]

Escalating numbers of poor residents quickly became a problem too pressing for middle-class Philadelphians to ignore. A town meeting in February 1817 commissioned a group of prominent merchants and professional men to raise relief funds for the burgeoning ranks of the needy. But they also commissioned these men "to investigate the causes of mendicity" and to recommend plans "for preventing, in the future, the occurrence of so great an extent of misery." For these men, like many other residents, the increasing number of dependent poor did not signal hopeful prospects for the city's future. It was a trend that needed to be quickly arrested before it worsened. The committee distributed a list of questions to the city's poor-relief officials to gather a consensus of opinion about the nature, extent, and causes of pauperism in Philadelphia. Their findings were issued as the *Report of the Library Committee of the Pennsylvania Society for the Promotion of Public Economy.*[18]

For the first time in Philadelphia's history, inquiries were made into the actual nature of poverty in the city: Who were the poor? What caused their impoverishment? What proportions were women, blacks, and foreigners? What role did pawnbrokers, marital desertion, or the consumption of alcohol play? To these questions the report offered answers that were often con-

tradictory or distorted. Despite evidence of the gender, racial, and ethnic dimensions of the city's poverty problem, the committee chose not to focus on
these factors.[19] Rather, they issued a dramatic declaration that poverty could
be traced almost entirely to the intemperate behavior of the poor. They cited
city officials who asserted that a shortage of employment was not the cause of
increasing poverty, but rather that "idleness, intemperance, and sickness"
were its most frequent and real causes. This argument that the poor were to
blame for their poverty was not entirely new, but from that moment on, it
became a forceful and persistent feature of an increasingly popular antagonism toward the poor.[20]

The conclusions of this first systematic study fueled a growing suspicion of
poverty and poor relief that marked a turning point in the culture of urban
benevolence. The editor of the New York *Commercial Advertiser* publicized
widely the Pennsylvania Society for the Promotion of Public Economy's effort, and within a few months New York citizens had commissioned a similar
study that blamed intemperance as the primary cause of poverty and severely
criticized poor-relief expenses. New York and Baltimore soon established Societies for the Prevention of Pauperism. By 1820, poor inhabitants and public relief officials alike found themselves vilified in nearly every sizable city in
the North. Prior to that moment, many urban Northerners still perceived
poverty as a natural product of economic or other misfortunes, as an example of God's providence. But with the flowering of belief in each individual's capacity for economic advancement—the foundation of nineteenth-
century liberalism—came the assumption that poverty was something
unnatural, even un-American, in a land of opportunity. These increasingly
popular liberal ideas helped convince middle-class Northerners of the moral
rectitude of their own passionate economic self-interest, while persuading
them that others' destitution was no longer a natural, or morally acceptable,
condition. The committee's first query—"What description of persons are
most improvident?"—and newspapers' responses that the poor were "victims
of their own improvidence and viciousness" illustrate these rapidly changing
cultural attitudes about poverty. The term "improvident" not only implied
that the indigent were directly responsible for their own poverty, but also removed the responsibility from God. In a Protestant religious culture, few
were likely to miss the implication of this wording: poverty resulted from the
improvidence of an individual, not the providence of God. From this perspective, greater numbers of the urban middle classes would develop a deep-
ening distrust of the poor.[21]

The Library Committee report was the first expression of a decade-long
fixation with the problem of poverty and poor relief in Philadelphia. Despite
the committee's recommendation for "a radical change in the present mode
of administering charitable assistance," Philadelphians made no immediate

changes in their poor-relief policies. Instead, from 1817 until the poor laws were revised in 1828, leading Philadelphians examined, studied, complained about, and denounced the problem of poverty and the methods used to relieve it. Typifying all of this was a growing dissatisfaction with the excessive burden of poor taxes and a simmering resentment over the ever-increasing throng of dependent poor.[22]

Within a few years, postwar economic doldrums turned into a full-scale national depression, the first in American history. The Panic of 1819 contributed to an economic stagnation that lingered through 1822, further exacerbating the poverty problem in northern cities.[23] Young industries, especially textiles, which had flourished during the protected era of embargo and war, were forced to abandon their operations. Unemployment ballooned. Conservative estimates at the time pointed to at least 7,500 displaced workers in Philadelphia, while others estimated that perhaps as many as 20,000 workers in the urban area had been dismissed. Economic distress indiscriminately struck nearly all groups in the community, but hit especially hard those individuals and families dependent on wage labor. The personal finances of many city residents simply crumbled. Over 1,800 Philadelphia men and women were imprisoned for debt in 1819 alone, and sheriff sales of foreclosed property rose tremendously. As Robert Ralston noted at the beginning of the panic, "the distress is beyond . . . description. Many failures have occur'd and many more will take place."[24] Hardships were compounded by the recurrence of epidemics and inclement weather in the city. An outbreak of typhus occurred in 1820 for the second time in two years, only to be followed the same autumn by another of the periodic panics about yellow fever in Philadelphia. By the beginning of 1821, the city was caught in the grips of its coldest January in four decades. Both rivers froze over, and Philadelphia's commercial economy ground to a halt.[25]

A tremendous burden was placed on available poor-relief services. The number of people receiving public assistance mushroomed from 3,145 in 1814 to over 5,500 in 1820, the largest single-year figure for the entire first half of the nineteenth century. An additional eight thousand residents sought relief at the soup kitchens and offices of private charitable societies.[26] As such, the city's charitable institutions, both public and private, staggered under the weight of greater demands for assistance. Since the 1780s, Philadelphia's municipal authorities (known as the Guardians of the Poor) had administered public poor relief through a system that supplemented admission to the almshouse for some of the poor with weekly cash allowances (pensions) for others. As poverty steadily increased after 1815, the balance began to tilt toward ever greater expenditures on what officials called "outdoor relief" (cash pensions) rather than on the almshouse.[27]

From the viewpoint of Philadelphia's public poor-relief officials, they had no other choice but to tighten their belts and reduce their expenditures for assistance. The panic not only swelled the ranks of the poor, but also severely reduced the incomes of middle-class and wealthy residents, who shouldered the poor-tax burden in the city. Thus, while poor-tax levies increased dramatically during the depression, the ability to collect those revenues diminished. During the height of the panic, the Guardians of the Poor decided to reduce the number of people receiving monetary assistance and curtail the amount paid to each individual. Likewise, the almshouse managers discharged from their care all the inmates whom they deemed capable of supporting themselves.[28] Economy and savings may have been the intended outcome of these actions, but this policy also had the unavoidable effect of making poverty more visible in Philadelphia. Street-begging and long lines at soup kitchens and private charities represented the increasingly evident signs that poverty had become a more common feature of life in the city.[29]

Resentment toward the poor and dissatisfaction with the relief system intensified throughout the 1820s. Few commentators agreed about where so many additional poor people had come from. Exaggerated claims were made about the excessive burden of former slaves on the poor-relief system, despite the known fact that the proportion of laboring black residents was actually declining during these years. Other critics blamed the influx of new foreigners, complaining that the generosity of Philadelphia's charitable institutions drew the profligate like a magnet to the city. Irish immigration had in fact grown steadily since 1815, with perhaps 200–500 new arrivals from Ireland each week during peak summer months.[30] Few contemporaries, however, recognized what historians now know: that the burgeoning poverty problem had less to do with immigration than with the market revolution, the transition to industrial capitalism, and the concomitant spread of wage labor in Philadelphia's economy. Greater commercialization and market production, both in the rural hinterland and in the city, along with new manufacturing enterprises, placed an ever-increasing number of people under the precarious conditions of seasonal employment. Perhaps it is understandable that wealthy and middle-class residents came to view this mobile class of wage laborers as a more distant and foreign group. Traditional and customary bonds among individuals, families, and communities, forged across wealth and status boundaries in the master's workshop, the nearby market, or the local church, began to break down as the new commercial economy expanded. Wage earners became visible only when economic hardships exposed the fissures in communal and family support networks and they were forced to request public or private assistance. In the eyes of the middle class, a poor person had changed from a neighbor into a stranger— a profound change, and few could clearly make sense of it. Many Philadelphians were certain only, as Mathew Carey phrased it, that the number of paupers in the city was "oppressively great."[31]

Women encountered the lion's share of this increasing poverty, just as they had in the eighteenth century (and still do in contemporary America). Between 1811 and 1829, women received about 90 percent of the outdoor cash relief from Philadelphia poor officials. Although less likely to be admitted into the almshouse, women still accounted for a sizable majority (often as great as two to one) of those receiving public assistance before 1828.[32] Other cities, such as New York, Charleston, and Petersburg, Virginia, faced similar problems with increasing female poverty.[33] Urban laboring women tried to survive on inadequate and inequitable wages. Neither textile employment, where female operatives could be hired for half the wages of a male spinner or weaver, nor the sewing trades with their exploitative putting-out system offered laboring women a sufficient living wage. The family system that still governed women's wage-earning made women workers more vulnerable to maltreatment by male sweatshop employers, and it kept their poverty less visible. Moreover, the population mobility that accompanied wage labor resulted in frequent cases of laboring men deserting their wives and families. The ledgers of urban poor-relief officials are filled with the characteristic explanations for a woman's impoverishment—"husband in prison," "husband bad fellow," "husband at sea," or "husband has abandoned her." Philadelphia's Guardians of the Poor reported a sharp increase in 1820 in wives with children abandoned by their husbands "who seek remote and distant places for employment." Mobility remained one of the few ways laboring men survived in a wage-labor system that offered them seasonal work and no employment security; yet their wives and children often experienced that movement as abandonment and privation. (Women with children rarely could exploit that mobility as easily as men.) Female-headed households grew steadily after 1815, and black women for the first time experienced this hardship more frequently than white women. Despite these realities, most contemporary discussions of poverty overlooked the predominance of women among the poor. The generic phrase "the poor" still dominated the discourse surrounding poor relief and the moral failings of the indigent. Little effort was made to distinguish the unique poverty of working women.[34]

Middle-class Philadelphians experienced the hardest pinch of the poverty problem in their purses. Poor-tax levies remained relatively high throughout the early 1820s. The annual poor-tax assessment for the years 1817–25 averaged over $130,000, compared to an average levy of $77,416 for the years 1800–1810. Indignation over public expenditures for the poor suddenly became more vocal. Samuel Emlen complained to Roberts Vaux that if the poor tax continued to rise as rapidly as it had, everyone would be a pauper by the end of the century. It is not surprising, then, that city officials had difficulty collecting the revenues demanded. Many residents simply turned the tax collector away empty-handed. In 1823 city officials received only $40,000 of the $100,000 levied.[35]

Philadelphia's leaders continued to investigate, study, and ruminate over the problem of poverty during the 1820s, but reform of the system came slowly. Other cities and states, by contrast, summarily acted to revise their poor laws much earlier in the 1820s. The final straw on the backs of tax-paying Philadelphians came in 1827 when a citizens' committee report examining other cities' poor-relief systems discovered that Philadelphia residents were paying more than twice the per capita poor rates of New Yorkers and nearly three times the rates of residents of Baltimore and Boston.[36] By 1828, the Pennsylvania legislature authorized a sweeping reform of the city's poor-relief system, not only creating a new almshouse outside the city limits, but also demanding the complete abolition of outdoor cash payments once the almshouse was completed. Philadelphia's public officials chose institutionalization as the only solution—the only deterrent—for the idle and profligate who had supposedly overrun their city. Ironically, the one city in America that was slowest to act, most cautious and indecisive in accepting changing ideas about poverty, would by the end of the 1820s carry out the most thorough and severe dismantling of the urban poor-relief structure inherited from the post-revolutionary generation. After that, the message of Philadelphia public officials was unmistakable—if you are poor, you may live in the almshouse, but do not expect cash relief.[37]

After a decade of scrutiny into the city's poverty dilemma, a well-established distrust of the poor's character became fixed in the minds of a sizable segment of the population. Older communal notions of the "worthy" and "unworthy" poor slipped silently from the rhetoric of poor-relief critics. Investigations of the welfare system now lamented the loss of the face-to-face resolution of poverty that had existed just a generation before. Public rhetoric concurred with a belief that if the worthy poor had vanished, then all poor people must be impoverished by their own vices. Understanding and sympathy toward poor women, such as Mary Wright, who had suffered hardships, faded from public discourse. Suddenly, "the poor" was replaced by the term "pauper," which implied a shiftless, idle, or intemperate person, less deserving of sympathy than the needy, distressed, or less fortunate. For more and more well-to-do Philadelphians, the city's financial woes and social problems could now be traced to what they perceived to be the morally suspect behavior of the poor. They did not have to attribute the city's poverty problem to the vagaries of a capitalist economy or even to the workings of God's providence. Now the middle class had a set of ideas confirming their belief that the poor were to blame for their own condition.[38]

Encountering the Feminization of Poverty

Dissatisfaction with public poor relief in the 1820s spilled over into a vociferous assault on private benevolent societies, operated primarily by religiously motivated volunteer activists. Fears that public expenditures had gotten out of hand now "excited a spirit of hostility" against private charities. Deeply felt suspicions of indiscriminate almsgiving pulsed through the strong oral culture of the city. Whether in taverns or coffeehouses, marketplaces or work spaces, many Philadelphians wondered aloud whether the able-bodied and undeserving were being indulged by benevolent organizations. Newspapers frequently accused benevolent societies of encouraging idleness and pauperism by being too indiscriminate in their assistance to the poor, by making dependence an easy alternative to industry. Public resentment over poor relief was so strong, Mathew Carey noted, that every day Philadelphians "hear loud complaints on the subject," with "eloquent orators declaiming against benevolent societies."[39] Under these circumstances, rumors easily developed that exorbitant sums were being lavished on undeserving paupers by private charities, further magnifying the escalating suspicions of private charities.[40]

Is it any wonder, then, that charitable societies felt besieged as their benevolent efforts elicited frequent criticism? Indeed, nearly every private charity mentioned the "discouraging circumstances" and public prejudice they encountered after 1820.[41] Accusations of promoting the very vices they wished to eradicate came as a serious blow to religious charities. It questioned the very foundations of their Christian activism, forcing them to rethink the presumptions that justified their benevolence. Their responses to the pressures of growing public impatience with pauperism reveal how new attitudes about poverty reshaped the strategies and objectives of urban benevolence. At the same time, their reactions exposed the divergent ways benevolent activists grappled with the gendered character of poverty in an urban economy characterized by market capitalism and a wage-earning labor force.

Religious benevolent societies immediately found themselves placed on the defensive. Some tried to refute distorted public conceptions about the nature and benefit of their charitable efforts. "Few errors [are] more pernicious, or more destitute of foundation," Mathew Carey repeatedly declared, than the claim that benevolent societies promote idleness and dissipation. Carey, a retired successful publisher, devoted much of his public writings during the 1820s to the issue of poverty and poor relief and became an outspoken defender of charitable organizations against such unfounded criticism.[42] The Female Hospitable Society thanked Carey in 1828 for his efforts to "combat the erroneous idea . . . that these charities increase pauperism." In the twenty years since they created their society, these women confidently asserted, "we can prove *we have been instrumental by timely aid* . . . in keeping hundreds out of the Alms-House." In a similar way, the Dorcas Society of Philadelphia objected vigorously to those who tried to smear the reputation of benevolent associations by exploiting fears of injudicious almsgiving. Some charities, especially women's societies, insisted that the virtuous and helpless poor ought not to be sacrificed on the altar of a hard-hearted fallacy that indiscriminate charity might injure society.[43]

But other private charities easily capitulated to prevailing public opinion rather than challenge their critics, hoping to turn the suspicions of city residents in their favor. Some charities, such as Philadelphia's Northern Soup Society, openly acknowledged that "indiscriminate charity" has "a direct tendency to increase pauperism." They hoped to convince a skeptical public that their society was different. Every effort would be made, these charities reminded the public, to evaluate the merits of all persons applying for relief, ensuring that only the truly deserving were assisted. These societies tried to allay their fellow citizens' fears that they had "unintentionally bestowed a premium on idleness." Nevertheless, by assenting to the basic premise that poor relief breeds pauperism, these benevolent activists further perpetuated popular prejudices against the poor.[44]

One important exception to this trend can be discovered in Philadelphia's African American community. African Americans rarely blamed the poor for their poverty because they recognized that their neighbors were impoverished by racial and economic conditions beyond their control. The vicissitudes they encountered in a wage-labor economy were only compounded by blatant racism. The valedictorian of a free black school in New York in 1819 wondered aloud, "Why should I strive hard, and acquire all the constituents of a man, if the prevailing genius of the land admit me not as such, or but in an inferior degree!" He mused despondently about his prospects for work, "Shall I be a mechanic? No one will employ me; white boys won't work with me. Shall I be a merchant? No one will have me in his office; white clerks won't associate with me. Drudgery and servitude, then, are my prospective portion. Can you be surprised at my discouragement?"[45] Free black residents knew that they accounted for an unjustly high percentage of the city's poor, and yet they received only a paltry share of public assistance and charity from white societies. African Americans, then, turned to mutual benefit associations to provide social insurance for contributing members and their families, while strengthening the free black community amid white prejudice. By 1831, more than sixty mutual benefit societies had been created by black men and women in Philadelphia. The Daughters of Africa, typical of these organizations, was founded during the depression in the winter of 1821. Hundreds of women joined the society (several of them capable only of signing their names with a mark) and paid pennies per week for dues. They received, in return, a little assistance whenever they might fall sick for a short period of time and burial funds in case of the death of a husband or child. During a given week in March 1823, several women claimed benefits of between $0.75 and $1.50 for a week of illness. Critics who harangued about the poor not being industrious, frugal, or investors must have simply ignored these mutual benefit associations. Yet, although they did not blame the poor for their poverty, African American benevolent societies did criticize the behavior of their poor members. The minute book of the Daughters of Africa is filled with instances in which the society disciplined members for disorderly, immoral, or unlawful actions. This was not a strategy for emulating the middle class; these women had little hope of ever moving out of the laboring classes. Rather, it constituted a method of self-regulation that was necessary for poor black women in an era when poverty and blackness were objects of derision among a majority of the white population.[46]

To stave off mounting criticism, white benevolent societies endorsed work relief as the distinguishing feature of private benevolence. Work was certainly not a new concept for charities. Since the 1790s, urban charitable societies had placed some stress on the advantages of supplying work opportunities as part of their charity. The Quaker women of the Female Society for the Relief of the Distressed created a house of industry in 1798 to provide spinning or needlework for impoverished women. But prior to 1820 benevolent societies had never devoted their primary attention to employment, nor had they aggressively promoted work as the principal selling point for their societies.[47] This all began to change in the 1820s. To survive the onslaught of skepticism about private benevolence, society members gradually played down their cash assistance and sang the praises of work relief as the true expression of Christian charity. They wished to convince skeptical critics that their organizations abided by the adage that it was better to give a man a fishing pole than to give him a fish—or more accurately in Philadelphia, to give a woman a needle and thread rather than fuel or rent.

Still, Protestant laypeople searched without certainty for a way to resolve their activities beneath the pressure of hardening public sentiments. Two benevolent societies in the 1820s—the Female Hospitable Society and the Provident Society in Philadelphia—offer a telling glimpse into the different ways white middle-class men and women responded to the critical assault on benevolent societies. The Female Hospitable Society was established prior to the poor-relief crisis of the 1820s, operated solely by women, and outwardly religious and Protestant. The Provident Society, by contrast, was founded in the midst of the 1820s poverty controversy and was operated by men without any overt pretensions of being a religious organization. Each society had a singular tale, and their respective stories together expose the ways in which gender defined the controversies surrounding poverty and benevolent activism in the early nineteenth-century city. Middle-class benevolent men and women each experienced and perceived poverty in different, gendered ways, and at certain moments the societies they created boldly embraced opposing positions, determined in part by how each confronted the feminization of poverty in American cities.

An interdenominational group of women founded the Female Hospitable Society when Philadelphia's working poor faced the economic hardships of an embargo in 1808. The society began with only forty members, but within two years it had grown to nearly two hundred, each paying a two-dollar annual contribution. At its peak just prior to 1820, the roll of subscribers had grown to seven hundred.[48] The managers who ran the operations of the society were women of the newly formed middle-class rather than the wives and daughters of Philadelphia's elite. None of the women, nor their fathers or husbands, would have appeared on a list of the city's wealthiest citizens. Most came from families where the head of the household was a small-scale shopkeeper, merchant, or retailer. Mary Snyder, Elizabeth Van Pelt, and Margaret Silver, among the most active members, were the spouses of a grocer, a dentist, and a merchant, respectively.[49] The same core group of women activists labored in the society from the 1810s to the 1840s. Their explicit design was to create a society "for the relief of the sick, the aged, the indigent, the widow, the orphan, and the destitute stranger." Active members distributed clothing, bread, and other sundry items to poor families, established a small-scale manufactory to provide spinning and sewing work for poor women, and also distributed Bibles, tracts, and prayer books for their spiritual comfort. The society derived its financial resources almost entirely from the donations and subscriptions of its members.[50]

From the beginning, the women of the Female Hospitable Society evinced their compassion and sympathy toward the poor. They emphasized repeatedly that no great moral difference existed between themselves and those they assisted. In their minds, falling into poverty represented a peril that nearly every class in the community faced. These women knew from face-to-face contact with poor women that indigence emanated from factors often beyond an individual's control. Female poverty most commonly resulted from inadequate employment and the insecurity of depending on laboring men for their livelihood. Their own experiences convinced these women that it was neither truthful nor fair to equate poverty with idleness and profligacy.[51] Amid economic distresses and shifting public reactions toward the poor after 1820, Female Hospitable Society members struggled to meet their compassionate objectives. Demands for their assistance grew with the onset of the depression. By 1818, the women reported that they had twice as many applicants for aid as they could help—and still they were ready to take on this challenge. The "depressed state of things," they announced, "will call for redoubled exertions on our part." But the managers of the Female Hospitable Society never had the opportunity. Conditions in the early 1820s severely reduced the society's resources. Diminished incomes among all classes and a widespread skepticism of the merits of benevolent societies resulted in fewer donations and greater difficulty in selling the work produced by their charges. Their annual receipts dropped from nearly four thousand dollars in 1817 to less than eight hundred by 1822.[52]

Despite their declining treasury, the women of the Female Hospitable Society challenged public prejudices about the character of the poor and the value of benevolent societies throughout the early 1820s. No doubt, society members felt a great deal of outside pressure as resentments brewed over the poverty problem in Philadelphia. Their annual publications spoke frequently about the "discouraging circumstances" they faced in carrying out their objectives and combating a skeptical and hostile public. Nonetheless, these women chose to stand firm against the tide of public sentiment, refusing to accept the notion that the city's poor were suffering from their own improvidence and vice. At the height of the depression they testified that "almost all the misery we have witnessed" this past winter "has arisen from want of *sufficient employment.*" Intemperance, they contended, more frequently developed as a by-product of poverty rather than being its cause. Nothing was more unfair, they stated, than judging all of the indigent by the vicious habits of a few. "The innocent ought not . . . to suffer for the guilty," they argued, "and giving the poor a *bad name* in a body, is adding to their distresses," and destroying their moral right to the relief they deserve. Such sentiments made the women of the Female Hospitable Society, along with Mathew Carey and African American mutual relief societies, the lone defenders of the poor at a time when the indigent were assailed from all sides. Yet their efforts to sway public opinion could not prevent the numerous defections from their membership ranks. From a high point of seven hundred members just eight years earlier, the number of their supporters dwindled to 107 in 1828 and remained near that figure for the next decade.[53]

The Female Hospitable Society could stand firm against the shifting tide of public sentiment for only so long, and within a few years the managers had acquiesced to the reigning perspective critical of poverty and its relief. By the 1830s, the society's reports began stressing that the nature of their relief was restricted to employment for the able-bodied poor. The seal and symbol of the society, with the motto "As Employment is Independence, so Idleness is the worst kind of Slavery," became more and more prominent in their publications. It displaced a print from the early 1820s portraying an idyllic image of a young woman spinning at a wheel outside a farmhouse, while others were busily harvesting in the background (figures 2 and 3). Thus a pre-industrial vision of work and a traditional view of poverty and communal values gave way as the women adopted a view of poverty and free labor based on the liberal doctrines of individualism and self-determination. By 1831, the women of the Female Hospitable Society had reissued their constitution and explicitly changed the purpose of the society from "the relief of the sick, the aged, the indigent, etc." to the employment and relief of the same. Four years later, they retreated further from their defense of the integrity of the poor, acknowledging that "in most instances, especially in our highly favoured country, poverty and its attendant sufferings are the consequences of improvidence and vice." Still, the outcome of their transformation should not detract from the battle they waged. Although the idea of poverty as a character flaw ultimately won out, the Female Hospitable Society fought courageously against that notion for a considerable time even though many other benevolent activists capitulated to the view of poverty consistent with liberalism and free-labor and free-market capitalism. Their more intimate contact with impoverished women and their developing ideas about womanhood had convinced them for two decades that poverty did not reflect any inherent moral differences between classes.[54]

Whereas these women activists resisted liberalism's revisioning of the meaning of poverty, the men of the Provident Society embraced the new conception of the poor even though that ultimately limited their effectiveness as benevolent benefactors. Organized in 1824, the Provident Society included many of the affluent and actively benevolent men who had shaped Philadelphia's benevolent culture since the 1790s, including Bishop William White, Roberts Vaux, and Robert Ralston. Three-quarters of these men had also served in other private benevolent societies. And although these men belonged to eight different denominations, the Provident Society never claimed to be a religious society. They did not use the city's clergy or churches to raise money or solicit volunteers, their publications lacked any explicitly Christian language justifying their endeavors, and they offered no religious solutions to the poverty problem, neither for the giver nor for the recipient of charity.

The Provident Society managers felt they possessed a remedy to resolve the woes of excessive poor taxes in Philadelphia. Work relief in a monitored environment would be far more efficient, they believed, than distributing cash payments to needy families. It offered an incentive to the industrious poor and drove away the supposedly lazy poor. By providing employment for indigent residents, the society hoped they had devised a plan whereby the in-

FIGURE 2. This idyllic image of female labor, the earliest symbol of the Female Hospitable Society, evoked notions of a pre-industrial farm economy. *Poulson's American Daily Advertiser,* 13 Jan. 1821. Courtesy of the Library Company of Philadelphia.

FIGURE 3. The Female Hospitable Society later employed a symbol and motto at the top of their annual reports emphasizing the idea that the poor were responsible for their own condition as well as for their own uplift. *The Twenty-Seventh Annual Meeting of the Female Hospitable Society* (Philadelphia, 1835). Courtesy of the Historical Society of Pennsylvania.

dustrious would be "saved from the degradation of dependence," and the public might be relieved of an excessive tax burden. In its first years, the treasury of the Provident Society was plentiful and its goals set high. In the first year alone, the society secured over $7,500 in donations and amassed total receipts of nearly $13,000. By comparison, that figure was equal to one-eighth of the total city poor-relief expenditures and was four times what the Female Hospitable Society received that same year. It was easily more money than any other private poor-relief charity had at its disposal throughout the 1820s. With the apparent financial and moral support of a sizable part of the philanthropic community, the managers proceeded to put their plan into operation. Their first step was to establish a house of industry in the western part of the city, where the poor could come for employment when they had exhausted all other possibilities.[55]

From the outset, the men of the Provident Society were caught in a bind. On the one hand, they considered themselves compassionate men; after all, most of them had distinguished themselves by their generous charity for two decades. When they first created the society, they wanted the public to know they were not motivated by a contempt for the poor. In one of their earliest statements they declared that "it is unworthy of us, as men and Christians, to sit still and condemn the poor. . . . They are not all confirmed in intemperance and indolence." Provident Society members wanted to demonstrate that private benevolence could still work, that compassion could coexist with the capitalist and entrepreneurial economic ideals they also embraced. On the other hand, these men shared the prevailing skepticism and hostility toward poverty in a supposed land of opportunity. With few exceptions, they had all achieved their fortunes from humble beginnings and felt they knew personally the values of industry and thrift. Over half of the society's managers were merchants and professionals, and many of them looked back on their successes as vindication of their own character. As such, their sympathies for the poor quickly waned. Statements expressing sympathy for the poor did not appear again in the society's reports. Within a few years these men had a difficult time convincing benevolent-minded Philadelphians that the Provident Society's actions, let alone their rhetoric, were motivated by compassion.[56]

The Provident Society managers' high hopes for a successful marriage of benevolence and free-labor market capitalism immediately soured. The principal reason was their inability to comprehend the gendered nature of the problem they confronted. From the beginning, the Provident Society proved incapable of affecting the one social group they had set out to reform—indigent men. They hoped that by encouraging labor and thrift they might arrest the vices they viewed as the bane of poor neighborhoods and the peculiar traits of poverty-stricken men—dependence, idleness, and intemperance. But because the society's managers were afraid they might compete against existing industries in the city, they resolved to pay only "extremely low wages," hoping the poor would seek work elsewhere. Thus they were left with offering sewing work for women and miscellaneous labor around the workhouse for men. It should not have surprised them, although it did, that "very few males . . . availed themselves of the opportunity," while "hundreds of women crowded to the House."[57] These men uncritically embraced the wage-labor system and consequently failed to address the ways in which the inequities of that system fell heavily on poor women. Their actions revealed their incognizance of the extent of female poverty and the disparity between the wages men and women could earn outside of charitable institutions. After the first year, when hopes of establishing a house of industry had vanished, the Provident Society's assistance was confined to providing putting-out sewing work for poor laboring women. In short, they became proprietors of a sweatshop. They learned abruptly that this would not provide a quick fix to the city's poverty problem.

The Provident Society's intention not to compete with existing industries ironically left them vying with an industry—textile manufacturing—that already exploited Philadelphia's dependent poor. Unlike the Slater or Lowell systems in New England, Philadelphia's textile industry was initially dominated by the city's poor-relief officials. The Guardians of the Poor became the city's largest textile manufacturing enterprise between 1800 and 1815, employing over 250 women spinning coarse and fine cotton, combined with almshouse residents who were compelled to work at spinning and weaving. Public poor-relief authorities, along with manufacturing promoters like Tench Coxe, were complicit in driving down wages for textile production, ensuring that this work would always remain the desperate work of the dependent poor. Talk of encouraging industry or independence proved meaningless when the work they promoted was a dead-end job that kept poor women continually dependent on the poor-relief system rather than their own enterprises. What these men wanted was an industrious poor, who kept busy with work, who did not become economically independent or drain the public coffers, and yet who provided a compliant labor force to supply the cheap yarn and cloth that fueled the city's expansion and the nation's economic independence from Europe.[58]

This enterprise marked one of the stages in the transition away from a commercial economy based on bound labor and toward a "free-labor" economy rooted in industrialism. The shift from a slaveowning to a "free-labor" society has always been accompanied by a convulsive period when the measure of freedom for laborers remained questionable. Hence the transformation in American attitudes about poverty was inseparable from the decline of traditional bound labor. As historian Edmund Morgan has noted, slavery allowed colonial Americans to resolve the age-old problem of how to ensure proper control over the dependent and unruly poor. So when unfree labor began to decline rapidly in the North, it was no accident that new efforts emerged to subordinate the poor. The numerous cases of recalcitrant runaway slaves and indentured servants brought before Philadelphia's courts between 1790 and 1830 indicate that African Americans and the working poor were not willing to accept severe limitations on their freedom once bound labor became an anomaly. Textile manufacturers and sweatshop practices of the Provident Society can be seen as similar concerted efforts to limit the independence and freedom of women laborers.[59]

The Provident Society's tight-fisted approach to wages provoked a sharp rebuke from Mathew Carey. Carey devoted much of his writings after 1820 to a defense of the interests of distressed female seamstresses. Yet he was also one of the early republic's most ardent promoters of manufacturing and advocates of government protection (tariffs) for American industries. Carey expected that manufacturing interests would be tempered by a heavy dose of justice or paternalism. The expansion of northern industries, he thought, promised the best solution to the problem of unemployment and poverty.[60]

Carey thus attributed women needleworkers' impoverished condition to the inadequate wages they received. By offering these women only twelve and one-half cents per shirt, Carey contended, the Provident Society did not pay enough for seamstresses to survive, even at the barest subsistence level. He estimated that even if they tirelessly worked without interruption from children for twelve to fifteen hours a day, these needlewomen would still be left with only nine cents per day for food, clothing, and fuel after paying their rent.[61]

The tragic misery of women laborers eventually led Carey to visit their homes to see for himself the deprivation they were forced to endure. His account reveals the passion behind Carey's convictions, but it also foreshadows a style of sentimentalizing poor women that would grow in popularity later in the antebellum era:

> I visited a room in Shippen street, . . . which contained no furniture, but a miserable bed, covered with a pair of ragged blankets. Three small chunks lay on the hearth. The day was intensely cold. The occupant, a woman, far too slenderly clad, had two children, one about five years old, the other about fifteen months. Both were inadequately dressed for the season, and were *destitute of shoes and stockings. The younger child had had its hands and feet severely frost-bitten, and the inside of the fingers so much cracked with frost, that a small blade of straw might lie in the fissures!*—What a hideous case in such a city as Philadelphia!

Few alternatives existed for many of Philadelphia's poor women. Hundreds lined up to receive even this scant pittance offered by the Provident

Society. It was a testimony to the industry and virtue of the city's poor women, Carey reported, that on a single day more than one thousand women applied at the door of the Provident Society to make shirts at twelve and one-half cents, some travelling as far as two miles, although it was known that none would receive more than four shirts per week. Carey's criticism struck especially hard because the society's managers were encountering decreasing financial support at the same time.[62] The Provident Society's response to this critique confirmed that these men preferred economy and savings over sympathy and compassion. After all, they argued, women were poorly paid in many urban industries. Why should their enterprise be any different? Increasing wages would bankrupt the society, they insisted, for it would have "annihilated all its funds and broken up the society." For Carey, this defense was nothing more than a smoke screen. The Female Hospitable Society had never paid less than eighteen and three-fourths cents per shirt during its twenty-year existence; therefore, Carey was convinced that the Provident Society's policy was neither humane nor benevolent.[63]

The contrasting experiences of these two societies begs the question of the role gender played in the controversy over poverty and benevolence in the 1820s. Women's charity organizations offered one of the lone voices among white middle-class benevolent activists in defense of the poor against charges that their character was vicious and intemperate. Benevolent women were more likely than their male counterparts to challenge the hostile attacks leveled (primarily by men) against benevolent societies. The Female Hospitable Society carried on a decade-long crusade to exonerate the integrity of the destitute women they assisted and the propriety of that aid. Mathew Carey's impassioned advocacy for female wage laborers and private charities is perhaps the exception that proves the rule. No other prominent white man defended the female laboring poor in Philadelphia during the same era. This is not to say that hostility toward the poor and toward private charities had to follow gendered lines, but only that in antebellum cities such as Philadelphia it often did. Face-to-face interaction with poor women and an affinity for paternalism, rather than any essential features of either sex, determined whether middle-class activists were likely to challenge these hostile representations of the poor.

In the process, white women activists perhaps affirmed, in their minds, the popular nineteenth-century belief that women were innately more benevolent and compassionate than men. With greater regularity, middle-class men and women spoke of this as a distinctive feature of the female character. By the 1830s poor-relief activists, like many others in the middle class, became both the recipients and purveyors of this set of ideas about sexual difference. The women of the Female Hospitable Society asserted that "to our sex in an especial manner appears to be assigned the delightful task of alleviating human woe." Philadelphia's Union Benevolent Association declared that women were "more sympathetic, more self-denying, gentler," and "by their constitution and habits more suitable for the work" of benevolence. A Philadelphia minister maintained that "the heart of *man* may be avaricious, and cold and unmoved" by the pleas of charity, but he had never met a woman who was. In making this distinction, he gave voice to a perspective that middle-class white benevolent women were coming to accept as natural.[64]

Conversely, white middle-class men more commonly expressed opinions that attributed poverty to the vices of the poor. Male charities and reform organizations were often more restrictive and selective in dispensing their charity. Clearly, the cold-hearted view of poverty that emerged in the 1820s and the strong tugs on their purse strings from poor-tax collectors had a stronger effect on benevolent men. Such men knew that public discourses on poverty frequently characterized softness toward pauperism as an unmanly trait. New York's Society for the Prevention of Pauperism called it an "effeminate notion" to maintain "that pauperism is one of the conditions of the social existence." Weakness, irrationality, helplessness—all terms commonly used to describe either women or effeminacy—were invoked repeatedly by critics of benevolent sentiments. Thomas Cooper, whose *Lectures on the Elements of Political Economy* (1826) directly addressed Philadelphia's poor-relief crisis, lambasted as unmanly any person who yielded to his compassion and gave to the poor beggar asking for charity. "These are the ethics of sentimental novelists," he wrote, flowing from "that morbid sensibility that induces a weak female to indulge all her charitable dispositions" without rational reflection, "perfectly careless, and unconscious whether this indulgence be wrong or right."[65] By now the imperative to be a "man of feeling" had faded from white middle-class ideals of manliness. Small wonder, then, that even activist men adopted a hard-edged critique of the dependent poor. The contradictions inherent in the actions of the Provident Society managers illustrate this dilemma. Although they pledged not to look on the poor with contempt, they failed to understand or sympathize with men who stayed away from the menial work and insufficient wages they offered. Their affirmation of a genuine concern to assist poor women was circumvented by their decision to be stingy with wages for seamstresses. This contradictory behavior reflected a glaring unawareness of the experiences of the working poor and, most especially, of the gender dimension of the poverty problem in Philadelphia.

Middle-class men's and women's divergent attitudes toward poverty and benevolence originated in the circuitous way in which the charitable community addressed the problem of female poverty. It should have been apparent as early as the 1817 Library Committee report that the hardships of mounting pauperism rested unfairly on the city's laboring women. The report conceded that wage inequity between men and women was "a matter of serious regret," and male desertion in the city was "lamentably extensive."[66] Still, throughout the 1820s, Philadelphia citizens continued to discuss the poverty problem as a problem among men—specifically the product of the twin vices of idleness and intemperance. Newspapers often led the charge, lamenting the many "respectable men" who were applying for public or private assistance. All discussions of able-bodied paupers employed a gendered language that assumed the poverty problem could be solved by redressing the improvident behavior of laboring men. Intemperance was a masculine problem. Contemporaries considered female drunkenness too delicate a subject to be addressed, so the decision to blame the poor's condition on intemperance indicates that a gender-specific explanation for poverty governed the kind of solutions that benevolent activists attempted. Although the feminization of poverty was a factual reality, none of the prevailing ideologies of that era—economic, political, or gender—could conceive a solution to poverty that endorsed women's behavior as autonomous economic agents. No framework of ideas adequately acknowledged the prevalence of wage-earning women in a system that provided no opportunities for their financial independence or upward mobility.[67]

The idea of dependency lay at the heart of the different gendered understandings of poverty. Within the ideology of republicanism still ensconced in American thinking, dependency loomed as an evil to be avoided by all white men in the new republic. And as new concepts of middle-class manhood championed male entrepreneurial striving, poverty appeared as a threat to manliness. Every man was expected to be independent, prosperous, self-interested, and autonomous. This successful man should be an independent force needing little assistance from friends or kin. By contrast, men whose poverty made them dependent were portrayed as moral failures and as less than fully men.[68] But according to this same ideology, there was not the same fear that women would be made dependent. Rather, dependency was cast as an accepted facet of women's lives, part of the female character necessary to protect them in a world inhabited by unvirtuous men. This was the principal reason why benevolent men could not easily come to grips with the reality of female poverty. Their strategies to combat pauperism, designed to increase the independence of the recipient, did not correspond with the widely shared view of women's dependency that they upheld.

At the same time, some of Philadelphia's benevolent women, such as the members of the Female Hospitable Society, came to a different conclusion—that a woman's dependency was the primary cause of her poverty. Women activists remained keenly aware that poverty often developed as the adverse by-product of a woman's dependence on men for financial security. Laboring women in northern cities were frequently pushed into the ranks of the indigent by the breakdown of this dependence, whether on account of death, desertion, or intemperance. Hence women's charities remained much more resistant to efforts to label the poor as idle and vicious. Their exposure to the women who needed assistance convinced them otherwise.

Shifting attitudes toward the poor and dissatisfaction with poor relief profoundly altered the workings of private benevolence in northern cities such as Philadelphia. Whether they quickly assented or remained sternly defensive for a while, benevolent activists eventually came to accept the idea that poverty resulted from the improvident behavior of the poor. By the mid-1830s, voices refuting this perspective became more difficult to hear, even among benevolent women. Bitterly hostile public opinion proved too great for even the strongest of the benevolent associations to withstand. Benevolent societies that survived the 1820s became almost formulaic in their emphasis on the benefits of work relief, seeing employment as the only proper and Christian charity for the indigent. It was in this climate that a growing body of reform-minded urban residents began to promote spiritual solutions for the dilemmas of poverty.

Spiritualizing Poverty

Throughout the 1820s, Protestants in northern cities began directing more of their energy and support toward societies that stressed evangelism, religious training, and moral reform, and less toward those that proffered relief or even employment. This transformation of benevolent sensibilities corresponded with the tremendous emotional and spiritual upheaval of popular piety, revival meetings, and religious experimentation that historians have designated the Second Great Awakening. Wherever that awakening flourished, people cathartically embraced a new individualistic concept of self—a "new birth"—achieved by self-mastery over temptations and desires, and accompanied by a passionate zeal for saving the souls of others. Churches and individuals who espoused evangelical sympathies multiplied rapidly in northern cities throughout the 1820s. Sunday schools, Bible societies, and tract and missionary societies suddenly emerged as the engines of this religious awakening in the urban North, prompting one minister to call it "the age of evangelic invention."[69]

The shift toward evangelistic benevolence was exhibited in the new type of Sunday schools that began flourishing in every northern community. Philadelphians had first experimented with Sunday schools in the 1790s, when apprenticeships had fallen into disfavor and laboring-class children worked six days a week without mandatory public schools. The First Day School Society (founded in 1790) offered basic education in reading and writing to prepare children (of both sexes) to become virtuous citizens, thereby displaying the blending of both humanitarian and religious objectives that characterized early benevolent societies. In the new religious climate of the nineteenth century, evangelical Sunday schools were more interested in converting young souls than in teaching them basic literacy. The Sunday School Union's reports, for instance, were more attentive to counting children who had experienced a "saving benefit" than they were in reporting their educational progress. And like a sudden gust of wind, new evangelical Sunday schools blew past their older rivals. The First Day School Society operated only a handful of schools between 1790 and 1810, but Philadelphia's evangelicals opened forty-one new Sunday schools between 1811 and 1817. By the early 1820s, one in every four school-age children in Philadelphia was being instructed in nearly seventy schools with over 850 volunteer teachers. The Philadelphia Sunday and Adult School Union, founded in 1817 to coordinate all of these activities, expanded within seven years to become the American Sunday School Union, one of the largest religious enterprises in the nation.[70]

Evangelicals spun a web of benevolent activities within an ever-active network of enterprises. Tract societies provided the texts for Sunday schools. Sunday scholars raised money for Bible societies. Bible societies supplied domestic and foreign missionaries with the Scriptures. Religious newspapers and magazines trumpeted the successes of all these missionary labors. And incessant correspondence between like-minded activists in other communities kept northern evangelicals involved in a national religious culture of benevolence. Women in Boston, for example, organized the Female Bible Society soon after they initiated correspondence with a sister organization in Philadelphia.[71] By this whirlwind of religious activism, evangelistic societies watched their fortunes rapidly eclipse those of traditional charities throughout the turbulent 1820s. The membership ranks of Philadelphia's charitable societies were decimated by the city's poor-relief crisis. Valiant efforts by individual societies could not prevent hundreds of financial supporters from withdrawing their membership and assistance over the course of the decade. Recall that the Female Hospitable Society membership dropped from 700 to 107 during those ten years, and the Provident Society's more than one thousand original subscribers shrank to fewer than three hundred in only five years. Other charities endured the same decline. The Female Association and the Philadelphia Benevolent Society reported dwindling support, and St. Joseph's Catholic Orphan Society watched its subscribers drop from three hundred to only seven during this time. The writing seemed to be on the wall. Public hostility toward the poor and benevolent societies had irretrievably diminished support for organizations that provided private charitable relief for Philadelphia's poor.[72]

Religious societies whose primary objective was to save souls passed through this poverty controversy without the damage incurred by charitable societies.

After suffering a dry period of financial support during the first years of the depression, Bible, missionary, tract, and other similar societies continued to grow and amass large popular financial backing throughout the 1820s. The amount of money that flooded into evangelical societies throughout America, especially in the North, was astonishing. The American Bible Society receipts more than doubled between 1828 and 1830, growing from $76,000 to over $170,000. By the end of the 1820s the revenue of the eight national evangelical societies rivaled what the federal government spent on internal improvements. Some urban evangelical societies might have floundered (not all the records have survived), but the overall trend was prosperity. The most prominent evangelical associations in Philadelphia had a combined budget in 1828 greater than that available for the city's poor officials, and twice the amount received by the thirty-five societies devoted to poor relief, education, and reform. The mere fact that organizations like the Female Bible Society could retain a consistent level of support during the tight-fisted 1820s attests to the growing popularity of evangelical benevolence. Keep in mind too that the financial demands on evangelical organizations were not nearly as great as those on charitable societies. It was cheaper to give a poor person religious tracts than firewood and cheaper to run Sunday schools with volunteer labor than to hire full-time teachers for charity schools. Thus, the surpluses for evangelical societies multiplied rapidly.[73]

City residents were readily aware of the disparity between the state of evangelical and relief societies, and that the new evangelical vision of benevolent action had captured the hearts and purses of many more supporters. Mathew Carey observed that these "religious" societies were on the whole "tolerably well supported" and too "sufficiently numerous" to warrant inclusion in his plan to increase revenues for the city's charities. This complaint became a recurrent theme for Carey—that great sums of money were raised for foreign missionary societies while the plight of female wage earners remained unresolved in American cities. He estimated that as much as $100,000 was raised annually in the four largest American cities for foreign missions.[74]

The northern middle classes certainly spoke with their pocketbooks, and they consequently tilted the balance of benevolent activity toward an evangelical perspective. After 1820, religious activists were much less likely to join both types of societies—humanitarian and missionary—than they had in the recent past. As poor relief came under heated assault, urban evangelicals were progressively knocked off—or they jumped off voluntarily—the fence they had previously straddled between humanitarian and evangelistic benevolence. It was rare now to find activists like the Ralstons and Bethunes who labored for both types of philanthropy. Benevolent-minded evangelicals began supporting only evangelistic societies. By 1821 Philadelphia's Female Association reported that its subscribers were annually dwindling and that many had withdrawn "in order to patronize newer societies." Although one-fifth of the Female Domestic Missionary Society managers during its first three years (1817–20) also served as managers of the Female Hospitable Society, only one woman could be found working for both societies during the next ten years. Evangelical men and women were consciously choosing to express their benevolent piety through Sunday school, Bible, tract, and home missionary societies, and not through charities to relieve the material needs of the poor.[75]

Changing attitudes about poverty in the 1820s and the shifting priorities of benevolent activists were not unrelated events; they were two sides of the redefinition of poverty in nineteenth-century America. Both were expressions of a new perspective that emphasized the spiritual needs of the poor and made an individual's moral character the critical focus of benevolent and reform activities. For a growing number of benevolent contributors, the means of salvation—the written word of God in the form of a Bible, tract, or sermon—was a more important gift for a poor person than a morsel of bread. In the midst of the depression in 1822, when working families could find little employment and had difficulty providing food for themselves, the Auxiliary Bible Society of Philadelphia reminded its patrons to focus on a different dimension of the city's problems: "Are not hundreds perishing around us amid all the horrors of Spiritual Famine?" A speaker at a Bible society anniversary repeated the same message. "Were we met to provide no better thing for our fellow man than a perishing weed to cover his flesh, or the perishing food that sustains his life," he remarked, then there would be little cause for rejoicing. But he continued, "No Sir: ours is a higher charity. . . . We are met to spread the Bible of God." The definitions of poverty and true benevolence toward the poor had now experienced a profound transformation. Just as poverty became dissociated from God's providence, evangelical revivalist theology began to de-emphasize the sovereign God of Calvinism and stress instead each individual's moral free agency. Now both those who succeeded in securing their own salvation and those who secured their own economic independence—not the downtrodden or the oppressed—could be hailed the truly blessed by God.[76]

If the choice was now between charity or the gospel, evangelicals emphatically chose the gospel. These shifting priorities surfaced in a decision Thomas G. Allen made in 1831. Allen, a young Episcopal minister, declined an offer to serve as general agent for the Philadelphia Benevolent Society, a three-day-a-week position that paid an annual salary of $500. For Allen, like many middle-class evangelicals, the choice between spreading the gospel and relieving the impoverished had become an easy one. In rejecting the society's offer, Allen admonished them that unless their efforts were made "with an immediate reference to the influence of Gospel truth," unless they privileged evangelism over poor relief, they should expect to look in vain "for any extensive or permanent moral results."[77]

White evangelical ministers became more vocal during the 1820s in attributing the plight of pauperism to the vices they felt typified the character of the poor. Rare now were statements like Jacob Janeway's that the poor were somehow especially blessed by God. Again with the exception of African American churches, suspicion and judgment more frequently flowed from the pens of the city's white clergy. One Philadelphia minister consecrated Malthusian ideas in an anonymous pamphlet, *The Christian Principle in Relation to Pauperism*, declaring poor laws immoral and contrary to the Scriptures. The Christian principle regarding poverty, this minister declared, could be summed up in the words of St. Paul: "if any one will not work, neither shall he eat." Christians therefore should exempt themselves from charity toward those they considered viciously responsible for their own poverty: "Religion requires us to feed the hungry and to clothe the naked, only when the distress for which they solicit compassion, is involuntary." Presbyterian minister James Patterson warned that the poor tax would continue to grow until measures were taken "to prevent the increase of vice and immorality." Without religious instruction for the city's poor, Patterson declared, "the very foundations of society" were threatened. Evangelical ministers such as Patterson expected a resolution of the poverty problem in the activities of evangelical societies that molded the character of the poor—Sunday schools, home missionary societies, and the temperance movement. The author of *The Christian Principle* agreed: "Let the vast sums now squandered on poor-houses, be appropriated to the erection and maintenance of schools. . . . let the Bible be put into the hands, and its truth into the minds, of the children of the indigent . . . and we shall soon see . . . a generation of intelligent, honest, independent, industrious and valuable citizens." A gendered conception of poverty and dependence again surfaced here. Although the author of *The Christian Principle* spoke generically of the poor, in actuality, his solutions presumed an economic and political agency that made sense only when applied to white men. White men alone could be expected to develop into "independent, industrious and valuable citizens" as long as industry, independence, and citizenship were explicit markers of manliness in the early republic.[78]

Presbyterian clergyman Ezra Stiles Ely exhibited one of the most remarkable reversals in attitude toward the poor during this time, exemplifying the new priorities of evangelical activism and the popular animosity toward the impoverished. Prior to his arrival in Philadelphia, Ely had spent four years as chaplain to the New York City Almshouse and Hospital. The journal he kept during his ministry there exhibited the blending of humanitarian and missionary sensibilities that initially characterized urban benevolence at the turn of the nineteenth century. No doubt, Ely saw sinners in need of redemption as he made his rounds through the almshouse, but the tragedy of their poverty also tugged at his heart. "O! it is astonishing," he lamented on one occasion, "that the heirs of heaven should be found in such circumstances." Ely wrote with sympathy for his impoverished flock, knowing the pain and injustice of poor young women whose husbands had died or deserted them and who worked diligently for wages too low to support their families.[79] Ely's perspective on poor relief, however, hardened during the 1820s as public sentiments alleged that improvidence caused poverty and indiscriminate charity encouraged pauperism. In an article entitled "Prevention of Pauperism," Ely declared that the majority of paupers landed in urban almshouses because of their own "drunkenness, idleness, extravagance, improvidence, laziness, lust, and the righteous curse of unchastity." Taking this attitude even farther, he maintained that they ought to be turned out of the poorhouse until they demonstrated a thorough reformation of morals. Poor-relief officials should likewise inform those poor who received outdoor relief that they would be denied firewood next winter in order to frighten them into laying up some store in a fuel savings fund. From that moment forward, Ely directed his benevolent efforts exclusively toward evangelism and moral reform. He labored on behalf of the Presbyterian education society, the American Sunday School Union, and other agencies of evangelical reform, gaining his most notable fame in his call for a Christian political party.[80]

One final example, the story of the Female Domestic Missionary Society of Philadelphia, illustrates how evangelical reformers transformed the meaning of benevolent activism as they gained ascendancy in the culture of religious benevolence. In summer 1816, this small weekly gathering of mostly Presbyterian women decided to perform their Christian duty toward those living in the city's poorhouse, hospital, and prison. They were unconcerned about relieving the physical needs of the inmates in these institutions; saving of souls was their all-consuming passion. As their annual report stated, "Thou who hast a soul to be saved, pause and reflect! Is not the value of the never-dying soul, more than the whole universe of matter?" These women thus organized themselves into a society and raised funds to support Francis Ballantine as their missionary both in those institutions and in working-class neighborhoods in the city's outlying districts. Within the first year, the women decided to begin visiting the poor in the districts themselves "for the purpose of conversing with them on religious subjects; and for distributing Bibles and Tracts among them." Nearly five hundred women contributed as annual subscribers during the first year, and the society raised over one thousand dollars.[81]

Francis Ballantine recorded in his journal one of the rare instances in which the voice of a recipient of religious benevolence can be heard. One September morning, he observed the women of the society as they tried to coax the almshouse residents into attending their worship service. A society member, whom Ballantine called "Mrs. S.," met a poor woman in the almshouse yard and invited her to join them in an upstairs room for preaching and worship. The woman refused, and as Mrs. S. walked away she overheard the woman say to another, "If they would give us more of their charity, and less praying and preaching, we should thank them." Ballantine probably never intended to disclose how the working poor interpreted the religious charity they received. He viewed the poorhouse residents as object lessons in a different moral tale. His journal was quick to recount the many favorable reactions to the missionary society's appeals, and he even found a moral in the story of this antagonistic poor woman. Within a few weeks he reported that she was a "serious and attentive" listener at his missionary services. We will never know how representative that woman's initial reaction was or how many other poorhouse residents shared her displeasure that their material needs were slighted in favor of their salvation. The unsolicited opinion of an anonymous poor woman, however, exposes the crucial change in the meaning and definition of benevolent activism that occurred in the early nineteenth century.[82]

The women of the Female Domestic Missionary Society embraced a spiritualized concept of poverty and championed their evangelistic goals as the best solution for the poor. They reinterpreted the commands to relieve the poor issued by the ancient Hebrew prophets, maintaining instead that a gospel message satisfied biblical injunctions that called on them not to "turn aside the needy" or "oppress the poor." They spiritualized the meaning of "needy" to imply that what the poor needed was salvation. Yet they also rejected the contention that work relief was the preferred method for assisting the poor. Instead, they insisted that "many of the poor are not willing to be employed" and that Bible and missionary societies could better address the problem of poverty because they would instill in the minds of the poor "that industry brings its own reward; that idleness is the root from which great evils spring." Although their official reports were filled with concern for "sinners," these middle-class women easily conflated "sinners" with the indigent. As Ballantine phrased it, "how often are poor sinners left . . . wedded to their sins, and in love with iniquity." When religious reformers began to spiritualize the meaning of poverty, "sinners" became a middle-class evangelical code word for the laboring poor. A short time after the poverty problem developed in northern cities, middle-class Protestants, both men and women, had begun to embrace a new benevolent ideal that spiritualized the condition of the poor and aspired to moral rather than material solutions to the conundrum of poverty in a supposed land of plenty.[83]

Perhaps the most significant consequence of this shift toward a spiritualization of charity lay in the new gendered conception of benevolent behavior

that it produced. By the time an evangelical benevolent agenda had superseded post-revolutionary humanitarianism, reforming men and women had
come to talk about the meaning of women and benevolent activism in strik-
ingly different ways than before. By the 1820s, middle-class men and women,
both black and white, began using a new gendered language to depict both
the meaning of benevolent activism and the differences between men and
women. The language of civic virtue, which late-eighteenth-century reformers applied equally to men's and women's public actions, now nearly disappeared from discussions of female activism. Decades before, Benjamin Rush
had referred to benevolence as that "virtue which must not be constrained,"
and poets praised the earliest female societies for performing "virtue's
work," indicating a framework for public action that closely blended republican and Christian ideals.

In its place, nineteenth-century ministers, essayists, and benevolent promoters now spoke more frequently of a woman's "influence," rather than
her virtue, when they discussed her benevolent activism (figure 4).[84] One of
the most straightforward statements of this ideology of women's benevolent
activism came from the pen of George Washington Doane, Episcopal Bishop
of New Jersey. In an essay entitled *Woman's Mission*, he argued that women
were meant to exercise an "influence," a specially endowed regenerative role
in society, but not to exercise "power," by which he meant political activity,
including the right to vote. In Doane's words, "We claim for them no less an
office than that of instruments (under God) for the regeneration of the
world. . . . Can any of the warmest advocates of the political rights of woman
claim or exert for her a more exalted mission,—a nobler destiny!" Doane was
not expressing an ideology constructed exclusively by men; both women and
men of the white middle class wrote and spoke this language of difference, as
did urban black middle-class leaders in their newspapers. But as Doane's
essay indicates, champions of the notions of benevolent femininity clearly
wanted to circumvent an expansion of women's power in public, thereby ensuring the identification of manhood with political authority. This ideology
of female influence certainly did not stop women from taking public political actions, but it did serve to delegitimize those actions within prevailing
middle-class gender conventions.[85]

This gender ideology rested on the assumption that women were naturally
endowed with the ability to convert human souls, correct their vices, and administer to their needs. Woman was "fitted by nature" for this work, one minister stated, since "God has endowed her with qualities peculiarly adapted to
these offices." One society declared that women, "by their constitution and
habits," were ideally suited for benevolent work.[86] As benevolence took on a
more evangelistic dimension after 1820, women began to be described as more
innately benevolent than men. Women's organizations commonly alluded to

FEMALE

INFLUENCE AND OBLIGATIONS

FIGURE 4. The idea of female influence pervaded conceptions of women and benevolent activism, especially with the spread of evangelical reforms, such as Sunday schools and Bible societies. "Female Influence and Obligations," *Publications of the American Tract Society* (New York, 1842). Courtesy of the Brown University Library.

their unique redemptive capabilities. "We are not insensible," one society reminded the public, "to the high obligations which rest on our sex to seek for the transformation of the world." Along with these sentiments came assurances that women somehow possessed a piety distinct from men, that they were "naturally prone to be religious," that theirs was "peculiarly the religion of the heart."[87] Women's significant role in promoting revivals and converting family members during the Second Great Awakening confirmed this image. With each passing year between 1800 and 1840, women numerically surpassed men in forming the legions of Sunday school, missionary, and other religious activists.[88]

Consequently, by the 1830s popular perceptions began to imbue religious benevolence with feminine meanings. The language and symbols surrounding religious activism shed the masculine connotations inherent in the idea of public virtue and took on the distinctly feminine traits of a woman's influence. This significant shift in language illustrates what historians have called the "feminization of religion" in nineteenth-century America, a change that might just as accurately be labeled the demasculinization of religion. Although women had outnumbered men in Protestant churches since the late colonial era, the preponderance of female membership continued to rise during the second quarter of the nineteenth century. This growing imbalance within the churches, combined with an increasing emphasis on child-centered spirituality and sentimentalized religious beliefs, contributed to the appearance of a feminized, or demasculinized, evangelical faith. All this reinforced the gender coding of religious activism and commitment as feminine.[89] Whatever analytical phrase we employ, the response of Protestant men to these changes in the gendered meaning of religious activism remains to be examined by historians and will be considered in the next chapter.

Sentimentalizing the Poor

For the next two decades, the poor and the dilemmas of urban poverty in the North were pushed aside by policy makers and middle-class reformers. Throughout the 1830s and into the 1840s, in the midst of a depression, charities struggled valiantly to provide some assistance to people facing the hardships of an often cruel wage-labor economy. Evangelical reformers, on the other hand, devoted their attentions to reforming the vices of the urban poor through temperance, sabbatarian, and antiprostitution reforms.

By the 1840s and 1850s, however, urban fiction writers returned the attention of middle-class audiences to the plight of the urban poor, but with a different twist. At mid-century, dozens of novelists gazed upon the problems of impoverished urban workers, producing tales of the hardships confronted by newsboys, match girls, factory operatives, and mechanics. Most common were those tales of the exploitation of women needleworkers or seamstresses. Novels about the trials of seamstresses at once exposed and sensationalized the condition of women workers, repeating nearly every argument against the abuse of women wage earners that Mathew Carey had first voiced in the 1820s.[90] Needleworkers were compelled to accept barbarously low wages (often as little as fourteen cents for a long day's labor), forced to live in squalid garrets without furniture or heat, and subjected to the chicanery of greedy sweatshop owners. Novelists portrayed the most extreme cases of oppression, exaggerating low wages for literary effect, and making Carey's descriptions of workers' conditions appear almost tame by comparison. "How many thousands of females are there," one novelist queries, "who commence their toil at early dawn, working until midnight, who earn, on an average, from twenty to thirty-seven and a half cents per day[?] . . . There is no class of the community who are so oppressed as the female portions, and what many of them suffer is beyond the comprehension of many of our citizens."[91]

These white middle-class stories were for white middle-class audiences. Readers were continually reminded that the poor seamstresses portrayed in these tales had invariably fallen from comfortable or affluent standing into a state of impoverishment. Despite references to the working poor, the protagonists rarely had been born into the urban working class. Widow Willson, in Maria L. Buckley's *Amanda Willson* (1856) was "once in affluent circumstances," while Mrs. Talbot in Buckley's *Sketch of the Working Classes* (1856) had been "reared in the lap of luxury and care" before marrying a gentleman merchant. Both Lizzy Glenn and Mrs. Gaston in T. S. Arthur's *Lizzy Glenn; or, The Trials of a Seamstress* (1859) had likewise been reduced from their former conditions of respectability and middle-class standing. Charles Burdett paints one of his seamstresses as "the daughter of a worthy man" and the widow of "an industrious, economical, and temperate" mechanic in *The Elliott Family; or the Trials of New-York Seamstresses* (1850).[92] In all these novels, women are forced into poverty by the loss of a male provider. Husbands or fathers typically lose their wealth through risky speculation or business failures, only to die soon after. T. S. Arthur poignantly describes this dilemma facing working women: "The manly stay upon which a woman has leaned suddenly fails; and she finds self-support an imperative necessity; yet she has no skill, no strength, no developed resources. In all probability she is a mother. In this case she must not only stand alone, but sustain her helpless children."[93]

These characters were certainly victims of urban poverty, but they were also downwardly mobile women who had slipped from the stability of middle-class domesticity. Middle-class reading audiences were no longer asked to identify with protagonists across class lines. Instead, they were left to ponder the vulnerability of sustaining class security and to remember that class identity remained dependent on a successful functioning of the gender system.

Wealthy women philanthropists had prepared middle-class readers for this perspective on poverty during the 1830s when they established women's exchange societies that offered self-help charity to well-to-do women who had fallen into financial misfortune or, as they phrased it, women forced to confront the "imaginary stigma . . . attached to woman's labors" rather than "the actual sting of poverty." Some of the same women who had struggled valiantly in the 1820s to defend the treatment of poor working women had now switched their attentions to preserving class status and domestic identity through charities such as Philadelphia's Ladies Depository.[94]

Writers of this urban fiction ensured that their audiences could identify the unmistakable markers of class and race that stood neatly conflated for them. T. S. Arthur carefully portrays Lizzy Glenn as a woman who should elicit sympathy from almost anyone, except perhaps an evil sweatshop owner. He depicts her as tall and slender with light-brown hair and hazel eyes. Although her cheeks were sunken to indicate her new poverty, "her forehead was high and very white." Just so readers did not miss it, Arthur reminds them that Lizzy is white, as were all of the other poor seamstresses in this sentimental genre. "She's a touch above the vulgar," one of the sweatshop tailors reminded his employer, and Arthur notes that her voice indicated that she "had moved in a circle of refinement and intelligence." Not surprisingly, none of the urban fiction told the story of the poor African American worker, male or female, or the Irish immigrant woman who typically worked as a seamstress in the nonfictionalized city.[95]

The eventual plot resolution in these novels illustrates that urban seamstress tales were meant to ease middle-class readers into a sentimental view of poor working women. In most stories, the denouement finds the poor seamstress marrying a man who can return her to a life without toil and hence help her regain her middle-class status. Lizzy Glenn finds and marries her long-lost fiance, William Perkins, and consequently both she and Mrs. Gaston are freed from ever again working for sweatshop proprietors. Maria Maxwell's *Ernest Grey; or, The Sins of Society; a Tale of New York Life* (1855) concludes when Lizzy Roberts marries Richard Kane, who becomes "every year more prosperous and respected," so that Lizzy and her friend and fellow seamstress Margaret can live out their lives without ever having to work again.[96] The notion that women could be independent and autonomous workers remained largely absent from this urban fiction. And although authors hoped that their writings might alter the wealthy's comportment toward the working poor, readers were given no reason to think that respectable women would work unless forced into it by the demise of a male provider.

These novels were thus more concerned with addressing gender inequities and declining status in the middle classes than they were with addressing the real dilemmas of urban poverty for working women. Urban novelists rarely portrayed poverty as a product of class oppression. They strove instead to distance their reading audiences from those who exploited women workers, who were usually marked not by class but by moral, ethnic, or racial difference. In one of the most sensational portrayals of the exploitation of women laborers, Charles Burdett describes the deceptions practiced by urban cap makers, who swindled labor from hundreds of desperate women by promising to teach them a trade and then releasing them right before they qualified for receiving wages. Other cap makers were guilty of amassing a large stock of caps produced by women laborers and then leaving town before paying their workers. Yet all of Burdett's capmaker characters are depicted as Jews, not discernible members of the Protestant middle class.[97]

Typically these stories also attributed a villainous role to elite women who were more concerned with obtaining their luxuries at the cheapest cost. These haughty and spendthrift women were then often contrasted to benevolent benefactors or poor women who displayed compassion toward poor needleworkers. In this way, urban seamstress fiction nostalgically invoked the imagery of late-eighteenth-century notions of benevolence and poverty— contrasting luxury with virtuous benevolence and depicting poverty distinct from the culpability of the new middle class.

It seems at times that poverty's greatest threat in these novels rested in its capacity to strip a woman of true womanhood, especially her supposedly inherent feminine capacity for compassion and charity. Lizzy Roberts wonders whether her poverty had removed her feminine disposition toward unselfishness because she feels compelled to ignore other women's needs in order to ensure her own survival. Urban seamstress novels unintentionally suggested that these signs of womanhood were merely the markers of class privilege rather than of gender—the privilege of not having to labor for one's survival and of having free time for charitable activism. Yet ultimately these novels confirmed a gender-specific idea of compassion. Their pages were filled with accounts of women's innate tenderness, especially in the repeated kindnesses that poor working women offer to one another. When a grocer displays sympathy for a starving needlewoman, Arthur reminds his readers that the grocer was after all "a woman and a mother." With "the delicacy of true feeling" one working-class woman assists another, while a wealthy man responds to a beggar by launching into a verbal tirade "against the lazy, improvident poor." The dangers of poverty in this sentimentalized world of fallen middle-class women surface not in economic oppression, but in the constant fear that a woman's true benevolent femininity might be lost.[98]

Although conveying lurid and sensationalistic images of poor working women, mid-century urban fiction ultimately evoked a sentimental view of poverty that looked nostalgically back to an age before market capitalism had fixed a pattern of systematic exploitation of wage laborers. In response to the feminization of poverty, these stories offered nothing more thoughtful than previous benevolent reformers had displayed. Instead, tales of poor working women emerged as a forum for addressing middle-class anxieties about gender and the tenuous foundations of domesticity.

The ascendancy of an evangelical vision of benevolence and the demise of religious poor-relief societies during the 1820s occurred simultaneously, feeding on each other and working to create and confirm a new culture of benevolence in the city. Definitions of benevolent activity and conceptions of poverty had begun to shift before the Panic of 1819 rocked Philadelphians' postwar optimism. Constricted incomes and a deluge of newcomers wandering the streets searching for employment or extending an outstretched hand accelerated the changing meaning of benevolence during the 1820s. A recognition of the spiraling cost of the poverty problem persuaded religious reformers that answers to these social problems rested in an individual's free will and personal responsibility. Some middle-class women at first resisted, but ultimately capitulated, to the prevailing perceptions of poverty and benevolence. This transformation of benevolence toward individualistic and spiritualized solutions to social problems continued throughout much of the nineteenth century. Not until the social gospel and progressive reform movements at the end of the century would white middle-class religious activists again challenge the assumption that preaching an evangelical gospel was more valuable than responding to the temporal needs of the poor or the economic causes of poverty.

Welfare history has a tendency to sound eerily familiar, revealing voices whose message echoes into the present. Blaming poor women for their poverty and yet not providing an ideological structure for their independence, championing work relief but not providing sufficient employment, and labeling the indigent "idle" or "worthless," all express a similar blindness to the gendered dimensions and capitalist causes of poverty in American society. The poor have all too frequently become twin victims, assuming both the labels of "deserving" and "undeserving"—deserving of their impoverishment but undeserving of assistance because of their alleged vices. During the 1820s, poor-relief critics latched onto intemperance as the peculiar vice of the poor, illustrating their new attention to moralistic and spiritualized definitions of benevolent activism, but effectively masking the gendered history of drink in the early republic.

CHAPTER 3

Drink

It is really astonishing how much mischief one man can accomplish
when he steps out of his proper sphere of action and engages in
matters in which he has no concern.

Dialogue between the Devil and a Teetotaler (1844)

Americans in the new republic, like European colonists before them,
loved to drink. They consumed alcohol with astonishing frequency
and in prodigious quantities. Few of life's occasions or activities escaped some association with drinking. Early Americans consumed wine,
beer, or rum whenever they were given an opportunity for celebration or
hospitality. They drank at weddings, they imbibed at funerals, and they
drank both before and after church worship. No respectable barn raising,
harvest, auction, dance, political election, fire-company meeting, or civic celebration would have been complete without its participants sharing some alcoholic libation. Early Americans drank at work during the day, and they
quaffed in taverns and their homes when the day was through. Their own
health, they reasoned, was more apt to be threatened by consuming the local
water supply than by drinking beer or wine. Thus medical treatments relied
on wine and spirits, and few people ever challenged their medicinal efficacy
for a host of health problems.[1]

During the colonial era most residents in seaport towns drank beer, wine,
or cider on a daily basis, but by the end of the Revolutionary War and continuing into the new republic Americans began consuming distilled
liquors—which contemporaries called "ardent spirits" (rum, gin, or whiskey)—in greater quantities than ever before or ever since. Rum consumption had begun to rise by the 1750s, and soon cities such as Boston and
Philadelphia became competitors in a booming rum-distilling industry. But
after the Revolution, distilling rum became less desirable as West Indian mo-
lasses supplies dried up, and as American merchants and manufacturers

shied away from industries dependent on European colonial economies.[2] Rapidly, whiskey eclipsed rum as the drink of Americans. Westward migration beyond the Appalachian mountains made whiskey a more profitable way for farmers to sell their grain in eastern markets. It remained prohibitively expensive to ship wagonloads of grain across the mountains before the advent of canals or railroads, but distilling grain into whiskey allowed farmers to sell their surplus in distant markets, often at four times the profit. Whiskey production had become so essential to western Pennsylvania farmers that they openly staged a rebellion against the new federal government in 1794 over the excise tax on distilled liquors. For these reasons, whiskey became plentiful and cheap in the early republic. By 1820, rye whiskey sold for as little as thirty cents per gallon in Philadelphia. Nearly everyone could afford to purchase and drink hard liquor by the gallon; and that is just what they did. Whiskey consumption skyrocketed in the decades after 1790. The average drinking-age person was swilling nearly ten gallons of distilled spirits each year by 1830—nearly twice what he or she might have consumed in 1790 and almost four times what twenty-first-century Americans drink.[3]

Consequently, in the 1820s northern men and women initiated a temperance movement to address what they perceived as the nation's collective addiction to ardent spirits. The problem of drink was inextricably bound up with specific notions about manhood and womanhood in this era and tied to the deep social transformations that Northerners experienced during the transition to market capitalism and industrialization. It seemed no less possible to reform people's drinking behavior without resorting to concepts of gender than it would to reform their sex lives—and Philadelphia's most famous temperance advocate would try to reform both. Activists formulated new gendered conceptions of benevolence and devised new strategies in order to reconcile profound social changes with their developing class-based ideas about individuals and families. Some of these reformers concentrated explicitly on drinking, while others carried the gospel of self-discipline and restraint into other arenas. African American reformers recognized the gendered constructs of drinking and temperance and used this knowledge to generate definitions of gender in African American communities as well as agency for social and economic survival or advancement in northern society.

At the center of this story, especially in northern cities such as Philadelphia, stood the problematic figure of the young man. For middle-class Protestant reformers (both black and white), urban young men exhibited the dilemmas connected with the new expressions of masculine identity in a market economy. Beginning around 1830, northern urban moralists unleashed a torrent of books and essays directed explicitly at the problems of young men in the city. "Public speakers every where," one of these writers noted, were expressing their deep anxieties about the "character, temptations, dangers and prospects" of young males.[4] In response, urban Protestants established distinct "young men's societies" as vehicles for developing a competing ideal of disciplined manhood. These Jacksonian-era young men's reform societies, together with the temperance movement, set their sights on a reformation of masculine behavior and represented drinking as the battleground for a challenge to patterns of aggressive masculinity that had developed since the Revolution. White women either became the unseen silent partners in the temperance movement or stood as the symbolic victims in narratives of drinking men's failures. In either case, temperance reform masked the real experiences of both women's drinking and women's temperance activism.

It is important to note here that the sources addressing young men, women, and temperance do not always lend themselves to straightforward distinctions of race or class. Certain discourses about drink and about gender were clearly exclusive, serving explicit class and racial agendas for the white middle class. Others were intentionally uncertain and ambiguous, and still others were openly inclusive, crossing both race and class boundaries. It is not always easy to measure the degree or extent of class or racial differences in these sources. By embracing this complexity, we can expose the intriguing, if not always clear, interplay of class, race, and gender without resorting to simplistic conclusions about the class or racial divisions in the history of drink, gender, and temperance.

Despite the visible connections between men and drinking in American culture, historians have only superficially explored the relationship between gender and alcohol consumption. What, for example, was the relationship between male drinking and representations of the masculine self in early America? Why did men feel the need to drink in the exclusive company of other men? Why did men drink more than women? On what occasions and in what places did women drink, and how was their drinking explained in a culture that associated drinking with masculine behavior? Perhaps because men and drinking have seemed so universal in American culture, historians have assumed that the gendered meaning of drink has remained unchanged across time. To move beyond this shortsightedness, we must examine not only the relationship between gender conventions and men's and women's drinking patterns, but also the type of gendered imaginings that influenced the strategies and actions of antebellum temperance reformers.

Men, Women, and Drinking in Early America

Drinking was not limited to men, either before or after the Revolution, and yet drinking served as an undeniable feature of masculine self-identity

and gender construction in early America. Male cultures of drinking[5] developed in American cities toward the end of the eighteenth century and eventually became the object of class and gender controversy during the nineteenth century. In most instances, men chose to drink with other men or to
drink in places or at events where women "as a gender" were excluded.[6] Men
drank in taverns and coffeehouses, in workshops and on auction floors, and
in one another's homes. In every case, there were undoubtedly women present, but seldom were they invited or expected to participate in the drinking
ritual. More often than not, drinking itself was an experience shared with
other men only. Despite William Penn's warning that drunkenness "unmans
men," early American men endowed their drinking habits with the power to
mediate their masculine identity within the context of social relationships
with other men.[7]

During the eighteenth century, drinking did not automatically signify a
person's class standing in cities like Philadelphia. Whether a man chose to
drink, where he met others for drinking, what he imbibed, and with whom
he drank—none of these constituted the markers of class distinction in
northern cities. Ministers and magistrates certainly condemned drunkenness as a personal or moral failing, but all classes of white men drank alcohol
together. The civic ceremonies of eighteenth-century life—militia musters,
elections, and court days—were occasions when white men shared in the di-
versions of drink and participated in the give-and-take of treating. Only in
the nineteenth century did the members of an emergent white middle class
begin to make drinking a defining feature of class. By then, they began to
portray those who could moderate or abstain from alcohol consumption as
respectable, as persons who possessed *character*—the cultural signifier of the
middle class. Those who wished to drink during or after work, and anyone
who frequented taverns and bars, they marked off as members of the lower
(and dangerous) classes.[8]

The diary of Jacob Hiltzheimer of Philadelphia illuminates the important
features of male drinking cultures that existed during the revolutionary era.
A German-born livestock breeder who served as a state legislator throughout
the 1780s, Hiltzheimer became active in numerous voluntary associations
and public institutions, including a local fire company and the vestry of the
German Reformed Church. At first glance, Hiltzheimer appears in his diary
to have been a social gadabout and an inveterate name-dropper. His pages
are filled with daily records of the numerous men with whom he dined,
drank, or visited. For example: "January 24. [1766]—Attended a cider frolic
at Greenwich Hall with the following gentlemen: Robert Smith, Robert
Erwin, William Jones, Richard Footman, Mr. Adcock, Captain Mushett,
Philip Kinsey, James Johnston, William Lloyd, F. Trimble, Humphrey Robe-
son, and Samuel Hassell." On further investigation, it becomes apparent,

however, that Hiltzheimer's gadding also reveals the patterns of sociability that surrounded men's relationships of friendship, commerce, and politics transacted in taverns or within the hospitality of their homes. Much like Dr. Alexander Hamilton's habit during his travels in the 1740s, Hiltzheimer supped and drank with men of varying degrees of wealth and power, although ideally, he tried to socialize with a company of gentlemen. His drinking partners included Thomas Mifflin, major general in the Continental Army and later governor of Pennsylvania, as well as Timothy Matlack, who rose from economic obscurity to political prominence when radical artisans seized political leadership during the Revolution. Matlack, a brewer's son whom the Friends meeting dismissed for his accumulating debts, was notorious before the Revolution for excelling in such masculine popular recreations as horse racing, cock fighting, and bull baiting. Hiltzheimer frequented taverns with Matlack during the 1760s and joined him in many of these same pursuits.[9]

Gentlemen in the eighteenth century often drank with men of differing economic statuses without fears that this might jeopardize their standing; in fact, it helped to confirm their hierarchical position. When a gentleman treated others to a bowl of punch at a local tavern, opened a cask of wine to celebrate his recent political election, or attended a horse race or cock fight, he used those occasions to demonstrate his superior hospitality, wealth, and independence, while cementing the bonds of deference and patronage. Gentlemen and laborers could frequent the same taverns and occasionally drink, dine, or join together in various pastimes without threatening the social order. That a New York aristocrat such as James Delancey would travel to Philadelphia to participate in a cock fight with Matlack underscores that a male culture of sociability and drinking coexisted with and reinforced the hierarchical divisions in American society on the eve of the Revolution.[10]

Traditional tavern life, then, was a hubbub of boisterous white men, often with different circles of companions and various agendas. John Lewis Krimmel's painting of an early-nineteenth-century Pennsylvania tavern (figure 5) reveals nearly all of the elements of early American tavern culture. Behind the bar we can find punch bowls, glass decanters, and pewter tankards to accommodate the various drinking appetites of customers. Newspapers and almanacs hang from the walls reflecting the intersection between oral and print cultures in the republic. Artisans wearing their work aprons share drinks together, while men of various ages and class positions (including a man dressed as a Quaker) converse, drink, read newspapers, or await the mail or stage's arrival. A woman and child appear only to implore a husband and father to return home, and, because Pennsylvania laws prohibited taverns from serving liquor to servants or slaves, no African American (slave or

FIGURE 5. The masculine camaraderie of work, politics, and (oral and print) communication were important features of early American tavern culture, as were mounting gender tensions, illustrated by a woman and child imploring a drinking father to return home. John Lewis Krimmel, *Village Tavern*, 1813–14. Courtesy of the Toledo Museum of Art, Toledo, Ohio.

free) is anywhere in sight. Actually, Philadelphia taverns had more of an atmosphere of functioning chaos than Krimmel's painting depicts. Phliadelphians used them for meetings of civic associations and clubs; for empanelling juries; for conducting local, state, and even congressional government; for discussing local gossip and political opinions; and for socializing over food and drink—often many or all of these functions happening at the same time.[11]

For elite white men, toasting was a ritual that both confirmed the communalism of male camaraderie through drink and demonstrated a gentleman's grace and civility. By the time of the Revolution, drinking toasts became a ubiquitous feature of male social and political gatherings. Saluting other men's health emerged as the most frequent ritual in this practice. Jacob Hiltzheimer reported in 1766 that he had dined on the Schuylkill River with about 380 people; "several healths were drunk, among them Dr. Franklin, which gave great satisfaction to the company." Toasts also became a medium for expressing political and patriotic commitments. During the Revolution, men hailed the well-being of heroes from Washington to Lafayette, and even raised forty-five toasts of "Wilkes and Liberty" to commemorate the British radical Whig agitator's famous pamphlet, *North Briton No. 45*. Loyalists, on the other hand, toasted the king or drank to the damnation of Congress. Toasts also offered colonial gentlemen an opportunity to display their eloquence and wit, while exhibiting the rituals of civility that separated them from ordinary working men. When George Roberts Twelves Hewes, a common Boston shoemaker, accepted an invitation for a New Year's Day visit to John Hancock's palatial home in 1763, he recalled his frightful nervousness when Hancock ordered a servant to bring wine, proposed that they drink to each other's health, and then proceeded to clink glasses with him, an act that Hewes had never seen before. Other common folks did not fare as well as Hewes in the competitive battle of wit and grace that gentlemen often contrived out of the rituals of drink and sociability.[12]

But as the Revolution began to subvert the deferential posturing that had held together the hierarchical relationships between white men in America, it became more common for American men to conceive of drinking in a context of equality. Some men experienced this as a gain, others as a loss. Nonelite men began to expect that the shared experience of a communal drink among equals in a tavern would now reflect rather than refract the social and political equality they desired outside of the tavern. To share a glass of wine or rum, then, began to imply a true feeling of equality rather than deference among ordinary men. The immediate reaction of Philadelphia's elite was to seek out and establish spaces where men of similar standing could drink and socialize away from the common folk. In 1773, approximately fifty elite men founded City Tavern at a cost of three thousand pounds to be shared among the subscribers; it was followed in the 1780s by George and Robert Grays' gardens on the Schuylkill, a patrician space insulated from contentious partisan politics. At the same time, laborers and artisans adopted their own taverns as spaces where they might encourage political and cultural affinities, such as William Bradford's Old London Coffee House, the Four Alls, or the Wilkes and Liberty tavern.[13]

Still, a central feature of men and drinking in the late eighteenth century was its gender exclusivity. Jacob Hiltzheimer's description of his family's outings on July 4, 1787, illustrates both the social relationships of male drinking and the gendered division of drink:

July 4.—Went on horseback to Captain Von Heer's, at the Falls of Schuylkill, and there dined with the following: Andrew Geyer, Nathan Boys, William Richards, Samuel McLane, Peter Ozeas, Philip Pancake, Street Commissioners; Peter January, Peter Kraft, John Purdon, George Latimore, and ——— Sneider. Coming home I overtook a company of gentlemen who had dined at Mrs. Keepler's country seat. Colonel Jacob Morgan asked me to go with him to Funk's Tavern. There had good punch, after which we parted and I got home before ten o'clock. My wife and two daughters, Kitty and Hannah, went to Primefield and there drank tea.

Hiltzheimer frequently met his fellow street commissioners at a tavern to conduct their business, or he drank with them after the completion of their work, such as inspecting a new bridge or the cleaning of streets; on this occasion he included them among the gentlemen with whom he socialized on a holiday. But his wife and daughters did not join him for the dining or drinking; rather, he felt the need to record that they went elsewhere and drank tea. And whenever he went for an outing with his wife or daughters, he always recorded that he too drank tea, not wine or punch, with such mixed company. Rum-punch drinking, by contrast, was performed almost always in the presence of other men only. Male friends or acquaintances regularly invited Hiltzheimer to drink a bowl to celebrate the marriage of a son or daughter, the birth of a child, the completion of a building, or an election to political office. In no instance does he record that wives or daughters joined in these rites presumably offered to celebrate a man's accomplishments, despite the fact that marriages and births were impossible without women.[14]

Toasting also reinforced the notion that drinking was a man's prerogative, as well as a defining feature of manliness. In addition to drinking "healths," nearly every ritualized gathering for drinking involved the customary toast to the "fair sex." As if they needed another reminder that women were absent from the tavern table or at the punch bowl, drinking men conspicuously acquainted themselves yet again with their all-male fellowship by offering toasts to women and womanhood. Gentleman also engaged in battles of wit to outperform one another in the eloquence of their toasts. Dr. Hamilton recalled a night at the Governor's Club in Philadelphia in 1744 when the men drank several toasts, "among which were some celebrated ones of the female sex." By devising a symbolic womanhood, which might represent political virtue or domestic bliss at best, and unbridled male sexual desire at worst, and then fusing that with a custom of male drinking, eighteenth-century men were able to emphasize the patriarchal privileges that came with the social world of drinking and manhood.[15]

By making the rituals and spaces of drinking the nearly exclusive realm of men, northern white men had begun to use drinking as a means of constituting a male-exclusive public sphere. If, as Habermas has suggested, the public sphere emerged where collective public opinion was created, then drinking and tavern culture became inseparable from the expanding political consciousness that accompanied the development of newspapers and a print culture. During the American Revolution, taverns and coffeehouses provided one of the central spaces where political opinion and nation building originated. Men debated imperial rule, taxation, independence, revolution, and constitutions. Tavern speech, the oral culture of male public political debate, influenced in turn the print culture of pamphlets and newspapers. The gender exclusivity of drinking and taverns paralleled the ways in which white men tried to partition off the developing public sphere as a realm for men alone.[16]

Most white men in eighteenth-century Philadelphia did not wait for an evening repast or a special celebration to drink. Alcohol had become a customary feature of working life. On the one hand, masters and employers saw this as an opportunity to demonstrate their paternalism and patronage. Patrons would insist upon treating laborers both during and after the completion of work. Stone masons and carpenters who constructed George Washington's presidential home in Philadelphia in 1792–93 were first treated to food and drink when the cornerstone had been set, once again when they completed the first floor, and then at least three times more when they finished the second and third floors and began work on the roof rafters.[17] Workingmen also developed a ritualized culture of drink at the workshop. Craftsmen and laborers expected, and at times demanded, that part of their compensation include a daily allotment of alcohol. At the half-dozen paper mills in and around Philadelphia, the customary practice was for every journeyman to receive a half-pint of spirits at eleven o'clock each morning, and young apprentices were welcomed into the fraternity by fetching the bottles. Each workplace developed its own rituals that prompted men to stop and share a drink—the completion of an order, a co-tradesman's birthday, a journeyman's first day at the shop, or the presence of a visitor. Seamen pledged oaths of loyalty to each other and sealed them with a drink, or baptized a sailor's first crossing of the equator with a rite of ducking in water and treating shipmates to a bottle of brandy.[18] These kinds of drinking rituals constituted the pre-industrial patterns of labor and production that characterized white men's lives in colonial and revolutionary Philadelphia. Most white men who labored for someone else during that era lived under the same roof and shared both bread and beer with their masters. The reciprocal relationships of dependence and compensation were cemented by such exchanges between masters and journeyman or employers and laborers in the workplace, especially before wage payment began to sever those relationships.[19]

During the expansion of industrialization in the early republic, when far greater numbers of workers became wage earners rather than bound or family laborers, the presence of cheap and plentiful whiskey, and an ideological undercurrent that asserted every man's equality, proved to be an explosively disruptive combination in American cities. Workers continued to drink at prodigious rates and openly resisted efforts by employers to disconnect drinking from work. When employers refused to supply beer or whiskey, makeshift taverns, groceries, and grog shops popped up in working-class neighborhoods to fill the void, providing still other folks with a new entrepreneurial opportunity. According to the new labor history of the last generation, drink played an important role in the way workers forged an integrative working-class culture by cleaving to traditional leisure patterns and embracing a producer ideology rooted in republicanism. Labor historians thus portrayed workers' drinking behavior as an essentially positive experience, as the bulwark from which workers resisted the economic and cultural hegemony of moralizing capitalists.[20]

For some groups of journeyman artisans, this narrative represents an accurate portrayal of their historical experience, but for many other workers it remains an overly idealistic picture of alcohol and working-class life. Often laborers in the most hazardous and exploitative situations—canal workers, miners, or any man whose only skill was his strength—were the ones on whom employers lavished copious amounts of hard liquor. And working men were led to believe the lie that whiskey gave them additional strength to endure grueling physical labor in a hot or cold climate. A quick glance at the Philadelphia Mayor's Court docket tells a different story—the destructive and counterproductive consequences that alcohol abuse could mean for workers' lives. George Greiner's mother and father certainly did not consider drinking a liberating experience when their son repeatedly became intoxicated and had to be incarcerated to prevent him from killing them; nor did Mrs. Kelly, whose son John got so drunk that he beat her "in the most cruel and barbarous manner"; nor did Agnes Madden, whose husband Levin would abuse her both physically and verbally when he went off on a spree. The influx of cheap whiskey meant that traditional drinking customs, developed when cider or beer was consumed, could suddenly have more perilous consequences, as male workers struggled valiantly to cling to traditions that allowed them to resist the industrial transformation of their working lives.[21]

Just because women were regularly excluded from these rituals of male drinking, we should not assume that no women drank or became intoxicated in early America. Because women were compelled to drink in places that were more private than public and because ideas surrounding women and drinking were so closely tied to emerging ideologies of class, domesticity, and sexual difference, we will probably never know the actual extent of women's consumption of alcohol during this era. The records on which historians must rely to discern women's drinking are themselves caught between the twin ideological constructions of male drinking and temperance reform. In other words, much of the drinking that women did (like the women themselves) remains invisible because men primarily left behind records of their own drinking with other men and because temperance reformers had difficulty reconciling drinking women with their images of women as the inherently moral victims of men's intemperance. It is only in the silences and fissures of these sources that some glimpses of women and drinking can be discovered.

The relationship of women to taverns, drinking rituals, and drunkenness illuminates the same ideological forces working to hide the visibility of women in the economic and political arenas of the new republic. Although gentlemen such as Hiltzheimer and Hamilton rarely wrote about sharing a drink with a woman in a tavern, women were certainly present in eighteenth-century taverns. In fact, women were often the proprietors; a quarter of Philadelphia's eighteenth-century taverns were operated by women. White widows either held their own licenses to operate taverns or assumed responsibility when their husbands died. In the wake of the Revolutionary War, female tavernkeepers constituted a viable presence as independent economic agents, much like other working women, whose labor was critical to the transition to a market economy. Also, white and black women constituted the labor force that served food and beverages to taverngoers in the city. If we include the many unlicensed dramshops that supplied customers with a quick drink without the amenities of a tavern, then women might well have exceeded one-quarter of the liquor proprietors. Because black proprietors would have had difficulty procuring a license and sizable property for regulated taverns, black men and women probably managed or worked in a substantial number of tippling houses and dramshops that remain hidden from surviving records.[22]

The visible economic presence of women in taverns contradicts the invisibility of respectable women in male narratives of drinking. This contradiction was usually concealed by the association of women in taverns with an implied sexual licentiousness. When Dr. Hamilton made references to young women in taverns, he always did so in the context of his gentlemen friends taking liberties with these women or posing as someone else in order to seduce them. Hannah Callender Sansom noted in her diary that she was forced to assume that the "basest" interest motivated all the men she encountered when she, like many other women, had to stop in taverns during her travels. Furthermore, because women tavernkeepers tended to be poorer or operated unlicensed dramshops, they may indeed have combined tavernkeeping with prostitution or they might have had greater difficulty preventing men and prostitutes from beginning or consummating their trysts in their establishments. In either case, women in public houses for various reasons became associated with "public women" or prostitutes; as one historian has phrased it, prostitution became "the name given to female agency in the public realm" in the late eighteenth century. This association with sexual licentiousness masked both women's connection with drink and their increasing economic presence in the city.[23]

While the opinions of some observers suggest that women never actually consumed ardent spirits, local criminal court records in Philadelphia or New York show that women drank as frequently as men and appeared nearly as often on charges of public intoxication. In February 1824, for example, city watchmen in Philadelphia charged Mary Reev with "having been continually drunk for weeks" and making loud noises throughout the night to the perpetual annoyance of her neighbors. Women drank alone, they drank with their husbands or lovers, and they drank with one another. The five women who were all charged on the same day with being "idle drunken vagrants" might well have enjoyed a spree together before unluckily encountering a city watchman.[24]

Women, like men, drank at work, although with less ease. African American women were prohibited from drinking in licensed taverns before the Revolution, just as were black men, and their dependence on domestic employment meant that they usually remained under the watchful eye of masters and mistresses; they could not as easily escape to the drinking spaces that male laborers (white and black) frequented. It is not hard to imagine, however, that women often shared in the drinking breaks that interrupted the routine of an artisan's shop. There is also a smattering of evidence that women workers retained their own symbolic exchanges of drink that accompanied their work. For example, Thursday was the customary washing day in Philadelphia, and washerwomen were usually supplied with a quart of cordials to drink during the work day. Yet, because women often led the transition into new forms of wage labor in locations such as factories, they likely experienced the termination of the reciprocal exchange of drink from employers to workers before many male laborers did.[25]

Women's drinking became entangled with the definitions of class and the cultural markers of respectability long before that was the case for men. William Cobbett criticized the incessant "tippling" of spirits by men and boys in the United States, but he thanked God that "women of any figure in life" abhorred the practice "as much as well-bred women in England." Phrases like "women of any figure" or "well-bred women" marked off nondrinking women by the language of class. With the advent of the temperance movement, male reformers fused this class ideal of drinking with the notion of women's inherent purity to obscure much of the female drinking that actually took place. In the minds of male reformers, true women did not drink, even if they had to admit that many female persons did drink. With no way to measure how often women drank, they assumed that respectable women did not do so. In short, the rhetoric and the reality of women's drinking seemed to be in a state of perpetual tension in the early republic. Gendered notions of womanhood draped a veil of confusion and short-sightedness over the issue of women's drinking and helped to direct the focus of the temperance movement on the reformation of men and manly vices.[26]

Drinking was inseparably tied to conventions of gender in early America. So when in the youthful days of the republic many Americans began to believe that excessive alcohol consumption endangered the republic and the lives of its citizens, it was not a great leap for men and women concerned about reforming American drinking habits to turn to concepts of gender when fashioning temperance reform. When they did, they focused their attentions on the young men (sons) who were most tempted to drink, on the older men (fathers) who led them astray, and on a generation of new men who embraced an ethic of self-restraint that became the hallmark of white middle-class manliness in the nineteenth century.

"Like a Mass of Combustible Material"

In June 1833, a group of youthful white citizens in Philadelphia decided to organize themselves into a Young Men's Association for Discouraging the Use of Tobacco. They wished to step beyond temperance reform and to demonstrate their manly self-denial by swearing off snuff, chew, or a smoke. Those who operated this society were not particularly noteworthy; they were middle-class men, with no particular prominence in politics, commerce, or the arts. Nor was there anything extraordinary in how they established their reform organization. They simply adapted the familiar strategies of organized benevolence ubiquitous in their civic landscape, drafted a constitution, and signed a pledge to abstain from recreational tobacco use.[27] The significance of these reformers' actions, however, lay beyond the problem they wished to address, resting instead on how they chose to identify themselves—as "young men."

In a little more than a decade, Philadelphia reformers, both white and black, created at least nineteen young men's associations for various reform purposes. By 1838, white reformers had established young men's Bible, tract, missionary, temperance, anti-vice, and colonization societies. Black activists established a handful of young men's associations of their own to promote temperance, mutual relief, and assistance for fugitive slaves, while black and white abolitionists together had created a young men's antislavery society.[28]

The creation of young men's societies signaled a revealing moment in antebellum urban history: these organizations provided a critical space where definitions of gender, particularly manhood, could be constructed, and their reform strategies coalesced with the gender discourses of the temperance movement. Temperance reformers and young men's societies became concerned during the same decades about older codes of manly behavior and about substituting new ideals of manliness in their place.

Today we might not consider these men as being especially young. Americans in the early republic employed little precision when classifying age groups, so "youth" or "young man" could connote a wide spectrum of ages ranging from fifteen to thirty-five years old.[29] The men who created and joined young men's societies could hardly be described as adolescents, even in the broadest meaning of the word; they were fairly well established and in the early stages of their careers. Young men's reformers tended to be clustered in a similar generation—men who were approaching or had recently turned thirty. The average age of a young men's society activist when he first joined was twenty-nine. One-third of the youthful reformers were over thirty, and two-thirds were over twenty-five. Life-cycle patterns also belied a picture of young men's societies filled with adolescent youths. Many members had made the transition into roles as husbands and independent householders. Almost 70 percent had already married when they joined a young men's society, and nearly half of the men were parents of small children.[30]

The creation of young men's reform societies corresponded with a fervent discourse about the status of young men and youth in the city. Although anxieties over youthful indiscretions had certainly plagued colonial parents, northern urban moralists became obsessed after 1830 with the relationship between young men and prevailing urban social problems. "Youth counselors" produced a new genre of advice literature, directing hundreds of books, lectures, and sermons specifically at young men. Albert Barnes, a Presbyterian minister, marveled at "the unusual number of books that are addressed particularly to young men," leading him to proclaim boldly that "at no period of the world has there been so decided a reference to young men in public doings as in our own times."[31]

We might expect to find a noticeable increase in young men flocking to the cities to precipitate this heightened concern, yet no new waves of young male immigrants entered northern cities during the Jacksonian era. The proportion of young men in Philadelphia, in fact, changed little between 1800 and 1860; the number of urban young men grew at a rate comparable with the rest of the city's population during the first half of the nineteenth century.[32]

How then can we explain this intense preoccupation with "young men," if it was not a product of demographic change? Historians who were influenced by 1960s youth culture and the writings of psychologists Erik Erikson and Kenneth Keniston have tried to uncover a youth movement or nascent category of adolescence in antebellum America.[33] But youth was not the principal cause for these concerns; this fixation on young males emanated more strongly from gender issues than from age. Contemporaries focused their fears on young *men* rather than on youth in general. It was the formative dilemmas of entering manhood in this era that prompted a discourse on urban young men, and it was issues of masculine identity that fueled the formation of these societies. (In fact, one might argue that in every instance when Americans have become obsessed over a "crisis" in masculinity, they have fixated on youth as the symbolic embodiment of manhood in the making.)[34] Urban activists rarely established separate "young women's" societies during this era, despite an abundance of young women in cities and churches and the dominant place female associations assumed in benevolent work in northern cities. Women reformers found no compelling reason to divide themselves by age or to establish distinct age-specific societies. Young women tended to be identified by their womanhood rather than their youth. Women of all ages found themselves encompassed within the emerging ideology that conflated benevolent activism with womanliness and gave benevolent behavior an explicitly feminine meaning. Within this ideology of benevolent femininity, a woman was a woman regardless of her age, whereas men somehow needed to be divided. To understand the reasons why certain male reformers needed to establish young men's societies, then, we must focus our attention on what they perceived to be the distressing developments in men's behavior in the early republic.

Urban moralists were among the many voices during the 1830s who had become uneasy about the changing experiences of men and shifting patterns of masculine behavior since the American Revolution. The rising rate of alcohol consumption was only part of their concern. Deep fears for the situation of young men represented anxieties over the revolution in men's lives and in ideals of manliness in the early republic. A new order of unrestrained self-interest rose atop the ruins of the hierarchical world that had governed white men's lives for the past few centuries. Nowhere was this change more conspicuous than in men's commercial activities. Thousands of white men of middling rank plunged wholeheartedly into a headlong chase for wealth and fortune. Ideological barriers to success and mobility were torn away, and an unfettered pursuit of prosperity became a nationwide obsession, filling men's conscious desires and unconscious dreams. "Everyone is a man of business," one Philadelphia attorney noticed, now that this new order had removed "every sensation of restraint."[35]

Thomas Haliburton's shrewd and enterprising salesman character, Sam

Slick, voiced this entrepreneurial urgency in his own rustic vernacular. "Your great men are nothin' but rich men," Slick chortled, "and I can tell you for your comfort, there's nothin' to hinder you from bein' rich too, if you will take the same means as they did." Self-interest, as Alexis de Tocqueville observed, became elevated above virtue as the defining characteristic of white northern men. Newspapers began to lament that self-interest and profit-seeking seemed to have penetrated all levels of American society, "from the petty dealer in the market, to the great marketplace of power"; in the behavior of all men "there is no *honesty*, or *probity*, no *private*, no *public virtue*." The only remaining barrier preventing a man from rising to whatever heights he desired, in this view, was his own lack of aggression.[36]

A new ideal of white middle-class manhood emerged to justify and explain these entrepreneurial strivings. American men began depicting themselves as possessing a character of action, an image that historian Charles Rosenberg has called the "masculine achiever"—active, dynamic, aggressive, and exploiting the opportunities that new economic or political structures made possible. The masculine achiever often remained as aggressive and competitive in personal relationships as he did in business ones.[37]

Philadelphia men had a perfect model for this aggressive masculinity in Stephen Girard, the merchant-banker who through his own resourcefulness seemingly turned everything he touched into golden profits. Although undoubtedly the wealthiest man in America when he died in 1831, Girard, whom one biographer dubbed the "Lonely Midas," never found satisfaction in his personal relationships. He had his wife committed for alleged insanity, disowned a daughter she bore in the 1790s, and left the bulk of his $6 million estate to endow a school for poor white orphans—as much a testimony to a man without friends or family as to his generosity. This ideal of entrepreneurial aggressiveness and self-interested venturing marked the origins of the nineteenth-century obsession with the "self-made man," a formulaic description of success and manhood in America.[38]

Despite the obsession with self-made success, Northerners were aware that this was hardly a stable or trouble-free time for such men. Along with the risks of entrepreneurial venturing came the far-too-common reality of failure, debt, and unemployment. Rising rates of violence and alcohol consumption emerged as two telling signs of the stresses that confronted white men of the emerging middle classes. The brief period between 1780 and 1825, for example, witnessed more multiple murders than any other era in American history prior to 1875, stories of suicides became a regular feature in daily newspapers, and per capita alcohol consumption skyrocketed to unprecedented heights, with the average American man drinking a sizable portion of the seventy million gallons of hard liquor consumed each year. If aggression and action were part of the new masculine character of white men, it appeared that so too were violence and lustful drinking. Even mental health reformers began to wonder whether this new society was stretching men to the breaking point.[39]

Advice literature written specifically for young men in the 1830s voiced these same fears that new expressions of masculine behavior had become problematic and that a healthy society was threatened by the conduct of young men. The vices most feared by evangelicals—drinking, prostitution, and theaters—appeared to be particularly directed toward young men. As Henry Boardman stated before a young men's society: "These are the altars on which talent and reputation and virtue are sacrificed. They smoke with the blood of human victims." From this perspective, young men were assaulted by temptations from all fronts, and their youthfulness (without developed habits of character or control of their passions) made them especially vulnerable to such an onslaught. A young man was, in the words of William Engles, like "a mass of combustible material, which one spark of unholy fire may inflame." He could be "volatile, reckless and impatient of restraint."[40]

Just as often as youth counselors expressed fears of urban vice, they lamented the dangers associated with a young man's early pursuit of wealth. Liberal ideals of economic behavior, which legitimized the unsullied quest for rapid riches, served as a dangerous tempter for Christian young men, as dreams of instant wealth choked the seeds of piety and benevolence. Never had the danger been greater, remarked Albert Barnes, "that all the great barriers of virtue should be trampled down under the influence of one raging, master, almost uncontrollable passion" for immediate wealth. Other youth advisers feared the "peculiar money-spirit of the age," where young men's lust for "this world's goods" seemed to have no "reasonable and moderate bounds." Youth counselors, then, echoed the deep fear in Jacksonian America that young men were leaping ahead, or being pushed, too quickly into an active public life. But drinking, sexual licentiousness, and greed were not merely the problems of youth. They were also the inverted images of that same aggressive masculinity flourishing during the early republic. In short, white urban moralists feared passage into manhood—and the frightening traits of an aggressive and self-interested masculinity—as much as they feared the season of youth. These youths were too quickly becoming men.[41]

The fears of youth counselors exposes the masculine counterpart of the nineteenth-century gender discourse on female influence. Moralists voiced their concern about a masculine influence that represented an inversion of a woman's redemptive role. All men, but young men in particular, were susceptible to the corrupting influences of unscrupulous and deceptive associates and companions. Male youth were thought to be the targets of "the vicious influence" of ungodly men, seeking to "ensnare" them or lead them off onto the path of folly and vice. Friends and acquaintances might not be what they first appeared to be; indeed, youth counselors brought to life the figure of the "confidence man" decades before he appeared in the pages of Herman Melville's novel. Masculine influence, then, involved men's ability to tempt, deceive, entice, or corrupt other men, and thereby undo the influence of a woman's piety and her moral compass for their lives. Moralists' fears were not just that youths were fast becoming men, but also that they were evading the moral influence of the feminine.[42]

The meanings and definitions of manhood, then, assumed an even more contested quality. When Philadelphia's first penny-press paper, the *Public Ledger*, began publishing accounts of the daily docket of the mayor's court in the mid-1830s, middle-class Philadelphians became increasingly aware of rival images of masculinity that either challenged or reinforced the vision of manliness espoused by middle-class reformers. The mayor's court served as the point of first contact for local neighborhoods with the criminal justice system. These local courts became places where working-class men and women could settle disputes through private prosecution, while at the same time enhancing the spectacle of the courtroom as "a grand, free popular theater, with friends and neighbors as the performers." Among the acts these folks performed—intentionally or not—were gender and manhood.[43]

Again, "young men" moved to center stage in this drama. Too frequently, the mayor's court accounts depict behavior that was marked as young, masculine, and class-specific. Among the typical proceedings were: George Watson, "a genteel looking young man," prosecuted for drunkenness; Hugh Lindler, "a young man of genteel appearance," charged with brawling and drunkenness; John Morgan, described as "a *genteel* looking man, but who last night did not act very *genteely*," similarly charged, as was "a dandified and genteel looking personage," known as Robin Robbinet.[44]

Of course, numerous working-class men also appeared before the alderman, displaying bawdy, drunken, and violent behavior. When a newly arrived French immigrant wondered aloud in court, "Vat for kind of liberty dat be, ven me no can drink what I like, as much as I like?" he simultaneously confirmed middle-class stereotypes and yet voiced the challenge of a democratic and working man's masculinity, with its conflation of freedom and drink. Still, the frequent references to "genteel looking young men" illustrate that white middle-class men were engaged in a battle over gender identity that was not exclusively an attempt at class domination against working-class men. It also involved, significantly, a conflict *within* the middle class over rival forms of masculinity. Middle-class men did not share one agreed-upon concept of manliness. Masculine identity was in a contested state during the Jacksonian era, a contest between those dandified young men aspiring to gentility who frequented taverns, gaming houses, brothels, and theaters in the corners of less respectable working-class and black neighborhoods and reformers in young men's societies who chose benevolent activism as a badge of their own respectability and usefulness.[45]

Images of black working-class masculinity also appeared in the dramas of the local courts. One common image emerged in narratives involving the typical (or stereotypical) seaman. Court accounts often referred to sailors, or "sailor-like" men, whose behavior pushed the boundaries of aggressive, disorderly, and "manly" actions. When "two sailor looking chaps" were brought before the alderman charged with being drunk and noisy, only one of them was actually a seaman; the other was an oyster huckster, a trade predominantly filled by African Americans. In the same way, dock workers were stereotyped as "dark" or "black" in the court records, suggesting that seafaring work and the laboring life that surrounded it constituted (at least in middle-class eyes) a form of working-class blackness, even though less than 10 percent of the black laboring force worked as mariners. (Remarkably, the average age of black sailors and dock workers was nearly identical to the age of the young men's reformers.)[46] A seafaring life exposed black sailors to a unique egalitarian work experience unknown among most black laborers and produced a robust masculinity that was as disorderly on shore as it was rigidly ordered at sea. Furthermore, mariners possessed a rare item for a northern black man—a certificate attesting that he was "a citizen of the United States" to protect him from impressment by hostile navies.[47]

A seaman's work and his badge of citizenship were two, oft-times contradictory, markers of African American working-class manhood. These images were likely situated alongside enduring depictions of urban African Americans' reputed affinity for stylish dress, frolics, and dancing, further contributing to perceptions of black workers' masculinity. Black and white leaders, as well as European travelers, expressed fascination and alarm at how newly freed blacks supposedly dressed beyond their means or class standing and danced or drank either to celebrate their freedom or to challenge their marginality.[48]

Penny-press newspapers and the earliest sensationalist urban fiction combined with the vivid imaginations of reformers to expose urban audiences to discordant expressions of masculine behavior and self-presentation. Middle-class readers, both black and white, became fully cognizant not only of the competing manly ideals among those aspiring to gentility, but also of the egalitarian and raucous masculinity of white and black working-class men, whose behavior, more often than not, revolved around drinking alcohol. These rival patterns of masculine behavior quickly became the object of pressing concern for urban reformers.

Youthful Energy and Usefulness

Not surprisingly, when the situation of young American males provoked such intense concern, Philadelphia reformers organized new associations during the 1830s and labeled them "young men's" societies. Religious reformers found in benevolent societies a partial resolution to the dilemmas facing young men in the metropolis. Benevolence allowed such men to assert their usefulness, build character through self-discipline and compassion, and find a manly expression for their piety in a feminized religious culture. Young men's reform societies therefore present us with a splendid opportunity to explore the ways that notions of gender developed in antebellum cities. Young men's reformers situated themselves, and their reform causes, so as to advance their own visions of an ideal manliness. After all, these reformers understood that the markings of true manhood were unsettled and contested in an industrializing city.[49] Yet the rhetoric and actions of white and black young reformers also reveal that battles over definitions of manhood were not fought solely in terms of class dominance or social control. Often these conflicts were waged as reformers endeavored to transcend class and racial boundaries. Although both white and black young men's reformers hoped to reframe an ideal of urban manliness to include reforming activism, they differed in how each appropriated dominant ideas about civic action and manhood, and whether they constituted their own manhood as part of a familial or generational conflict. In the effort to identify manliness with reform activism, these reformers constructed notions of manhood that were in opposition to other men rather than directly in opposition to the category of "woman." In doing so, they obscured their shared participation in one arena of religious behavior that they knew was predominantly occupied by and associated with women.

Philadelphia's experience mirrored young men's actions in other American cities. Bible, missionary, temperance, colonization, and antislavery societies, all bearing the moniker "young men's," emerged in New York, Boston, Baltimore, Pittsburgh, Providence, Albany, New Haven, Cincinnati, and other cities and towns during the 1820s and 1830s. In Baltimore, reformers founded a young men's society to resist the institution of lotteries, while Boston's young men organized an Anti-Masonic association, and groups of young African American men organized numerous "colored young men's" societies in cities from New York to Pittsburgh.[50] Recall that these reformers identified themselves as "young men," even though they might not have been especially young. Many of them had already married and recently become fathers. Perhaps these young men saw reform societies as an opportunity to enact fatherly relationships with other men, outside of the constricted

domesticity of the home, much like the middle-class men who joined fraternal lodges at this time.[51] Or perhaps they were searching for ways to reconcile
prevailing middle-class notions of manliness with their own newly established
domesticity, claiming the shared space of benevolence and home as a manly
realm. In either case, age, family life, and even geographical origin indicate
that these young reformers were not adolescents and confirm that these societies were concerned more with men and manhood than with the problems of adolescent males.[52]

White young men reformers shared the same religious and occupational
characteristics as other male reformers. They were cut from the same broad-
cloth of the middle class as other urban activists. Young men's societies paralleled closely the religious composition of their parent or principal society.
An identical proportion of Presbyterians and Quakers, for instance, joined
the Young Men's Colonization Society as joined the Pennsylvania Colonization Society, and the same held true for Philadelphia's antislavery societies.
In similar fashion, the same percentages of professionals, merchants, and
shopkeepers could be found in young men's temperance, colonization, and
antislavery societies as existed in their parent societies. Class or religious differences thus fail to explain why these men did not simply join temperance,
missionary, or antislavery societies that already existed in the city. They created young men's societies because they were convinced that the loosely defined category of "young men" offered the best opportunity to introduce an
ideological statement about masculinity in the city.[53]

These activists were trying to advance an ideal of manhood befitting men
of all ages, but especially young men. Young reformers insisted that their vision of manliness had been forged in opposition to the aggressive and ac-
quisitive masculinity that had developed during the post-revolutionary generation. As a result, young men's societies possessed a characteristic unique
among other religious benevolent societies: the young men were both the
agents and objects of reform. Young men's societies had the dual objective of
accomplishing a specific benevolent cause, such as promoting temperance
or distributing Bibles, while at the same time encouraging a reformation in
the character of the young men who made up the society.

Hence, the publications of these societies often concentrated as much on
young men as on the reform cause. These associations continually accentu-
ated what they saw as the primary characteristics of their youthful members:
activity, energy, and vigor. The youthful life, according to one society's lecturer, was "another word for motion and activity." "To become stagnant," he
stated, "is to die." "Enterprising" was the adjective most frequently employed
when describing a young man's life. This was the driving spark that fired a
young man's pursuit of material prosperity. The potent energy that made

young men, in William Engles's phrase, "a mass of combustible material," vulnerable to urban temptations and vices, was ironically the same quality that made them especially suited for activism. Young men's societies, then, hoped to channel this energy into usefulness and thereby invigorate the new reform causes in the city.[54] Job R. Tyson, an attorney, exulted in the hope that a Young Men's Colonization Society would give new life to the movement by "infus[ing] into its veins the inspiriting virtue of youthful blood, with impulsive energy." Members of the Young Men's Tract Society boasted of their new usefulness: "We are young men. We have but just commenced our career in benevolence. . . . This then is the time to secure us as the advocates of pure and disinterested benevolence."[55]

Indeed, a young activist needed a healthy dose of energy and self-discipline to accomplish his benevolent duties. He had to sacrifice his only day off each week, spending several hours teaching Sunday school classes, distributing tracts, or participating in committee meetings. He had to forgo the recreations enjoyed by his contemporaries and relinquish the extra income he might derive from working on Sundays. Gideon Burton, a dry goods clerk, and Lewis Ashhurst, a new merchant, knew these sacrifices personally. During a typical week in January 1835, Ashhurst either attended several services at Episcopal churches, collected subscriptions for the education society, attended the executive committee meeting of a missionary society, went to a Sunday school celebration, or solicited a lecturer for the young men's society. Burton's schedule was no less hectic. He arose before breakfast on Sundays to distribute tracts in the market. From there he proceeded to a Bible class at St. Andrew's Episcopal Church. Following the morning service, he took a twenty-five-minute walk to Southwark where he taught in the mission Sunday school. Burton then made his way back to St. Andrew's for afternoon services at 3:30. He also attended all weekly services, including evening prayer meetings and lectures. Squeezed between these commitments were his committee and managers' meetings for the tract and Sabbath societies.[56] These two young men had found a way to channel their youthful energy into practical expressions of evangelical manly piety. Additionally, each demonstrated to would-be creditors, employers, or future partners that they were young men whose piety had not been diminished by prevailing obsessions with entrepreneurial successes.

It was no easy task to cultivate this youthful zeal, and it often brought the young reformer directly into confrontations with another generation's ideals of masculinity. It is not hard to imagine that a previous generation of merchants, such as Stephen Girard or Robert Morris, would have found this religious busyness unnecessary and a hindrance to entrepreneurial aspirations. But Gideon Burton, an aspiring merchant, was keenly aware that as a young reformer he was performing a different brand of masculinity than many older men. As president of the Young Men's Tract Society, Burton distributed tracts to people working in the Sunday markets. He later recalled that the "greatest cross that I had to take up in my Christian experience, was to go before breakfast to these market people and give them tracts, for I would see the older merchants coming along."[57] This last phrase is telling: in their activism, youthful reformers consciously asserted a distinctive style of manly evangelical activism, even in the face of older men's habits. Burton knew that the merchant princes of the new republic had not distracted themselves from their quest for wealth by labors they considered the province of ministers and women. By his actions, a young reformer like Burton tried to promote a different standard of masculine behavior, one in which piety and religious activism would not be sacrificed for the advancement of self-interest, greed, or personal pleasure.

African American young men's reformers also maintained that a connection existed between reforming activism and manliness, yet with subtle but important differences. By the 1830s, a cadre of young activists emerged among Philadelphia's black elite, assuming their place at the center of free black leadership at both the local and national levels. They organized "colored young men's societies" and played a prominent role in the six black national conventions held in Philadelphia during that decade. Black activists looked to the conventions to "give vent to our feelings as men, who feel oppression, and . . . to speak like men wishing to be free."[58]

Whereas white reformers were distinguishing themselves from their fathers' patterns of masculinity—drinking, vice, or commercial avarice— black young men's reformers did not cast their efforts as a generational challenge. In part, this can be explained by their ambivalence as elite black men toward the language of manly citizenship passed down from the mythical founding fathers who had excluded them at the nation's origin. However, these young black reformers were not ambivalent about another set of founding fathers because they held a privileged genealogy as the sons of the first generation of elite black leadership who forged Philadelphia's free black community between 1780 and 1820. The young men of the Forten, Gordon, Douglass, and Gloucester families embraced reform work as an extension of their community's ongoing struggles for inclusion in the public sphere. They understood their reforming activism as a continuation of the battle that their fathers had waged against white efforts to exclude them from the markings of true manliness in the American republic. And they embraced temperance reform as one of the best means of asserting their independence and manliness.[59]

White Working Men's Bodies and the Slavery of Intemperance

More than any other antebellum reform movement, the temperance campaign brought together concerns about young men and masculine identity
into a thoroughgoing crusade to reform the behavior of men and promote
an ideal of true manliness built on an ethic of self-discipline and restraint.
Temperance reformers hoped to triumph over competing models of manhood by subverting the manliness associated with drinking men. For temperance reformers, then, all the evil influences that threatened to ensnare men
during this era coalesced into one great all-consuming monster.

Temperance reform cannot be fully understood without first taking into
consideration the social dislocations produced by industrialization in the
North. Between 1815 and 1850, industrial expansion profoundly transformed Philadelphia's economy and the everyday lives of its workers. An
emergence of domestic markets shifted the focus of merchant capital away
from foreign commerce and toward local manufacturing. A transportation
boom of canals and railroads, beginning in the 1820s, connected Philadelphia businesses with the Pennsylvania backcountry, reducing freight costs
and stimulating industrial development. Railroads linked Philadelphia with
Harrisburg and Trenton as early as 1834 and with Baltimore and Wilming-
ton just four years later. Iron and machine tool industries flourished, and
clothing and textiles emerged as the leading sector of the city's industrial
surge. By the 1850s Philadelphia had become America's largest textile-pro-
ducing city. Its manufacturers relied more on immigrant textile workers with
handicraft skills from Britain and Ireland than did New England mills, which
utilized a landless native population and machine technology. As a result,
smaller-scale manufactories, sweatshops, and factories emerged throughout
the city's outlying districts, the northern suburbs of Northern Liberties and
Kensington, and the southern suburbs of Southwark and Moyamensing.

Industrialization began to register its effects both on workers and on the
class dynamics of the city. Traditional artisan work environments changed
dramatically. The crafts system, which had regulated workers' lives for centuries, began to disintegrate. Masters with access to capital or credit separated themselves from the daily life of the workplace and remade themselves
as manufacturers. Poorer masters and journeymen slipped permanently into
the status of wage laborers, as the putting-out system and the division of
labor expanded throughout the industrial sector. Wage-earning employees
began to see their interests as different from those of master craftsmen and
manufacturers. As nonmanual work increasingly became separated from
manual labor, the middle classes looked for ways to confirm their different
work status in cultural ways that transcended the workplace.[60]

Consequently, class-based residential patterns emerged, redrawing the neighborhoods of the urban North. In Philadelphia, wealthier middle-class folk moved to more elegant western wards of the city, and laboring families moved out of center city and into the various neighborhoods that lay adjacent to their workshops in the northern and southern districts.[61] Some outlying neighborhoods, however, became attractive to both middle-class and working-class families at the same time, because of lower property costs or proximity to workplaces. Northern Liberties, for example, became after 1810 a neighborhood with competing constituents. Aspiring entrepreneurs and land speculators had been moving there since the Revolution. Its southernmost wards housed the new middle classes—retailers, shopkeepers, manufacturers, and wealthy artisans. The northernmost wards, by contrast, attracted thousands of laborers looking for affordable rents near manufacturing shops. George Foster, a New York reporter who authored *New York by Gas-Light,* lumped Northern Liberties together with the rest of the suburbs, describing them as "infested with a set of the most graceless vagabonds and unmitigated ruffians" ("b'hoys") who swarmed together in gangs. Although Philadelphia developed a less notorious version of the street life and sporting culture on the Bowery in New York, class segregation of the city's neighborhoods still encouraged openly aggressive displays of working-class leisure that gave working men and women their own class-specific public spaces, while also luring some middle-class young men into working-class neighborhoods for the attractions offered by the sporting life.[62]

With such volatile class topography, Northern Liberties became one of the pivotal sites in Philadelphia where evangelical revivalists and temperance reformers could test their designs for bringing salvation and sobriety to their working-class neighbors. As early as 1814, James Patterson launched a full-scale urban revival out of his First Presbyterian Church there. Employing Finney-like methods, a full decade before Charles Finney, and borrowing techniques from Methodist evangelists, Patterson transformed a weekly prayer meeting into a "protracted meeting" and preached to overflowing crowds for seventy-six consecutive nights, followed by ninety more on another occasion. He often preached from a soap box in the district's narrow lanes and employed a fire-and-brimstone style of extemporaneous exhortation that raised the emotional excitement of his services to a fevered pitch. Some women fainted under the stress of their convictions; others cried out boldly, "Lord have mercy upon me!" One hundred eighty new members were added to Patterson's church during the seven-month revival, and other city churches also reported their rolls swelling with converts. Patterson's colleagues in the Philadelphia Presbytery criticized the emotional excesses of the revivals and Patterson's encouragement of "lay preaching." Affluent center-city churches left revivalist techniques to the Methodists, Baptists, and Presbyterians out in the industrial suburbs.[63]

When enthusiasm began to wane in the mid-1820s, Patterson extended an invitation to Charles Finney to come to Philadelphia, and the controversial revivalist made his first foray into a major eastern city in Patterson's Northern Liberties church. Within two months, after a cold reception from conservative Old School Presbyterian churches in center city, Finney berated Philadelphia as an "AntiRevival city" and confined his in-church preaching to Patterson's meeting house.[64] Finney's revivals in Philadelphia never stirred the kind of expansive responses he experienced in western New York or New York City. Despite a few dramatic conversions, Finney could make no claim to·have transformed Philadelphia as he did the city of Rochester two years later.[65]

City temperance reformers, much like the urban revivalists they admired and emulated, set their sights on the industrial suburbs. There they hoped to convince master craftsmen and manufacturers of the liabilities of drinking at work and to convince journeymen and laborers that a temperate life could guarantee greater health and prosperity. Although only 20 percent of Philadelphia's temperance reformers lived in Northern Liberties, they sent their agents principally there, or to other industrial neighborhoods such as Kensington and Southwark. When the state temperance society hired a dynamic young lecturer named Sylvester Graham in 1830 to be their agent, he devoted his Philadelphia labors to neighborhood audiences in Northern Liberties and Kensington.

Middle-class Northerners were apparently primed and ready to join temperance societies when the American Temperance Society was founded in Massachusetts in 1826. In a few short years, local temperance societies materialized in towns and cities throughout the North, and white middle-class women and men flocked to join them. By 1829 the American Temperance Society estimated that close to one thousand societies existed with a combined membership of nearly one hundred thousand. By the mid-1830s they boasted that as many as one million individuals had pledged to abstain from ardent spirits, a 500–1,000 percent increase in only five years. If these figures are correct, then one out of every nine adults in 1835 had signed a temperance pledge, nearly as many as belonged to all the churches in the country (one in eight) in the same year.[66] New England and upstate New York founded the preponderance of new temperance societies, but mid-Atlantic cities such as Philadelphia and New York also participated in this first wave of temperance enthusiasm. By 1834 Philadelphia could boast over thirty temperance societies with nearly 4,500 members.[67]

Temperance activists created a model of reform that linked the techniques of evangelical benevolence with the strategies of urban revivalists. The earliest temperance societies differed little in their organization from the Bible, tract, or Sunday school societies that dotted the landscape of the city's religious culture. The only variance was that temperance society members committed themselves to a behavioral standard—the "pledge"—to abstain from drinking distilled liquor.[68] Early temperance reformers cut their teeth on evangelistic societies during the 1820s. Nearly half of the Pennsylvania Temperance Society managers had been active in Bible, Sunday school, or tract societies. Temperance began as a movement to change people's attitudes about drinking and to alert them to the dangers of intemperate behavior. It was a campaign of persuasion—which nineteenth-century Americans called "moral suasion." The reformation of intemperate drinking habits, reformers insisted, must be secured by appeals to conscience and not primarily through legislative action.[69]

From the beginning, temperance reformers in Philadelphia tried to present their movement as a scientific as well as a moralistic reform. Since evangelical activists at this time saw no inherent conflict between science and religion, they exploited whatever new knowledge or technology served their purposes. They tried to capitalize on the populace's growing concerns about personal health and the body, promising tangible health benefits in addition to the moral or economic advantages of temperance. In addition, temperance societies became obsessed with statistics, the numerical proof of their campaign. More than any other reform, temperance agents were enamored with numbers, hoping such scientific evidence would morally persuade drinkers. They reeled off these numbers at every opportunity to show the full extent of the national drinking problem or the projected savings that could result from temperance. In fact, temperance reformers had a great deal to boast about. After only one decade, they could point to a radical reversal in the nation's drinking habits: Americans no longer drank at the prodigious rate they had since the revolutionary era. The annual consumption of hard liquor per drinking-age person, which had skyrocketed from five to nearly ten gallons between 1790 and 1830, plummeted back to five gallons by 1840 and then down further to three and a half gallons by 1850, never again to reach the levels it had during the first third of the nineteenth century. After its first two years, the Pennsylvania Temperance Society was claiming credit for a diminished consumption of distilled spirits in the state by nearly one-half million gallons.[70]

With this emphasis on the science of temperance, it is not surprising that physicians played a prominent role in Philadelphia's temperance movement. Clergymen dominated temperance societies in New England, but nearly 30 percent of Philadelphia's temperance society managers were medical professionals. Physicians wrote regularly for temperance publications, and the Philadelphia Medical Society produced an oft-cited study concluding that intemperance was responsible for one-sixth of all deaths in the city. In 1829, two of Philadelphia's most active temperance-advocating physicians, John Bell and D. Francis Condie, began publishing a bi-weekly medical magazine designed for a lay readership, entitled the *Journal of Health*, which devoted as much attention to promoting temperance as it did to any other issue. In many ways, the *Journal of Health* seemed to be ahead of its time—encouraging physical exercise, reduced meat consumption, vegetarianism, and vaccinations, while shying away from a humoral system of blood-letting and warning against fraudulent patent medicines. At the same time, the journal also published a report from a doctor who claimed he could authenticate cases in which alcoholics had died of spontaneous combustion, the alcohol igniting in their bodies "without any external application." It would seem that even for temperance physicians, when it came to moral suasion, demonstrating that a drunkard could die while "suffering the torments of hell" still trumped a rational appeal to personal health. If readers remained skeptical about the science, some readers perhaps noticed parallels to popular descriptions of young men, as masses of "combustible material" capable of being inflamed by one drop of their unholy passion for drink.[71]

With both physicians and evangelical activists leading its temperance campaign, it made sense that the Pennsylvania Temperance Society would hire Sylvester Graham as their agent and full-time temperance lecturer in June 1830. Graham had already shown a predilection for theories of physiology and health reform consistent with those in the *Journal of Health*. Yet Philadelphia temperance reformers also felt they were acquiring an urban revivalist in Graham, because he had recently been ordained an evangelist. Within the next few months, newspapers were reporting that Graham had lectured before crowded houses in Kensington and Northern Liberties, delighting audiences of all degrees of society, from professionals to artisans (and likely women as well as men). Such flowery descriptions of Graham's spell-binding lectures must be read with a dose of skepticism, since throughout Graham's brief career he always seemed to provoke equal measures of adulation and hostility among his audiences.[72]

In all likelihood, Graham made a special effort to address the temptations and evil influences facing young men and to relate a pivotal encounter from his own youth that steeled his determination to advance the temperance cause. He described his tale as "one of those peculiar trials which young men too seldom have the moral courage to endure." As a young man, Graham had accepted an invitation to a party at a tavern with the promise that no alcohol would be served. But soon after arriving, Graham discovered that his associates had tricked him as they tried to persuade him to join in drinking rounds of "rum-sling." When Graham failed to yield, they resorted to ridicule, taunting, "He is *too stingy* to call for his glass and that is the reason he won't drink!" Such an accusation, Graham recalled, was "almost intolerable." So he purchased a drink, placed it firmly on the table, and bid his friends "good night." Of course, as in any good melodrama, Graham's determination ended the drinking affair, saved his friends from the consequences of a "debauch," and confirmed Graham in his life work.[73]

Graham concentrated his temperance work on preaching to manufacturers and mechanics in an effort to convince them that the benefits of abstinence outweighed the masculine rituals of workplace drinking. The reform paper *Genius of Temperance* raved over the consequences of Graham's labors in one manufactory in Northern Liberties. Prior to his arrival, the paper reported, "all the hands in the establishment used ardent spirits daily," both at work and at home, and they would have "continued on in their dangerous and ruinous habits till they heard Mr. Graham's lectures." But now they came to the "cool and deliberate conclusion" that "they were, in no respects, benefited by the use of ardent spirits" and resolved to drink nothing but water.[74] From the description of Graham's lectures in the *Journal of Health*, stating that he employed "the aids of chemistry and physiology" to show that liquor temporarily excites the body only to leave it weaker afterward, Graham apparently was already moving beyond a moral censure of drinking and toward his systematic vision of health reform that emphasized the dangers of all kinds of stimulants on the body.[75]

Graham quickly shifted his concerns away from drinking and the workplace and launched into a series of evening lectures in large urban venues on what he called "the organic structure of man" and "the science of human life." By 1831 he was addressing audiences as large as two thousand in New York, Boston, and Philadelphia, and by 1832 he was receiving more than $200 per night in New York for these lectures.[76] The sizable fortune now at Graham's disposal made it much easier for him to resign his temperance society position in Philadelphia. Although temperance remained a central theme in his talks, Graham soon expanded the logic of abstemiousness to include abstaining from stimulants of any kind—meats, heavily spiced foods, tea, coffee, alcohol, and sexual indulgence. Graham began to deliver lectures on the dangers of sexual excess, eventually publishing *A Lecture to Young Men on Chastity* (1834), which ran through fifteen printings over the next ten years. In his *Lecture to Young Men*, Graham simultaneously addressed the prevailing fears of urban moralists about young men, championed the ethic of self-restrained manliness associated with temperance, and unveiled his own unique vision of sex, health, and body reform.[77]

The *Lecture to Young Men* reveals Graham's apprehension not only about sexual excess in all its various guises, but also regarding uncontrolled and unrestrained passions in all areas of life. By describing the nervous system and the body's essential functions (digestive system, brain, and genital organs) as integrally related, Graham proposed that too much stimulation could lead to overall debility and sickness in a man's body. Yet Graham rejected the argument espoused by other contemporary sex reformers, which one historian has called "the spermatic economy": that semen was an essential fluid for a man's energy and that expending it too frequently depleted his virility and manliness. Instead, Graham insisted that "the importance of semen to the system" had been "exceedingly overrated." In his mind, the great danger for men lay not in the loss of this valuable fluid, but in "the peculiar excitement of the nervous system" that accompanied sexual indulgence. Graham summarized this premise in these words:

> SEXUAL DESIRE, cherished by the mind and dwelt on by the imagination, not only increases the excitability . . . of the genital organs themselves, but always throws an influence . . . over the whole nervous domain; . . . if this excitement is frequently repeated, or long continued, it inevitably induces an increased degree of irritability and debility,. . . And hence, those LASCIVIOUS DAY-DREAMS, and *amorous reveries*, in which young people too generally . . . are exceedingly apt to indulge, are often the sources of general debility, effeminacy, disordered functions, and permanent disease, and even premature death, without the actual exercise of the genital organs![78]

Graham turned to the appetites of the stomach to find the cause of this excitement. Parents who trained their children to eat too much meat or highly seasoned food, or to drink tea, coffee, wine, or various other stimulants made them victims of their own passions, producing "these lascivious and exceedingly pernicious day-dreams of the young." What Graham feared was too much stimulation of the passions, whether it be anger, fear, grief, sexual desire, or appetite. By this logic, masturbation ("self-pollution"), extra-marital sex, and even sex between husband and wife could seriously endanger a man's health. Graham thus concluded that men needed to substitute self-denial for sexual desire and to incorporate a regimen of exercise and a diet that included fruits, vegetables, and coarsely ground grain, thus making Graham flour and the "Graham cracker" perhaps the longest lasting legacy of his ideas. And herein lies for Graham the connection to temperance. He perceived intemperance not as a problem of alcohol, drunkenness, or indolence, but as a problem of overstimulation. It was all stimulants that he opposed; wine and spirits just happened to be among the era's most visible example of stimulants.[79]

Graham bridged the gap between the moralists' obsession with young men, the discourse surrounding "influence," and the relationship between the logic of temperance and reforming masculine behavior. Graham gave a sexualized and embodied presence to the dangerous influence that tempted young men to seek stimulants. Contemporary reformers considered Graham not only a temperance, health, and sex reformer, but a reformer of men and manhood as well. When Henry B. Stanton wrote to Theodore Weld about the qualities they desired for new faculty at Lane Seminary, he stated, "We want *men* here, to *make men*," and immediately he inquired whether it might be possible to procure Graham as the professor of natural sciences.[80]

Graham was replaced as temperance society agent by Thomas P. Hunt, a North Carolina Presbyterian minister whose career was also colorful and provocative and who led the temperance movement into a new phase. Like Graham, Hunt concentrated on Philadelphia's industrial suburbs. But unlike Graham, he moved his family into a modest cottage on the border of Penn's Township and Northern Liberties. Hunt proved to be a virulent critic of the urban wealthy classes and considered himself an ardent defender of working men. He leveled his strongest assaults not on the drinking habits of laborers, but on the greed and immorality of the liquor traffic. Unfailing in his "thrashing" of liquor vendors, Hunt once described liquor selling "as the vilest, meanest, most earth-cursing and hell-filling business ever followed." This message for working-class Philadelphians grew ever more appealing as the panic in 1837 stretched into a four-year depression. Hunt's meetings in suburban churches resulted in over five hundred new temperance converts during the first two months of 1837; and nearly 250 voluntary fire company members signed the pledge after just a few weeks of Hunt's labors. Hunt thus forged a link between the earliest temperance reformers and the next wave of temperance organizations that emerged by the late 1830s and 1840s.[81]

By the late 1830s, then, the temperance movement was infused with a new group of reformers from working-class backgrounds who envisioned a very different agenda for the movement. Temperance now shed its resemblance to evangelical benevolence and began to assume the characteristics of a popular movement that at times transcended class and race. Working-class support for temperance first appeared with the formation of temperance beneficial societies. Faced with the economic hardships of a depression, urban artisans devised a strategy to merge the idea of mutual benefit societies with a communal reform of workingmen's drinking habits. Temperance workers now convened both in the streets and in churches and meeting halls, not as missionaries to a different class in society but as groups of fellow workers and former drinkers wishing to support one another in their adoption of a temperate style of life. After 1840, the new temperance reform received an additional jumpstart in working-class communities with the remarkable growth of Washingtonian societies. Named after the Washington Temperance Society in Baltimore, where former drinkers helped one another break free from their dependence on alcohol, the Washingtonians appealed to a broad swath of both middle-class and working-class men and women. By 1841, they claimed to have amassed two hundred thousand adherents in the North, and two years later they estimated that their followers numbered in the millions.[82]

By the early 1840s, Washingtonian societies incorporated temperance benefit associations into a nationwide movement that reached out to ex-drinkers and made temperance popular among urban workers. For the first time, ordinary laborers who had often been influenced by the new revivalism formed their own independent temperance organizations. Between 70 and 85 percent of the members of these new societies were drawn from the ranks of journeymen artisans and unskilled laborers. Recent converts to evangelical churches in Philadelphia suburbs, such as weaver Alexander Fulton or tanner Benjamin Sewell, discovered an outlet for the self-discipline that their evangelical conversion inspired.[83] Temperance beneficial societies, craft-oriented groups such as the Carpenter's Temperance Society, and fraternal lodges called the Sons and Daughters of Temperance emerged seemingly overnight in every ward in the city. With these new organizations, the number of temperance supporters grew dramatically. Local sources began to estimate that the total number in greater Philadelphia had grown to 17,000 by 1841, with over 4,000 new supporters in the first two months of that year alone.[84]

These two different phases of the temperance movement produced a striking contrast in philosophies, rooted in the changing core of Protestant ideas. Middle-class evangelicals preached a limited temperance gospel, much like the Calvinist theology that many of its supporters still embraced. These temperance reformers expended little effort to assist individuals whom today we might describe as alcoholics, defining "the confirmed drunkard" as hopeless and lost. Their temperance gospel was for the elect—for occasional drinkers and the sober; for those who had no control over their drinking, they offered only limited atonement.[85] Both Washingtonian societies and temperance beneficial societies, on the other hand, sought out "the confirmed drunkard" whom older temperance societies had written off, offering mutual support and shared experiences. They reinvigorated the temperance movement by giving it a mass appeal. Working-class reformers preached a temperance gospel that was no longer limited to the sober. It was now freely open to all who chose to accept it—like the Arminian theology that rapidly eclipsed Calvinism in American culture. With that change, more and more temperance supporters adopted total abstinence ("teetotal") as the true pledge of the temperate.[86]

African Americans in the North embraced the new wave of temperance organizations, and working-class black men and women often espoused total abstinence with greater zeal than white reformers. Throughout the 1830s, black national conventions (dominated by Philadelphia and New York young male activists) encouraged the formation of total abstinence societies in order to counteract racist assertions of their moral or intellectual inferiority. By 1842, at least ten black temperance societies were active in Philadelphia, and there were even more in New York City. The Moyamensing Temperance Society, a Washingtonian-style organization of former drinkers in Philadelphia's black neighborhood, claimed to have administered the teetotal pledge to as many as one thousand men and women in the early 1840s. African American laborers, in the wake of cholera epidemics and the panic of 1837, had motivations for embracing abstinence similar to white workers, but they also held a different interpretation of the meaning of temperance and manhood.[87]

At the moment when working men and women embraced temperance activism, a common motif in temperance rhetoric—the association of intemperance with slavery—assumed greater resonance and appeared more frequently in temperance discourse. White reformers had, since the first sparks of temperance advocacy, invoked the argument that intemperate drinking was analogous to enslavement. In the late 1820s, Lyman Beecher reminded his readers that intemperance was as socially destructive as the slave trade. "We have heard of the horrors of the middle passage," Beecher intoned, but "bring together the victims of intemperance" and the "sights of wo" would be "quite as appalling." It involved no great leap outside the circle of ideas about drink and temperance to associate alcohol abuse (or even moderate drinking) with dependence and abstinence with independence—indeed, dependence is still the term commonly employed to describe substance abuse. But in the antebellum decades, this language carried an especially strong appeal for white working men who clung to an ideology of "artisan republicanism" amid the dislocations associated with urban industrialization. Albert Barnes relied on these ideas of republicanism and independence, connecting temperance and freedom, in his 1835 speech before the Mechanics and Workingmen's Temperance Society of Philadelphia. To be temperate, then, was decidedly not to be a slave. So as native-born working-class men adopted an identity that distinguished them from the negative image of black slavery, temperance became an equally powerful marker of whiteness for the working men who embraced the reform.[88]

Because the privileges of whiteness could be procured through adopting the temperance ethic, it is not surprising to find a close relationship between temperance actions and nativism in the years following the influx of working-class supporters to the movement. Some white workers began to embrace a temperate style at the same time that the first waves of Irish immigrants began converging on Philadelphia's outer neighborhoods. Temperance issues fed the growing animosity between native-born Protestants and Irish-born Catholics. The cultural positioning of Irish immigrants outside the category of whiteness required the consolidation of conceptions of whiteness attached to free native-born workers. It was at this stage, then, that native-born laborers began to contrast the image of the independent temperate white working man against the stereotype of the dependent drinking Irish laborer.[89]

In this heated context, African Americans remained conscious of the racial and gender implications in the developing discourses surrounding drinking and temperance. Many urban black leaders were convinced that their only hope of being recognized as "men and citizens," and their best strategy for economic survival, rested in a complete identification with the temperance cause. Black national conventions regularly asserted that no other segment of the population had "as deep an interest in the promotion of the cause of Temperance" as free people of color in the North.[90] When the convention movement devolved into the American Moral Reform Society in 1836, Philadelphia black activists managed the organization, and temperance and education became the society's highest priorities. If temperance implied a triumph over a state of dependence, black activists knew this meant that abstaining from drink offered one of the best means of asserting true independence and manhood. Black temperance activists exploited the intemperance-slavery analogy with as great a fervor as white reformers. William Whipper declared that intemperance was as great an evil as slavery in a speech before Philadelphia's Colored Temperance Society in 1834. Before white men would accept them as their equals, Whipper contended, black men "must be superior in morals"—"we must be more pure than they, before we can be duly respected." For northern free blacks, then, the metaphor linking slavery and intemperance was a personal one, yet also more than personal—it was collective and political. Urban black reformers desired both independence and freedom, and thus they regarded temperance and antislavery as inseparable movements during the 1830s and 1840s.[91]

Yet the assertion of black manhood through temperance activism was fraught with difficulties for African American reformers. It required them to put aside the idea of a unified black citizenry in order to advance a bourgeois criticism of the masculinity of working-class black men. Although young black leaders hoped to speak for the entire free black community, they also knew that maintaining the respectability derived from temperance was as essential to their middle-class status as it was to their position as citizens and men. Black temperance activists challenged rival black working-class masculinity by depicting men addicted to drink as dependent, inferior, and enslaved. They accordingly targeted black seamen and dock workers by establishing temperance boarding houses as alternatives to the public houses and taverns that such working men commonly patronized. By highlighting distinctions among urban black men and by conflating gender and class, these reformers made temperance a measure of class rather than a characteristic of freedom.[92] Still, temperance was overwhelmingly adopted in northern black communities after 1840, leading one historian to claim that "intemperance had become more of a white problem than a black one."[93] Temperance activism, however, placed black reformers in the dangerous position of asserting their superior independence and manliness before antitemperance white working men, especially Irish immigrant men, their most hostile economic competitors. With drinking and temperance so interwoven with the meanings of manhood in the antebellum North, this development led directly to violent conflict.

One of the most devastating race riots ever experienced by antebellum Northerners directly involved black temperance and young men's reformers. As a result of their efforts to assert their status as men and citizens, black men became the direct targets of white mob violence. On August 1, 1842, on the alternative independence day celebrated by urban blacks to commemorate Britain's abolition of slavery, temperance leaders from Philadelphia's largest black neighborhood organized a parade, and twelve hundred supporters joined the procession. White onlookers took offense at a banner raised by the Young Men's Vigilant Society depicting a slave freed from his chains with a rising sun and sinking slave ship in the background. Some onlookers rationalized their violent outburst with the assertion that the banner depicted the slave rebellion in Haiti. The marchers were attacked by a crowd of white laborers (the *National Anti-Slavery Standard* claimed the mob was composed almost entirely of Irishmen) and, when the paraders fought back, the clash escalated into a full-scale riot. White rioters burned to the ground the Second African Presbyterian Church and Smith Beneficial Hall, severely beat dozens of black residents who set foot in the streets, and sent hundreds of black families fleeing for the safety of the New Jersey woods while their homes were ransacked or destroyed. The riots led young reformer Robert Purvis to lament that he was "convinced of our utter and complete nothingness in public estimation." Black reformers such as Purvis understood that the contested nature of manhood in the antebellum North could often be settled on the life or death ground of racial violence.[94]

Temperance and the Cultural Battle over Manhood

Temperance reform clearly illustrates how urban reformers constructed an ideal manliness around the disciplined respectability that marked their generation and, more ambiguously, their class. The temperance movement, in fact, became a battle over the nature of manhood in antebellum America. With numerous popular culture media at their disposal, temperance writers deluged their readers with images of family conflict incited by drinking men, painting portraits of drunken husbands and fathers who subjected their families to violent rage or economic and moral ruin. The architects of temperance popular culture exploited the same problem of generational alienation that young men's reformers had introduced.

As the second phase of the movement flourished, temperance culture quickly took on a new and exciting character. Reformers now pushed far beyond the staid techniques of its earliest societies, jettisoning the previous obsession with statistics and moderation. Washingtonian organizations and total abstinence societies reinvigorated temperance reform with bold strategies and methods, most of which were rooted in the newly thriving print media and popular entertainment in the antebellum North. Songs, hymns, poems, books, pamphlets, engravings, and cartoons were employed to enlist supporters and to rally faithful believers. Tales of destruction to families, livelihoods, and character following the first sip from the bottle soon abounded in sentimental novels. Theatrical promoters and playwrights adapted many of these temperance tales into popular melodramas for the stage, offering another medium for the temperance message. Reformers also exploited music to further spread temperance ideas. Activists with a gift for verse, and many more without a gift, penned temperance songs for all occasions, and publishers released compilation songbooks, with John Marsh's *Temperance Hymnbook and Minstrel* among the most popular. Like ballads printed in the form of broadsides that peddlers and shopkeepers sold, temperance songs were written to be sung to well-recognized tunes and provided immediate commercial successes for their publishers. These songs ranged from hymns to comic tunes to melodramatic numbers, but they invariably echoed the same moral message as the temperance novels and dramas.[95]

Post-1830s temperance reformers, especially the Washingtonians, also devised drink-free alternatives to the leisure-time activities of urban residents. They created temperance hotels and temperance taverns for travelers. They organized children and youth clubs, called the "Cold Water Army," throughout northern cities. To reach even larger audiences, working-class temperance advocates transformed popular celebrations and amusements into alcohol-free urban entertainment. Temperance fairs, picnics, concerts, and dances were common in Philadelphia during the 1840s. Independence Day festivities and parades easily stood as the most grand and popular occasions sponsored by temperance supporters. Orations, songs, toasts (with water, of course), and feasts marked these annual celebrations, as temperance advocates emphasized the connections between their activities and the republican traditions of the revolutionary era. Never before had Americans seen so many novel means to spread a reform message. Reformers began to resemble political promoters like Thurlow Weed or carnival showmen like P. T. Barnum.[96]

As temperance reformers discovered that moral suasion could be presented in the guise of entertainment, undeniably the largest cottage industry spawned by the movement was sensational and sentimental fiction, published separately as short stories or novels, or serialized in magazines and penny-press newspapers. Temperance fiction dramatized personal and family battles with alcohol abuse, always presenting the same moral lesson of economic and social ruin that began with a man's moderate drinking, and occasionally telling of his redemption secured by his introduction to the habits of self-discipline and abstinence. Philadelphia writer T. S. Arthur, the most prolific author of sentimental novels in antebellum America, provided readers with a spate of stories beginning in the 1840s with *Six Nights with the Washingtonians* (1842) and *Temperance Tales* (1843) and culminating in his most popular tale, *Ten Nights in a Bar-Room* (1854).[97] Temperance stories supplied the central plot ideas for much of the sentimental fiction consumed by Americans in the first half of the nineteenth century. The most memorable of these tales were adapted into plays and occasionally became enormously successful popular dramas. During the mid-1840s a play called *The Drunkard* opened in Philadelphia, Boston, Cincinnati, and Brooklyn, before settling into a record run at Barnum's 3,000–seat American Museum in New York City. By the 1850s, temperance dramas and *Uncle Tom's Cabin* frequently shared billing in urban theaters. Temperance reformers exploited the blurred line between respectable writing and sensationalism; and it seemed that entertainers were equally willing to profit from the lurid and provocative tales told by temperance writers.[98]

Clashes between fathers and sons became the ubiquitous plot device in temperance stories, plays, and songs. Writers depicted fathers as the instruments of their sons' ruin by introducing them to strong drink at a young age. As one temperance poem phrased it:

> "'Tis but a drop," the father said,
>   And gave it to his son;
> But little did he think a work
>   Of death was then begun.[99]

Temperance fiction did not invent this narrative of the corrupting influence of fathers; nearly every temperance society in the country had been telling tales of fathers killing their sons since the movement first gained popularity. For example, the American Temperance Society printed a tale from "a Merchant in New York," wherein he claimed that all the neighborhood grocers had "gone down to the grave" in the past few years, and in nearly every instance, a father was responsible for sending his sons to a "drunkard's grave."[100] A similar narrative appeared in the popular penny presses. The *Public Ledger* reported in 1837 the story of a young man who "had the appearance of an intelligent and respectable mechanic," yet brought his two-year-old son into a bar and ordered him to drink from a glass of brandy. The paper editorialized in the vein of temperance writers: "How many drunkards are made from such beginnings! How many heart broken mothers are sorrowing over their fallen offspring, brought to disgrace and ruin by a father's folly!" From the beginning, then, temperance reformers underscored the destructive influence that fathers had on their families, and especially on their sons (figure 6).[101]

Temperance novelists fastened onto this theme of the destructive influence of fathers more often than any other argument, and then proceeded to carry it to new heights of sensationalism. T. S. Arthur honed this tale of a father's legacy to perfection during his two decades of writing temperance fiction. In "The Ruined Family" (1843), Arthur spins the tale of Mr. Graham, "a merchant of high standing in Philadelphia," and the family he nearly destroyed. Graham had, since "early manhood," freely imbibed wines and brandies, not realizing the dangers of such indulgence. Social drinking led inevitably to drunkenness, and Graham abandoned his business and brought his estate into ruin before his premature death. Meanwhile, the story continues, his eldest child and only son Alfred, then twenty-one, followed his father's path into dissipation. Indiscreet in the choice of companions and inclined toward solo drinking binges, Alfred spent several lost days in a drunken stupor. If not for the kindness of a stranger who introduced him to the temperance pledge, the son would have met the same fate as his father.[102]

In *Ten Nights in a Bar-Room,* Arthur brings together nearly all the themes of antebellum temperance fiction and wraps them in a sensational tale of men destroying their families. Perhaps this explains why the novel became one of the best-selling books of the century, with over 400,000 copies sold. Arthur depicts the innocent young Frank Slade as destined for ruin when his father, Simon Slade, decided to take up tavern-keeping, thereby exposing his children to the corrupting influence of alcohol and barrooms: "From the day the tavern opened, and Frank drew into his lungs full draughts of the changed atmosphere . . . the work of moral deterioration commenced." For Arthur, the elder Slade is as guilty as if he had systematically planned his son's demise. "How almost hopeless is the case of a boy," Arthur pleads, "surrounded, as Frank was, by the corrupting, debasing associations of a barroom! Had his father meditated his ruin, he could not have more surely laid his plans for the fearful consummation; and he reaped as he had sown." *Ten Nights* abounds with other examples of men destroying their families. Joe Morgan's drinking resulted in his daughter Mary's dramatic death, when she, on one of her angelic errands to retrieve her father from a tavern, was struck in the head by a heavy glass tumbler angrily thrown by Simon Slade. Mary's death, however, brought about the salvation of her father, who never drank again, and at the end of the dark novel he was the only person better

FIGURE 6. This illustration from popular temperance fiction sensationally depicts the de-structive influence of a drinking father and men's drunkenness as the special burden of women in the home. "The Drunkard's Home," *The National Temperance Offering, and Sons and Daughters of Temperance Gift*, ed. S. F. Cary (New York, 1850). Courtesy of the Brown University Library.

off than when it began. Meanwhile, Judge Hammond exposed his son Willy to the pernicious influences of tavern life, only to witness his son's and wife's nearly simultaneous deaths, as a result of the gambling and drinking that produced Willy's downfall. In a case of poetic justice, and an ironic patricidal twist, Frank Slade eventually killed his own father by hurling a brandy bottle at his head. In Arthur's powerful temperance moral, the bottle both killed Slade and resulted in the final ruin of his son.

Within this context, *Ten Nights* fixes its gaze on the dangerous influences and temptations that young men face. Like the urban youth advice litera-ture, Arthur pictures an environment where the evil influence of designing associates can lure any young man into a cycle of destruction. As one character interjected: "Your sons are not safe; nor are mine. We cannot tell the day nor the hour when they may weakly yield to the solicitation of some companion, and enter the wide open door of ruin." Arthur's young men are potential victims of a "masculine influence" that worked at odds with the regenerative influence of the feminine. For Arthur, the tavern represents more than a physical space; it signifies as well the system of market capitalism that produced those menacing attributes associated with a new masculine identity in the nineteenth century. At one point Arthur describes Simon Slade as "selfish, grasping, unscrupulous, and passionate"—in other words, all the characteristics of aggressive masculine behavior (the "masculine achiever") that developed in the early republic. While self-interested actions situated entrepreneurial men in a position to distinguish themselves from working men and domestic women, that same passionate selfishness engendered a destructive force unless properly reigned in. "With a selfish desire to get gain," Arthur portrays Slade as "embarked in the trade of corruption, ruin, and death."[103]

Temperance fiction always preached that the best resolution for the deathly destruction inherent in masculine passions resided in the formation of a strong character built on the exercise of self-restraint. In *Ten Nights*, Arthur emphasizes this point through his portrayal of men's faces. Once a man came under the influence of a drinking life, Arthur's narrator depicts his facial features as thickened and increasingly sensual, as slipping from the qualities of manliness into those portrayed as animalistic. Judge Lyman's face had changed terribly in just a few years: "the swollen lips and cheeks gave to his countenance a look of all-predominating sensuality. True manliness had bowed itself in debasing submission to the bestial." The young men who nightly patronize Slade's tavern elicit the description that "there was scarcely one of them whose face did not show marks of sensuality." Simon Slade's countenance not only displayed his "strongly marked selfishness," but "his face had grown decidedly bad in expression, as well as gross and sensual." "There was, too, a certain thickness of speech, that gave another corroborating sign of evil progress." And finally, Frank Slade's downfall is also measured in his countenance: "He had grown into a stout man—though his face presented little that was manly, in the true sense of the word. It was disgustingly sensual." This fascination with faces represented more than a literary device. Arthur invokes the middle-class anxiety that reputation and respectability, principal markers of the middle classes, might often be merely an outward illusion reflected on a face or a mask to be donned. As historians Karen Halttunen and Mark Carnes have noted, masks and faces were crucial to the cultural production of class and gender in the nineteenth century. Arthur tries to convince his readers that the true attributes of intemperate men could not be hidden behind a mask of reputation or respectability and that the character of self-restrained men of temperance was an inner quality that needed to be nurtured amid the corrupting influences of aggressive men.[104]

Small wonder, then, that Philadelphia's young men's temperance reformers saw the temperance crusade as a clash between generations—as a contest between competing versions of manliness. Fathers of the previous generation became both real and symbolic antagonists for young men's reformers and temperance activists alike. Young men became convinced that they could not wait for their elders to secure this reformation.[105] Hence Philadelphia's Young Men's Temperance Society pleaded with apprentices or clerks to ask their masters, merchants, or even their mothers about the benefits of joining a temperance association. But intentionally, the society did not ask young men to seek their fathers' advice; fathers were the ones most likely to lead them astray. Young male reformers assumed that fathers were capable of destroying their sons. The critical divide separating the drinking habits of men following the Revolution and those who entered manhood in the 1830s was now played out as the differences between fathers and sons. Not surprisingly, memoirs of "self-made" men, which found their inspiration in this era, commonly emphasized the ways they distanced themselves from their fathers or their fathers' intemperate habits.[106]

These reformers' tendency to construct gender out of familial conflict can be seen in the temperance movement's obsession with the American Revolution and the heroic tradition of the founding fathers. A generation of young sons declared their independence from the image and behavior of their revolutionary fathers. The American Temperance Union pleaded with young men: "You are called to achieve your country's independence; to hand down moral freedom to the generations that come after you. By the spirit of our fathers who pledged their lives, . . . we entreat you. . . . Dare to be temperate. Resolve to be free."[107] With a symbolically patricidal twist, temperance advocates named their organizations Washingtonians or Sons of Temperance, scheduled their celebrations on national holidays in order to contrast manly temperance against Fourth of July revelry, and grafted patriotic lyrics onto familiar nationalistic tunes when composing temperance songs. William B. Tappan, a young men's activist, captured this spirit in verse: "Our Declaration?" Tappan intoned "'tis the PLEDGE; Our Sword's good work?—the *silent* STILL." The enemy?—Ardent spirits, and "'Tee-total,' [our] BUNKER HILL!"[108]

By fusing the language of patriotism and citizenship, which consistently marked manliness for middle-class white men, together with an implicit critique of their fathers' generation, these young reformers articulated a gendered vision of their reform activism. At a Fourth of July meeting in 1828, Philadelphia's Young Men's Temperance Society resolved that the intemperate habits of the previous generation were "calculated to impair the existence of our republican institutions, and to render as a dead letter the glorious Declaration of Independence." The revolutionary generation had introduced, as they saw it, the tyranny of "King Alcohol," and now young temperance reformers had chosen to declare their independence from a masculinity linked with drink.[109] Beneath this patriotic rhetoric lay the subtle but unmistakable message that these reformers believed they were engaged in a more important revolution, that temperance reform involved a symbolic assertion of the superior manliness of the sons of the founding fathers.

White Women, Womanhood, and Temperance

White male reformers made few, if any, direct references to the fact that their reforming activities took them into a realm increasingly inhabited by women and marked as feminine in the nineteenth-century discourse surrounding religion and reform. If we look only at the public statements of these young male reformers, it might appear as though women were not a part of the story—and yet, once again, they were. Women reformers and the new conventions of domesticity were silently present even if young male reformers chose not to address them directly. Women activists had already begun redrawing the gendered landscape of reform and redefining the gendered language of religiosity. Young male reformers certainly were cognizant of this cultural dynamic; they knew it from the experiences of their own wives, as well as from the competitive fundraising between men's and women's reform societies. Yet young men's reformers chose to promote a definition of manhood that did not explicitly place women (of their own class or race) as the opposite of manliness. By casting their actions as a generational struggle that demonstrated their superior manliness against fathers (both real and metaphorical), young white male reformers defined an ideal manhood against the opposing figure of the older intemperate man. In other words, they proved they were true men by showing they were different from other males who compromised their manhood by drinking. They represented their true manliness not as a product of sexual difference, but as a distinction between men of different generations, classes, or moral characters. In this way, male reformers could mask the fact that they were entering into a feminized realm of religion and reform—that they were acting "like women." Instead, they envisioned a familial conflict not against mothers, whom domestic conventions held responsible for ensuring a young man's pious character, but rather against a generation of fathers whose aggressive behavior (both personal and commercial) made it increasingly hard to reconcile manliness with piety, charity, or domestic intimacy.

Because temperance reform and women in public seem so inseparably linked in American culture by the end of the nineteenth century and because temperance work was a principal source of suffragist activism, it might come as a surprise that at its beginning temperance did not lead to an expanded public presence for white women. Although women took an active part in the crusade from its inception, at no time in the nineteenth century were they less visible as activists than during the first phase of the movement (1826–37). Temperance societies welcomed women members, but kept the leadership on both local and national levels firmly in the hands of men. Much like earlier drinking rituals, women might be allowed in the door, but they were not invited to participate equally at the table. Not one northern city could claim a women's temperance society before 1837, and only a few isolated towns in New England had female temperance organizations. Still, temperance activists estimated that women constituted between 35 and 60 percent of the membership of male-led societies in the early 1830s. More commonly during this period, women worked for the cause outside the structure of societies. They encouraged family members to abstain, boycotted stores where ardent spirits were sold, and worked to keep temperance standards a matter of church policy in their congregations.[110]

Male temperance reformers tried, with unflagging tenacity, to relegate women to either of two largely symbolic roles in the logic of temperance reform—either they were portrayed as helpless victims of male drinking or they were championed for their domestic influence that tamed men's drinking appetites or redeemed wayward husbands and sons. Even if temperance women had no firsthand knowledge of drunken men's destructive powers in their own families, temperance publications ubiquitously reminded them of their role as victims of men's intemperance. "Alcohol has been the bane of woman's happiness; the mildew of her budding bliss," teetotal advocates reminded women. "It has robbed her of her husband, and prematurely buried the son of her earliest affection in a disgraceful tomb."[111] Albert Barnes declared that women suffered more than all others where intemperance prevailed. "Woman, in the march of this pestilence, has bled at every pore," he wrote. "Whoever is the drunkard, she is the sufferer. Thousands have sighed and groaned in vain: thousands bound to profligate husbands still weep and wail."[112]

Male temperance reformers continually emphasized that the movement could not succeed without the efforts of women, but at the same time denied women any positions of agency or leadership. Such a formulation could make sense only within the convoluted logic of a woman's influence. Combining symbols of both victim and influence, John Chambers told a temperance festival in 1838 that "no effort to purify a depraved public sentiment

can ever succeed without female influence; and as woman is the greatest sufferer in the burning tide which sweeps over the land from intemperance, her
influence should be secured, in every possible way, to advance the Temperance reformation."[113] With increasing frequency, male temperance leaders'
emphasis on female moral influence was offset by efforts to ensure that the
constricted boundaries of a woman's activism remained secure. There
should be "no sacrifice of delicacy," a temperance publication insisted without any subtlety, "no stepping beyond your proper sphere."[114] These pictures
of women's personal interest in temperance's success resonated with early-
nineteenth-century notions of gender and domesticity that white middle-
class women both consumed and produced. There were no models of activist
women in temperance popular culture—only hapless victims of drunken violence and bankruptcy or the quiet influence of piety and purity at home.
Ironically, then, despite late-nineteenth-century connections between temperance and an expanded public political presence for women, temperance
began as a retrenchment, a step away from the aggressive public role that
poor-relief benevolent societies had played in the early republic.

Just as membership and new strategies flourished during the second phase
of antebellum temperance reform beginning in the late 1830s, white women
began to assume more prominent roles as the movement attracted greater
working-class and nativist support. The virtual invisibility of black women's
temperance actions in northern cities before the Civil War, however, remains a tremendous shortcoming in antebellum reform sources. White societies left almost no record of black women's organizations; African American
newspapers wrote frequently about temperance activism, yet consistently
represented both drinkers and reformers as men. This paucity of evidence
does not mean the absence of black women's activism, only that their labors
were likely ignored by others. (Black abolitionist women, such as Francis
Watkins and Mary Ann Shadd, often wrote and spoke on behalf of temperance causes.) The few available sources reveal that African American women
could outdistance black men in their commitment to the cause. When black
clergymen organized a week-long moral-reform rally in Troy, New York, in
1837, the newly created black women's total abstinence society gathered
sixty-eight members, while the men's group mustered only twenty-six. It is
very likely that growing working-class interest in temperance corresponded
with new local associations of black women, who were already conversant
with mutual benefit societies.[115]

Women formed their own societies with an agenda of total abstinence. Female total abstinence societies, Martha Washington associations, and Daughters of Temperance groups emerged alongside their male counterparts in
Philadelphia. One newspaper estimated that as many as sixteen thousand

women were active in Philadelphia's temperance movement. The Female Total Abstinence Society in 1838 spoke of all women being "united in a holy phalanx to arrest an evil which has poured its bitterest causes upon the head of women." In contrast to previous temperance groups, Martha Washington societies made a concerted effort to reclaim alcoholic women, who were welcomed as members in large numbers during the early years. By addressing the issue of female alcoholics, these working-class temperance women were the first to correct the elision of women's drinking in male-dominated temperance rhetoric. In their minds, formerly alcoholic women did not sacrifice their claims to true womanhood merely because they had once been dependent on drink. Still, Martha Washington activists did fear that drinking women produced an inversion of the moral pattern of influence within the family, as drunken husbands led their wives into the slavery of intemperance. As one historian has shown, working-class women who formed Martha Washington societies shared with other temperance reformers a "deep absorption in the affairs of the home and the conviction that the use of alcohol was inimical to family happiness." Washingtonian women did not, however, merely make a middle-class ideology of true womanhood their own. They built a domestic rationale for temperance from their own experiences, and from the vulnerable position that working women and their families occupied in the industrial economy. Their society reports were filled with personal testimonies of the baneful effects of alcoholism in their own families and pleas for the "moral resurrection" of homes through the pledge of total abstinence. From that moment forward, women tirelessly labored for the temperance crusade, no longer willing to bequeath the moral leadership on this issue to men. By the end of the nineteenth century, the temperance cause was kept alive almost exclusively by the spirited efforts of both black and white women in America.[116]

The contested nature of gender and temperance reform was never as simple as middle-class definitions of manliness clashing with working-class expressions of masculinity, or vice versa. Philadelphia's young men reformers and temperance activists illustrate that manhood was contested not only across classes and races, but within them as well. That conflict exposes the process by which gender is constituted to mask racial and class differences. By examining that dynamic, we can begin to unravel the ways American men constructed various forms of masculinity, as social theorist Victor Seidler phrases it, in order to see and talk only of others and yet appear "strangely invisible to themselves." Philadelphia's young male reformers invoked generational conflict and citizenship to obscure the complexity of masculine identities, and to mask their shared need with women for a reforming presence and a pious character.[117]

Still, at the heart of the temperance debate remained ideas of independence and dependence. And African American reformers exposed the ways in which the language of slavery and freedom—intemperance and temperance—revealed the racial dimensions of those gender ideologies during an era when the United States became severely divided over the issue of slavery and the desire for equality by people of African ancestry.

CHAPTER 4

Slavery

I have a mind to be a man
Among white men and free,
and OLD LIBERIA!
Is not the place for me!!
JOSHUA SIMPSON, "Old Liberia Is Not the Place for Me"
(1852)

He set out on a journey with great uncertainty about his survival. At best he harbored a distant hope that life's cruel fates might turn for the better; at worst he feared a bitter end to his life without ever knowing its rewards. It was a perilous voyage, across a tempestuous ocean, in a wooden vessel. Difficult to distinguish from cargo, tightly packed, he was squeezed into a space resembling a tomb, straining even to move. Death his constant musing, he headed toward a land unknown and toward a place where the promise of freedom was equally unsure. Perhaps a memory of the god Yemoja, "mother of waters," briefly entered his thoughts; he offered prayers to his god for safe passage and deliverance.

The cultural experiences of African peoples in the Americas have been shaped by journeys—journeys of body, soul, and memory. The first image that this description conjures for the history of the Atlantic world is the infamous Middle Passage of slaves forcibly removed from their ancestral homes. Memories of that passage resonated in the collective and personal consciousness of generations of African Americans well into the nineteenth century. Yet this same imagery appeared in many other voyages during the antebellum years, voyages perhaps less familiar but still significant for what they disclose about the imaginings of bondage, freedom, and national aspirations for African Americans.[1]

This imagery also appeared in the journey of a slave named Henry Brown, who in 1849, with the help of friends, enclosed himself into a wooden box three feet long and two feet deep and wide and had himself shipped from Richmond, Virginia, to Philadelphia, a twenty-seven-hour sea journey. For several of those hours he was placed on his head, straining under the pressure until he felt his "eyes were almost swollen out of their sockets," and the veins on his temple "seemed ready to burst." Henry "Box" Brown, as he became known through a white abolitionist "as-told-to" account of his escape, succeeded in his voyage to freedom when his box was opened in the home of Philadelphia abolitionists and underground railroad activists (figure 7). Brown (or his ghost writer) described the slave experience with the metaphor of sailing on an ocean amid a gathering storm, not knowing whether he might ever escape or even outlive the storm. "Long had seemed my journey," Brown stated, "and terribly hazardous had been my attempt to gain my birth-right; but it all seemed a comparatively light price to pay for the precious boon of *Liberty*."[2]

For African Americans before the Civil War, journeys toward freedom or toward a new homeland offered one of the most powerful symbols of the autonomy, humanity, and nationhood denied to them in the United States. It was no coincidence that fugitive slaves called their networks of flight an "underground railroad" or that Frederick Douglass named his newspaper after the North Star. Freedom was a passage; it involved crossing over a boundary that had kept one confined, like the exodus of the Israelites from Egypt that provided the archetypal story of African American Christianity.[3] For this reason, black responses to the perpetuation of slavery in America, and their struggle to secure its abolition, developed within the context of journeys of colonization and emigration that offered competing visions of another homeland or a black nation finally realized; and yet it was resistance to those alluring visions that secured the goal of true citizenship for African Americans in the United States.

When the American Colonization Society (ACS) began recruiting northern free blacks to establish a new colony in West Africa in the 1820s, Joseph Blake, a thirty-three-year-old Philadelphia ship carpenter, departed for an ocean journey of his own, fraught with similar uncertainties that at first seemed less precarious than the voyage of Henry Brown. He joined dozens of urban free blacks who turned a deaf ear to overwhelming black opposition to the colonization scheme and set sail for Liberia. Perhaps Blake, like many of his fellow colonists, considered Liberia his only hope for true freedom. A decade later, Blake wrote to the ACS secretary charging the society's white colonial agent in Liberia, Dr. Joseph Mechlin, Jr., with having seduced and "debauched" his wife, leaving Blake to support "a mulatto child" produced by their "criminal intercourse." The consequences for Blake were numerous. His wife had become "haughty, insolent, and disobedient," and "careless" about family matters. He expressed disillusionment that a man "put here to

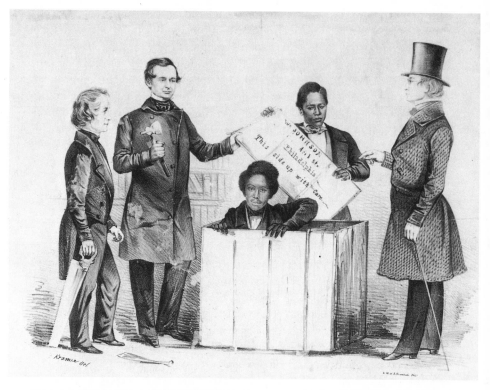

FIGURE 7. The account of Henry "Box" Brown's escape from slavery evoked images of voyages across water that symbolized African American journeys to freedom in the antebellum era. "The Resurrection of Henry Box Brown at Philadelphia." Courtesy of Friends Historical Library, Swarthmore College.

be our father, and our guide," and "our representative, an earthly protector," could perpetrate such an evil. At the same time, Blake worried about the repercussions for the colony's reputation. "Had I killed the man," he wrote, "it would have been a stigma casted upon the Colony, that never could have been rubbed off." So Blake appealed for redress, requesting a grant of waterfront land to build a shipyard, and threatened that if he were not compensated, he would "publish [Mechlin's] conduct to the whole world."[4]

Blake's experiences highlight how conceptions of manhood and debates over African colonization, both of which have been insufficiently addressed by historians, essentially fashioned the gendered and racial foundations of northern responses to the slavery problem prior to the Civil War. Those white colonization leaders whom Blake addressed certainly remained cognizant of the various masculine reactions he outlined for them. His possible manly responses ranged from violent revenge of his honor, to a reassertion of patriarchy in his family, to independence through property ownership, or finally, to exposure of the pretenses behind white colonizationists' claims of benevolence and paternalism. Although the ACS ignored Blake's pleas, for decades those same colonization society leaders had been actively promoting their reform movement as a vehicle for masculine identity for black colonists and white reformers alike.

This episode illustrates a gendered history of slavery and abolition different from that typically presented by historians. For some time, the history of antebellum abolitionists has been a fragmented narrative. For more than thirty years, women's historians have focused attention on the relationship between white women's abolitionist activism and the origins of feminism and the woman's rights movement.[5] And yet surveys of the abolitionist movement still fail to integrate gender as an analytical category, choosing instead to emphasize women as a problem ("the woman question" that produced an abolitionist schism) or to mention briefly the woman's rights movement.[6] Moreover, black abolitionists have been relegated to a separate literature, as general histories of the movement have situated white abolitionists as the central, and at times the only, players in the drama of antislavery reform.[7] Colonization and black emigration movements remain conspicuously absent from most histories of antislavery.[8] A comprehensive understanding of the ways in which gender shaped and influenced northern reformers' responses to slavery must not only reveal the gendered histories of the whole abolitionist movement—men and women, black and white, feminist and nonfeminist. It must also encompass the perspective of the abolitionists' greatest rivals for northern whites' sympathies—the colonizationists—as well as those northern blacks who favored emigration while expressing their hostility to white colonization schemes.

An examination of colonization, emigration, and abolitionist movements together provides the kind of holistic analysis that a history of gender and antislavery demands, and it situates the experiences of African Americans as integral to that narrative. As the southernmost northern city, Philadelphia possessed the largest and most influential free black community and experienced the most intense competition between colonizationist and abolitionist reformers. One important premise here is that manhood and colonization were inseparable elements of a comprehensive gender system that sustained antebellum movements designed to resolve the dilemmas of slavery, race, and the place of free African Americans in that society. Colonization reform assumed a masculine character from its inception and framed its solution to the slavery problem in political terms. The movement never attracted a sizable number of white women activists in the North, and its white spokesmen adopted a gendered discourse that simultaneously depicted colonizing as a masculine endeavor while questioning the masculinity of the

African American men who actually performed the work of colonizing. In doing so, they invoked a sexualized imagery of Africa that reinforced a convergent set of fears among northern whites about "amalgamation" and generated a climate favorable to race riots in northern cities during the antebellum years.

In the face of this gendered racial discourse, African Americans in the North asserted their own interpretations of the meanings of manhood and womanhood as they defended their place in American society and reconciled their discordant views over whether blacks should emigrate from the United States. These divergent perspectives on colonization and emigration demonstrate that free blacks, as much as white reformers, actively produced a comprehensive gendered discourse as they struggled to respond to the powerful forces of slavery and race in antebellum America. Black emigration plans exposed the relationship between gender, citizenship rights, and black nationalism, and opened a door for an expanded public presence for African American women.

In turn, the work of women antislavery activists reveals the significant differences between colonizationists and abolitionists. Since colonization reformers constituted the solutions to slavery as political, national, and masculine, they inadvertently assisted in creating a climate that by definition radicalized women's abolitionism, making it a direct affront to a male-dominated public sphere. Black women abolitionists played a central role in defining women's antislavery activism by guiding white women into a deeper understanding of racial prejudice, the hypocrisy of churches, and the plight of fugitive slaves. At the same time, white abolitionist women helped to develop a gendered discourse regarding race and slavery that was markedly different from that of their male counterparts in the colonization movement, a discourse rooted in a sentimentalized portrayal of slaves as feminized. They depicted "the slave" as more spiritual, more religious, more forgiving than white American men—descriptions that easily allowed white women abolitionists to see their own oppression mirrored in the experiences of all enslaved people.

"It Will Be Making a Man of Me"

Even before Joseph Blake was born, proposals for African colonization had circulated among late-eighteenth-century seaport towns. Colonization became a national reform movement in 1816 with the formation of the American Society for the Colonizing of Free People of Colour. Its stated purpose was to establish independent colonies in western Africa, to be populated by freed slaves and free-born African Americans who would bring "civi-

lization" and Christianity to the continent of Africa. The American Colonization Society seemed to promise all things to all people, posturing as the most
broadly appealing of all benevolent causes. It claimed to be a missionary enterprise, a remedy for the upper South's expanding free black population, a
conservative step toward gradual abolition, a solution to pauperism in northern cities, and the dawn of expanded commerce with Africa. As black critics
noted, "It is one thing at the south, and another at the north; it blows hot
and cold; it sends forth bitter and sweet." The American Colonization Society forged a link between those who desired the removal of free blacks in
both the North and South and those supporters of foreign mission enterprises just getting started in the 1810s. Because the society envisioned the
spread of Christianity in Africa, it received widespread support from most of
the major Protestant denominations in the country between 1816 and 1840.
Most northern colonizationists, such as the members of the Pennsylvania
Colonization Society, seemed convinced that the society would result in the
"safe, gradual, voluntary and entire abolition of slavery."[9]

The movement's underlying ideological premise was that white prejudice
against black people was so debasing and immutable that African Americans
could never be accorded equality unless they were removed from white society. "There appears to exist in the breasts of white men in this country,"
wrote white colonizationist Frederick Freeman, "a prejudice against the
colour of the African, which nothing short of divine power can remove."
With their pessimism rooted in a Calvinist-inspired vision of corporate reform, colonizationists voiced little hope for resolving these conditions. Black
and white abolitionists countered by insisting that these claims merely concealed the racism behind colonizationist actions. Colonization was "the offspring of Prejudice," black abolitionist Sarah Forten contended; she was convinced "that it originated more immediately from prejudice than from
philanthropy."[10]

From the outset, African Americans in the North responded with intense
opposition to the American Colonization Society. Three thousand free
blacks rallied together in Philadelphia in 1817, despite hints that some
black elites favored the idea, and declared their resolve to "renounce and
disdain every connection" with the plan. Colonization, they argued, was
merely a ruse by southern slaveholders to remove free blacks, so that they
would not inspire slaves with the hope of freedom or continue struggles for
their emancipation. African Americans knew full well that some of the colonization society's early publications spoke longingly of ridding the nation of
free black people. They had surely read descriptions of themselves as "an
idle, worthless, and thievish race," "a nuisance and a burden," and "condemned to a state of hopeless inferiority and degradation by their color."
The tone of these unveiled sentiments fueled their skepticism whenever

African Americans heard colonizationists declaring their benevolent intentions. If colonizationists truly felt compassion toward black Americans, their critics chided, then they would not hesitate to devote a like measure of their resources toward good schools and employment for those who remained on this side of the Atlantic. As one young New York man stated, "the Colonizationists want us to go to Liberia if we will; if we won't go there, we may go to hell." Black opponents stood alone for more than a decade, as white abolitionists failed to develop an ardent anticolonization critique until William Lloyd Garrison began publishing the *Liberator* in 1831, followed by his *Thoughts on African Colonization* the next year. From that point forward, white and black abolitionists echoed one another's cry that colonization was a racist scheme that both condoned and encouraged white racial prejudices.[11]

What is perhaps most remarkable about white colonization in the North is how few white women embraced the cause as their own or organized female societies to support it. A scarcity of white women activists within colonization societies is especially surprising given the movement's claim to be a missionary enterprise and the preeminence of white middle-class women in evangelistic benevolent societies. Yet women rarely appeared among colonization records and publications during the movement's first two decades. Societies operated exclusively by white men outnumbered women's colonization associations by as much as twenty to one, with over two hundred male auxiliaries organized between 1817 and 1831 compared to only nine female colonization societies, only two of which were in communities outside the slaveholding South. Moreover, most of these female societies originated in isolated small towns. White women in New York, Boston, Hartford, Providence, and Albany opted not to form colonization societies.[12] Many of the nation's leading white male abolitionists—Arthur and Lewis Tappan, Gerrit Smith, Samuel J. May, Theodore Weld, and Joshua Leavitt—had supported colonization in their early reform careers, before making their way into the camp of the immediate abolitionists. None of the leading white women antislavery activists—Lucretia Mott, Abby Kelley, Sarah and Angelina Grimké, or Lydia Maria Child—followed this route from colonizationist to abolitionist.[13]

One reason for the limited participation of white women may lie in the differences in the colonization society's origins, as compared with other reforms. Typically, benevolent causes began with local organizations whose members directed their assistance or reform initiatives toward local residents. This pattern allowed white bourgeois women to negotiate a shared space for their religious activism during the early republic. Only after several similar associations emerged in many different communities did a group of reformers organize a national organization to coordinate and expand these efforts. The American Bible Society (1816), American Tract Society (1825),

American Sunday School Union (1824), and the American Temperance Union (1836) were just a few of the national organizations formed according to this pattern. Colonization reform, however, began as a national society, and its founders had only a reluctant interest in developing local organizations that satisfied the specific needs of local communities. From the beginning, colonization was a centralized reform activity, to such a degree that the phrase "the colonization society" referred to the movement as a whole, as if only one such society existed.

A more convincing explanation as to why white middle-class men greatly outnumbered white women colonizationists can be found in the ways that gender conventions shaped the strategies and techniques of colonization reformers. From its inception, colonizationists framed their reform activity within a definitively masculine public arena, giving colonization a gendered—that is, masculine—character. Despite its posture as a religious and benevolent organization, the society maintained a political cast to its operations from the outset. The American Colonization Society was organized and headquartered in Washington, D.C., held its annual meetings in the Hall of the House of Representatives, and included among its officers such leading national political figures as Henry Clay, William Crawford, Daniel Webster, and Andrew Jackson. Henry Clay eventually served as the society's president and figurehead for nearly fifteen years (Frederick Douglass jibed that it marked the only occasion when Clay would be elected president).[14] In addition to operating among the nation's political elite, the American Colonization Society aggressively sought the assistance of state and federal governments to foster their objectives. Within weeks after the society's founding, they submitted petitions to Congress seeking financial assistance. Although their early hopes for congressional sponsorship were frustrated, colonizationists spent the next two decades pleading for congressional funds and naval support. They took any federal acknowledgment as an endorsement and sought and received money from southern state legislatures. So determined were they to get congressional and state funding, that the society neglected the development of state and local auxiliaries for fifteen years and then continued to appeal for government funds throughout the remainder of the antebellum era.[15]

Colonizationists also persistently blended colonization with patriotism, especially when appealing for support, suggesting that theirs was "the greatest scheme of combined benevolence and patriotism" known to any age, an activity worthy of true citizens (and hence true men). By the early 1830s, they had embraced a strategy of associating colonization with national identity, having sympathetic clergy deliver fundraising sermons every Fourth of July. This provided a consistent income for colonization societies, but it also reinforced distinctions between white "freemen" and African Americans, who found themselves regularly excluded from Fourth of July celebrations in northern cities. Whereas Methodist minister John H. Kennedy concluded his Fourth of July colonization sermon by heralding the privileges of Independence Day, a day "which will be held in joyful and thankful remembrance so long as Freemen breathe," Frederick Douglass felt compelled to remind a white audience in 1852: "This Fourth [of] July is *yours*, not *mine. You* may rejoice, *I* must mourn."[16] This blending of formal politics, patriotism, and religious authority illustrates the primarily masculine arena in which colonizationists chose to perform their reform activism. It also complicates the timing and pattern historians have usually attributed to the politicization of reform before the Civil War. Conventional interpretations attribute the shift toward political action and away from moral suasion to the rise of political abolitionism and the formation of the Liberty Party in 1840. Yet colonization reformers looked to political action more than a decade before abolitionists divided over the issue.[17]

Given their pursuit of an overtly masculine arena of patriotism and political activism, white colonizationists in Philadelphia experienced a resurgence of local activism when a Young Men's Colonization Society was organized in 1834. Recall that dozens of young men's societies emerged in Jacksonian-era cities, providing bourgeois men with an opportunity to demonstrate their character, compassion, usefulness, and manly piety within an evangelical culture. These reformers' concerns about masculinity surfaced in Job R. Tyson's speech before the Young Men's Colonization Society, criticizing the manliness of southern slaveholders. "Instead of the hardy race," Tyson declared, "we find them luxurious and effeminate, unequal to those vigorous exertions" required in a new country, and "emasculate by indulgence." Conversely, colonization reformers depicted themselves as "sons of enlightened and Christian freemen" engaged in an honorable and useful enterprise.[18]

Elliott Cresson was the hardest working colonizationist in Philadelphia and the leading activist in the Young Men's Colonization Society. A wealthy gentleman bachelor from a prominent family of merchants, Cresson was like many other Orthodox Friends who moved easily in and out of evangelical reform circles. But colonization became his life's work. Cresson single-handedly served as a liaison between southern slaveholders, the American Colonization Society, and Philadelphia colonizationists. He was a tireless promoter of the cause, writing letters, publishing public appeals, organizing societies, and editing a colonization newspaper. Cresson served on the executive committees of both the Pennsylvania Colonization Society and the Young Men's Colonization Society, and as an agent for the American Colonization Society. As a result, he became the lightning rod throughout the 1830s for opponents of colonization on both sides of the Atlantic. In 1831, the American Colonization Society sent him on a two-year mission to England to raise $100,000 from leading British humanitarians. Yet abolitionists, especially William Lloyd Garrison and black Baptist minister Nathaniel Paul, hounded Cresson's every step in England, convincing British antislavery men that Cresson's antislavery intentions were disingenuous. Soon Cresson found churches and philanthropists in Britain unreceptive to his pleas and returned home with his fundraising mission a dismal failure.[19]

Cresson, like other northern colonization reformers, found colonization compatible with a growing middle-class hostility toward poverty and poor relief in northern cities after 1817. Colonization reform began at the same moment that new market perspectives transformed traditional notions of poverty, more frequently blaming the poor for their own poverty and castigating private charities for increasing pauperism. Cresson, along with another Philadelphia colonizationist Roberts Vaux, was active in the Provident Society, which spearheaded this new hard-hearted approach to poor relief during the 1820s. By the late 1820s, the American Colonization Society regularly reported the conditions of pauperism among free blacks in northern cities, especially Philadelphia. Colonizationists, such as Cresson and Vaux, looked for solutions to the problems they associated with slavery and emancipation in the largely masculine-dominated realms of public politics and political economy.[20]

The defining features of colonizationists' activism evoked attributes of masculine action in a republic; yet the political bent of the movement was only one part of the gendered construction of colonization reform. The discourse surrounding colonization also exploited explicit gender imagery, especially conceptions of masculinity, to justify the removal of African Americans as the best solution to the slavery problem. Colonizationists appropriated what they perceived to be the lessons of history, nature, and the Scriptures, and constructed a rationale for their movement that combined an internal unity of ideas enveloped in a flurry of contradictions and deceptions. In the process, they contributed to the development of a discourse on race, sex, gender, and civilization that shaped the underpinnings of white supremacy and white male dominance for the remainder of the nineteenth century.[21]

Colonizationists frequently expressed the notion that the history and character of man demonstrated that he was naturally a colonizer. Although they sometimes employed the universal "man" of humanity, more frequently these reformers placed "man" as a masculine being at the center of their discourse. Although some men "talk of colonization as a new idea," Episcopal rector Stephen Tyng reminded a young men's meeting, "the whole history of man is a scheme of colonization. . . . [It] furnished our own existence as a Christian people, and as a nation of the earth." Other spokesmen invoked biblical narratives to confirm this point. Noah, Moses, and the nation of Is-

rael confirmed men's desire for conquest throughout human history. (Elliott Cresson even told the Massachusetts Legislature that Moses was president of the first colonization society.)[22] These reformers thus depicted colonizing not only as the natural and instinctive desire of men, but also as one
of the highest expressions of human development. Other spokesmen invoked American history to validate their view of conquest and settlement as
masculine characteristics. Colonizationists voiced continual veneration for
the earliest white European settlers in North America. One society counseled their supporters, when opponents challenged their actions, to think of
their "own pious ancestors" who courageously colonized this continent.

Just as history confirmed this universal masculine trait for them, antebellum reformers also imagined colonization within the context of a geograph-
ically and socially mobile society that they wished to encourage in the United
States. Colonization became synonymous with migration, and nothing was
considered more manly in this era than westward migration—except perhaps the closely equated idea of entrepreneurial "colonizing" in a market
economy. As a writer for the *Colonization Herald* stated, "Eager for wealth,
men will brave any dangers, and settle down in any place, if they may but increase their worldly store. They go still further, and make the ocean a home,
and leave the rolling billows a patrimony to their children, for the purposes
of pleasure or of profit." By the antebellum decades, westward migration
(and the consequent wars with American Indians) had become a symbol of
white manly courage and adventure. It also produced continual conflicts between white men and women over the frequency of such moves and the toll
they took on personal and familial relationships. Colonization supporters exploited these notions of manly migration and entrepreneurial industry when
defending their cause, thereby connecting manliness with their particular
brand of activism.[23]

The irony here is that white colonizationists were not the colonizers in this
scheme; at most they colonized vicariously. The true colonizers were African
Americans, a fact that often became blurred in that discourse. Although
white colonizationists liked to connect their reform activism to the heroic
manliness of colonizers past and present, in reality, they raised money, petitioned legislatures, and criticized abolitionists, while former slaves and free
blacks courageously built new communities on another continent. According to this white discourse, the power of colonizing as a sign of civilization
meant that emigrating to Africa would eventually make men out of African
American men. For this reason, white colonizationists exclusively referred to
black colonists as generically male, despite the fact that women emigrated to
Liberia in substantial numbers. A complementary set of ideas—that emigrating would make a "true woman" out of African American women—never appeared in colonization records.[24] This is especially striking since domesticity

and motherhood were such ubiquitous features of empire-building schemes in the nineteenth century. Apparently white colonizationists could not conceive of black women as agents in the spread of domesticity.[25]

Colonization publications returned again and again to this set of ideas about race, colonization, and gender. They started with the foundational premise that slavery had emasculated African American men, that black men had been debased below the level of manhood and could not possibly be elevated any higher while surrounded by white prejudice. "So [it is] with the coloured man," Rev. Spencer Cone declared before the New York City Colonization Society in 1836, "you might set him up in business; he might prove honest and upright, and might even grow rich; but if he should acquire the wealth of Stephen Girard, he would still remain a separate and degraded being." As General Robert Harper stated in the first annual report of the American Colonization Society; "You may manumit the slave, but you cannot make him a white man; he still remains a negro or a mulatto." Without ever calling it a miracle, colonizationists maintained that this same former slave could be miraculously transformed into a man by his migrating to and colonizing Africa. Once transported to new and prejudice-free surroundings in Africa, the *African Repository* declared, "they are excited by new motives . . . stimulated to industry and enterprise by prospects of the noblest and richest rewards, and made to cherish the manly and mighty spirit of an independent and self-governed people." To remove him "to the land of his fathers," Cone concluded, "would present the man [as] an entirely new being." Black opponents scoffed at this contradiction, stating, "Here we are ignorant, idle, a nuisance, and a drawback on the resources of the country. But as abandoned as we are, in Africa we shall civilize and christianize all that heathen country." This inconsistency led British abolitionist Charles Stuart to wonder how free blacks could at one moment be "declared as a body, to be little better than devils in the United States," while at the next "be commuted, by mere transportation to Africa, into almost angels!"(figure 8)[26] So common was this motif of miraculous transformation that even the most virulently racist supporters of colonization, such as the anonymous author of *Freemen Awake!*, resorted to it. After querying, "Why should the brave, honest hearted and generous *Indian* be driven from his home, and the deceitful and designing *nigger* be permitted to remain among us?" the author declared in the very next sentence, "The sooner the coast of Africa is planted with colonies of enlightened American Negroes, the sooner will that cursed traffic in negro slavery be wholly abolished." Upon emigrating to Africa, then, these men suddenly became "enlightened American Negroes," but remained the "deceitful and designing *nigger*" when residing in America.[27]

The converse of this logic impelled colonizationists to question the manliness of those who refused to emigrate to Africa. Perhaps the best example of

FIGURE 8. Abolitionist criticisms of African colonization reminded northern audiences (black and white) that colonizationists had pro-slavery motives and that they paradoxically represented African Americans as both "nuisances" and as manly agents of Christian missions. *Antislavery Almanac for 1839* (New York, [1838]). Courtesy of the Library Company of Philadelphia.

this reasoning appeared in the *Maryland Colonization Journal* in 1839. In a likely embellished account, a free black man entered the colonization society offices to declare his intent to emigrate to Africa. The journal recorded the visitor's description of his mounting economic difficulties: "Germans come, Irish come, and if any thing, it's harder for me to get on every year. I have a notion that IF I GO TO THE COLONY IT WILL BE MAKING A MAN OF ME." Rather than an accurate appraisal of black sentiments about colonization, this episode illustrates the interrelationship between race and gender in white colonizationist thought. Contrasting this man to those who chose to stay behind, the journal then commented: "He is worthy to be a freeman in fact, as well as in name, they are not. . . . He has enterprise, judgment and courage," while "they are blinded by ignorance, prejudice, or evil purposes."

The implications are hard to miss. The only black man who could be considered by colonizationists as intelligent, enterprising, courageous—in other words, a true man—was one who recognized that he could not live among white people and chose to go to Africa. All others were mired in ignorance, prejudice, or under the influence of evil forces. It became a common refrain of colonizationists to defame the manliness of those who refused to emigrate, or who opposed the colonization society. In language filled with white middle-class markers of manliness, the Philadelphia Young Men's Colonization Society criticized the lack of manly desire and character among free blacks who "prefer inglorious ease and indolence, to the self-denial and courageous adventure of emigration in search of hardy independence." By racializing such notions as self-denial, courage, adventure, and independence—making them the defining features of white middle-class manliness and thereby conflating whiteness and manhood—colonizationist rhetoric illustrates how inseparable race and gender were in nineteenth-century white discourses about the problem of slavery and its solutions. Perhaps this contributed to the appeal of the colonization movement for the northern white men who overwhelmingly dominated it—that it debased the manhood of black men in America while also vicariously enhancing the manliness of white colonizationist reformers.[28] It certainly explains why northern black men objected to the colonization scheme as an assault on their own manhood.

A corollary to this notion of an essentially masculine desire to colonize emerged in the striking gender and sexual imagery employed in colonizationists' portrayals of Africa. In contrast to abolitionists, colonizationists rarely wrote or spoke about the conditions of slavery in the South; but on the topic of Africa, they were effusive. First and foremost, white colonizationists' depictions of Africa were shaped by a set of ideas about the dichotomy between civilization and savagery, ubiquitous in descriptions of human development and racial "others" since the eighteenth century.[29]

At the same time, American colonizationists commonly represented Africa as a woman and portrayed African colonists in terms of aggressive male sexuality. This imagery appears from the earliest colonization literature through the entire antebellum era. Rev. Robert Finley of New Jersey, a founder of the colonization society, portrayed Africa as both a woman and a mother. Her bosom, he stated, "begins to warm with hope and her heart to beat with expectation and desire" for the arrival of African colonists. Colonizationists used only feminine pronouns when describing the continent, depicting Africa's interior as not sterile but "rich and fertile," with rivers "deep enough and long enough to bear freights of empires on their bosom." Colonizationists also explicitly depicted Africa as the object of masculine sexual conquest. As colonizing was associated with masculine prowess, so the object of that desire became a sexualized woman. In Alexander McGill's words, a "curious and restless and excited gaze" had been fixed on Africa by those desiring to colonize "her," just as America had been the object of similar desires three centuries before. It was an inevitable feature of masculine conquest, McGill implied: "Shall the instincts of humanity be powerless, because it is an old world that is now thrown open to enlightened men? Shall the migratory impulse of manly souls be repressed, because a mother, instead of a daughter, pleads . . . for one race alone to return . . . ?" Other colonization sources referred repeatedly to the need for colonists "to penetrate into the interior" and spread the seed of civilization in West Africa. Yet Africa was also represented as the "poor mother of slaves" who was "panting for the return of her absent sons and daughters." These statements evoked the dual mythical imagery of African American women slaves that Deborah Gray White has exposed, as both Jezebel and Mammy—not surprising considering the persistent sexualization of African American women in white discussions of slavery.[30]

White colonizationists, then, exploited sexual imaginings of male power that have underpinned colonial enterprises in other places and times. For example, a similarly sexualized literature of colonialism developed by the late nineteenth century, particularly in the fantasy fiction of Rider Haggard. In these imperialist male adventure quests, where "British boys could become men," the "penetration of Africa" constituted one of the central images, and white women were generally absent from the plots. As one scholar has noted, "the categories of colonizer and colonized" have frequently been "secured through notions of racial difference constructed in gender terms," as notions of virility were expressed through images of both emasculation and hypersexuality.[31] But although white colonizationists foreshadowed later imperialist discourses, their statements also conformed to the many instances in which antebellum social and political conflict, particularly surrounding the realm of reformers, had become sexualized.[32]

Amalgamation and the Terror of Racial Violence

With sexual imagery so prevalent in the discourse surrounding colonization, it is not surprising that supporters of the movement often let slip their own fears of social and sexual contact between white and black Americans, which they merged under the label "amalgamation."[33] Although colonization publications did not abound with alarmist rhetoric about sex or marriage between black and white Americans, the amalgamation argument still underpinned nearly every pronouncement of the necessity of separating the two races. Colonization polemics fell back on some reference to amalgamation whenever their defenses reached an end. The specter of amalgamation served, in part, as a convenient strategy for raising alarm among racist whites about the consequences arising from abolitionist plans for immediate emancipation. Colonizationists were not averse to exploiting those fears, and their use of amalgamation arguments certainly escalated following the advent of the immediate abolition movement. After 1830, anti-abolitionist rhetoric became the defining feature of northern colonizationists. Perhaps the most inflammatory of these expressions appeared in the anonymously authored *Freemen Awake!*, which denounced abolitionists as "nigger hearted amalgamation traitors."[34]

Yet amalgamation functioned as more than just a convenient device for terror. Ultimately, amalgamation rhetoric represented an interrelated pattern of ideas about race and politics that exploited sex and gender in order to deny political equality and ensure racial dominance through violence. Black male activists in the North understood the colonization scheme as part of the same developments that denied them political freedom and suffrage. Since the rights of political participation and citizenship consistently marked manliness in the American republic, northern black men logically considered their political exclusion as an assault on their own manhood. The first black national convention in 1830 lodged an attack against colonization "as citizens and men," reminding their audience that "many of our fathers, and some of us, have fought and bled for the liberty, independence, and peace which you now enjoy."[35] When Pennsylvania's Constitution was revised in 1838 to disfranchise free black men in the name of expanding white manhood suffrage, young black male reformers leapt forward to challenge it. Petitions, public meetings, and conventions, however, failed to reverse the political exclusion of free African Americans. Black activists again invoked the language of manhood and citizenship in their protests and appeals. Black abolitionists helped publish and distribute Robert Purvis's *Appeal of Forty Thousand Citizens* (1838), challenging white voters to reconsider disfranchisement. The *Appeal* forcefully stated that when one class of citizens "are wholly, and for ever, disfranchised and excluded" because of their skin color, they "have lost their check upon oppression . . . [and] their panoply of manhood," having been "thrown upon the mercy of a despotic majority." John C. Bowers was one of many black activists who saw a familiar and sinister enemy behind disfranchisement, declaring, "If we look minutely, we shall discover the demon of Colonization busy at work." Nearly every protest against disfranchisement called for black men to exert a unified and "manly" resolve against both colonization and political exclusion as two sides of the same evil coin. Both threatened their identity as "citizens and men."[36]

Northern black men knew they had to fashion a competing vision of manhood to counter the vision of masculinity espoused by white colonizationists.

Black activists correctly perceived the conflation of sex, black manhood, and political rights that reared its head in racist anti-abolitionist publications like *Freemen Awake!*, whose author declared:

> And who are the instigators of this demand of 40,000 negroes? Are they not men, ay! the very men who would take from a poor white female and give to a big buck nigger, and who would not take up arms in defense of the country that feeds them?
>   And for the sake of the country and future posterity, COLONIZE the *niggers! colonize them!* Southern men! Look to your rights! and . . . discountenance these hot-brained, squash-headed, pumpkin-hearted male and female amalgamation fanatics.

This pamphlet constituted an extreme example of white colonization thought and hardly represented the public rhetoric adopted by most white colonizationists in the North. Still, amalgamation threats (subtle or blatant) represented a sexualization of politics designed to maintain political and social inequality.[37]

Despite the cacophony of white voices expressing multifarious motives for colonization (from missionary zeal to racist fears), most African Americans in the North heard only the same tune—separation, removal, and segregation from white American society. Colonization hardly seemed any more benevolent than the treatment blacks received in legislative assemblies or in the streets. In 1829, the Pennsylvania Legislature resolved that removing free blacks was in "the best interests of our country," and then proceeded to endorse the American Colonization Society. Following Nat Turner's uprising in 1831, the legislature restricted the entry of free blacks into the state and repealed fugitive slave laws from the 1820s that had protected blacks from being kidnapped and sold back into slavery in the South.[38] African Americans in the North knew firsthand that white fears of immediate abolition (and amalgamation) could easily erupt into violence. Northern cities like Philadelphia and New York witnessed recurring anti-abolitionist and race rioting during the 1830s and 1840s. For three consecutive nights in August 1834, antiblack rioters demolished a black neighborhood, destroying two churches and numerous private dwellings in Philadelphia's outlying district of Moyamensing. African Americans feared for their own lives and for the continued existence of the free black community.[39]

A symbiotic relationship existed between colonization reformers and antiblack and anti-abolitionist violence that took place in northern cities. Colonization reformers were not directly responsible for the riots, and no colonization activist was known to have engaged in rioting in Philadelphia. Colonizationists did, however, directly benefit from public perceptions of abolitionists as agitators, since they could then present themselves as the proponents of an alternative strategy of moderation while offering to remove the free black population. Moreover, colonization spokesmen encouraged a climate conducive to mobs. Virulent colonizationists such as the author of *Freemen Awake!*, as well as more moderate voices such as Calvin Colton and Frederick Freeman, played on white racial fears in their speeches and writings. They cleverly reminded their audiences of the supposed prevalence of vice and crime among blacks and accused abolitionists of promoting amalgamation. Unless slaves were removed from society after emancipation, they suggested, the only alternatives were race war or race mixing. In perhaps the greatest irony associated with the cause, colonizationists fanned the flames of white prejudices while at the same time throwing up their hands in frustration that this racism was unalterable.[40]

This climate of racial fear surfaced in the most famous anti-abolition riot in Philadelphia—the burning of Pennsylvania Hall in May 1838. Abolitionists had constructed Pennsylvania Hall to provide themselves with a meeting place and a headquarters in the city. The building opened during the usual evangelical anniversary-week meetings in May 1838, as national abolitionist leaders, including William Lloyd Garrison, Theodore Weld and Angelina Grimké Weld (who married on the day Pennsylvania Hall opened), Maria Weston Chapman, and Abby Kelley, arrived to participate in four days of antislavery meetings. The building was destroyed by a white mob before the week was over. On the third evening, May 16, as abolitionists—men and women, black and white—gathered to hear speeches by Angelina Grimké Weld and Abby Kelley, rioters disrupted the proceedings by hurling stones through the windows. The meeting was disbanded, and white abolitionist women were allegedly seen escorted from the hall on the arms of black abolitionist men. The next day a crowd surrounded the hall until as many as three thousand people had assembled outside. City authorities refused to restrain the rioters. "It is *public opinion makes mobs!*" Mayor John Swift stated, "and ninety-nine out of a hundred of those with whom I converse are against you." By morning all that remained were the charred walls and foundation of Pennsylvania Hall. The next evening rioters set fire to the Friends Home for Colored Orphans and stopped just short of completely destroying two black churches, while Garrison was secretly transported out of Philadelphia via the underground railroad.[41]

The riots were sparked by fears of amalgamation that colonizationists and proslavery advocates alike had fueled. There was plenty of talk on the streets that day about the abolitionists' bending of gender and racial mores. A. J. Pleasonton recorded in his diary that he expected "some terrible outbreak of popular indignation" to occur in response to "the disgusting habits of indiscriminate intercourse between whites and blacks so repugnant to all the prejudices of our education," which abolitionists "are in the habit of practising in this very Abolition Hall." White Philadelphians had tolerated racially mixed antislavery associations before; yet now white women were addressing "promiscuous audiences" and socializing with black men in public. Indeed, the official police report excused the violence because it had been provoked by agitators who advocated a mixing of the races. How else could Philadelphia residents respond, the report concluded, when confronted by practices "subversive of the established orders of society," such as "the unusual union of black and white walking arm in arm in social intercourse." The Grand Jury of Philadelphia exonerated the rioters of all misconduct, placing the blame on the abolitionists for the violence that had ensued. After all, the Grand Jury argued, abolitionists had brought individuals "into close and familiar intercourse," whom popular prejudices had long "kept asunder." The foreman of the Grand Jury was none other than the indefatigable colonizationist Elliott Cresson. Nearly a decade later, a derisive broadside entitled "Abolition Hall" (figure 9) echoed the same gender and racial ideology, especially fears of interracial sex, that inspired the rioters. The lithograph depicted Pennsylvania Hall with abolitionist women hanging out of the widows as if from a brothel, while black and white couples strolled around the building with their multicolored offspring.[42]

Such a shock was the riot to Philadelphia abolitionists that they never recovered the momentum they had gained throughout the 1830s. Two weeks after the burning of Pennsylvania Hall, the American Colonization Society held the largest colonization meeting ever reported in Philadelphia. Before the summer was over, Philadelphia's evangelical abolitionists had separated from the Garrisonians in the Philadelphia Anti-Slavery Society and formed another organization called the Church Union Anti-Slavery Society. Churches throughout the city refused access to their buildings for fear of conflagration, leaving abolitionists with no public space to organize their meetings.[43]

Gender and Black Emigrationist Plans

Race riots marked just the tip of an iceberg of racial violence and ubiquitous denials of social and political equality for free blacks in the North, forcing many African Americans with each passing decade to debate the possibilities and liabilities of creating their own homeland outside of the United States. The journeys of African Americans again reverberated throughout the black community. As expected, northern blacks did not speak with one voice on either colonization in Africa or emigration elsewhere in the Americas. Still, a gendered discourse governed the controversy surrounding these

FIGURE 9. A derisive portrayal of Pennsylvania Hall prior to its being burned by a mob in 1838, this lithograph cartoon depicts the alleged social and sexual familiarity between white and black abolitionists. [Zip Coon,] "Abolition Hall." Courtesy of the Library Company of Philadelphia.

plans. Competing languages of masculinity remained at the center of how northern black men interpreted colonization and emigration schemes. A nuanced history must, then, account for divergent convictions that allowed some free blacks to support white-sponsored colonization plans in Liberia, while others favored independent black-initiated proposals for emigration, and still others opposed any efforts to abandon their native home in the United States. Comparing these diverse responses exposes the complex intersection of race and gender among all northern antislavery voices (black and white) and demonstrates the ways in which free blacks were constrained by, and yet subverted, the gendered discourses surrounding colonization. Free African Americans were not simply responding to dominant white conceptions of gender and race; rather, they created their own creolized interpretation of the meanings of manhood and womanhood within strategies for black nationalism, citizenship rights, and communal and individual survival.

Many free blacks found their position on the question of emigration changing repeatedly as the conditions of their daily lives, and their hopes and fears about social and political equality, shifted in the winds of white racial policies. Many leading African Americans in northern cities, such as James Forten and Richard Allen in Philadelphia, initially supported voluntary emigration to Africa when black Quaker sea captain Paul Cuffe promoted the idea at the beginning of the nineteenth century. Forten and Allen, along with Russell Parrott, organized an African Institution in Philadelphia to assist Cuffe in his plans. Cuffe's unexpected death and the formation of the American Colonization Society, however, changed the public stance of these urban black elites. When Forten observed three thousand men gathering at Bethel Church in 1817, and not one soul "in favor of going to Africa," he and other leading black men acquiesced to the overwhelming opposition among the people in their community. But as Forten was quick to note, "my opinion is that they will never become a people until they come out from amongst the white people, but as the majority is decidedly against me, I am determined to remain silent, except as to my opinion which I freely give when asked." Very few folks must have solicited Forten's private opinion because when meetings were organized to protest against the colonization society in August 1817 and again in November 1819, Forten was chosen to serve as chairman in each case (and Russell Parrott was chosen as secretary). While Forten's daughter Sarah remarked in 1837 that she had "never yet met one man or woman of Color" who did not despise the colonization society, she was probably too young to recall a time when her father's position was more ambiguous or that one of the sailmakers who worked for James Forten, Francis Devany, was among the earliest emigrants to Liberia.[44]

Although an overwhelming majority of African Americans expressed nothing but disdain for the American Colonization Society, a handful did embrace the colonization plan and set off on voyages across the Atlantic to Africa. The voices of Philadelphia's earliest black colonists might easily be missed amid the loud cries of their opponents. Perhaps some of them shared the feelings of a colonist from Philadelphia who wrote to the American Colonization Society in 1847, "for my part I am ready to go this moment, for I am convinced of the place and of its value [to] the colored race, and by our industry it may be in time as richly covered with cities, farms, and commerce as the great United States of America, which 300 years ago was a wilderness." Sixty men, women, and children from Philadelphia emigrated to Liberia on the colonization society's first four voyages between 1820 and 1823, roughly one-third of the initial emigrants.[45] Francis Devany, along with his wife and two children, joined this group. Devany had been at one time the slave of Langdon Cheeves of South Carolina, but after purchasing his freedom, he migrated to Philadelphia and worked as a sailmaker. After his migration to Liberia in 1823, Devany accumulated a small sailing vessel and a net worth of at least $20,000, and served as High Sheriff for the colony.[46]

Black colonists to Liberia often voiced similar descriptions of manliness that had been so common in white colonizationist discourse. Augustus Washington, a daguerreotype artist from New England, not only boasted of Liberia as free blacks' ideal home "for the development of their manhood and intellect," but also spoke of the African continent "on whose bosom reposes in exuberance and wild extravagance all the fruits of . . . a tropical clime." He even harkened back to the history of Plymouth Rock and Jamestown to connect African colonizing with manly independence.[47] Black colonists almost universally conceded the idea that racial prejudice was so unalterable in America that Africa offered a place for true freedom and manhood. John Russwurm, co-editor of *Freedom's Journal*, the first black newspaper in the United States, stated prior to his emigration in 1829 that every man of color, "if he have the feelings of a man," ought to be aware "of the degraded station he holds in society, and from which it is impossible to rise." Baptist missionary Lott Cary, a former slave from Virginia and one of the earliest colonists in Liberia, reportedly stated, "I am an African, and in this country, however meritorious my conduct and respectable my character, I cannot receive the credit due to either. I wish to go to a country where I shall be estimated by my merits, not by my complexion." By the 1850s, these same sentiments led Martin Delany to long for a time when people of color in America would be "a migratory people," and the day when their children might "maintain that position and manly bearing" that stems from freedom and independence."[48]

The letters that black colonists wrote from Liberia provide a wealth of material on transnational African American journeys during the antebellum years, but they also present some intriguing problems for interpretation. It would be naïve to assume that black colonists in Liberia shared all the same assumptions and values as the white colonizationists who sent them, and unfair to write these emigrants off as veritable "Uncle Toms" who betrayed their families and millions of other slaves by emigrating and then writing something positive about Liberia. Colonists needed to act strategically when writing to former slave masters and colonization officials, especially when requesting their families' freedom and paid passage to join them overseas. Nestled within nearly every letter, even those most overtly enthusiastic about the prospects of Liberia and full of praise for the generosity of white colonizationists, can be discovered some glimpse of colonists' resistance and independence, some tone of criticism of their colonization patrons. For instance, letters frequently praised the colonization plan as "the cause of God," and yet in the next breath criticized colonization agents for their inability to understand the pain of families separated by the Atlantic Ocean.[49]

What support northern blacks showed for colonization in Liberia quickly waned. News of horrendous mortality rates awaiting Liberian colonists contributed mightily to this declining interest. Only twenty-one of those sixty Philadelphia colonists were still alive and residing in Liberia by 1831. Vast numbers died of malaria and other fevers soon after arriving, and high death rates continued for decades. Francis Devany lost his wife and both of his children within the first few months. Devany's ship marked the end of any significant emigration by northern blacks during the antebellum years. Only nine other emigrants from Pennsylvania sailed between 1830 and 1847 (when Liberia declared its independence), replaced instead by hundreds of slaves and former slaves from Virginia, North Carolina, and Maryland.[50] When "A Colored Philadelphian" wrote to the *Liberator* that the colonization society was busy trying to ship free people of color off to their almost certain deaths, there was more truth than exaggeration in his words. Although over 4,500 African Americans left for Liberia between 1820 and 1843, a colony census in 1843 revealed a population of just over 2,000.[51]

Joseph Blake's misfortune in Liberia, with which this chapter began, evokes even greater meaning in light of a white discourse that viewed colonizing as sexual conquest. His disillusionment festered from the failed promise of independent manhood via colonization. Blake encountered instead an eerily similar experience of sexual exploitation, economic dependence, and denial of justice and political power that slaves and free blacks in America knew all too well. Perhaps Blake would have come to embrace—along with the great majority of northern African Americans—the gendered language of the abolitionist song from the 1850s, "Old Liberia Is Not the Place for Me":

> You say "it is a goodly land,
> Where milk and honey flow;
> And every *Jack* will be a *man*
> Who there may choose to go."
> You say that "God appointed there
> The black man's destiny;"
> Yet old Liberia
> Is not the place for me.
>
> . . . .
> I deem this as my native land,
> And here I'm bound to stay.
> *I have a mind to be a man*
> *Among white men and free;*
> *and OLD LIBERIA!*
> *Is not the place for me!!*[52]

Still, the impulse to seek real freedom outside the United States was never far from the minds of some northern blacks. White schemes of removal always provoked widespread suspicion and contempt; but plans for emigration that originated from African Americans met with eager, if cautious, consideration. During the mid-1820s, when the white middle classes berated the urban poor and condemned poor-relief expenditures, a black-sponsored movement to emigrate to Haiti captured the attention of many African Americans in the North. Philadelphia's black community had maintained a special interest in that independent black nation ever since the arrival of refugees from St. Domingue in the 1790s. When Haitian President Jean Pierre Boyer promised in early 1824 that his government would transport African Americans willing to emigrate to Haiti and grant them lands for homesteads, the first Haytien Emigration Society was organized in New York City. Similar societies appeared in Baltimore and Philadelphia that summer, and by autumn as many as fifteen ships full of hopeful black emigrants had set sail from eastern seaports. Within only a few months, two thousand had departed from Philadelphia alone (out of a total of nearly eight thousand). Philadelphia's anticolonization black leaders assumed a prominent role in the Haitian emigration; Richard Allen was chosen president of Philadelphia's society, and his son secretary, while James Forten, Quomony Clarkson, and other leading colonization foes served on the board of managers. But enthusiasm for Haitian emigration subsided nearly as quickly as it had flourished. Urban free blacks found neither the language and religious differences nor the farm work and the contempt of native citizens to their liking. By spring 1825, emigrants had returned by the thousands. After that, emigration plans would not again attract widespread interest among northern blacks until after the passage of the Fugitive Slave Act in 1850; and even then, emigration became more popular in the West than in northeastern ports such as Philadelphia.[53]

The great mass of African Americans in the North chose to build homes and institutions of their own in the United States: "This is our home and this is our country." "Here we were born, and here we will die." These became the most common refrains in black opposition to colonization. Many free blacks agreed with David Walker's assertion that "America is more our country than it is the whites'—we have enriched it with our blood and tears."[54] They defiantly resolved that their journeys had ended, and they would look nowhere else for a homeland. Black antipathy toward white colonization schemes grew so strong that African Americans began distancing themselves from any association with Africa, while insisting upon their American nationality and citizenship. Since the late eighteenth century, northern free blacks had attached the name "African" to nearly all of their self-determined institutions, willingly proclaiming their connection to that continent. By the 1830s, however, northern blacks abandoned the name "African" for their numerous churches, mutual aid societies, and schools, choosing instead to embrace the designation "colored" (or "people of color") and naming their societies in tribute to African American leaders or prominent abolitionists. The United Daughters of Wilberforce, Female Clarkson Society, United Daughters of Allen, and Citizen Daughters of Philadelphia soon joined the roster of black benevolent societies that had previously included the Daughters of Africa, the African Female Benevolent Society, and the Daughters of Zion Angolan Ethiopian Society. By 1838, New York's black public-school teachers had convinced the school board to change the name of their schools from "African" to "Colored." Some African Americans even professed that they were mystified at the notion of their connection to Africa. "What do I know of Africa?" asked one black abolitionist in 1852, explaining, "I am part Indian and part German." Likewise, a group of New York blacks affirmed that they could not trace their ancestry exclusively to Africa: "We trace it to Englishmen, Irishmen, Scotchmen; to the German; to the Asiatic, as well as to Africa. The best blood of Virginia courses through our veins." In this manner, some black activists turned the amalgamation argument on its head. Along with their birth on American soil, generations of coerced interracial intercourse did not make free blacks a foreign people. It made their ancestry definitively American.[55]

With this conviction that they were native-born Americans and entitled to the same citizenship rights as other free persons, northern blacks experienced a devastating blow with the passage of the Fugitive Slave Act in 1850. It was like a knife in the heart to African Americans who still held hopes that the republic's noble ideals might apply to all its inhabitants. The sense of betrayal and fear that struck black Americans cannot be overstated. The Fugitive Slave Act flagrantly denied northern blacks due process of law, giving them no legal means for defending themselves, and making every black man and woman a target for slavery's bounty hunters. Martin Delany called it "the crowning act of infamy" toward the black community, and Harriet Jacobs described it as "the beginning of a reign of terror to the colored population." Black churches and community institutions watched their membership shrink overnight as thousands of terrorized former slaves sought protection across the border in Canada.[56] More than any other event, the Fugitive Slave Law produced deep ideological divisions among black reformers. Many African Americans began to see emigration as their only hope for a secure and self-governing community, while the majority continued to stand firm in their determination never to be driven from their native land.

In the wake of the Fugitive Slave Act, Martin Delany and Frederick Douglass personified these opposing viewpoints on black emigration. Although it has become commonplace for historians to identify Delany with the beginning of black nationalism and to associate Douglass with integrationist principles, these two leading black activists shared many beliefs. Both held a deep hatred for the American Colonization Society, a passion for the elevation of black Americans, and a conviction that racial uplift must be the "work of our own hands." The two men had worked together during the 1840s as co-editors of Douglass's newspaper, the *North Star*, and until 1850 they seemed to complement one another quite effectively.[57] But events in 1850 led Delany to become embittered about the fate of black Americans. The same year as the Fugitive Slave Act, Delany was forced to withdraw from Harvard Medical School when white students objected to the presence of black students. He then proceeded to publish *The Condition, Elevation, Emigration, and Destiny of the Colored People of the United States* (1852), declaring that free blacks were no better off than slaves and that they must immediately begin to emigrate to Central and South America and to the Caribbean. Although Douglass expressed outrage at the Fugitive Slave Act, he refused to waver from the defiant stance he had outlined a year before: "Our minds are made up to live here if we can, or die here if we must," Douglass declared. "While our brethren are in bondage on these shores; it is idle to think of inducing any considerable number of the free colored people to quit this for a foreign land." So Douglass planned a national black convention in Rochester in 1853, where black reformers, including Philadelphians Robert Purvis and James J. G. Bias, joined him in condemning colonization and the Fugitive Slave Law and calling for immediate abolition and citizenship rights for black men "as Americans." Delany, however, organized a National Emigration Convention the following year in Cleveland for those who shared his opinion that "our case is a hopeless one" and that the only remedy for the disease of white racism was emigration elsewhere in the Americas.[58]

Gendered language permeated the disagreements between Delany and Douglass, and between emigrationists and nonemigrationists. Delany repeatedly referred to emigration as "a bold and manly course of independent action" and "adventurous deeds of manly daring." Douglass, however, contrasted the "cowardly" actions of the National Emigration Convention with the "manly position" assumed by the Rochester convention. In his mind, staying in the United States and fighting for the freedom of slaves and freemen alike was the "manly" course of action. In part, these examples of masculine bravado were indicative of the male-dominated language of political conflict in the antebellum era; Delany and Douglass, in other words were not so far removed from the rhetoric of Lincoln and Douglas.[59] For Delany, however, notions of manliness represented the essence of the colonizing and emigrating enterprise, and yet he distanced himself in subtle ways from the language of white colonizationists. Delany unmistakably characterized emigration with a masculine vocabulary of adventure and independence, but he also subverted the prevailing expansionist notions of white Americans. Delany insisted on referring to Africa as the "fatherland," perhaps consciously rejecting white colonizationist imagery of Africa as a woman. He also developed an argument for black emigration that inverted the "manifest destiny" rhetoric that dominated white expansionism. Delany maintained that he could "see the 'finger of God'" in the historical developments that produced majority populations of people of color in the nations south of the United States. It was therefore God's destiny for black Americans to be united with these people, and one day to "form a glorious union of South American States." God, he wrote, "as certain as he has ever designed any thing, has designed this great portion of the New World, for us, the colored races." Like imperialist writers, Delany proceeded to associate this expanding new empire with the elevation of motherhood in the black nation. "Our females must be qualified, because they are to be the mothers of our children," he wrote; and "no people are ever elevated above the condition of their *females*; hence, the condition of the *mother* determines the condition of the child."[60]

To maintain their consistency, black emigrationists had to walk a fine line between unflinching hostility toward white colonization societies and an openness toward proposals for black independence and national autonomy. Thus emigrationists exploited both the discourse that associated colonizing with masculine adventure and enterprise and the rhetoric that represented opposition to white prejudice as a manly action. Both of these threads are certainly evident in the rhetorical twists and turns that Delany took in his emigration philosophy. H. Ford Douglass of Illinois also evinced how black emigrationists exploited both forms of masculine rhetoric for their own purposes. In a speech before the National Emigration Convention in 1854, Douglass proclaimed, "I can hate this government without being disloyal, because it has stricken down my manhood, and treated me as a saleable commodity." But he continued, "Is not the history of the world, the history of emigration? . . . Let us then be up and doing. To stand still is to stagnate and die."[61]

Finally, in contrast to the limited role of white women in colonization reform, African American women played a more active part in emigration plans. Black men's efforts to frame their opposition to colonization within a set of ideas about manhood, citizenship, and political participation tended to marginalize black women, who were already made invisible in white colonization discourses. But a few northern black women found emigration plans more liberating than anticolonization protests. Over 30 percent of the delegates to the National Emigration Convention in 1854 were African American women. Four women were elected to serve on the finance committee, one was chosen as a vice president, and women played an active role in crafting the resolutions drafted by the convention.[62]

African American women emigrationists have been overshadowed by their prominent male counterparts, especially Delany, Henry Highland Garnet, and Henry Bibb. Mary Ann Shadd is an exception. Shadd received her antislavery training in the house of her abolitionist father, Abraham Shadd, who forcefully resisted both colonization and disfranchisement as a leader in the black convention movement during the 1830s, and whose family secretly assisted fugitive slaves in their escapes to freedom along the underground railroad. Shadd received her education in schools outside Philadelphia before teaching in Norristown, Pennsylvania, and New York City. She began to be noticed by African Americans in Philadelphia when she started writing letters to Frederick Douglass's *North Star* and published a pamphlet, "Hints to the Colored People of the North," in 1849. After the passage of the Fugitive Slave Act the next year, Shadd emigrated north of the border and quickly gained prominence as a schoolteacher and then newspaper editor among emigrationists in Canada.[63]

Mary Ann Shadd's position as editor of the *Provincial Freeman* was unmatched by any other black women activist in the United States. She steadfastly defended her views that Canada (not Africa or Central America) was the best location for black emigration and remained adamant that free blacks should try to integrate into white Canadian society rather than establishing separate communities and institutions. Those political views, along with her outspoken criticism of black clergymen, placed her in immediate conflict with other Canadian emigrants, especially Henry and Mary Bibb, who ran a school and newspaper in a nearby town. In the heated discussions among northern blacks over emigration, Shadd frequently resorted to the masculinist rhetoric that framed emigrationist discussions. Like Maria Stewart two decades earlier, Shadd commonly invoked representations of black masculinity to challenge African Americans to defend their liberties and sustain their autonomy and independence. The motto of her newspaper—"Self-Reliance Is the Fine Road to Independence"—highlighted the way Shadd subverted gendered (masculine) conceptions of "independence" that reigned in antebellum America by asserting her own independence in her political convictions and her livelihood. As she stated in the *Provincial Freeman,* "woman's work was anything she put her mind or hand to do." Shadd's career and autonomous political convictions as North America's first black woman newspaper editor subverted prevailing gender conventions in a manner as radical as any white woman abolitionist. By exploiting the boundaries of this gendered discourse, black emigrationists cleared a path for wider participation by black women activists.[64]

But neither Shadd nor Delany were successful in convincing the majority of African Americans in northern cities to emigrate. Shadd delivered numerous lectures in Philadelphia between 1852 and 1855 on behalf of emigrationist plans; garnered the loyal services of William Still, the underground railroad activist; and was even the beneficiary of a fund-raising concert by the black singing star, Elizabeth Taylor Greenfield (the "Black

Swan"). Still, Philadelphia's black community agreed with anti-emigra-
tionists such as Frederick Douglass and Robert Purvis that "neither Colonization nor Emigration, is a remedy for the ills of the Colored American. He
cannot emigrate from himself. He cannot destroy his own identity." They
chose, instead, to remain and continue the struggle for emancipation and
the full privileges of citizenship, at least for black men.[65]

"We Are Thy Sisters"—"They Are Our Sisters"

Recognizing that white colonizationist men fashioned a reform movement
where public politics would supersede moral suasion, and enveloped it in a
discourse that inscribed racial difference in explicitly sexualized and gendered ways, helps to unravel the puzzle of why white women's activism was so
remarkably limited in the northern colonization movement. Certainly, the
conservatism of the men and women who gravitated toward colonization societies (many of them from Calvinist and evangelical backgrounds) contributed to their timidity in challenging gender conventions, especially compared with other reformers.[66] Fears of race mixing and supposedly improper
social intercourse also might explain why white women were reluctant to join
a reform movement whose implicit goal was to bolster the true manliness of
black men.

Those white women who did become actively involved in colonization restricted their reforming efforts to establishing schools for children in the
African colonies. In 1832, Philadelphia women established the Ladies
Liberia School Association to support several schools established by white
emissaries but taught by African American colonists in Liberia. The managers of the Ladies Liberia Association included a smattering of Presbyterian, Quaker, Methodist, and Episcopal women, several of whom were the
wives and daughters of leading male colonizationists in Philadelphia. At least
one-quarter of them worked in at least one other religious benevolent society, including the association's treasurer, Anna R. (Grimké) Frost, the sister
of abolitionists Angelina and Sarah Grimké. Women colonizationists were
given little freedom or autonomy to push beyond this restrictive definition of
benevolent activism. The women in the Ladies Liberia School Association
did not even run their own meetings. When they met for an annual gathering, ministers and male colonizationist activists called the meeting to order,
read the women's annual report, and gave the speeches and sermons to the
audience.[67] By contrast, other reforming women in northern cities had been
running their own meetings, writing their own reports, and shaping their
policies since the earliest women's benevolent societies were founded in the
1790s.[68]

Eventually, many northern women's colonization efforts during the 1830s and 1840s looked to the Ladies Liberia Association for their model. Catharine Beecher endorsed the Philadelphia Ladies Association in her assault on the indecorous activism of women abolitionists in general and the Grimké sisters in particular. Beecher organized a women's colonization society in Cincinnati to parallel and assist the Philadelphia association's efforts "to promote education and religion in Africa." This type of women's activism—its child-centered focus, emphasizing the "benign influence" of womanly benevolence in contrast to the political power that allegedly "unsexed" abolitionist women—placed white women's colonization activism within the conservative framework of the gendered understanding of women and benevolence that had emerged since the 1820s. The language of female influence offered a more passive, domestic, and less overtly politicized notion of women's activism, and colonization women seemed eager to embrace this definition. For Beecher, women's colonization actions marked "the just bounds of female influence" and signaled the differences between true womanliness on the one hand and the gender transgressions of abolitionist women on the other. As Beecher argued in her *Essay on Slavery and Abolitionism* (1837), women should restrict their activism to those "peaceful and benevolent principles" found only in "the domestic and social circle." Once a woman "begins to feel the promptings of ambition, or the thirst for power," Beecher insisted, abolitionism leads her "into the arena of political collision," assuming the "attitude of a combatant," and "throws her out of her appropriate sphere." Beecher repeatedly invoked this pugilistic metaphor ("combatants"), which easily could have connoted the antebellum "manly arts" of boxing and politics, both of which constituted male-exclusive arenas of public life.[69]

The choice by women's colonization societies to concentrate their efforts on children and schooling, rather than on adult black men, illustrates the gender conventions that shaped the various responses to slavery among northern reformers and highlights the divergence between colonizationist and abolitionist women. Because colonization was represented as a process by which white men benevolently helped to create a new masculine identity for African American men, many white women found it hard to sympathize or identify with men's colonizing adventures. In many ways, the outlook of women colonizationists reflects the inverse of the identification that abolitionist women claimed with slaves, and especially with slave women. White women could not identify their own experiences with colonizers and emigrants in the same way that white abolitionist women, as we will see, insisted that their own experiences as women mirrored the enslavement of African Americans.

Beginning in the 1830s, the immediate abolitionist movement challenged the benevolent assumptions of white colonizationists and eventually led some northern reforming women toward a sustained radical critique of their own subordination. But when sixty-two abolitionists assembled in Philadelphia in December 1833 to create the American Anti-Slavery Society, their convention reinforced the existing strata of invisibility in antebellum public culture. Only three black men were among the society's founding members, despite the fact that free blacks, even with their more limited resources, had kept the nascent abolitionist movement afloat by their generous support of Garrison's *Liberator*. And although a small group of white women were permitted to attend and contribute to the discussions over the wording of the society's Declaration of Sentiments, none of the male abolitionists considered inviting those women to join the society. Black women, the most invisible group in public, were entirely absent from the proceedings. Clearly, these abolitionists began their campaign with no intention of radically disrupting the gender and racial hierarchies of American life. It would not be long, however, before white and black abolitionists alike developed critiques of gender and racial inequalities that exposed both the promises and the shortcomings of the abolitionist movement. Decades later some of the more radical abolitionists would look back with regret at their failure to open a door to diversity at the origins of their movement. As Samuel J. May recalled, "we *men* were then so blind, so obtuse, that we did not recognize those women as members of our Convention, and insist upon their subscribing their names to our 'Declaration of Sentiments and Purposes.'"[70]

Women abolitionists contested the assumptions about public activism, gender, and slavery that colonizationist and proslavery men and women advanced during the antebellum years. By challenging the ideas that confined white women colonizationists to a limited domain of reform, abolitionist women redefined the rights and province of reforming women's actions and thus developed one of the earliest feminist perspectives in American culture. Yet while they expounded the most radical pronouncements on behalf of the equality of African Americans and women since the founding of the republic, they also fell far short of realizing those powerful ideals. Thus, the story of Philadelphia's female antislavery activists reveals two neglected themes: first, that African American women were critically important to the powerful set of criticisms embedded in the gendered philosophy of women abolitionists; and second, that a critical stance toward churches and clergymen (anticlericalism) provided the foundation for a budding feminist consciousness among these antislavery women, both black and white.

White and black women did not wait long before declaring their own place in the movement. Three days after the national antislavery society was organized, Philadelphia's women abolitionists created the Philadelphia Female Anti-Slavery Society. Black women accounted for nearly one-third of

the thirty-three founding members who attached their signatures to the society's new constitution, making it the first integrated antislavery society in
Pennsylvania. Male abolitionists in the city followed the women's lead and
created a Philadelphia Anti-Slavery Society four months later, a Young Men's
Anti-Slavery Society in 1835, and then a state antislavery society in 1837, all
of which were racially integrated. Declaring that "slavery, and the prejudice
against colour, are contrary to the laws of God" and to the principles of the
Declaration of Independence, the women of the female antislavery society
proclaimed it their duty "as professing Christians" to assail "the flagrant injustice and deep sin of slavery" and to advocate for "the right of the slave to
immediate emancipation." This language, from the preamble of the society's
constitution, illustrates three fundamental premises that all immediate abolitionists shared: that slavery was a personal sin rather than an unavoidable
evil, that slavery was antirepublican and inconsistent with the basic principles
outlined in the Declaration of Independence, and that Northerners were
complicit in the wrongs of slavery, or engaged in a "co-partnership of iniquity" with the slave states. From the movement's beginning, then, abolitionist women and men maintained that slavery was a moral issue, a political
issue, and a northern issue.[71]

For white abolitionists, the publication of Garrison's *Liberator* and the subsequent formation of antislavery societies throughout the North after 1831
marked a new departure for the cause of antislavery, the genesis of a new
abolitionist movement with its rallying cry of an "immediate abolition" of
slavery. But for African Americans in the North, these events embodied no
new revolution in perspective nor an apotheosis in reform activism. Rather,
it appeared to African Americans that white reformers had finally come
around to the convictions they themselves had long held regarding immediate emancipation. Indeed, in many ways, northern blacks were the tutors and
new white abolitionists the pupils in the ideas and strategies associated with
the causes of antislavery and race reform. Fugitive slaves and free African
Americans understood this at the time, as did many white abolitionists such
as Garrison, Weld, and the Grimkés; indeed, it has been historians who have
obscured that relationship.[72] Throughout the years before emancipation,
black men and women schooled white reformers in the various meanings of
abolitionism, and black women, in particular, guided Philadelphia's radical
abolitionist women in the earliest formulations of a race and feminist consciousness. At the forefront of Philadelphia's new abolitionist crusade in the
1830s, then, stood a cadre of dedicated African American women and men,
and white women, who refused to accept the basic premises of racial slavery
that undergirded the republic.

Two different groups of abolitionist women emerged in the antebellum
North, and Philadelphia's activists stood clearly on one side. Both groups

shared the defining abolitionist assumptions that slavery was a sin and that
northern society, including its churches, was complicit in that sin; their differences were rooted in their attitudes about the scope of a woman's appropriate activity and the relationship of churches to slavery. In one camp stood
those antislavery women closely associated with evangelical benevolence,
who resisted every call for expanding women's role as public speakers or
leaders in the national antislavery movement, and who excluded black
women from membership in their societies. Conservative white women activists in New York City became the principal voices for this group. In the
other camp stood the leaders of Boston's and Philadelphia's female antislavery societies, whose connection to liberal Protestant groups, such as Unitari-
ans or Hicksite Quakers, led them to a very different set of ideas about
churches and slavery. Boston's and Philadelphia's white abolitionist women
challenged the restrictions on female activism, supported women as public
lecturers, denounced race prejudice, and proclaimed northern black
women to be their equals and co-partners in the antislavery cause. These radical abolitionist women more readily embraced a "come-outer" spirit—a belief that abolitionists must withdraw ("come out") from corrupt and unright-
eous churches and fellowship only with people who condemned slavery and
slaveholders—and they more freely assailed clerical hierarchies as the source
of women's subjugation.[73]

Unlike white colonizationist women, Philadelphia's female abolitionists
launched themselves immediately into openly public and political activities.
They petitioned legislative bodies and spoke out in public forums on behalf
of the antislavery cause. Because colonizationist and proslavery men had already framed the slavery problem as a public (not domestic) and masculine
issue, women's entry onto these stages made their activism by definition a direct challenge to male authority and privilege. In their pursuit of these public actions, these women abolitionists possessed a political sophistication far
beyond that usually attributed to them by historians. They were aware that in
a political system that denied them any genuine power, they needed to
achieve some of their victories through the symbolic messages they publicized. Abolitionist women soon realized that this type of politics was not exclusively the domain of women, but proved true for many minority perspectives, including all abolitionists and African Americans. Indeed, the first
action of Philadelphia's abolitionist women carried this kind of symbolic political message. When they assembled to organize their society in December
1833, they turned to an African American man, James McCrummell, to preside over the meeting. Historians have often interpreted this as evidence that
these women were inexperienced in the operation of public organizations or
initially reticent about challenging gender conventions. Lucretia Mott remarked that she and other abolitionist women "had no idea of the meaning

of preambles and resolutions and votings" because a majority of them were Quakers who were more accustomed to gathering the "sense of the meeting" than tallying votes. Yet too often accounts of this event have focused only on this first part of Mott's explanation, which by itself hardly seems sufficient to explain their decision. After all, women had been laboring in voluntary associations and chairing their own meetings for nearly forty years, and it is hard to imagine that these abolitionists had been untouched by the female culture of benevolent activism prevalent in northern cities.[74] In fact, in the second part of her explanation, Mott suggested that there was more to this incident than merely female propriety or inexperience. These abolitionist women intended to express a subtle, but unmistakable, political statement when they chose McCrummell, a black antislavery activist and founding member of the American Anti-Slavery Society. "You know that at that time," Mott explained, "negroes, idiots and women were in legal documents classed together." Thus, she concluded, "we were very glad to get one of our own class . . . to come and aid us in forming that Society." The choice of McCrummell, then, represented a bold maneuver to emphasize the independence of groups forced into oppressive dependency and to attest to the political intellect of black Americans. And in contrast to their colonization counterparts in the Ladies Liberia Association, the Female Antislavery Society never again relied on a man to preside over their meetings.[75]

Northern abolitionist women manifested their earliest and most visible public actions in the petitions they sent to Congress and state legislatures. As early as 1831, Lucretia Mott and five others submitted a petition to Congress with the signatures of more than 2,300 Philadelphia women. By 1835, the American Antislavery Society had begun actively encouraging petition campaigns throughout the North. Women activists took up this enterprise as their own special mission, developing local, state, and sectional networks to coordinate and distribute petitions in every possible locality. Philadelphia's Female Anti-Slavery Society proved untiring in its petitioning labors. In 1836 the members published an address to Pennsylvania women urging their support, and together black and white women collected 3,300 signatures in Philadelphia County; the next year they collected an additional 5,000 signatures. Between 1835 and the mid-1840s, antislavery societies flooded Congress with petitions, directing them either to abolish slavery in the District of Columbia, deny the annexation of Texas, or end the interstate slave trade. Two out of every three signatures on those petitions were from women. Women abolitionists were convinced that "when all the maids and matrons of the land knock at the door of Congress, our Statesmen must legislate." When the House of Representatives responded with a gag rule that effectively tabled any antislavery petition without its being heard, the abolitionist cause suddenly gained even more sympathizers as it became identified with the right of free speech, and Congress found itself drowning in antislavery petitions. (It was estimated that all the petitions for 1837 could have filled a room twenty by thirty by fourteen feet, packed to the ceiling.) As one Mississippi senator declared in exasperation, there would be only a few abolition petitions "if the ladies and Sunday school children would let us alone."[76]

Petition canvassing hardly constituted the glamour work of antislavery reform; pounding the pavement with door-to-door requests for signatures was an arduous task for women abolitionists. Philadelphia's Female Anti-Slavery Society assigned members (both white and black women) to collect signatures in each of the wards of the city and outlying districts. They covered effectively the center-city neighborhoods in which they lived, but admittedly struggled to gather signatures in the less familiar working-class suburbs. Northern abolitionist women confessed that petition campaigns involved exhausting work that they sometimes dreaded. One activist estimated that she had walked twenty-one miles during one week of canvassing. "I never undertook anything that was so entirely distasteful to me," remarked Sarah Pugh. More often than not, these women faced unsympathetic or hostile faces on the other side of the doors they approached. "We go from house to house, sad, and sick at heart with the selfishness, and ignorance, and pride with which we are repulsed," remarked Philadelphia's female abolitionists. Yet the difficulties and rejections these women faced only encouraged them to persevere: congressional gag rules spurred them to send more petitions with more creatively worded requests. It also became readily apparent that women were more successful in gathering petition signatures than men, as male antislavery societies resorted to paid solicitors to complete their petition work rather than walk the streets of the city themselves. The men of the Philadelphia Anti-Slavery Society even requested that their female counterparts solicit contributions while they were out canvassing for petitions, attesting to the superiority of women activists in both tasks—fund-raising and petition gathering.[77]

Women's petitioning immediately raised an alarm from critics who maintained that slavery and abolition were political subjects and hence outside the province of women. Those female abolitionists who assembled each year between 1837 and 1839 in Antislavery Conventions of American Women thus had the task not only of publicizing and expanding women's canvassing efforts, but also of justifying their behavior in the face of prevailing gender conventions. In response, they formulated a spirited defense of women's petitioning, although not without a measure of conflict among themselves or contradictions between their new aspirations and the accepted ideology of benevolent womanhood. Women abolitionists responded to their critics' gender arguments by insisting at first that women had a "natural and inalienable" right to pursue such political actions as citizens. "Are we aliens because we are women?" asked Angelina Grimké in her *Appeal to the Women of the Nominally Free States*. "Are we bereft of citizenship because we are the *mothers, wives*, and *daughters* of a mighty people? Have *women* no country—no interest staked in public weal—no liabilities in common peril—no partnership in a nation's guilt and shame?" Abolitionist women maintained instead that this was "our only means of direct political action." They could not participate in enacting or enforcing legislation, nor elect those who did. Petitions thus offered the only method at women's disposal to effect legislative change. Angelina Grimké eventually arrived at the radical position that "it is woman's right to have a voice in all the laws and regulations by which she is to be *governed*, whether in Church or State." She concluded, "whatever it is *morally* right for a man to do, it is *morally* right for a woman to do."[78]

Not all female abolitionists were willing to go that far in asserting women's political rights. While abolitionist women asserted their right to a voice in political affairs, they also insisted that slavery and abolition were not political issues after all and that their sex gave them a special interest in the subject that legitimized their activism. These women ruptured the framework of slavery and politics that male colonizationists had established. Rather than advancing only the radical notion that women possessed the same citizenship rights as men, they also resorted to essentialist ideas about womanhood derived from the discourse on female influence. As Sarah T. Smith stated before the second women's convention in Philadelphia in 1838: "It is not true that it is merely a political question; it is likewise a question of justice, of humanity, of morality, of religion; a question which . . . enters deeply into the home." In short, slavery was a problem that affected the domestic realm that women could claim as their own, thus making antislavery activism an expression of a woman's familial concerns and influence. Both groups of abolitionist women (conservative and radical), as well as both white and black abolitionists, invoked this language of female influence. It expressed at once the safe contention that a woman's activism was merely an extension of her circumscribed domestic identity and the radical implication that there were no bounds to her reform actions. Perhaps this also represented an effort to maintain a united and strong antislavery sisterhood despite their divisions. The ideology of female influence also pervaded black and white abolitionist men's prescriptions for African American women's activism. Black newspapers were filled with paeans to women's influence for the elevation of the race; and Garrison voiced the same notions to Sarah Douglass, one of the leading black women in the Philadelphia Female Anti-Slavery Society.[79]

This belief that slavery was neither a political nor an exclusively masculine subject led female abolitionists to conclude that women possessed a special interest in abolitionism because of their sex. From their perspective, if southern women were slaveholders, if women in great numbers were the victims of that evil system, and if northern women of color were still oppressed by the racism that sustained slavery, then northern women, "as women," had a duty to labor for the abolition of slavery. *"They are our sisters,"* declared the Anti-Slavery Convention of American Women about women slaves, echoing the language of Sarah Forten's poem as the voice of black women in the North: "We are thy sisters. . . . Our skins may differ, but from thee we claim/ A sister's privilege and a sister's name." Abolitionist women, such as "A Colored Woman" from Hartford, Connecticut, turned petitioning into opportunities to encourage black and white women to reflect on the condition of slaves, particularly women slaves, and to act because these thoughts provoked a woman's sympathy.[80]

For Philadelphia's women abolitionists, petitioning and the affirmation of women's political rights as citizens became more complicated as the abolitionist crusade unfolded between the 1830s and 1850s. At first, they simply sidestepped the apparent discrepancy between petition drives and their simultaneous declarations that antislavery must be accomplished through moral suasion. A form of symbolic politics for these women seemed to be indistinguishable from other strategies of moral suasion. Yet by 1840, the American Anti-Slavery Society had divided over both women's leadership and an abolitionist political party. At that point, Garrisonian abolitionists, including Philadelphia's abolitionist women, gravitated toward a stance (called "non-resistance") that rejected all human governments because they were based on force and renounced voting and political campaigning as part of a Constitution corrupted by its covenant with slaveholders. Despite this, Philadelphia's female abolitionists continued to petition Congress for legislative solutions to slavery until the society disbanded after emancipation, although door-to-door canvassing for signatures began to die out in the early 1840s.[81]

The abolitionist controversy over public women intensified as some women reformers took to the rostrum and pulpit and became public speakers for the cause. These were certainly not the first women to speak to mixed-sex audiences in America—Quaker women, visionary women, and African American women preachers had been doing so since the seventeenth century. And the radical Englishwoman Frances Wright preceded abolitionist women orators as the most recent woman to be excoriated for daring to lift her voice in a public forum. But with the rise of the abolitionist movement, zealous female activists began to demand their right to speak in churches, legislative halls, and civic spaces. Two sisters transplanted from South Carolina emerged as the central figures in a maelstrom of controversy surrounding a new assertive public woman.

Sarah and Angelina Grimké were born into a prosperous South Carolina slaveholding family, but moved during the 1820s to Philadelphia, where they joined a meeting of Orthodox Quakers. In the early 1830s, Angelina briefly attended Catharine Beecher's female academy in Hartford, Connecticut. Both sisters possessed keen intellects and deeply felt ambitions, yet found few outlets for their gifts among Orthodox Friends, among whom they heard little discussion about the new antislavery movement. Angelina eventually joined the female antislavery society two years after it was organized. The close friendships she developed with black women reformers, along with the horrific race riots she witnessed in 1834, solidified her impassioned identification with the plight of slaves. When a personal letter she wrote to Garrison, describing immediate emancipation as a cause "worth dying for," was published in the *Liberator*, Angelina instantly gained national prominence among abolitionists. By summer 1836, she had published her *Appeal to the Christian Women of the South*, affirming the fundamental human rights of slaves and women's special duty to work for abolition. A few months later, both sisters had been appointed as agents of the American Antislavery Society and began lecturing before antislavery women in New York City. By 1837, the sisters had been invited to commence a lecture tour throughout New England.[82]

Imagine the powerful impression that these two women must have made on their audiences. Dressed primly in the plain clothes and bonnet of the Quaker style, diminutive in size and stature, Sarah and Angelina Grimké evoked an image of dour, restrained, delicate Victorian womanhood. Until, that is, they opened their mouths. Suddenly, with a fire and intensity rivaling any male orator, they began to recount the horrible cruelties and physical abuse they had seen inflicted on slaves during their youth in Charleston. What had been thought to be cruelties too unspeakable to be voiced in mixed company now escaped the eloquent lips of these two Southern "ladies." The Grimké sisters became something of a curiosity as they traveled the New England countryside. They spoke to packed houses in every community they entered. The expectation that their audiences might be restricted to "females only" quickly proved futile. Before long the sisters found themselves speaking to large mixed-sex (what contemporaries called "promiscuous") audiences. Angelina was clearly the more gifted orator; Samuel J. May recalled how he once witnessed her hold "six hundred hearers in fixed attention for two hours." And when an angry mob threatened to destroy Pennsylvania Hall, Angelina held her audience spellbound in their seats for nearly an hour, while bricks and stones rained in continuously through the windows. Garrison recalled that "her eloquence kindled, her eye flashed, and her cheeks glowed" that evening.[83]

As soon as the Grimké sisters began speaking before mixed-sex audiences, they encountered vociferous opposition from Congregational ministers in New England. In July 1837, the General Association of Congregational

Churches of Massachusetts issued a "Pastoral Letter" chastising Garrison and all abolitionists, and the Grimké sisters in particular. Couched in the gendered language reminiscent of Bishop Doane's distinction between feminine influence and masculine power, the Pastoral Letter admonished women abolitionists to adhere to their "appropriate duties and influence" and to refrain from dangerous activities that "threaten the female character with wide-spread and permanent injury." "The power of woman," the letter claimed, "is her dependence and weakness." These clergymen were comfortable with modest forms of a woman's benevolence, such as Sunday schools or prayer meetings. "But when she assumes the place and tone of man as a public reformer," they declared, "our care and protection of her seem unnecessary; we put ourselves in self-defence against her . . . and her character becomes unnatural." This statement apparently had no effect on the crowds who continued to attend the sisters' lectures. Just days after it was published, fifteen hundred people packed Lowell's town hall to hear Angelina and Sarah Grimké lecture, and hundreds more were turned away.[84]

Angelina Grimké's response to the Pastoral Letter, and to white abolitionist men's objections to the sisters' emphasis on women's rights, was a tour de force, illustrating the inseparable connection these women abolitionists made between the rights of slaves and the rights of women. The antislavery cause, she insisted, was imperiled by those clergy who opposed the agency of women: "We are gravely told that we are out of our sphere even when we circulate petitions; out of our 'appropriate sphere' when we speak to women only." "They utterly deny *our right* to interfere" with any moral reform, she continued, and "if we dare to stand upright and do our duty according to the dictates of *our own* consciences, why then we are compared to Fanny Wright and so on." She refused to back away from a confrontation, declaring that "*the time* to assert a right is *the* time when *that* right is denied." If women did not establish their right to speak on the moral issue of slavery, she chided her male colleagues, then there existed little hope for the work of emancipation itself. "Can you not see that women *could* do, and *would* do a hundred times more for the slave if she were not fettered?" As Grimké saw it, the opposition to women's public speaking threatened the whole enterprise of antislavery; it was a "deep laid scheme" to silence the voices of those who would most naturally sympathize with the slave, and a slippery slope that would remove women entirely from the field of moral reform and antislavery. "If we surrender the right to *speak* to the public this year, we must surrender the right to petition next year and the right to *write* the year after and so on. What *then* can *woman* do for the slave when she is herself under the feet of man and shamed into *silence?*"[85]

It was a small step, then, for white abolitionist women such as the Grimké sisters to move from a conviction that women abolitionists were downtrodden by men to a perspective that identified the plight of all women with the oppression of slaves. In her *Appeal to the Women of the Nominally Free States*, published the following year, Grimké declared that when white women were denied the right to act in public, they might as well "be termed 'the white slaves of the North.'" Abby Kelley agreed that women's labors on behalf of the slave had opened their eyes to their own enslavement: "In striving to strike *his* chains off, we found, most surely, that *we* were manacled ourselves." Angelina Grimké stated it this way in her *Letters to Catharine Beecher*: "The investigation of the rights of the slave has led me to a better understanding of my own."[86]

Despite the exaggerated fears of orthodox clergy over the Grimké sisters' public speaking tours, multitudes of abolitionist women were not clamoring to assume a public rostrum. Very few women abolitionists, in fact, willingly stepped across the boundaries that policed their voices in public spaces. For every Grimké, Kelley, Mott, or Sojourner Truth, there were hundreds of others who, although deeply committed to the antislavery cause, were unwilling to become public speakers. Undoubtedly, many women must have been frightened or discouraged by the abuse that the Grimké sisters encountered, but, frankly, only a few brave and gifted men or women ever volunteered to become the public voices for the abolitionist movement. Despite requests, white and black abolitionist women hesitated to assert their individual voices in the public arena. For example, Philadelphia's female antislavery society pleaded for its members to write essays and deliver addresses for the society, but for nearly five years no members took them up on this request. Despite this reticence, abolitionist women strongly supported those few who became public speakers, and they identified with the abusive treatment meted out to their more vocal sisters. Whatever persecution Abby Kelley, Lucretia Mott, Sojourner Truth, or Angelina Grimké experienced was interpreted as an assault on all abolitionist women. It offered further proof of the enslavement of all women. They considered the suppression of their own rights and freedoms bound up in the denial of a public stage for abolitionist women.[87]

Abolitionist women's forays into the public arena of speaking and petitioning led them into repeated conflicts with churches and clergymen, exposing and fostering the anticlericalism that characterized radical women abolitionists in the urban North. From the beginning, abolitionists faced a dilemma about the moral responsibility that churches should assume regarding slavery. After all, these were devout and committed Christians who shared two conflicting assumptions: an abiding confidence in the unique redemptive power of Protestant churches in their era, and an unyielding intolerance for institutions that supported or turned a blind eye to slavery's sinful effects. Here was the rub; because every abolitionist embraced each of these two notions to differing degrees, confrontations and disagreements were unavoidable. And because women made up a sizable majority in Protestant churches and believed that they were the cohesive bond that held those churches together, abolitionist women became deeply concerned about their churches' moral responses to the evil of slavery. Indeed, the criticisms of corrupt churches and excessively powerful clergymen that characterized these radical abolitionist women's anticlericalism provided the foundation for their emerging feminist consciousness.

With their own history of discrimination in white Protestant churches, Philadelphia's black women abolitionists generated a critique of churches that reverberated throughout the abolitionist community. Moreover, African American women tutored white abolitionists in the consequences arising from the churches' failure to promote equality. Many northern blacks had already developed their own "come-outer" approach toward northern churches when they formed separate congregations rather than continuing to be treated as second-class Christians in white churches. Prominent black activists and newspaper editors openly criticized white Protestant churches for their hypocritical failure to condemn slaveholding. Frederick Douglass, the most celebrated of numerous critical voices, concluded his *Narrative*, "I love the pure, peaceable, and impartial Christianity of Christ: I therefore hate the corrupt, slaveholding, women-whipping, cradle-plundering, partial and hypocritical Christianity of this land."

Black abolitionists, and especially black women, deeply influenced the way their white compatriots viewed the hypocrisy of Northern churches. Sarah Mapps Douglass contributed to the Grimké sisters' criticism of the Society of Friends by recounting the prejudice she and her mother, Grace Douglass, had encountered in the segregated back bench at Quaker meetings: a white Friend was positioned at each end of that bench to ensure that no white Friends would sit there. Sarah recalled her own tears when she heard a half dozen times per meeting, "'This bench is for the black people,'" and she wondered indignantly, "are these people Christians?" Several other black Philadelphians reported to her that they left the Friends' meeting because of this treatment. In the words of one man, "'They make the *highest* profession of any sect of Christians, and are the most deficient in practice.'" Some black women also manifested their anticlerical sentiments in criticisms of clergymen in black churches. Mary Ann Shadd's first exposure in the black reforming community came in a letter to Douglass's *North Star*, where she denounced "the influence of a corrupt clergy among us, sapping our every means," and "inculcating ignorance as a duty, superstition as true religion."[88]

According to radical female abolitionists in Boston and Philadelphia, women could never assume their rightful place in the crusade to emancipate slaves until they challenged corrupt churches, misguided interpretations of the Bible, and the inordinate power of clergymen. In their minds, an ortho-dox clerical power structure kept women confined to a restricted sphere of activity. At the first women's convention in New York City in 1837, Angelina Grimké nearly divided the assembly when she offered a resolution champi-oning expanded women's rights while blaming women's subjugation on or-thodox churches and clergy. Grimké proposed that "the time has come for woman to move in that sphere which Providence has assigned her, and no longer remain satisfied in the circumscribed limits with which corrupt cus-tom and a perverted application of Scripture have encircled her." It was this "perverted application of Scripture" that prevented women from exercising their rightful duty to "plead the cause of the oppressed," and from laboring in every way (with voice, pen, or purse) "to overthrow the horrible system of American slavery." Grimké's resolution provoked an immediate, and heated, debate. Her opponents, mostly from the Ladies New York City Anti-Slavery Society, objected to the resolution because it advocated a break from women's customary roles and assailed biblical orthodoxy. They opposed sep-arating from churches, convinced in their minds that evangelical churches were God's chosen instruments for a new millennial age, and therefore de-manded to be listed as dissenters to Grimké's resolution. The women's con-vention avoided a permanent breach, but clearly an antichurch perspective marked the unmistakable dividing line between radical feminist and conser-vative evangelical women abolitionists. Radical abolitionist women in Philadephia and New England continued their antichurch criticisms throughout the remainder of the pre–Civil War years.[89]

This relationship between anticlericalism and a radical critique of gender conventions is not surprising; anticlerical sentiments constituted a popular feature of democratic movements in the early republic. They provided a common language for numerous dissidents hoping to strike at aristocratic pretensions and authoritarian privilege, and they offered a vital source for egalitarian ideas. These ideas were especially common among religious groups that espoused anti-reform and liberal theological viewpoints, such as Hicksite Quakers, Universalists, antimission Baptists, and primitive Methodists. These groups found their favorite targets in Calvinist dogma, ec-clesiastical authority, and educated and overpaid ministers, whom they branded with derogatory labels such as "orthodoxy," "priestcraft," and "hireling priests." The voices of anticlericalism did not necessarily reject Christianity or religious expression. In fact, these critics were often more de-voutly religious than their typical American neighbors. Because the majority of Philadelphia's Female Anti-Slavery Society's white members were Hicksite Quakers, anticlerical attitudes filtered quickly into these women abolition-ists' views. Their anticlericalism represented not only a democratic assault on the special privileges of a clerical aristocracy, but also a gendered critique of masculine privilege embedded in church institutions and biblical interpretations that had kept women in subjection to men for centuries.[90]

The controversy provoked by the Grimké sisters' public speaking illustrates the interrelationship of anticlericalism and feminism for radical women abolitionists. The sisters interpreted the hostility they encountered from New England clergymen not only as an assault on the rights of women, but also as part of a plot by an excessively powerful clerical aristocracy. From the sisters' perspective, the Pastoral Letter represented the fears of hireling priests and male ministers who hoped to preserve their prerogatives through gender exclusion. "The ministers seemed panic struck," Angelina Grimké remarked, for "if it can be fairly established that women *can lecture,* then why may they not preach and if *they* can preach, then woe! woe be unto that Clerical Domination which now rules the world under the various names of Gen'l Assemblies, Congregational Associations, etc." In a similar vein, Maria Weston Chapman penned a satirical poem, "The Times That Try Men's Souls," in answer to the Pastoral Letter, evincing the combined themes of anticlericalism and feminism:

> Our clergy have preached on the sin and the shame
>   Of woman, when out of "her sphere,"
> And labored *divinely* to ruin her fame,
>   And shorten this horrid career;
> But for spiritual guidance no longer they look
> To Fulsom, or Winslow, or learned Parson Cook.

The Pastoral Letter was one more sign of what Lucretia Mott called the "priestly thralldom" from which women were just beginning to liberate themselves. Slaves would never be freed and (white) women never liberated, radical women abolitionists asserted, until church leadership and clergy came to see the evils they continued to uphold.[91]

Mary Grew was perhaps the most outspoken critic of corrupt churches and clergymen among Philadelphia's women abolitionists. The New England-born daughter of an English Baptist minister, Mary Grew and her sister Susan moved to Philadelphia in 1834 and immediately joined the Female Anti-Slavery Society, where she was soon appointed to the Board of Managers and elected corresponding secretary, a position she held until the society's end in 1870. In that capacity, she wrote the society's annual reports and corresponded with hundreds of women abolitionists throughout the nation. In 1840, Grew penned the society's denunciation of American churches, North and South. "Slavery," she wrote, "is feeding upon the vitals of the church, diminishing its energies, paralysing its missionary operations, destroying the independence of its ministers, and dreadfully perverting its influence." By the late 1840s, she assumed the editorship of the *Pennsylvania Freeman*, the newspaper voice of the Pennsylvania Anti-Slavery Society, and wrote her first editorial on the issue of slavery and the churches.[92] Like other radical women abolitionists, Mary Grew's anticlerical ideas shaped her developing feminist consciousness. She became an untiring advocate for women's rights throughout the nineteenth century, signing the call for the first national woman's rights convention in Worcester, Massachusetts, in 1850, laboring on the business committee of the fifth national convention in Philadelphia, and serving as president of the Pennsylvania Woman Suffrage Association from 1869 until 1892.[93]

Ironically, Mary Grew's anticlericalism developed under the shadow of her father, a Baptist minister, who considered it his particular calling to remind other abolitionists that the Bible (in his opinion) confirmed a woman's subordination to men. Henry Grew made a habit of following Mary to abolitionist and woman's rights meetings, speaking against women's equality, even when his daughter was prominently featured at those meetings. In 1840, Mary Grew attended the World Anti-Slavery Convention in London as a delegate from the Philadelphia Female Anti-Slavery Society. But after she was refused a seat in the convention along with the other American women delegates, Henry Grew rose to state that the admission of women would violate not only British custom, but "the ordinance of Almighty God!" prompting Lucretia Mott to note that Henry "betrayed some inconsistency." An even more dramatic episode unfolded in 1854, while Mary Grew was sitting on the speaker's platform at the fifth Woman's Rights Convention in Philadelphia. Rev. Grew rose to express his disagreement with the proceedings, and then quoted several verses from the Bible to prove that God intended "that man should be superior in power and authority to woman."[94] What Mary Grew thought at that moment, we can only imagine; she must have heard those words many times before, perhaps around the fireside of her own home, but she rejected them nonetheless. She listened as Lucretia Mott systematically dismantled her father's biblical argument in front of a crowd of her feminist peers. Mott declared that it was "not Christianity, but priestcraft" that placed woman in her present state of subjection. Garrison then questioned bringing the Bible in to settle this dispute: "Would Mr. Grew say that woman can not preach, in the face of such a preacher as LUCRETIA MOTT?" But Mott rose immediately "to substitute friend Grew's own daughter, Mary Grew, who has already spoken on this platform!!" Nowhere in the hundreds of letters Mary wrote, nor in the diary she kept in 1840, did she express her feelings or opinion about her father's behavior or his views on women. But she knew in a very personal way that any reform agenda that wished to emancipate slaves and all women had to confront the theological positions of American churches and their powerful clergy. She knew this meant she must directly defy her father; and defy him she did through her writings and her feminist abolitionist activism.[95]

Radical abolitionist women throughout the North, but especially in Philadelphia, looked to Lucretia Mott as the most articulate spokesperson in their two-front assault on orthodox religion and women's inequality. Mott, a Hicksite Friend and female preacher, was among the most articulate voices of liberal Protestantism in the antebellum era. Time after time, Mott opined, the Scriptures had been distorted to justify "the existing abuses of society." In Mott's opinion, a "noble gift of reason" had been "divinely bestowed upon us," and the Bible needed to be evaluated within the framework of one's own experience and knowledge of the truth. "The time has come," she declared, "for woman to read and interpret Scripture for herself; too long have we learned God's will from the lips of man and closed our eyes on the great book of nature, and the safer teaching of our own souls." With these assumptions, the moral foundations of slavery and sexual dominance were sure to be shaken. Radical abolitionist women in Philadelphia, as voiced by Lucretia Mott and Mary Grew, but inspired by their black women co-laborers' perspective, relied on this type of anticlerical criticism for the foundation of their maturing feminist viewpoint.[96]

Along with this frontal assault on corrupt churches, radical abolitionist women also insisted that it was the duty of antislavery activists to conquer the racism (or "prejudice against color," as they commonly called it) that reigned in the hearts of white Americans.[97] Without a doubt, hostility toward racism emanated from the unrelenting reminders voiced by black women in the movement. As tireless teachers, black abolitionists introduced sympathetic white reformers to the realities of racial prejudice. Recall that it was black protests that first taught white reformers that the colonization plan was rooted in prejudice. African American women tutored the Grimké sisters in the pervasiveness of race prejudice, and black men repeatedly spoke to Philadelphia's female antislavery society on the "shameful prejudice" that declared black men inferior to white men. James Forten, Jr., for example, ridiculed slavery's preposterous racial ideas: "tie our feet and seal our mouths, and then exclaim, 'see how superior we are to these people!'" And at every women's antislavery convention during the 1830s, free black women made impassioned appeals against the pervasive race prejudice in the North. When Anne Weston offered a resolution at the first convention condemning "the unreasonable and unholy prejudice" behind the colonization society, her plea initiated a slew of "touching appeals" from women of color. This prompted Angelina Grimké to condemn the "unnatural prejudice against our colored population" and plead for "every woman to pray to be delivered from such an unholy feeling," so they could associate with every person "as though the color of the skin was of no more consequence than that of the hair or the eyes." In the eloquent plea of a black woman named Clarissa Lawrence, who held the rapt attention of women abolitionists at the 1839 convention: "We meet the monster prejudice *every where*. . . . It kills its thousands every day; it follows us every where, even to the grave; . . . You must pray it down. . . . Place yourselves, dear friends, in our stead. . . . Go on, I entreat you. A brighter day is dawning."[98]

Abolitionists thus became the first group in the United States to develop a popular discourse on race prejudice. Colonizationists opened the door by emphasizing the immutable and unreformable prejudice of white Americans against people of African descent. But radical abolitionists were the first to represent white American racism as a central feature of American culture, and the first to express a public commitment to racial equality. As radical abolitionist women explained, if slavery were a sin, and white Northerners were complicit in that sin, then misguided beliefs and feelings (prejudice) constituted the source of that sin. No one among northern whites, not even abolitionists, was exempt from guilt. "Prejudice against color," Sarah Grimké declared, "is the very spirit of slavery." It was a fire that consumed "the happiness and energies of the free people of color." Philadelphia's black and white women abolitionists echoed that language, declaring of African Americans that race prejudice "blasts their hopes, and, consequently, destroys their energies." The ultimate intent for white women activists was reforming their own behavior even more than their nonabolitionist neighbors'. If prejudice is ever to be eradicated, remarked the female antislavery society, "the first thing for *us* to do is to search carefully our own hearts, to ascertain that no vestige of it is lurking there."[99]

Not all white abolitionists shared this commitment to racial equality, and even radical whites fell short of their professed desires for a racially inclusive reform movement; yet many white abolitionist women in Philadelphia and New England considered it a sign of true antislavery devotion to work side by side with black women reformers. Many of these women, as Hicksite Quakers, must have been familiar with Elias Hicks's statement: "We are not better for being white, than others for being black." Still, there was nothing customary about establishing a racially integrated reform society (figure 10). In fifty years of benevolent and reform activism in Philadelphia, there had never been one. New York City's white abolitionist women certainly felt they could form a legitimate antislavery society and still refuse to admit black women as members; and subsequent violence like the Pennsylvania Hall riot proved that racial cooperation was not without its risks. In the face of these obstacles, black and white abolitionist women tried to confront racism through a series of interrelated objectives that revealed the radical transformation they envisioned for social relationships. Unfortunately, this was a

Yᴱ ABOLITIONISTS IN COUNCIL—Yᴱ ORATOR OF Yᴱ DAY DENOUNCING Yᴱ UNION, MAY, 1859.

FIGURE 10. Intended to be derogatory depictions of wild disorder at abolitionist meetings, contemporary prints reveal the presence of white women, black women, and black men in the public arena of antislavery activism. "Ye Abolitionists in Council," *Harper's Weekly* (May 28, 1859). Courtesy of Swarthmore College Library.

standard for radical reform that white abolitionist women often failed to achieve. The strategies these women proposed for combating racism ranged widely, including appeals to full color-blind equality, greater social interaction among white and black Northerners, eliminating segregation in northern churches, laboring to improve the condition of free blacks' lives, and identifying with the social and legal restrictions under which people of color lived their lives.[100]

Radical female abolitionists tried to encourage white abolitionists to live their lives as model relationships of racial equality. At the first women's convention, Angelina Grimké pleaded with women abolitionists to "mingle with our oppressed brethren and sisters," so as to know firsthand the crushing blows of racial prejudice. The next year, Sarah Grimké offered a resolution declaring it an abolitionist's duty to identify with African Americans, sit with them in churches, walk with them in the streets, visit their homes, and invite them into one's own home, just as one would unthinkingly do for white citizens. Apparently, this was too much for a minority of more cautious white women abolitionists, who voted against her resolution. But throughout the

1830s, some women abolitionists continued to hope that they could change the hearts of northern white women, publishing *An Appeal to American Women, on Prejudice against Color* in 1839, despite signs that few white abolitionists, let alone nonabolitionists, in the North were free of race prejudice. Angelina Grimké even appealed to women of color not to forsake white reformers: "You must be willing to mingle with us whilst we have the prejudice, because it is only by associating with you that we shall ever be able to overcome it." In the end, only a few white women made radical efforts to challenge the racial barriers that existed in antebellum America, by working alongside black women in antislavery societies. Only a few developed close friendships with black reformers, and a few symbolically identified with blacks by attending their churches and staying in their homes.[101]

With dreams of a new racism-free America, Philadelphia's Female Anti-Slavery Society welcomed both white and black women as members and leaders when it began its labors in 1833. Black women accounted for as many as eighteen to twenty of the initial one hundred members of the society. Among these, Margaretta and Sarah Forten, Sarah McCrummell, Hetty Burr, and Grace and Sarah Douglass worked on important committees and served as officers and managers for several decades. Yet despite this core of activists, very few other African American women joined the society after its first two years. Between 1836 and 1840, eighty-six new members joined the society, but only one was an African American woman. By then, the society had become convinced that racial prejudice among white abolitionists was the reason for black women's limited participation. They resolved again to denounce such prejudice and publicized an invitation "to our colored sisters to cooperate with us in our labors." White racial attitudes certainly accounted for part of this dilemma; yet Philadelphia's female abolitionists also seemed unaware of the ways that class determined perceptions of racial difference in the antebellum city. After all, African American women abolitionists were either wealthy elites from families with incomes in the top 2 percent of the city's population or independent women (teachers, shopkeepers, or milliners). Working-class black women might have felt less than fully welcome in the society. Class affinities perhaps made it easier for white middle-class women to establish connections with wealthy and highly educated black women, such as the women of the Forten and Purvis families, and working-class black women had little in common with African American elites in the organization. The society thus made few inroads among working-class black women, except during petition drives.[102]

African American women's reluctant involvement must have also stemmed from the lack of attention that the society's white abolitionist women paid to the basic needs of the African American community. The society had begun with high ideals of improving the condition of urban free

blacks. During their first year, they formed a committee to evaluate the education received by black students in the city and then opened a school for
them. The school, which was taught by a white woman and supervised by a
committee comprising only white members, never attracted substantial en-
rollment. By 1838, the female antislavery society began receiving criticism
for "inconsistently neglecting" the education "of our colored population,"
and so they decided to assume financial responsibility and oversight for a
school run by Sarah M. Douglass. Within two years, Douglass formally withdrew the school from the society's control, declining the three-hundred-dol-
lar annual salary. Perhaps she was tired of their meddling, but Douglass's
letter to the society also indicated that she wished to establish her independence; the school had been initially founded and supported by her affluent
parents and she now wanted, in her words, to "support myself." By 1849, the
female antislavery society had abandoned all financial assistance to black
schools, claiming they could no longer afford the expense. Working black
women remained unconvinced that the society was concerned with the best
interests of the urban black community or the independence of African
American women.[103]

For antebellum northern blacks, it was evident, as it has been for historians since the Civil Rights Movement, that white abolitionists were not free
from the racist thinking that pervaded American culture.[104] "Our white
friends are deceived when they imagine they are free from prejudice against
color," observed the *Colored American*. Sarah Forten explained to Angelina
Grimké that "even our professed friends have not yet rid themselves" of this
"all pervading, all-powerful prejudice." African Americans knew that white
abolitionists were the only segment of white society that advocated human
freedom and civil rights regardless of skin color, but they also knew that
many could be more deeply concerned about reforming the consciences of
white Northerners (including abolitionists) than about working for true
freedom and equality for black Americans. As Wendell Phillips confessed in
1851, "If we never free a slave, we have at least freed ourselves in the effort to
emancipate our brother." White abolitionists simply failed to live up to the
high ideals they had set for racial equality. Black reformers were continually
slighted and denied positions of authority in the movement, and black activists, including Martin Delany, criticized abolitionists for refusing to hire
African Americans in their businesses or at their antislavery newspapers.
With few exceptions, black abolitionists were never elected as senior officers
in antislavery societies, including Philadelphia's female antislavery society,
where white women always served as the president and corresponding secretary, the two most powerful positions in the society.[105]

The story of Philadelphia's women abolitionists is a complex narrative, not
easily reduced to a portrait of white reformers' racial inconsistencies. For, al-

though they fell short of achieving their stated goal of racial justice, Philadelphia's female abolitionists nevertheless continued to engage in actions that defied the relationships of power that circumscribed the lives of African Americans and women. Throughout the antebellum era, these abolitionist women attacked the system of slavery through forms of defiant resistance that at times involved breaking the law. Notably, many female abolitionists became active supporters of underground railroad efforts to assist slaves running away to freedom. In 1842, the society declared that "we love to watch the signs of slavery's downfall" and praised the efforts of the Philadelphia Vigilant Committee and its women's auxiliary, the Female Vigilant Association. Vigilance committees were the first public organizations committed to spiriting fugitive slaves safely away from bondage to freedom. Philadelphia's association was led by Robert Purvis, husband of society member Harriet Forten, and it thrived between 1838 and 1842, guiding nearly three hundred slaves to freedom during 1842 alone. But the brutal race riots that same year led to a lapse in the Vigilant Committee until it was reorganized after the Fugitive Slave Act of 1850, under the leadership of black minister William Still. In vigilance committees, black and white activists labored together at risk of imprisonment and violence. The female antislavery society publicized the efforts of vigilant committees and donated hundreds of dollars for their support. By 1849, the society openly expressed its support for any efforts that aided the flight of slaves, maintaining that such actions render slave property insecure, diminish its market value, and thus "weakens the system of slavery." Esther Moore, the white abolitionist who was first president of the society, withdrew in 1846 to devote her energies to the vigilant committee's work; and Lucretia Mott's home was regularly used as a shelter for fugitive slaves. Fugitive slave efforts continued to be one of the female society's principal concerns from the 1840s until the Civil War.[106]

For decades, historians have attributed the permanent schism among northern antislavery activists in 1840 to two issues—the dispute between the advocates of moral suasion and political action, and the conflict over the "woman question." This interpretation is not only a misnomer, it also reinforces a male-centered view of antislavery history. The internal conflict among abolitionists was never a "woman question"; it was a gender dispute, and one that centered as much around definitions of manhood as it did around questions of womanhood. When Garrisonian supporters elected Abby Kelley to serve on the executive committee of the American Anti-Slavery Society and a dissenting group withdrew to form their own antislavery society, it sealed a division that had been festering for years. Northern abolitionists divided in 1840 over the issues that defined manliness in antebellum America (perhaps it is time to call their disagreement the "man question"). The seceding abolitionists, led by Arthur and Lewis Tappan, separated from the national society because the Garrisonians drifted toward positions that threatened abolitionists' identity as manly men in that culture. Accepting women in positions of authority, allowing women's voices onto the public stage, and repudiating the defining mark of manliness in antebellum public life—the act of voting—proved to be too threatening to the masculine identity of some white abolitionist men. They could not foresee a moment when they would willingly relinquish the privileges of male dominance and slip into the gender ambiguity that characterized more radical Garrisonian abolitionists. Hence for these dissenting male reformers, choosing to secede because of the election of a woman, and forming a political party (the Liberty Party), constituted two sides of the same coin of the gender dispute confronting abolitionists in 1840.[107]

Black and white women abolitionists developed one of the most radical critiques of gender and racial inequality that Americans encountered in the nation's first century. Colonization reformers had inadvertently assisted in creating a climate that by definition radicalized women's antislavery activism by constituting the solutions to slavery as political, national, and masculine. By our standards, these abolitionist women's strategies and accomplishments seem limited; yet their appeals for basic human rights and for political and social power for the disenfranchised and powerless produced the first sustained effort by women to force the nation to realize its ideal that "all men and women are created equal"—words that women abolitionists helped to craft at the Seneca Falls Womans' Rights Convention in 1848.[108] The feminist perspective these activists developed was shaped by insistent tutelage from African American women, and a persistent resistance to the power of churches and male clergy.

Gendered Difference in the Symbol of a Slave

For the vast majority of white Americans in the North, slavery existed only in their imaginations. That is to say, by the 1830s few white Northerners had any firsthand knowledge of the "peculiar institution" of the South nor any personal observations of the life experiences of real slaves and slaveholders. This was not true for African Americans in the North, the majority of whom encountered slavery either in their memories, their family histories, their neighbors' stories, or their own recent experiences. Certainly some free black families in Philadelphia by the 1830s had not known enslavement for several generations, but they were only a small minority. When the new abolitionist movement began, therefore, antislavery activists needed both to create mental images of the lived experience of slavery and to convince their fellow Northerners, white and black, that these images demanded a particular moral response. Indeed, the expectation was that these imaginings of slavery would stimulate a set of right feelings—sympathy, compassion, and indignation—that would in turn produce right actions—charity, petitions, legislation, abolition, and a prejudice-free society. Abolitionist writings did not maintain hard and fast distinctions between fiction and reality, since most of their conceptions of slavery were produced by asking northern audiences to imagine the cruelties experienced by slaves and the sins committed by slaveholders. Authenticity and moral rectitude were more valued attributes than realism in these writings. The content of the literature that abolitionists produced—whether narratives of slaves, recollections of white Southerners, or the poems, speeches, sermons, stories, or novels of northern abolitionists—was real and yet imagined. And white abolitionists based their perceptions of slavery on the knowledge that many of them learned from black abolitionists in the North.

In this imaginative world, abolitionists and especially antislavery women, employed a markedly different gender discourse regarding race and slavery than that produced by their colonization counterparts. Whereas colonizationists wrote rarely about slavery and mostly about Africa, northern abolitionists wrote profusely about the conditions of slaves in all genres. Like others in the antebellum North, white abolitionists were influenced by and contributed to discourses that conflated racial and gender differences. In their efforts to demonstrate their unprejudiced view of African Americans, white abolitionists projected a gendered conception of difference on black slaves. They created an imagery of slaves that was largely an abstraction that targeted a vast sentimental reading public. By sentimentalizing slaves, antislavery writers depicted all enslaved people with characteristics that were clearly understood in that culture to be feminine. This eased the identification of white women abolitionists with slaves; they could then see themselves in both the oppression encountered and the character exhibited by the enslaved.

Soon after the antebellum antislavery movement began, African Americans produced a considerable body of abolitionist literature in independent black newspapers and the antislavery press. Although very few African American women became public speakers during the early years of the movement, they did take up their pens with great alacrity and vigor, making regular contributions to papers such as Garrison's *Liberator*.[109] In their narratives, poems, and speeches, black reformers tried to elicit the sympathies of white and black Northerners toward the plight of their brothers and sisters in bondage. Antislavery activists always claimed that they aimed their missives at the heart; and their writings confirmed that moral suasion necessitated that they stir the feelings of their audiences. African American reformers were among the earliest antebellum abolitionists to craft their antislavery appeals around the concept of sympathy. James Forten, Jr., told the women of the Philadelphia Female Anti-Slavery Society, "Yours . . . is the cause of sympathy, and therefore it calls aloud for the aid of woman." His brother Robert had made a similar point to the same audience two years before. Sarah Douglass, along with Margaretta and Sarah Forten, filled the pages of the *Liberator* and other papers with their essays and poems regarding slavery, all designed in Douglass's words to stir up a "feeling of deep sympathy for our brethren and sisters" held in bondage.[110] This language of feelings and sympathy evoked the culture of sentiment and man of feeling from the eighteenth century, blending it with new perspectives on human rights, pain, and suffering, and with a flourishing literature of domestic sentimentalism during the first half of the nineteenth century.[111]

Philadelphia's black women abolitionists, particularly the Forten sisters and Sarah Douglass, penned a number of works that forced readers to confront the tragedy of how slaveholders cruelly separated slaves from their families. Narratives of slave family separations served as one of the strongest methods of evoking sympathy for the conditions of slaves, and these writers commonly turned to the separation of mothers from their children as the most tragic aspect of slavery. In a poem entitled "A Mother's Grief," Sarah Forten recounts the awful pain of a woman who has lost her son in what could have been any woman's grief, but when the author is identified as "a young lady of color," the story then conjures up the loss of a slave woman, whose child has been wrenched from her side. The grieving mother cries out, "There's nothing left for me to love, This earth holds nothing dear, Since *he*, my sweet—my gentle one, Is now no longer here." Sarah Douglass echoed these ideas in her poem, "The Mother and Her Captive Boy."[112] In keeping with the conventions of domestic sentimental fiction, these images of grieving mothers were intended to touch the hearts of reading women and persuade them that feelings of sympathy must lead them to support abolition. Family separations were the real-life tragedies of slaves, yet also the distinctive focus of women antislavery writers. By the 1850s, the most celebrated black woman poet, Frances Ellen Watkins (Harper) perfected these same appeals to sympathy through tales of grieving mothers in poems such as "The Slave Mother," "The Slave Auction," and "The Fugitive's Wife." Watkins asked her readers to hear the shrieks of a broken-hearted mother:

> They tear him from her circling arms,
>   Her last and fond embrace.
> Oh! Never more may her sad eyes
>   Gaze on his mournful face.
> No marvel, then, these bitter shrieks

Disturb the listening air:
She is a mother, and her heart
Is breaking in despair.[113]

Within a short time, such appeals to sympathy had become ubiquitous in antislavery writings. Men and women abolitionists, white and black, resorted to similar tugs on the heartstrings of their northern audiences. Harry B. Stanton once remarked that "nothing can be done to abolish slavery, unless we are waked up to feel." For African Americans, this involved an act that established their direct connection to friends, families, and an imagined national community of black Americans. As Frederick Douglass stated, "We are one people—one in general complexion, one in a common degradation, one in popular estimation."[114]

Yet for white abolitionists, this act of summoning sympathy was part of a larger discourse tied to a sentimentalized view of slaves. White abolitionist writers and speakers tended to portray slaves as abstractions rather than as real human beings with vices as well as virtues. Slaves possessed a symbolic power that transcended their real experiences, and for numerous purposes abolitionists wished to invoke that symbolism. They tapped into the vein of sentimentalism that dominated speech and writing for middle-class Americans in the mid-nineteenth century. Sentimentalist literature fixed its gaze on themes of suffering, enslavement, freedom, family, and the control of sexual passion—all central to the imaginative project of antislavery, whether published in abolitionist newspapers or in the most popular novel of the century.[115]

This language of sympathy and feelings was explicitly gendered; and it was invoked as often to reinforce concepts of womanhood that assumed a woman's natural feelings of sympathy as it was to demonstrate the callous and unfeeling masculine behavior of slavery's supporters. Recall that James Forten, Jr., told the female antislavery society that "the cause of sympathy" was the special mission of women, to which Mary Grew must have assented, since she suggested at the second women's convention that women especially should be moved by "the unparalleled sufferings of the slave." In like manner, Angelina Grimké vented her frustration at Catharine Beecher's hard-hearted contempt for abolitionism by remarking to a friend, "I have no hope of converting C[atharine] because I fear she has not the heart of a woman."[116] This comment also highlights the type of men that abolitionists typically characterized as bereft of human feelings and compassion: those who epitomized a self-interested, aggressive masculinity that middle-class moralists feared and who advanced beyond respectable manliness into a condition of inhumanity that made them no longer men. "Oh! How callous, how destitute of feeling, must that person be," reflected Forten, "who can think of the wrongs done to the innocent and unoffending captive, and not drop one tear of pity." When abolitionists imagined the type of man who was too uncaring to feel for the sufferings of slaves, they immediately summoned images of colonization, un-Christian tyranny, and the selfishness, greed, and avarice that alienated men from compassionate feelings.[117]

Abolitionist writers powerfully associated an absence of sympathy with an inhumanity devoid of true manhood in their accounts of the sexual abuse of black women under slavery. This horrific cruelty (along with the forced separation of slave families) made southern slaveholders, in abolitionist rhetoric, less than human. In this way, abolitionists inverted those proslavery portrayals of slaves as subhuman, arguing instead that slave masters had slid into a state of barbarism. Frederick Douglass's *Narrative* is filled with references to the savagery and "fiendish barbarity" of southern slaveholders, while a Philadelphia black abolitionist woman described slaveholders as "fiends" with "remorseless hearts."[118] Abolitionists then proceeded to turn around the amalgamation arguments that were leveled against them by their colonization and proslavery opponents. It was southern slaveholders, not northern abolitionists, who fostered the sexual unions of white and black. In one of the earliest issues of the *Liberator*, Garrison returned the slaveholder's question, "How should you like to have a black man marry your daughter?" with the reply that slaveholders "should be the last persons" to ask that question, "for they seemed to be enamoured with amalgamation." The *Anti-Slavery Record* wrote that abolition should, in fact, check the spread of sex across the color line because slavery "produces amalgamation at the most rapid rate possible."[119] Abolitionists thus contrasted the unrestrained sexual aggression of white southern men against a true manliness that embodied the ideal of discipline and sexual self-control. It was not a coincidence, then, that many Garrisonian abolitionist men were caught up in the health reforms and self-mastery ideas advocated by Sylvester Graham. Theodore Weld was an avid disciple of Graham, and Weld joined his abolitionist labors with a broad reforming ethos that included physical exercise, manual labor, and sexual self-control. Weld wrote to his bride-to-be, Angelina Grimké, that at the approach of their marriage, "I have acquired *perfect self-control*, so far as any *expression* or *appearance* of deep feeling is visible to others."[120]

Male abolitionists, then, invoked these negative images of white southern masculine behavior in order to demonstrate a superior model of manliness for American men. The reasons for this should be apparent. Garrisonian abolitionist men in particular faced repeated criticisms that their reform actions jeopardized their standing as men. After all, they championed a movement of moral suasion, rejected political power through voting, encouraged the expression of feelings and sympathy, and allowed women to labor as their equals. Remember that more conservative male abolitionists had bolted from the Garrisonians and remade their antislavery crusade in the image of dominant, public, and political men. Therefore, attacking southern white masculinity became one means of establishing the abolitionists' superior vision of gender. As Henry "Box" Brown (or his white ghostwriters) described his former master, "He was by no means one of your indolent, do-nothing Southerners, so effeminate . . . but he was a savage-looking, dare-devil of a man, ready apparently for any emergency to which Beelzebub might call him, a real servant of the bottomless pit."[121] It was not easy for white male abolitionists to affirm their manliness when they occupied an ambiguous gendered space similar to that held by clergymen and when they embraced both sexual equality in relationships with women and deeply emotional and loving relationships with other men. Whereas some men like Parker Pillsbury or Samuel May advocated a form of "spiritual androgyny," Theodore Weld described himself as a "Backwoodsman untamed," while still others faced their opponents' barbs that they were henpecked men. Challenging the manliness of southern slaveholders helped settle white abolitionist men's ambivalence regarding their own manhood.[122]

White abolitionists thus employed this sentimentalized discourse on slavery, with its moral language of emotions and sympathy, to create a symbol of the slave that advanced their visions of gender and reform in the North. Although all northern abolitionists contributed to this discourse, white women found that it possessed greatest meaning for themselves and for their understanding of the condition of women. In the imaginings of white antislavery writers, the slave was portrayed as more naturally religious, more deeply spiritual, than slave masters or white men in general, or, for that matter, the white race as a whole. Slaves appeared as Christ-like, possessing the noblest inner virtues and embodying the essence of Christianity. They had, in the words of one abolitionist, "a strong religious tendency" and were "capable of any kind of self-denial and self-sacrifice." To prove this, white writers insisted that slaves were essentially docile, submissive, and, most important, forgiving. In one of the earliest manifestoes of the abolitionist movement, *An Appeal in Favor of That Class of Americans Called Africans* (1833), Lydia Maria Child described Africans and slaves using the adjectives gentle, kind, compassionate, sympathizing, tender, and benevolent, while emphasizing that slaves were slow to seek revenge. Indeed, no image was more common in this literature than the forgiving slave. Forgiving slaves, of course, served as symbolic opposites of the violent white southern slaveholders that abolitionists wished to condemn, but this portrait of an innate propensity for forgiveness was also intended to convince white American readers that abolition did not portend a bloodbath. For these reasons, the symbolic slave was represented as dependent, strongly attached to home, and the victim of primarily male oppression.[123]

In other words, this imagined slave (male or female) was more religious, more forgiving, more feeling, and more domestic than white American men; in fact, these descriptors matched nearly all the prevailing assumptions about white middle-class women at the time. Such imaginings led abolitionists to maintain that slaves and women were comparable: women were slaves and slaves were feminine. In the minds of abolitionists, both shared essential traits and similar positions of dependence and vulnerability. "In comparison with the Caucasian race," Child wrote in an essay entitled "The African Race," "I have often said that they were what woman is in comparison with man." Child was struck by the parallels between "the colored race" and women: both were "characterized by affection more than by intellect," had "a strong development of the religious sentiment," and a tendency toward submission, having been "kept in subjection by physical force" and considered more as property than individuals. Many other antislavery writers agreed with Child's assessment and portrayed all slaves (male and female) as essentially feminine in nature. As another abolitionist wrote, black Americans were "more feminine and tenderminded" than white Americans. By 1863, Theodore Tilton was telling New York audiences that because of their moral faculties, instincts, and intuitions, "the negro race is the feminine race of the world."[124]

This sentimentalized and feminized image of the slave found its consummate expression in the most widely read work of antislavery literature in the English-speaking world, Harriet Beecher Stowe's novel, *Uncle Tom's Cabin* (1852). Stowe marshaled all the devices of sentimentality—a child's innocence, dying and deathbeds, imprisonment and slaves, freedom, and, most important, families torn asunder—in an antislavery tale bearing conflicting messages. Indeed, the theme of sympathy for the separation of slave families drives Stowe's narrative. At one point a character states, "The most dreadful part of slavery . . . is its outrages on the feelings and affections,—the separating of families," a sentiment that Stowe repeats nearly verbatim in *The Key to Uncle Tom's Cabin* (1854), written to confirm the novel's authenticity. Stowe appeals directly to women and mothers in the North to channel their feelings into an exertion of female influence by examining their sympathies. "There is one thing that every individual can do," she concludes at the novel's end, "they can see to it that *they feel right.*" Right feeling will bring right action—this is the shared message of both the moral suasion and sentimentalism of white women's abolitionism.[125]

For Stowe, Uncle Tom became the representative of both the black American slave and the "African race," and, not surprisingly, he is presented in the same overtly feminized imagery of religiosity, forgiveness, and domesticity. In the first few paragraphs, he is introduced to the reader with a piety and honesty arising from the moment he "got religion" at a camp meeting. "Tom has a natural genius for religion," Augustine St. Claire declares later, and Stowe is quick to remind her readers, that "the negro is naturally more impressible to religious sentiment than the white." Tom (as are all "Africans") is patient, forbearing, and forgiving, as well as deeply affectionate and home-loving; and to complete the gender symbolism, Stowe asserts that the "African race" is "not naturally daring and enterprising." In short, Tom has all the qualities of a "true woman," and yet he also functions for Stowe, as for other white abolitionist women, as the antithesis of what they feared was wrong with white middle-class men. The power of *Uncle Tom's Cabin* for its northern bourgeois readership resided not only in its sensational look at southern slavery, but also in its message of domestic gender politics. Historian George Fredrickson argues that the black slave became "a symbol of something that seemed tragically lacking in white American civilization"; yet more precisely, it was something lacking in white American *men* that Fredrickson describes, as men became greedy, self-interested, captivated by "gross materialism," "unprincipled and demagogic" in partisan political squabbles, and fixated on expansionism and "manifest destiny" in these years.[126] For white abolitionist women, this gendered discourse of slavery, with its feminized image of the black slave, enhanced the appeal of the anti-slavery cause, allowing white women to see their own oppression mirrored in the experiences of all slaves and reinforcing a gendered critique of the aggressive, unfeeling, and self-interested masculine conduct of white middle-class men.

In contrast to this sentimental imagery, slave narratives of African American men, such as Frederick Douglass and Solomon Northup, exhibit instead an ever-present struggle of resistance that would demonstrate the manliness of enslaved men. Douglass's *Narrative* presents his physical and violent encounter with the slave-breaker, Mr. Covey, as the central drama in his lifetime of resistance as a slave. It was this event, he writes, that "revived within me a sense of my own manhood," and illustrates for his northern readers "how a slave was made a man."[127] In the aftermath of Stowe's *Uncle Tom's Cabin*, which Douglass embraced despite its problematic images and procolonization section, he wrote his own novella of the slave experience entitled "The Heroic Slave." In that work, Douglass fictionalizes the story of Madison Washington, a black slave who engineered a slave mutiny on board the American ship *Creole*, en route from Virginia to New Orleans in 1841. Invoking the memory of the American Revolution that this slave's name implied, Douglass narrates a tale of restrained violence by a black man, who was not only "of manly form" but whose resistance should strike a chord in "a true man's heart." Indeed, in both his *Narrative* and "The Heroic Slave," Douglass voices the rejection of the colonizationist and proslavery assumptions that denied African American men a claim to manhood in their native land.[128]

Such abolitionist imaginings take us back full circle to the journeys that shaped African American experiences in nineteenth-century America. Stowe's and Douglass's stories involve travels and voyages across bodies of water that resonate with the memories and experiences of Henry Box Brown and Joseph Blake. Those journeys are not peripheral tales about the margins of American life; rather, they constitute the central narratives of Americans, white and black, confronting the tragedies and dilemmas of slavery, race, and freedom. The vast majority of northern black men and women boldly declared that their journeys ended in the United States; that this would be their home and nation; and yet also that the battle was not over as long as they maintained the hope that "a brighter day is dawning."

A gendered history of Northerners' responses to the problem of slavery cannot be limited to the story of white abolitionists or even to abolitionists alone. We need to look beyond (as well as more deeply into) the relationship between white women and abolitionism and begin the more difficult task of exploring how race and gender as a whole sustained antebellum antislavery debates. The rhetoric and actions of colonizationists reveal the complexity and contradictions embedded in racialist thinking among the vast number of northern white reformers who never embraced abolitionism. They initiated a gendered framework for northern dialogues about slavery and racial equality that contextualized the radicalism of white and black antislavery women and men. By contrast, as abolitionists and emigrationists, African Americans profoundly shaped the conflicts over race, gender, and citizenship for all antebellum Americans in the North. Black Northerners tutored white abolitionists in racial justice and exploited the cultural language of gender to authenticate their claims to citizenship or nationhood. It was this language of citizenship and nationalism that would reappear in the violent controversies surrounding new Irish Catholic immigrants in the two decades before the Civil War.

CHAPTER 5

Immigration

I have stood in the streets of the Quaker City, while a fierce mob,
hungry for blood, howled onward, their ten thousand faces glaring
in the light of a burning church, whose dome went up to Heaven
in clouds of smoke and waves of fire.

GEORGE LIPPARD, *Quaker City; Or, The Monks of Monk Hall*
(1844)

Between May and July 1844, one of the worst incidents of ethnic and religious violence in the history of the United States erupted in the outlying districts of Philadelphia. In two separate week-long riots during
that spring and summer, Irish Catholics and native-born Protestants resorted
to gunfire, cannons, and arson to settle a bitter controversy over Bible reading in the public schools. In the wake of these riots, at least twenty-five residents lay dead and more than one hundred wounded, two churches had
been burned down, and dozens of homes had been destroyed. Frightened
Irish families fled the city and camped in nearby woods to escape the wrath
of nativists. Local authorities were powerless to stop the rioting, and, when
the state militia tried to quell the disturbances, their presence merely escalated the violence. These riots, like others in antebellum northern cities, exposed the inadequacies of traditional modes of restraining urban violence
and heightened the desire among urban residents for a professional police
force.[1] Amid ethnic conflict and bloody terror in the streets, native-born residents in northern cities turned anti-immigrant, anti-Irish, and anti-Catholic
bigotry into a new political movement. A full decade before the sudden rise
of the Know-Nothings in 1854, nativist political parties had already become a
powerful force in northern cities, especially New York and Philadelphia.
Their political rhetoric and electioneering guided an emerging racial nationalism in an age of expansionism, "manifest destiny," and the Mexican
War.

195

Although nativists emerged as an important force in antebellum partisan politics, they defined their own activism as a broadly cast reform movement, one concerned not only with the limits of the citizenry, but also with the mission of a Protestant nation and culture. Nativists both benefited from and participated in the causes that inspired other antebellum reformers, employing many of the same strategies advanced by evangelical activists—moral suasion, distributing the printed word, and enlisting clergymen as promoters. They also portrayed their crusade as the moral equivalent of the temperance movement. Thus for nativists, Irish immigrants represented the lack of self-control that bred intemperance and embodied the dangers of corruption emerging from an alliance of immigrant politics and liquor interests. Yet more than any other reform issue, conflict between Protestant nativists and Irish Catholic immigrants centered on the Bible. This is hardly surprising since Bible societies had long constituted the definitive expression of evangelical benevolence; but the controversy in the 1840s focused on public schools, testing the degree to which city residents were willing to embrace pluralism and religious liberty. In the jingoistic era of racial nationalism that characterized the 1840s and 1850s, pluralistic solutions were not forthcoming.

This conflation of anti-Catholicism with the culture of reform can be seen in an episode recounted in Protestant and nativist newspapers in 1843 under the title, "The Bible Rescued and a Soul Saved." A young Catholic girl reportedly had been given a Bible, but was then compelled by her family to throw it into a nearby pond. When "a poor inebriate" rescued "the precious treasure from its watery grave," the Bible was placed on display at the Young Men's Bible Society office and the drinking man awarded a new family Bible. That man subsequently discovered the error of his ways at a Methodist service and joined a temperance society and a local church. Thus, at a time when Protestants became enraged over Catholic efforts to protect their children from the sectarian use of a Protestant (King James) Bible in the public schools, anti-Catholicism, evangelical benevolence, temperance, and young men's reformers all became intertwined in a tale that bespoke cultural upheaval for native-born Protestants and foreshadowed violent persecution for Irish-born Catholics.[2]

During the decade preceding this violent conflict, new immigrants from northern Europe (predominantly Irish and German) had been steadily increasing. An emigrant to Philadelphia reported excitedly back to Ireland in 1836 that "thousands are coming yearly to this country [where] there is room for all—employment for all and success for many." Yet in hindsight, the growth of new immigrants before the riots pales in comparison with the legions who fled from Ireland following the Great Famine that began in 1845. Less than 2,000 new immigrants entered the port of Philadelphia in

1835, whereas nearly 6,000 stepped ashore in 1845, and in 1850, that number exceeded 10,000. All together, over 1.25 million Irish immigrants came to the United States between 1845 and 1854. Still, anti-Catholic and anti-immigrant zealots had no idea during the early 1840s what would be the entire scope of the new Irish Catholic presence in northern cities. In their minds, the number of "papists" was growing rapidly as new Irish immigrants were now overwhelmingly Catholic rather than Protestant. Indeed, during the ten years before the riots, the number of Catholics in Philadelphia had doubled.[3]

Contrary to what nativists presumed, Irish immigrants carried with them experiences and cultural references remarkably similar to their native-born American neighbors. Ireland had encountered economic and social changes not profoundly different from the market revolution that transformed the northeastern United States during the same years (1790–1840). Increasing demand for foodstuffs during the Napoleonic Wars and Britain's industrial expansion led Irish farm communities into greater involvement with distant markets, bringing imported manufactured goods into more and more households. A market-driven agriculture also encouraged expanding whiskey production as a more profitable use for harvested grain. Consequently, prosperous landholders grew even richer, while the vast majority of farm families found their economic conditions worsening as consumer prices, land values, and population pressures steadily increased. Tenants began subdividing their farms, so that by the early 1840s over half of Ireland's farms were too small to support the families that resided there. Young Irish sons and daughters thus had only two choices: emigrate abroad (to England or the United States), or remain at home in deeper impoverishment.[4] Irish immigrants encountered bourgeois responses to Ireland's social transformation that must have made antebellum American culture seem quite familiar. During the early nineteenth century, Irish men and women frequently heard liberal (Malthusean) economic theories from British authorities, telling them that poverty derived from a poor person's improvidence and that its relief must start with independence and industry. They also witnessed evangelical revivals and the birth of a temperance movement (to counteract rising whiskey production and consumption); and they devoted considerable attention to youth problems, participated in mass democratic political rallies, developed a strong national identity out of their colonial status in the British empire, and embraced a public-school system despite nationalist battles over its curriculum.[5] So while nativists chose to see utterly different Catholic strangers when Irish immigrants arrived, Irish men and women recognized patterns of behavior that made America seem at once reassuring and hostile.

Nativism developed alongside several important shifts in antebellum politics and reform during the 1840s. First, popular participatory democracy for white Americans flourished; nearly every state adopted universal white manhood suffrage by eliminating property qualifications for voting, while at the same moment disfranchising free black citizens. The presidential election of 1840 marked the first mass-appeal, party-organized election in the United States. More than 80 percent of white men turned out to vote in an election that was part revival and part mass entertainment. White men and women attended barbecues, political rallies, orations, and parades, all festooned with the banners and slogans of partisan politics. The log-cabin-and-hard-cider campaign of the Whig candidate William Henry Harrison, featuring the catchy jingle, "Tippecanoe and Tyler, Too," masterfully defeated Democrat Martin Van Buren, the archetype of a professional politician. From that election through the remainder of the pre–Civil War years, politics, as one newspaper editor admitted, seemed "to enter into everything." At the same time, political parties made a concerted effort to recruit women for both symbolic and practical service in electoral campaigns. White women moved no closer to obtaining the right to vote, but they did assume a more central position in the organized activities of political parties.[6]

Second, urban Northerners began to look with greater frequency for government-sponsored solutions to social problems that had previously been addressed by voluntary associations. Public education, for example, evolved out of private charity schools. The New York City Free School Society (later the New York Public School Society) coordinated an array of the city's charity schools, yet it was financed by public funds and operated by a private board of trustees until the mid-nineteenth century. Between the 1830s and the 1850s, northern cities moved toward a thoroughly public, free, common-school educational system that supplanted the role that Sunday schools and charity schools had performed for several generations. By 1834, Pennsylvania had adopted a statewide public education system for all children. That same year, Philadelphia's Board of Controllers issued a set of resolutions to prevent the domination by any one religious denomination over the public schools, declaring their intention to discontinue all "religious exercises, books or lesson[s]" which were of a "sectarian character."[7]

Finally, reform movements began to recoil from moral suasion and move toward political action during this era. By 1840, abolitionists had divided into two antagonistic camps, creating a permanent fissure between those favoring and opposing electoral politics, exemplified in the new Liberty Party. Temperance reformers likewise pursued legislative solutions to control drinking, especially after the Maine Law in 1851, which thereafter committed the movement to the goal of legislative prohibition. Although temperance and antislavery activism provided the most visible examples, advocates for women's rights, prison reform, and prostitution reform also began to pursue political solutions for their concerns. Elections and legislative battles, by their very nature, tended to exclude white women and African Americans. The politicization of reform thus meant that disenfranchised groups now had to struggle even more strenuously to shape the public discourse surrounding reform.[8] The importance of these various political and reform developments for the emergence of nativism during the 1840s cannot be overstated. Like the earlier anti-Mason movement, nativism postured as both a reform movement and a political party. As such, it attracted the interest of white men and women at a time when reformers began to look toward the realm of politics, and political parties were courting the participation of all who might bring them electoral success. The Native American Party employed all the techniques of the new popular politics, including rallies, parades, orations, banners, and partisan newspapers; and they elicited the support of white women in nearly all these facets of party organizing.

When thousands of white native-born Americans began to believe that increasing Irish-Catholic immigration constituted a crisis for the republic, they invoked, like other reformers, gendered language and ideas to understand and respond to their predicament. Nativist conflict proved to be a gendered conflict. Anti-immigrant activists effectively utilized the gendered discourses so prevalent in northern benevolent culture to advance their agendas and their legitimacy as a reform movement. In the wake of the riots, women nativists exploited a political rhetoric of religion and domesticity to forge a bold claim for their role in the body politic. They then used their public political voice to advance a form of racial nationalism in an age of Anglo-Saxon expansionism. Nativist conflict also involved a controversy over manliness, as Irish immigrant men developed their own masculine ideals that at once affirmed gender values from Ireland and exploited the notion of "free white labor" to claim the privileges of white manhood in the United States. At the same time, in Protestant and nativist imaginations, in convent tales and other popular anti-Catholic writings, Irish-Catholic men emerged as masculine figures who provoked both prurient envy and political anxieties. The gendered discourse surrounding new immigrants exposed the vulnerability of white middle-class gender conventions in the nineteenth century. Before exploring these interrelated developments, it is crucial to understand the ethnic and religious controversies that produced these devastating uprisings in Philadelphia and the ways in which those conflicts emerged out of decades of religious reform in northern cities. Again, the controversies that developed in Philadelphia offer us a revealing portrait of urban experiences throughout the North before the Civil War.

Blood Spilled for Bibles

Nativist riots resulted from the culmination of the market revolution, which transformed seaports like Philadelphia and New York into manufacturing cities that attracted destitute wage-earners from the northern countryside and from impoverished Ireland. The first outbreak of nativist rioting began in Kensington, one of Philadelphia's northern industrial districts. Newly arrived Irish immigrants flocked to Kensington to find affordable (although substandard) housing near available work at the docks, metal works plants, and textile factories. Kensington was home as well to a traditional cottage industry of handloom weavers, who struggled to maintain a close-knit class solidarity in a craft threatened with extinction. Initially, the industrial expansion of cotton textiles in Philadelphia did not mean that all production became mechanized, unlike the factories in Lowell, Massachusetts, where power looms dominated by the 1830s. Rather, manufacturers and boss weavers built the nation's largest textile industry by relying upon handloom weavers who worked in their homes for very low wages. It was an arduous existence, starkly portrayed by novelist George Lippard: "Here we behold a house of time-worn brick, there a toppling frame; on every side the crash of looms, urged by weary hands even at this hour, disturbs the silence of the night." Journeymen weavers continually resisted their master-weaver employers' efforts to reduce wages, with effective strikes on several occasions. In 1842 and 1843, after a four-year depression and a rate reduction from 5¢ to 3¢ per yard, a union of Kensington's weavers went on strike. Their employers turned to scab workers, since the existing surplus of weavers had been augmented by a new supply of Irish immigrants. Striking weavers resorted to violence, entering homes and destroying the looms of scab weavers and then rioting against the sheriff and militia outside the Nanny Goat Market in January 1843.[9]

The weavers' riots exposed the complexity of ethnic conflict and the changing dynamic produced by new immigrants. Kensington's weaving population was overwhelmingly Irish-born. The majority were Catholics, although a substantial minority of both boss and journeymen weavers were Irish Protestants. So although much of the strike violence was directed at poorer and new immigrant weavers who had little solidarity with the strikers, the conflict was rarely motivated by either ethnic or religious enmity. Both Irish Protestant and Catholic weavers, instead, developed a class animosity toward their middle-class bosses, who were as likely to be Irish Catholics as native-born American Protestants, and vented their anger at the scabs (who were most often Irish Catholics) and at local magistrates (who were both Irish Catholics and native-born Americans). The weavers' strike, then, marked the last phase of an era of heightened working-class cohesiveness, rather than a precursor to nativist conflict among workers.[10]

Yet, in several significant ways, the weavers' strike in Kensington set the stage for the nativist riots that followed. First, wealthy Irish Catholic political leaders, such as Hugh Clark in Kensington, discovered that they could gain greater political prominence by defending Irish Catholic cultural interests against a proselytizing Protestant culture than they could by disregarding their constituents' economic hardships. Clark had amassed a small fortune as a boss weaver and land speculator, but found himself in difficult political straits when as a Kensington alderman he was responsible for arresting rioting weavers. Within months, Clark had shifted his attention to defending the interests of Catholic students who were subjected to Protestant Bible-reading in public schools. He quickly perceived that although religious and ethnic conflict might make him a lightning rod for nativists, it would deflect the hostility of neighborhood workers whom he economically exploited. Second, for the mainstream and nativist press, violence among Kensington's weavers came to represent a telling example of the riotous character and antirepublican sensibilities of Irish Catholics in general. These writers depicted the whole population of Irish residents as a lawless, violent threat to American institutions. The complexity of working-class ethnic discord became easily concealed behind a narrative of Bible-hating Catholics and Bible-loving Protestants.[11]

By the early 1840s, two different groups of nativists—religious nativists and political nativists—became increasingly visible in northern cities. Although they strongly influenced one another, the groups remained distinct, with leaderships that rarely intersected.[12] Each camp attracted a different type of nativist with a different agenda. Both feared a foreign enemy—only they disagreed over exactly who that enemy was and how best to confront it. Religious nativists tried to resist the Catholic threat by the powers of persuasion, by publicizing the dangers that "Popery" posed to American civil and religious institutions. They wished to keep alive the spirit of anti-Catholicism that had thrived since the 1830s, when the Ursuline convent outside Boston was destroyed and Maria Monk published her titillating tale of seduction and murder. In Philadelphia, nearly one hundred Protestant clergymen joined together in November 1842 to create the American Protestant Association, whose principal objective was to encourage and equip ministers to preach regularly against Catholicism. (Catholics liked to refer to it as the "American persecution association.") They distributed one hundred thousand copies of their inaugural address, established monthly lectures that soon became weekly events, and claimed thousands of supporters by 1844. For this cadre of nativists, their struggle was a religious crusade, an ages-old controversy rooted in the historical strife and theological disputes between Protestants and Catholics, and wrapped up in the conspiratorial packaging of the early republic's No-Popery literature.[13]

Political nativists, by contrast, thought the republic's greatest menace resided in the political power exerted by new immigrant men, especially the boatloads of Irishmen who settled in the narrow alleys of the city's working districts. Hence, they pursued an explicitly legislative agenda. They sought stark revisions in the naturalization laws, extending the residence requirement from five to twenty-one years before an immigrant could qualify for citizenship and voting rights. Political nativists thought this agenda could be best achieved through a new political party—the American Republican Party (or, as it was popularly known, the Native American Party). First organized in the late 1830s, the party took root slowly in Philadelphia. Once the Bible-in-the-public-schools conflict erupted, nativists succeeded in organizing local ward associations throughout the city and districts, although total membership still remained very small prior to the riots.[14] The Bible controversy temporarily wedded religious and political nativists, who had previously moved on separate tracks, and together they composed a symbiotic phalanx of anti-Catholic and anti-immigrant hysteria. Although eventually the nativist conflict slipped from the hands of evangelical ministers and was assumed by the political nativists, once violence broke out, nameless rioters carried anti-Irish Catholic fighting beyond the expectations of either organized group of nativists.

Nativism and the riots of 1844 can be fully understood, therefore, only in the context of a religious culture shaped by decades of benevolent activism since the American Revolution. This reform culture informed the religious issues that touched Philadelphia Protestants' most sensitive nerves. It not only set the stage for this social drama, but also provided the central tension for the plot that unfolded.

What historians have rarely noted is that this culture of benevolence, with its various strategies and techniques popularized by urban evangelical Protestants, was also visible in the religious institutions created by American Catholics. Urban Catholics and Protestants produced associations that were remarkably similar, despite their leaders' claims that each group was distinct. Non-Protestants, including both Catholics and Jews, adopted the principles of voluntarism common on both sides of the Atlantic and embraced specific charities that evangelical Protestants had claimed as their own.[15] By the early 1840s, Philadelphia's Catholics were publishing tracts, organizing Sunday schools, founding orphan asylums, administering poor relief, and even establishing young men's societies. And nowhere did Catholic and Protestant reformers' experiences overlap more than in the battle against alcohol. At the moment when Washingtonian societies were redefining the temperance rank-and-file in the United States, American Catholics enthusiastically embraced a total-abstinence movement that originated in Ireland under the charismatic direction of Father Theobald Mathew. The Irish temperance movement was a stunning triumph for Father Mathew, whose popularity as a preacher and healer at open-air meetings invited comparisons with evangelical revivals. Within a year of founding his temperance society in 1838, Father Mathew had convinced nearly one-quarter million Irish to join him, personally administering the pledge to as many as twenty-five thousand people per day on several occasions. In June 1840, Philadelphia Catholics formed the Pennsylvania Catholic Total Abstinence Society, and, by summer's end, five thousand had taken the pledge. Within months, every parish church in Philadelphia had its own temperance society. Clearly, both middle-class respectability and working-class mutualism inspired reform activism that transcended religious differences; still, nativist bigotry aspired to obscure the obvious similarities between Protestants and Catholics.[16]

A dispute over Bible reading in the public schools sparked the turmoil between Irish Catholics and native-born Protestants in Philadelphia because it reached down to the twin cornerstones of an evangelical benevolent culture—Bible societies and educational charities. Since the nation's founding, these two causes had constituted the core of Protestant activism in northern cities. And at a time when education for the city's children was passing from charity and Sunday schools to public schools, the question of religion's role became even more acute. Sunday school and Bible society activists had maintained for more than a generation that teaching children virtue and religion was the key to preserving republican principles such as civil liberty and self-government. Evangelicals were not satisfied, therefore, with relegating the Bible only to a school's opening prayers or exercises. A writer for the *Episcopal Recorder* stated that "our common schools" must be "penetrated with the influence of the Gospel," or the country's Protestant and republican institutions would be destroyed. A writer to the *Catholic Herald* captured this public spirit when he declared, "the Bible is a watchword, and a word of magic influence on the public mind." So when Catholics began to demand civil and religious liberties that an American republican government should have guaranteed—freedom of conscience—they exposed the tensions between a Protestant national culture and republican freedoms, and they unleashed anti-Catholic demagogues who began a vituperative campaign to convince the public that Catholics were the natural enemies of the Bible and, thus, unfit to be American citizens.[17]

Religious nativists filled pamphlet after pamphlet with a catalog of papal crimes against the free use and distribution of the Scriptures. In the immediate aftermath of the riots, anti-Catholic polemics such as *Rome's Policy toward the Bible, The Pope and the Presbyterians,* and *A Voice from Rome* reiterated centuries-old arguments about the Roman Church's hostility to the Bible. But nativists now added a new twist, focusing on papal hostility toward Bible societies, the consummate expression of evangelical benevolence. Anti-Catholic writers made much of several public pronouncements by popes against these societies. With poor timing for Philadelphia's Catholics, a Papal Bull was issued on May 8, 1844, praising local pastors who cautioned their congregations "against the insidious maneuvers of the Bible Societies" and lamenting those "imprudent Catholics who had gone over to these societies." The *Catholic Herald* remained faithful to the church's position and criticized Bible societies as late as November 1843.[18] Nativists whipped up anti-Catholic hysteria even more by publicizing stories of Bible burnings by Catholic priests. They exploited an incident in upstate New York in October 1842, in which a Canadian missionary priest, angered over Bibles his parishioners received from local Bible societies, burned all of the copies he could gather (figure 11). Months later, Protestant furor intensified when New York City's official Catholic paper declared it "an act not only justifiable but praiseworthy" if priests chose "to burn or otherwise destroy a spurious or corrupt copy of the Bible." Rumors and tales of Bible burnings became a stock feature of anti-Catholic lectures and publications, searing graphic images of Bible-destroying priests upon the Protestant imagination.[19]

Within this anti-Catholic milieu, any challenges to the Bible's place in American culture could unite disparate groups of nativists looking for an excuse to rail against immigrants or Catholics. The ethnic-religious dispute over Bible reading in public schools began in New York City. In 1840, Bishop John Hughes requested that Catholics receive a share of the city's funds allocated to the New York Public School Society, arguing that the public-school curriculum was sectarian and anti-Catholic, especially its use of the King James Bible. When their request was denied, Hughes encouraged New York Catholics to form their own political party and to establish a separate parochial school system for their own children. In reaction to Hughes's efforts, a Native American Party briefly flourished in New York.[20]

Philadelphia's Catholic leadership likewise hoped to escape the Protestant sectarianism and anti-Catholicism that pervaded their city's public schools. Francis Patrick Kenrick, the Irish-born Bishop of Philadelphia, waged a low-key campaign throughout the early 1840s to make public education acceptable to Catholic parents and children. Although Kenrick seemed emboldened by Catholic efforts in New York, he lacked Hughes's combative personality and preferred a reasoned exchange of arguments. Still, Kenrick objected to the sectarian features he perceived in the public-school curriculum—school books published by the American Sunday School Union, history books that were blatantly anti-Catholic, Protestant hymn singing, and reading from the King James Bible. In his mind, the school board's policy of nondenominationalism was merely a mask for sectarian Protestantism. In November 1842, Kenrick outlined Catholic grievances in a carefully worded statement to the Board of Controllers. He subtly reminded the Board that he

FIGURE 11. Images and stories of Bible burnings by Catholic priests were a staple of nativist propaganda, which incited anti-Catholic riots such as those in Philadelphia in 1844. "Catholic Priests Burning Bibles at Champlain, N.Y., 1842," Edward Beecher, *The Papal Conspiracy Exposed* . . . (New York, 1855). Courtesy of the Library Company of Philadelphia.

was not advocating the exclusion of the King James Bible (a distinction few nativists could see in the ensuing conflict), only that Catholic children be excused from Protestant devotional services and have access to their own Catholic (Douay) version of the Bible.[21] After thoughtful reflection, the school board adopted two resolutions in January 1843, declaring that no children "whose parents are conscientiously opposed" would be required to attend daily Bible readings, and that children whose parents "desire any particular version of the Bible, without note or comment," would be supplied with one.[22] Unfortunately for Kenrick and Philadelphia's Catholics, the provision of "without note or comment" effectively excluded the Catholic Bible because that version contained explanatory notes and commentary. The school board, in effect, made a futile attempt at compromise, freeing Catholic children from required reading of the Protestant Bible, yet still excluding the Catholic Bible from the schools.

Nativists then proceeded to condemn Catholics for attempting to exclude the Bible from the public schools. The episode unleashed a barrage of anti-Catholic rhetoric, with Protestant newspapers scoffing at Catholic appeals to "rights of conscience" as "ridiculous and farcical."[23] By early 1844, Walter Colton, a Navy chaplain, penned a caustic assault on Kenrick and Philadelphia Catholics in his pamphlet, *The Bible in Public Schools*. Colton predicted chaos and disorder if Bibles were suddenly excluded from the schools. "We must never forget," he exclaimed, "that this is a Protestant land." Fanning the coals of anti-Catholicism, Colton anointed schools as the battleground for preserving a Protestant culture, inciting every nativist to "stand by these schools and protect them as he would his heart's blood." The interference of foreign priests and foreign power, he proclaimed, "should perish at their threshold."[24] Yet Kenrick refused to cower in the face of this demagoguery. If nativists had their wishes, he wrote, they would "take charge of our youth, and provide them with a Bible, hymns and prayers, . . . and we must sit down contented, and be silent, if not grateful." With one small step, they would soon "provide us with a national religion . . . by means of a National Protestant education."[25] In his own way, Kenrick arrived at a criticism of the evangelical benevolent enterprise that its earliest critics, such as Hicksite Quakers, had voiced during the 1820s. Both spoke of threats to religious liberty and a union of church and state. But Irish Catholic clerics and laity knew quite well from their experiences in Ireland that schools could be battlefields for cultural conflicts over nationalism. They hoped for local control at best, so Catholic teachers could read Catholic books to Catholic children in neighborhood public schools; but if that was not possible, then they wished to be excused from readings from Protestant Bibles or anti-Catholic textbooks.[26]

The final provocation in the ongoing Bible controversy arose in early 1844 from Hugh Clark's stance as a defender of Irish Catholic children in Kensington. Clark, who was then a director of Kensington's school district, was accused by another director of ordering a teacher to stop reading the Protestant Bible to her students. Clark admitted that he had become "very much annoyed by constant complaints by Catholic parents" over the Bible issue and that he thought it wise to discontinue morning Bible readings until the issue was resolved. The local school district fully exonerated him after it was clear that Clark never ordered any teachers to dispense with Bible readings. The incident, however, united the fury of both religious and political nativists. In early March, the American Protestant Association convened a rally of six thousand at Independence Square, where ministers delivered impassioned speeches against the dangers of "Romanism" and clamored for direct elections of school officials in an effort to maintain Protestant control of the schools.[27]

Nativists exploited the Bible-in-the-public-schools controversy and quickly precipitated the deadly riots of 1844. On Friday afternoon, May 3, the Native American Party planned a mass rally in Kensington, at a site strategically chosen to exhibit their anti-immigrant rage before a largely Irish immigrant neighborhood.[28] Nativists decided to stage this assembly adjacent to a schoolhouse, around the corner from a Catholic church and an Irish fire company, and two blocks from the home of boss weaver Hugh Clark. This was the same neighborhood where the weavers' strike of the previous year had occurred. Throughout the day, nativists constructed a large platform while local residents looked on uneasily, and by three o'clock about three hundred nativists had gathered to hear speakers rail against the threat of foreigners and endorse restrictions in the nation's naturalization laws. A crowd of local Irish Catholic residents, jeering and taunting the speakers, eventually drove the nativists from the rally site, forcing them to reconvene briefly in a nearby temperance hall, where they defiantly resolved to meet again.

The next two days passed with relative quiet, but on the following Monday, May 6, nativist politicians rescheduled their disrupted rally. This time three thousand people converged near the schoolhouse in Kensington. At four o'clock an American flag was raised, and nativist leaders began asserting their rights to peaceful assembly and denouncing unrestrained immigration as a threat to such republican institutions as electoral democracy and schools. Several Irish carters proceeded to drive their wagons through the crowd and dump loads of dirt in front of the platform. Tensions between nativists and Irish Catholic residents intensified with each passing minute. Just as nativist leader Lewis Levin took the platform, a sudden cloudburst sent nativists scurrying for cover under the shelter of the nearby Nanny Goat Market. Irish residents struggled to prevent them from entering. One Irishman supposedly shouted, "Keep the damned natives out of the market house; this ground don't belong to them, it's ours!" Pushing and shoving quickly degenerated into a full-scale brawl. The American flag was allegedly torn in the scuffle, and moments later someone fired the first shot. For the next hour, nativists and residents exchanged gunfire and skirmished with clubs and bricks, until nativists eventually drove the Irish from the market and adjoining streets. By the time Sheriff Morton McMichael and his deputies had restored order to the marketplace, five people—all nativists—had been shot and numerous homes had been stoned.

This bloody skirmish in an Irish neighborhood gave anti-immigrant groups exactly the pretext they needed to incite a collective uprising against Irish Catholics. The next day nativists plotted their retaliation while stoking the fires of anti-Catholicism in broadsides and newspapers. The *Native American* proclaimed that "another St. Bartholomew's day has begun in the streets of Philadelphia" and urged fellow citizens to arm themselves against the "bloody hand of the Pope." Handbills posted throughout the city exhorted: "LET EVERY MAN COME PREPARED TO DEFEND HIMSELF." Six thousand people gathered that afternoon for a nativist rally in center city, where a few speakers pleaded for peaceful resistance. The militants, however, carried the day, condemning the previous day's "outrages" and accusing foreigners of attempting to remove the Bible from the public schools.[29] The huge crowd then marched toward Kensington, with one person carrying the tattered American flag along with a banner proclaiming: "This is the FLAG that was trampled underfoot by Irish Papists." Irish Catholics in Kensington also prepared for violence. When the marchers arrived, some of them heavily armed, Irish Catholic resisters fired on them from the upper floors of the Hibernian Hose Company, killing at least four and wounding eleven others. The nativists, who outnumbered their rivals, soon began setting fire to houses throughout the neighborhood. After an hour of fighting and arson, the sheriff and several militia companies effectively quashed the mêlée, but not before nativists had destroyed dozens of houses. Irish families fled the district that evening, many of them hastily sleeping in the nearby woods without food or supplies. Native residents and Irish Protestants placed American flags in their windows, hoping to fend off additional nativist violence.

Like many riots since the seventeenth century, Philadelphia's ethnic rioting attracted those barred from the realm of conventional electoral politics. Traditionally, riots offered a space where such excluded groups found their political voice. Not surprisingly, two categorical opposites of men—boys and women—actively took part in these riots. Sidney George Fisher noted in his diary that boys were engaged in the shootings and arson and that "women, too, were busy, as in the French Revolution, cheering on the men & carrying weapons to them." Fisher's comments were sufficiently vague, implying that women from both sides—Irish Catholic and nativist Protestant—were active participants. The penny-press paper, the *Public Ledger*, reported that Irish women were involved during the first day of rioting, with "some of the women actually throwing missiles," while others "incited the men to vigorous action" by cheering and rallying them on. Throughout the following weeks, both nativist and Irish immigrant women were arrested at various times for inciting or encouraging rioting. One nativist named Isabella Hamilton, described by the *Public Ledger* as a "very genteelly dressed woman," was arraigned on charges of attempting to incite a riot by "using threatening and denunciatory language against the Catholics and the Pope." General George Cadwalader, commander of the state militia, testified after the July fighting between nativists and state troops in Southwark that nativist women "were our greatest foes." For boys, these riots might have been their first steps into a political realm that welcomed them; but for women, the riots offered them a traditional yet momentary voice in a much less welcoming public arena.[30]

Gangs of nativists continued to riot for a third day, systematically destroying property in Irish sections of Kensington, including Hugh Clark's home and his brother Patrick's tavern. Before night's end, nativists had burned down two churches, St. Michael's and St. Augustine's, as well as the convent house of the Sisters of Charity. In an ironic twist, nativists presumably burned Catholic Bibles when they tossed the extensive libraries at Clark's home and at St. Augustine's church (one of the largest rare collections of Augustinian texts in America) into the streets to fuel bonfires. Although these church burnings effectively ended the riots, Philadelphians remained in a state of panic and under martial law for several more days. Bishop Kenrick fled the city and declared all Catholic churches closed the following Sunday for fear of violence. A New York Catholic newspaper implicitly questioned the manliness of nativist rioters in a poem entitled, "Reign of Terror," that chastised "these self-abasing slaves—this blue-law canting crew—these brawling *braves*—these 'Native' knaves." Bishop Kenrick, however, counseled Philadelphia Catholics to respond peacefully and do nothing to excite nativist anger. He admitted that Catholics hesitated to publish their own account of the riots for fear that their printing houses might be destroyed.[31]

The riots subsided, but the climate of ethnic and religious hostility endured. While sober-minded Philadelphians spoke of the city's disgrace and shame, local courts teemed with cases of arrested rioters and new episodes of inflammatory language and violence between Protestants and Catholics. In early June, a criminal courts trial commenced for an English Protestant woman, Caroline Sweeney, accused of murdering her Irish Catholic husband. Dominick Sweeney, a shoemaker, was discovered lying in a pool of blood in his home after being stabbed seven times. Neighbors testified that they heard a man shriek and fall, and afterwards heard Caroline Sweeney exclaim, "there, you ———— Catholic, take that!" Mrs. Sweeney's defense rested on her claim that her husband had attempted to stab her and that, in struggling to wrestle the knife from him, he fell on it and killed himself. Nevertheless, she exploited nativist attitudes toward Irish Catholics by telling the courts that the dispute arose over her refusal to give her husband money to buy liquor, that Dominick was a violent man, and "that he was a Catholic and did not like her not being of the same religion." Caroline Sweeney was convicted of voluntary manslaughter, but the incident illustrates the volatility of ethnic hatred and nativist sentiments. Later in June, a Philadelphia grand jury blamed the riots on "the efforts of a portion of the community to exclude the Bible from our Public Schools."[32] Furthermore, local magistrates, the sheriff, as well as state militia leaders heard endless criticisms from prominent Philadelphians for failing to act decisively and forcefully to quell the violence.

While Philadelphia's Catholic leadership pursued a noncombative strategy, political nativists fixed on Independence Day festivities with hopes of converting spasms of anti-Catholic hatred into an organized political movement. Rioters, after all, were neither reformers nor political actors and by themselves proffered no sign of a movement. Nativists needed to find some way to redirect vehement ethnic animosities toward the advancement of their political objectives. The Native American Party planned an elaborate

Fourth of July parade to demonstrate widespread nativist support in the city. Fearing another conflagration, city authorities also made preparations to stave off any additional violence.

Fourth of July celebrations had been the special domain of temperance activists for most of the prior decade. Recall that temperance reformers asserted their superior manliness and patriotism by identifying with the founding fathers and promoting a new "revolution" that enabled men, in nativist Lewis Levin's words, to "maintain their *glorious independence*," which fostered "health, happiness, respectability and worldly prosperity."[33] Temperance reformers thus organized rallies and ceremonies as an alternative to traditional Independence Day drinking celebrations. During the early 1840s, as many as fifteen to twenty temperance societies marched in Fourth of July parades in Philadelphia. Nativists, borrowing the tactics of temperance reformers, hoped to convince middle-class residents that they were co-laborers in a like-minded reform cause. Incidentally, they also expropriated a public ceremony in which urban Catholics had become increasingly visible. Catholics had organized temperance societies only since 1840, yet they soon surpassed Protestant and Washingtonian temperance reformers in the size of their Fourth of July processions. In 1841, twenty Protestant societies formed a procession with seven hundred marchers, while the Catholic procession, described by the *Public Ledger* as "large and truly imposing," mustered nearly three thousand participants, who marched behind banners bearing the Madonna and child, and the cross. The next year the Catholic temperance procession brought between seven and eight thousand supporters into the streets, parading behind banners bearing images of Washington, an eagle, and the flag. Bishop Michael O'Connor of Pittsburgh thought the parades were glorious, but he noted that Bishop Kenrick was apprehensive about such visible demonstrations by the city's Catholics. When nativists organized their grand Independence Day procession in 1844, then, they wanted both to co-opt the strategies of temperance reformers and to put an end to Catholic displays of patriotic citizenship.[34]

Nativists dramatized the city's shifting political allegiances with their huge parade and picnic supper on the Fourth of July. After weeks of planning, upward of five thousand men and women marched before an audience as large as one hundred thousand. Dozens of American Republican associations from each city ward marched together under elaborately designed banners with pictures and phrases communicating the popular iconography of the nativist movement. The images reflected a blending of the sacred and secular, of Protestantism and republicanism. The most common symbols were the Goddess Liberty, the American flag, busts and portraits of Washington (restating his farewell address: "Beware of Foreign Influence"), and an open Bible, usually placed in juxtaposition to a schoolhouse. The thousands who watched from the streets were treated to slogans such as "Beware of the insidious wiles of foreign influence," "Revision of our Naturalization Laws," and "Our fathers gave us the Bible, we will not yield it to a foreign hand."[35] When the day passed without any violent clashes, city officials let out a premature sigh of relief, and some Protestant papers attributed the calm to the powerful influence of temperance.[36] But Irish Catholics in the district of Southwark decided to take no chances and guarded a local Catholic church with firearms, setting the stage for another outburst of nativist violence.

The July riots took place in a section of Philadelphia where nativists had perhaps their strongest local support. Southwark was home to workers closely connected to the traditional seaport economy. It provided the nearest housing for dock workers, sailors, and artisans in the shipping industry, as well as for other traditional craftsmen like carpenters and shoemakers. These laborers suffered most severely during the 1837–42 depression: they experienced firsthand the competition from new Irish laborers on the docks, and they had the most to fear from the city's continuing industrial expansion. As a result, nativism constituted both a seething anger and a potent political force in Southwark.[37] The neighborhood's Catholic church, St. Philip de Neri, had been threatened but unharmed during the May riots, but William Dunn, brother of the parish priest, received permission from the governor to arm a local militia company to defend it against any possible Independence Day violence. The holiday passed peacefully, but the next day some passersby noticed men bringing muskets into the church and rumors spread that it was heavily fortified. After the burnings in May, Catholics were determined to defend their houses of worship; nativists, still incensed over what they perceived as an ambush in Kensington, were equally determined not to tolerate armed Irish Catholics. By early evening, a crowd of one thousand had converged on St. Philip's demanding that the sheriff remove the arms from the building. (At least two of the three Southwark aldermen present were active members of the Native American Party.) Although Sheriff McMichael and his deputies brought out twenty muskets, the crowd demanded that they be allowed to search for additional weapons, eventually disbanding after a search committee was selected and a company of local troops arrived very late that evening.[38]

For the next three days, St. Philip's became the site for battles between state and local militia units and nativist rioters. Late Saturday evening, when General Cadwalader ordered his troops to fire on a crowd that refused to disperse, a former Whig congressman named Charles Naylor rushed forward and yelled, "My God, don't shoot! Don't shoot!" He was promptly taken prisoner and guarded inside the church by the Montgomery Hibernian Greens, a militia company composed of Irish Catholics. The rioters soon fixed their attention on Naylor and his Irish captors, acclaiming Naylor as a nativist hero

and "a great Bible man" and returning on Sunday to try to secure his release.[39] Eventually, the Hibernian Greens received orders to release Naylor to
local aldermen, leaving the mob's rage focused on the Irish militia company.
Two Native American Party leaders, Lewis Levin and Thomas Grover, attempted to prevent another church burning and secure the removal of the
Hibernian Greens by convincing the militia company that Native American
Party leaders would guarantee protection of the building, as well as their safe
withdrawal. But as the twenty-four men from the Hibernian Greens marched
out of St. Philip's, they were pelted with stones and bricks and forced to run
for their lives. One Irish militiaman was beaten and left for dead. Soon state
troops under Cadwalader seized control of the church, rioters hauled cannons from the waterfront, and soldiers and rioters engaged in sporadic but
bloody skirmishes throughout the night. When the fighting had stopped,
two soldiers and thirteen civilians had been killed, twenty-three soldiers and
twenty-six civilians wounded.

The ethnic-religious controversy over Bibles in the schools was never far
removed from this conflict that had now degenerated into a civil war between rioters and state troops. George S. Roberts, a Philadelphia gentleman,
described for a later grand jury the mindset of rioters and the "religious discussions" he encountered as he wandered among them. Roberts was convinced that the rioters were a band of "Bible-canting scoundrels" who possessed the shallowest of religious knowledge. He would have agreed with
another critic who suggested that the rioters "would not have known the difference between the Protestant and Catholic Bible if it had been placed in
their hands." Despite arguing with many of the men in the crowd, Roberts
was unable to dissuade any of them from the belief that "the law made King
James' Bible the only lawful Bible, and it was their (the Catholics') duty to receive it as such."[40]

Nativism's popularity soared after the May and July riots. A fledgling political movement with perhaps only five hundred members before the violence,
the Native American Party now numbered its supporters in the tens of thousands. Two new newspapers, the *American Advocate* and the *Native Eagle,*
joined the *Native American* and the *Daily Sun* as partisans. When November
elections rolled around, the party succeeded in capturing three of the four
U.S. congressional seats from Philadelphia and sending nine nativist men to
the state legislature. The following year nativists also captured control of the
municipal government of New York City. Lewis Levin was among Philadelphia's new nativist congressmen. He was reelected two more times, becoming the most prominent national figure in the nativist party during the
1840s.[41]

"All Women Are Patriots"

By the time the smoke had cleared from the riots that spring, Philadelphia's nativists had assembled a movement that reconfigured the political landscape. Native Americans, as they called themselves, created ward associations, mutual benefit societies, and secret fraternal organizations in every section of the city and its industrial suburbs. Feeling invigorated by their participation in nativist rallies that summer, white native-born women also stepped into the fray of anti-immigrant politics, expanding their visibility in the movement. Nativist women prepared elaborate banners that marchers carried during the immense Fourth of July procession and gave speeches as their banners were presented. By late summer and early fall, these female nativists were organizing mass meetings for women and founding female Native American associations and benevolent societies throughout the city. In September 1844, they also began publishing their own newspaper, the *American Woman*, the first political newspaper in the republic operated exclusively by women. Harriet Probasco, widow of printer Simon Probasco, assumed the place of editor and publisher, and she employed three other women to assist her. These women and their contributors fashioned a weekly paper that published essays on literature, history, women's patriotism, and reform activities, as well as nativist party politics, thus affirming in their own minds the central role of white women in defining American nationality.[42]

Female nativists were intent on making the *American Woman* into a medium of communication that presented the voices of women only. They refused contributions from male writers, declaring in their inaugural issue that all original editorial content "will be exclusively furnished by those of our own sex." Every original line, they insisted, will be "the production of the female mind." Nativist women reveled in the opportunity this newspaper provided to express their political and social opinions, to demonstrate the capabilities of white women, and to encourage other white women to follow their lead. Scattered throughout its pages were discussions of women's education and literary production, and pleas for young women to "study, study, study," to master all they could read, so that they might then write in a commanding fashion. In addition to empowering other women, the publishers wished to use the *American Woman* to compel men to hear their voices. Believing they possessed a peculiarly female perspective on the current social and political crisis, they wanted "the *men* of the land to know what the *women* have got to say to them."[43]

Nativist women used the *American Woman* to challenge the gender restrictions that defined public political speech and actions as the exclusive domain of men. They voiced a demand for the empowerment of women rarely articulated outside of the radical abolitionist movement, and several years

before the Seneca Falls woman's rights convention. Harriet Probasco elo-
quently proclaimed the right of women to participate in all facets of public
life, "We have tongues, and shall we not speak? We have heads, and shall we
not think? We have hearts, and shall we not feel? We have much responsibility, and shall we not discharge our duties?" As one contributor wrote, a
woman's "intermeddling with politics results from the fact that she is the primary element of the body politic. There can be no political body without
her. Whether active or inactive, she still interferes, and the only question is,
shall it be an interference of light or darkness?" In tandem with their bigotry,
these nativists made some of the boldest claims by any antebellum activists
for the political significance of women in the republic.[44]

In their minds, the present crisis—a deluge of new immigrants corrupting
elections and municipal government, Bibles suddenly banished from schools
or burned in bonfires, and young boys slain in the streets—justified women's
forceful entry into the realm of politics. "In view of these things," nativist
women asked, "who but an ignorant, inflated, self-conceited politician would
gainsay woman's right to take, at the present crisis, an extraordinary interest
in public affairs?" Female nativists resorted to a familiar argument for
women's political action, habitually alluding to the history of women's patriotism during the American Revolution. "Are we not in the midst of a Revolution?" Lewis Levin asked one gathering of nativist women; and their re-
sounding affirmation was echoed countless times in their writings and
speeches. Female nativists interpreted Philadelphia's ethnic conflicts as a national crisis resembling the Revolutionary War, and they looked to every aspect of women's involvement in the Revolution (from economic boycotts to
battlefield glory) as confirmation of their right to combat "anarchy, misrule
and foreign influence." Moreover, nativist men affirmed this view of
women's patriotism, agreeing with the *Public Ledger*'s defense of women's
role in nativist politics on the grounds that "*all* women, in every country, are
patriots of the soil, or in other words, attached to their country as their
home."[45]

Women nativists insisted that the Bible–and–schools controversy war-
ranted their bold actions. From their perspective, women had a special interest in the moral training of children and in the dissemination of the Scriptures in America. If one "asked why women are so deeply interested in the
present struggle," the *American Woman* answered that it was "because our
dearest rights have been assailed by a foreign power. That the rights of the
BIBLE, and of children, are particularly dear to women (especially to mothers) is acknowledged by all." Epitomizing their viewpoint was an original bal-
lad, entitled "We'll Not Give Up the Bible." It was unthinkable, in their
minds, to encourage women to be active in Bible societies and Sunday
schools, and then to deny them a political response when those reforms in-

tersected with public policy. Philadelphia's female nativists combined this ideology of women's benevolent activism with a conspiratorial anti-Catholicism. If the Bible was threatened, then American liberties were endangered, and women had a responsibility to ensure that political men did not miss that point. "Can not every man see," they declared, "that the war against the Bible by the Romanists, is the entering wedge to the subversion of the liberty of this country?" These nativist women repeatedly invoked references to "Bible bonfires" while endorsing female Bible societies and Sunday school associations.[46]

Without possessing the right to vote or to hold public office, nativist women's political actions were severely circumscribed; and in fact, they really had no intention of challenging that essential exclusion of women from formal politics. As Mrs. Catharine Shurlock stated in her speech before an association of nativist men, "We cannot stand by you side by side, and shoulder to shoulder, in your councils and deliberations—this we ask not. This is not woman's sphere." What they did insist upon was to be acknowledged as "co-laborers" in the nativist crusade, to express freely their opinions on those issues central to that cause, and to use their pens and voices to define an American nationalism. In the process, they encouraged other women nativists not to fear acting "the part of politicians" even within their own "appropriate sphere." They knew full well that their actions and words would make them susceptible to criticisms that they had inverted sex roles or unsexed themselves. One newspaper commented colloquially about the *American Woman*'s observations on recent elections: "There now, isn't that talking like a man?" And a sympathetic newspaper editor praised both the "feminine grace" and the "masculine energy" exhibited by nativist women's writings and wondered whether "our American women have more manliness of intellect than our men." Nativist women refused to retreat in the face of these criticisms. One contributor to the *American Woman* even reversed the traditional gender stereotypes by suggesting that women were more rational in their approach to the immigrant crisis than nativist men, who proceeded "through the medium of feeling."[47]

Female nativists discovered their first vehicle for political action during the preparations for the massive Fourth of July procession in 1844. Taking advantage of the symbolic value that women carried in party politicking, and perhaps following the example of Whig women during the election of 1840, nativist women prepared elaborate banners to be carried by men parading on behalf of local ward associations. The iconographic messages that nativists conveyed through the streets carried the convictions of nativist women. Local newspapers devoted pages to describing the scenes depicted on each banner. Typically the banners contained some combination of the figures of Lady Liberty, George Washington, Washington's mother, an open

Bible, an American flag, a serpent, and the motto "Beware of Foreign Influence." Nativist women were not content with symbolic voices alone. Both married and unmarried women gave political speeches on the occasion of presenting their banners, urging men toward greater zeal in their nativist labors and letting those men know that nativist women intended to speak out as long as the nation continued to be threatened by the political power of foreigners.[48]

At times, nativist women's politics led them to look beyond a narrow conspiratorial fixation on "Popish foreigners" and to address the economic and legal oppression of women. They became, for example, outspoken advocates for the thousands of women workers exploited by low wages. Espousing the female critique of liberal explanations for poverty first formulated in the 1820s, the *American Woman* suggested that it was not "idleness or improvidence" that caused the proliferation of poverty, but rather "that robbery which withholds from labour its honest wages." Women workers' wages were simply too meager to escape impoverishment. Male and female nativists alike directly appealed to workers dependent on wage earning, and working women, including seamstresses and factory workers, filled the membership rolls of nativist associations. Harriet Probasco reminded her readers of her own identity as a working woman, describing in the *American Woman* her printing-office business in language reminiscent of the persona of the industrious artisan assumed by Benjamin Franklin: "This business she personally superintends with all its multifarious concerns. She makes all her own purchases of paper, type, &c., pays all her hands, reads all her proofs, is her own clerk, . . . is her own post-*boy*, . . . manages her own large household, directs the education of her children, and is a member of various societies."

Ironically, this working-class condemnation of the injustices of wage labor might have also included the numerous Irish women who had recently begun to work in textile factories or the needle trades. For nativist women, anti-immigrant sentiments might have derived from factors other than economic competition or a distinct class consciousness. Unfortunately, too little evidence exists to determine how these activists felt about Irish women entering that workforce. It is certainly easy to imagine that some of them remained undisturbed by job advertisements that read "No Irish Need Apply!" Their intense antagonism was not directed against Irish immigrant women, but rather against certain men—those who induced immigrants to work for depressed wages and those who encouraged immigrants to vote en masse. In light of this kind of economic feminism, nativists also championed the cause of creating married women's property laws, and they fashioned their local nativist organizations into mutual benefit societies to provide a buffer for fellow native-born women against the vagaries of a wage-labor economy. Nativism was neither exclusively a middle-class nor a working-class ideology; however, it did manifest itself in different ways for different classes.[49]

White women active in the nativist campaign clearly promoted a set of ideas that extended beyond the Native American Party's agenda to revise the naturalization laws for new immigrants. Using the forum of the *American Woman*, nativist women also became outspoken proponents of the ideology of true womanhood and domesticity, writing endlessly about women's appropriate behavior and characteristics. One week they printed essays on a woman's temper, female beauty, flowers, and advice to mothers; the next they devoted more than a full page to a piece on "Health-Dress," warning of the dangers of tight-fitting clothes and extravagant spending. Articles such as "A Good Wife," "The Best Housewife," "Woman as She Should Be," "A Mother's Love," and "Domestic Happiness" all perpetuated dominant white middle-class notions of womanhood, associating a woman's true destiny with the home. "Woman is naturally domestic," Harriet Probasco proclaimed, and if her mind is "properly constituted," then "all her joys, her hopes, her wishes" will be centered on "that loveliest spot on earth, called *home*." Nativist women writers affirmed many of the prevalent elements of that domestic ideology, including notions of a woman's passionlessness and her spiritual superiority.[50] Nativist women knew, then, that they had to walk a fine line between their professions that women were essential to the political process and their conformity to the powerful expectations of this Victorian domestic ideology. When challenged by an opponent who suggested that perhaps a woman had better remain at home and mend her husband's stockings than attend political meetings, one activist replied: "'Sir, allow me to say to you, that a Native American lady never goes *out*, until the holes in her husband's stockings are mended.'" Just as abolitionist women recognized, nativist women knew that their assertive public actions were always better shielded by a well-ordered and respected household; this explains why the Grimké sisters always appeared more vulnerable to criticism than Lucretia Mott.[51]

These women made the reforming spirit of nativism one of their primary justifications for speaking out in public against Irish Catholic immigration. The conflation of "true womanhood" with both moral reform and domesticity helped nativists ease their way into women's politicking. Some women must have been attracted to the nativist cause because it emphasized moral reform, whereas male nativist leaders encouraged their participation because it adorned the movement with a moralistic image.[52] The domestic ideology convinced female nativists that Bible reading, the education of young children, and the drinking habits of men were their own causes. White middle-class women had also grown in prominence as teachers, both in Sunday schools and common schools, in the North by the 1840s. So when the Bible-and-public-schools controversy erupted in New York and Philadelphia, nativist women asserted that "all that woman holds dear and sacred, has been threatened by the ruthless hand of foreign influence." One writer declared that American wives and mothers "will never—no, never submit to the dictation of Jesuit *Bachelors* (!) in the training of our children!"[53]

Given the relationship of evangelical reform to antebellum nativism, it is not surprising that nativist women resorted to the discourse of female influence. Their writings overflowed with references to women's influence, both to position their political actions as a conservative force rather than as a challenge to gender roles and to invoke the claim that women possessed a natural endowment for that work. In her prospectus introducing the first issue of the *American Woman*, Harriet Probasco declared that "female influence is the novel, conservative principle of all countries." On another occasion, after asserting that a woman's patriotism demanded her voice in the political writings of the paper, Probasco wrote: "The influence of woman, in human affairs, has always been of controlling importance." Very quickly, "female influence" became the motto of nativist women.[54]

But unlike its previous manifestations, nativist women frequently contrasted female influence with its dangerous opposite, the "foreign influence" of the Catholic Church, a long-standing Protestant stereotype grafted onto a nationalist foreign policy slogan. As Mrs. Deiadamia Taylor stated in a Fourth of July speech, if only "Native Americans" would take back the ballot box and administer the laws, then she might finally cry out, "fear not, our national institutions are safe, the reign of foreign influence is now over." In an early editorial in the *American Woman*, Harriet Probasco declared that foreign influence sought to remove the Bible from the public schools, produced the riots in Southwark, and placed the victims of the riots in their graves.[55] By definition, foreign influence represented the opposite characteristics of female influence, suggesting instead the seduction, sensuality, and deception that characterized confidence men and designing priests who supposedly threatened to beguile unsuspecting young women and men, much like the dangerous associates who led urban young men astray in men's advice literature.

Nativist women were able to reconcile their own aggressive political activism with these paeans before the altar of domesticity precisely because they associated domesticity with the greater national and racial identity of a Protestant, Anglo-Saxon United States. As scholars of American culture have noted, domesticity assumed a central place in the project of empire-building and racial nationalism, and, significantly, at the same moment that nativist conflicts erupted in the 1840s.[56] This explains why Harriet Probasco and the *American Woman* could state on the one hand that "Woman is naturally domestic" and that "all her joys, her hopes, her wishes" are centered "on that loveliest spot on earth, called *home*"; and on the other hand proclaim that "she is the primary element in the body politic" and that the "affairs of the home can never be regarded as secure, while the affairs of the nation are un-settled."[57] Nativist women maintained that sexual difference—by which they meant the privileges and responsibilities of domesticity—was the boundary that separated white American women from culturally and racially inferior women throughout the rest of the world. This belief justified their political actions and ensured that such politicking did not mean that a woman had stepped beyond "her appropriate sphere." It also meant that differences be-tween Anglo-Saxon women and Irish immigrant women came to represent the supposed cultural superiority that Americans brought with them in their numerous missionary enterprises or incidents of national conquest (whether in Asia, in Mexico, or among American Indians). Nativist women's political activism assured men that if they did not "guard the temple of liberty, their women would be reduced to the level of their sex in other parts of the world." As the *American Woman* explained: "The truth lies here:—if woman be thrown back into Oriental listlessness, their situation will be that of the men. Man in China is nothing, because woman, in China, is nothing. . . . The progress of civilization has every where been retarded by the condition in which woman has been placed." Nativist women thus developed a dis-course about civilization, race, and nationalism as white Americans con-quered racial and ethnic "others" on their own continent, or watched those "others" disembark from emigrant ships in their own ports.[58]

During the three decades before the Civil War, white Americans had begun to develop a nationalism that defined what peoples rightly belonged to the nation through projects such as the forceful removal of American In-dians, the conquest of Mexico, the colonizing of Africa, and the expansion of the territorial limits of slavery. It is important to remember that a nation (or people) is no more rooted in nature than races are. Both are cultural cre-ations, produced in specific historical circumstances.[59] Nativist women con-tributed to defining the national polity of the United States by asserting a racial nationalism grounded in the empire-building project of domesticity and true womanhood. Not surprisingly, they were more effectively able to break into the realm of the masculine public than women with more radical social agendas such as abolitionism or woman's rights. Clearly, such conser-vative women have historically been more successful in winning access to the public stage because they present themselves as defenders of gendered pro-priety. As such icons of gendered order, nativist women stood in striking con-trast to the disorder associated with the masculinity of immigrant Irish men.

"But a *True* Man, like You, Man"

The nativist conflict was primarily a bitter contest to determine the nature of citizenry in the republic. And because citizenship rights were inseparable from masculine identity in nineteenth-century America, nativism spilled over into a controversy about manliness in northern cities. After all, the riots of 1844 pitted young men against one another in a largely masculine clash of ethnic and religious violence. Yet even before armed Protestants and Catholics displayed their belligerence in the streets of Philadelphia, nativist discourse relied on specific imaginings of gender in order to stir up fears of Catholicism and Irish immigrants. Whereas Irish immigrant men exhibited a distinct masculine identity in the antebellum city, nativist Protestants also summoned forth provocative imagery of Catholic priests and laymen, generating rival masculinities that destabilized prevailing ideas about gender. If the central issue was whether Irish immigrant men were qualified to take their place as citizens in a white republic—in other words, were they white?—then the process of defining that white citizen was tied to the ways antebellum Northerners talked about gender—were the Irish true men?

Soon after their arrival, Irish immigrant men discerned the reigning notions of white manliness in antebellum America. They also discovered myriad ways to establish masculine identities, partly in response to white gender and racial ideologies, but also based on gender concepts derived from traditional Irish culture and the experiences of famine and market capitalism in nineteenth-century Ireland. In other words, they brought with them certain assumptions about what constituted ideal manly behavior, and yet they also assimilated notions of white American working-class manhood that would ensure their partaking in the privileges bestowed on white men in a white republic.

Before examining the fears that nativists generated about Irish Catholic men, it is necessary to investigate the meanings of manhood for Irish immigrant men, whose lives metaphorically bridged an old world and a new. To reach a broader gendered understanding of Irish manhood, we need to analyze Irish men's drinking, violence, militarism, nationalism, and racial politics from their roots in Ireland to their diverse manifestations in northern U.S. cities. Irish American manhood cannot be reduced to a simple reference to Irish men drinking, brawling, or rioting. Irish men drank and Irish men were teetotalers; and native-born Americans also fought and drank prodigiously. Rather, what needs to be explored is the historical context surrounding the development of an Irish immigrant masculine identity that vied with white middle-class manliness, a context that highlights the complexities of motives and reasons for Irish men's drinking and fighting, and explores the other features of masculine identity that they embraced—nationalism, patriotism, and racial politics. Large numbers of Irish immigrant men drank and fought, not because of some cultural quality of Irishness, but because of specific historical circumstances in Ireland and their unique experiences as immigrants in an industrializing United States.

Too often historians have reflected the perspective of nineteenth-century Anglo-Americans and generalized about a single type of Irish masculine behavior. But instead of one universal Irish masculine identity, Irish immigrant men came from different regions, religions, and classes in Ireland, and they carried to America a set of contested ideals of masculinity derived from traditional Irish culture, defiance of English rule, and the social transformation of their homeland prior to the Great Famine. Irish men brought with them the heritage of a rural popular culture and then proceeded to adapt these traditions to a new urban environment. Although the vast majority had lived in small rural villages in Ireland, Irish immigrants became the first immigrant group in the United States to settle predominantly in cities. Unfortunately for many Irish families, steady work at decent wages proved to be scarce for unskilled laboring men in antebellum cities. Irish men found urban work to be seasonal and sporadic, and they often left women and children behind to pursue more advantageous employment in the countryside on large transportation projects, such as digging canals or laying tracks for railroads.[60]

Nowhere were conflicting masculine ideals from Ireland more apparent than in attitudes about drink. Irish Catholic men carried to the United States both a drinking culture of male sociability and a moral imperative of abstinence rooted in Father Mathew's temperance movement. Irish drinking habits were forged from a combination of social changes in nineteenth-century Ireland and the realities of the immigrant experience in the United States. Over a long duration, from the seventeenth to the nineteenth centuries, drinking in Ireland gradually changed from an occasional experience (prompted by special occasions such as festivals, fairs, wakes, or the entertainment of guests) to a regular experience (an everyday behavior in special male-exclusive indoor spaces, such as inns, taverns, or "shebeens"). For numerous reasons, whiskey consumption increased dramatically in Ireland during the late eighteenth and early nineteenth centuries. As Irish farm families encountered new market forces, greater profits could be gained by distilling harvested grain (or potatoes) into whiskey, and whiskey soon became more plentiful than ever. Irish families also discovered that whiskey production, especially illicit distillation, allowed them to rebel against English imperial rule by evading British regulations and excise taxes. And with each successive downturn in the fortunes of small farm families, poverty, emigration, an incomplete diet, and loneliness increased the consumption of alcohol. As one famine-era emigrant woman recalled, "My father he never was a steddy worker. He took to the drink early in life." It was during this transition that indoor drinkshops (pubs or shebeens) developed in Irish villages as male-exclusive spaces for socializing and drinking.[61]

Much like pub culture in England or America, Irish shebeens were places where men gathered to drink outside of the presence of their mothers, wives, and daughters. Of course, women could be present as proprietors, servers, or perhaps as prostitutes. Yet scholars of pubs and Irish culture have argued that drinking provided Irish men with a homosocial place to sublimate their sexual desires while living within a gender system that vigorously discouraged social interaction between the sexes. Especially in the famine years, parents and Catholic priests combined to prevent social contact between young men and women because family formation was economically unfeasible. Scholars have thus suggested that drinking with the lads became "a substitute for the company of women," pubs represented "female substitutes" for the "servicing of male needs," and intoxication ensured the diminishing of sexual desires.[62] One wonders, then, what happened to those sublimated sexual passions when thousands of men began taking the temperance pledge to abstain from alcohol consumption. Perhaps drinking was less a response to Irish Catholic sexual controls than a traditionalist response to the hardships of market capitalism. Thus the pledge meant a new, bourgeois rejection of traditionalism rather than an innovation in the realms of gender or sexuality.

In either case, Irish immigrant men found themselves in U.S. cities drawn between the familiar poles of same-sex drinking patterns and religious and economic incentives to abstain. In the United States, however, there were additional factors pushing and pulling in opposing directions. Liquor became a common means of exploitation in the economic exchange between laborers and employers at canal and railroad sites where thousands of Irish men flocked for wage work, leading them to drink to greater excess than they had in Ireland. In the cities, faced with a true shortage of livable wage employment, many Irish immigrant men opted for the entrepreneurial prospects that operating a drinking establishment offered them in the cities. A large proportion of new groceries and drinkshops were run by Irish immigrants in working-class Irish neighborhoods. As early as 1820, nearly one-third of the licenses for selling liquor in Philadelphia were given to men with Irish surnames. By 1840, Philadelphia possessed nearly one thousand licensed taverns and countless illegal grogshops, and New York City had as many as two thousand saloons, with a significant portion operated by Irish Americans. An immigrant man could establish a bar with no more effort than it took to set a plank across two barrels. Cheap liquor and his own gregarious personality might keep him in business for a long time before the authorities shut him down.[63]

But Anglo-American stereotypes of the Irishman reflected none of these complexities of motives and behavior behind Irish men's relationship to drink. Instead, native-born Americans constructed a popular image of Irish immigrant men as improvident drunks, further inciting their fears of immigrant political power as a defense of local liquor interests. Anglo-Americans were deluged with stock portrayals of Irish drunkenness in popular culture. John Brougham, a comedic actor and playwright, gave a classic portrayal of a comic Irish drunk in his play, *O'Flannigan and the Fairies*, which opens with ragged and hungry immigrant children wondering when their father will return, and their Irish mother lamenting that his drinking would lead the family to ruin. O'Flannigan enters as a stereotypical drunk:

> *O'Flan.:* Aha! Molly, darlin', here am I, core of my heart! . . .
> *Molly:* Here you are, Phil—but how? As usual, drunk!
> *O'Flan.:* The devil a drunk! Missus, only a thrifle sprung. [And after describing a dishonest bargain and a fight he got into.] . . . I couldn't do no less nor thrate, and that made a half-a-gallon fly like smoke! Oh, murther alive! The exercise has gav me a wonderful appetite for a dhrink.[64]

Stock characters served their purposes in the theater of public opinion; Irish men and inveterate drinking became a prevalent caricature of Irish American manliness.

In addition to drinking, male violence was an endemic feature of popular recreations in Ireland and part of the heritage that Irish men brought to America. "Hurling," the favorite indigenous sport among Catholic peasants, resembled a cross between cricket and field hockey, except that the players wielded much larger clubs and engaged in more violent physical clashes. One pair of travelers noted, "It is a fine, manly exercise, with sufficient of danger to produce excitement." In the heat of the contest, "men grapple, wrestle, and toss each other with amazing agility," and the sport was "often attended with dangerous, and sometimes fatal, results."[65] An even more violent popular recreation in Ireland were the "faction fights" that regularly erupted at fairs, festivals, and patterns (feasts for a patron saint). Faction fights grew out of regional and ancestral feuds and occurred with predictable regularity; they pitted groups of men numbering in the hundreds, who brandished heavy clubs (shillelaghs) and pummeled each other for an hour or two, while crowds of women supplied weapons and encouragement.[66] Irish novelist William Carleton contrasted the rapturous glee of faction fighting with the somber sectarian fighting that occurred between Orangemen and Catholics. "Paddy's at home here" at the faction fight, Carleton wrote, "he tosses his hat in the air, in the height of mirth. . . . To be sure, skulls and bones are broken, and lives lost; but they are lost in pleasant fighting—they are the consequences of the sport." Throughout the nineteenth century, Irish priests tried to suppress fighting, much as they encouraged the temperance crusade. Yet periodic displays of manly pugnacity defined the leisure activities of Irish peasant men. Fighting was rooted in the importance of kinship and clans in Ireland, and in Gaelic defiance of English dominance and the Protestant Ascendancy.[67]

It is easier to observe the persistence of Irish drinking behavior among immigrants than it is to see how Irish men transplanted or adapted the culture of fighting to an American environment. Contemporaries observed faction fighting on board ships transporting Irish immigrants across the Atlantic, and these clashes later erupted in the male-dominated work camps and shanty towns where canal and railroad workers labored in rural Pennsylvania, Maryland, and New York. Yet in cities like New York, Philadelphia, and Boston, where the greatest concentration of Irish immigrants settled, Irish men did not transplant the sports of faction fighting or hurling.[68] Instead, Irish men in the cities found other means to adapt the traditions of clan-based and recreational violence. Young Irish men expressed their masculine combativeness in street gangs, volunteer fire companies, and the sport of prizefighting. Although these activities frequently brought Irish immigrant men into violent contests with working-class Protestant and nativist men, their overall effect was to identify Irish men as a part of a white working class that defined its opposition to respectable white bourgeois manliness through a violent street life and sporting culture. Irish men held no monopoly on street gangs, fire companies, or boxing and gambling; other immigrants and native-born working-class men participated in comparable numbers. By adapting Irish popular recreations of fighting to an American environment, Irish men effectively forged a bond between versions of masculinity they knew in Ireland and a working-class male physicality they helped to fashion in American industrial cities.

During the years of nativist hostilities, street fighting between rival gangs and fire companies was a ubiquitous feature of urban life in New York and Philadelphia. Penny-press newspapers and social commentators continually complained about young male rowdies, or "B'hoys," who prowled the back alleys and occupied street corners, assaulting passersby or staging battles with rival gangs. It is estimated that at least one hundred gangs existed in Philadelphia between 1840 and 1870, bearing picaresque names such as the Rats, Bouncers, Jumpers, Skinners, Smashers, and Killers. In New York, the Bowery B'hoys were the most notorious of numerous youth gangs that prowled the city in the 1830s and 1840s.[69] In some white middle-class minds, these gangs were associated with Irish immigrants, even though they were just as likely to consist of native-born members. "B'hoy," after all, conjured a stereotypical Irish brogue, insinuating an undeveloped manhood or a "boy culture" that flaunted its rejection of bourgeois self-restraint and manliness.[70]

Street warfare, however, was not confined to criminal crews. Volunteer fire companies, despite performing an invaluable civic function, often by the 1840s had become affiliated with (if not peopled by) working-class gangs that fought out ethnic animosities in the city streets. Ironically, Bishop Kenrick expressed his relief in August 1845 that nativist violence would not be repeated from the previous summer, since "firemen have had riots among themselves without references to religious differences." What Kenrick failed to realize was that fireman riots were part and parcel of the same ethnic conflicts that resulted in gunfire and church burnings in 1844.[71] The Weccacoe Engine Company in Southwark bitterly divided in 1842, when Native American Party members succeeded in establishing a regulation that the company "be organized and its affairs conducted on the principle of total abstinence from intoxicating drinks." Irish and nontemperance American members withdrew and formed their own company, the Weccacoe Hose Company, one block away. By the mid-1840s, nativists and Irish Catholics had established opposing fire companies throughout Southwark and Moyamensing, which either sponsored street gangs or merely subsumed those gangs within their membership. Nativists organized the Shiffler Hose Company, backed by a gang called the Shifflers, both named after George Shiffler, the first Protestant casualty during the Kensington riots. Irish Catholics dominated a rival company called the Moyamensing Hose Company that worked in tandem with a gang known as the Killers. Throughout the late 1840s, then, these ethnic gangs and fire companies staged periodic battles, usually at the site of fires started by one group or the other. Traditional skirmishes between fire companies over the right to put out a blaze were transformed into ethnic battles that revealed a shared working-class rowdiness and physical violence. The key was that these performances differed sharply from restrained bourgeois and evangelical manhood.[72]

But Irish immigrant men did not join fire companies merely so they could fight other young men. Volunteer fire companies were also respected places for the expression of civic virtue in the republic. Ever since Benjamin Franklin established the first volunteer company in 1736, Philadelphia men had demonstrated their heroic service to the city and received the laurels of an admiring populace for their bravery and skill. Firemen were praised for exerting themselves "with the most becoming and manly spirit" and for risking "life and limb" to quell a disaster. In an age of voluntarism in the early republic, Irish emigrants quickly perceived the benefits arising from membership in a fire company. Fire companies resembled close-knit families, and firehouses permitted men to gather with other men, even if they had nothing more noble to do than drink and gamble; fire companies offered a visible civic brotherhood for the men who volunteered.[73]

Membership also offered Irish immigrants the opportunity to distance themselves—like other white workingmen—from African Americans, who were emphatically denied the right to form fire companies. When a group of young black men tried to establish the African Fire Association in 1818, nearly every existing fire company rallied to prevent it. They circulated a statement declaring that a black fire company "will be productive of serious injury to the peace and safety of citizens in time of fire" and encouraged "citizens of Philadelphia" to deny them any support, because "there are as many, if not more, companies already existing than are necessary at fires or properly supported." The implication, of course, was that free blacks were not considered citizens, that all fire companies were not necessary to prevent fires (in fact, it implied that more often they were up to mischief), and that fire companies represented a privilege of a white male citizen in the republic.[74] Yet when Irish immigrants began arriving in greater numbers during the 1840s, middle-class men had already begun to withdraw from volunteer firefighting, becoming more engrossed in their occupations and entrepreneurial pursuits as manifestations of their manliness in an industrial economy. This meant that fire companies became more prominently places for expressing working-class competitiveness and physical combativeness, and the urban elite began to see fire companies not as important civic enterprises, but as the domain of urban rowdies who posed a dangerous social problem. Between 1850 and 1870, cities throughout the nation replaced volunteer fire companies with paid municipal fire departments. Irish men might still have reaped some benefits from this change, because the new city fire and police departments were substantially staffed by Irish immigrant men or their sons.[75]

Finally, the sporting world of prizefighting offered another way for Irish men to adapt traditions of violent recreations in America. Pugilism thrived in northern cities where immigrant and ethnic enclaves combined the brawn of physical labor with the tensions born out of an industrial workplace. Irish-nativist animosities were frequently settled in symbolic bouts between prizefighters who represented a shared ethnic identity with their supporters. The celebrated match between Tom Hyer and Yankee Sullivan in 1849 pitted a native-born skilled tradesman and an Irish-born laborer in a battle that signified the ethnic and economic conflicts that separated the working classes of northern cities. Yet prizefighting also unified white working-class men in a popular pastime that subverted bourgeois values by exploiting the regimens of self-denial, temperance, and ambition for the enjoyment of pleasure, quick riches, and violence.[76]

Not all expressions of Irish immigrant masculinity were rooted in Irish popular recreations or confined to gangs and barroom behavior that white middle-class Americans considered unrespectable. Irish men not only confirmed their manliness within a set of gender values brought over from Ireland, but they also recognized the privileges they could derive from an identification with free white laboring manhood in America. During the years of unprecedented Irish immigration, Irish immigrant men made a concerted

effort to establish themselves as free whites, and thereby assert their difference from African Americans with whom they most commonly lived, and
with whom they shared the unskilled wage-work in the city's poorest neighborhoods. In other words, an Irish man could demonstrate that he was a true
man—not a slave, but a freeman and citizen—by participating in activities
that were the exclusive domain of white men. As historian David Roediger
has stated, Irish-Americans "treasured their whiteness, as entitling them to
both political rights and jobs."[77]

Soon after arriving in the United States, Irish immigrant men joined volunteer militia companies, claiming for themselves a badge of respectable
manliness and citizenship denied to free African Americans.[78] Prior to the
1844 riots, Irish men volunteered for a number of companies commanded
by native-born Americans, but they also established militia units of their own,
manned and commanded by Irish Catholic immigrants, including the Hibernian Greens and the Montgomery Hibernian Greens. Irish militia companies could display their patriotic manhood for native-born and immigrant
communities alike by appearing in full uniform at ethnic and political gatherings, such as Repeal Association meetings, and Fourth of July and St.
Patrick's Day parades.[79] After the riots, Irish militia units continued to flour-
ish, adding new companies such as the Emmett Guards, United Irish Rifles,
and Irish Volunteers. When the United States declared war on Mexico in
1846, Philadelphia sent four Irish militia companies and Irish volunteers accounted for at least one-fourth of the enlisted men under Zachary Taylor's
command. An Irish tavern-keeper from the city was one of the war's first ca-
sualties. As a result, Irish men were quick to extol their fellow immigrants'
patriotic service and heroism, counteracting years of nativists' allegations
that Irish immigrants were unfit to be U.S. citizens. A writer for the Catholic
Boston *Pilot* took aim at the nativists: "In times of peace we Irish are not fit to
enjoy 'life, liberty, and the pursuit of happiness,' but when the country needs
our aid, we are capital, glorious fellows."[80] Military service thus offered Irish
men an early opportunity to claim their status as white citizens and men.

An urban Irish American manhood developed most distinctly in the realm
of popular partisan politics as political action offered Irish men one of the
best opportunities for claiming their place in a white republic. The close
affinity that Irish voters and politicians developed with the Democratic Party
became one of the central features of American politics before the Civil
War.[81] Still, what often troubled nativists was the Irish immigrant's apparent
loyalty to a nationalism rooted in the politics of Ireland. Since Irish Catholic
immigrants believed they had been exiled from their homeland by English
tyranny, they retained an acute interest in nationalist movements in Ireland.
In the early 1840s, when nativism was spreading, American Irish Catholics
openly displayed their political passions by supporting the Repeal movement

that had been initiated by Irish nationalist Daniel O'Connell, known as the "Liberator" for ending the civil rights restrictions against Catholics. After a frustrating decade as a member of Britain's Parliament, O'Connell organized his legions of Irish Catholics to attempt to restore self-government to Ireland. The Repeal movement, which sought to repeal the Act of Union in order to ensure Irish self-government rather than British rule, was rooted in a nationalism that was not only Irish, but distinctly Irish Catholic. Irish nationalism developed out of the denial of Catholic civil rights and out of the immense poverty suffered disproportionately by Ireland's Catholics. Hence, the romantic nationalism behind the Repeal movement combined the political aspirations of the Catholic middle classes with the economic grievances of the Catholic peasantry to produce a shared conviction that for too long the true Irish Catholic nation had been denied its realization. In America, Irish Catholics immediately organized Repeal clubs in every city, raised money to be sent back to Dublin, and urged major U.S. political figures, including President John Tyler, to support the cause. Repeal meetings were often very open public displays, such as rallies and processions, making immigrant politics rooted in Ireland's nationalist struggles seem, to skeptical nativists, somehow "unAmerican."[82]

The Repeal movement revealed that Irish Americans possessed dual political loyalties that nativists could never fully comprehend. While deeply interested in affairs in Ireland, Irish immigrants also harbored strong allegiances to the American republic, especially to its racial privileges of whiteness. Despite their support for Repeal, many American Irish quickly soured on O'-Connell and his followers when those Irish nationalists began criticizing the United States for its practice of slavery. When seventy thousand Irish, lead by O'Connell and Father Mathew, signed "An Address of the People of Ireland to Their Countrymen and Countrywomen in America" in 1841, calling for the Irish in America to unite with the abolitionists and "treat the colored people as your equals," Irish Americans refused to equate the Repeal cause with an antislavery critique of the republic. When abolitionists tried to use the Address to rally Irish laborers to their cause, Irish immigrants responded with overwhelming hostility. Bishop Hughes questioned the authenticity of the Address, and a Boston Catholic paper stated that O'Connell had "no right to shackle the opinions of the Irishmen of America." The most common refrain for the Irish in America was the cry that they too would never countenance foreign interference in U.S. domestic institutions or politics. A group of Irish miners in Pennsylvania declared that we "consider ourselves in every respect as CITIZENS of this great and glorious republic" and consider "every attempt to address us, otherwise than as CITIZENS, upon the subject of the abolition of slavery, . . . as base and iniquitous." By alluding to white slavery, and by invoking their special privileges as white citizens, Irish Americans

indicated their deep allegiance to a republic built on a system of racial oppression, an allegiance they refused to make morally consistent with support
for liberty in Ireland. Indeed, Irish-American racial politics were most glar-
ingly revealed in the 1842 race riots, when Irish immigrants terrorized free
blacks just months after the Irish Address was published and following a
black celebration of the anniversary of the British emancipation of slaves in
the West Indies. In this case, anti-English Irish nationalism found its counterpart in the violent nationalism of Democratic racial politics.[83]

These sentiments provided one more reason why Irish immigrant men
were so closely wedded to the Democratic Party in the pre–Civil War years.
The Democrats were, after all, the one party that condemned nativism and
opposed abolitionism or any modification in the nation's system of racial
slavery. Indeed, the conflict over voting behavior of naturalized Irish citizens
grew out of the new "democratic" state constitutions, such as Pennsylvania's
new constitution of 1838 that promised the franchise to all white tax-paying
male citizens, while simultaneously stripping the right to vote from black
men. In addition to its racial politics, the Democratic Party also developed a
dynamic reciprocal relationship with Irish immigrants, providing local Irish
leaders with positions of authority and patronage while guaranteeing a large
loyal bloc of voters for the Party's candidates. The party provided jobs on
public works projects, protected immigrants against nativist legislation, and
symbolically championed Irish culture and festivities. It also gave Irish immigrant men an immediate association with U.S. nationalism.[84]

The lyrics of a Repeal movement song, invoking the memory of the
thwarted United Irishmen rebellion in 1798, fused together all of these masculinist notions embedded in an Irishman's patriotism, honor, nationalism,
slavery rhetoric, and even drinking:

> Who fears to speak of Ninety-Eight?
>   Who blushes at the name?
> When cowards mock the patriot's fate,
>   Who hangs his head for shame?
> He's all a knave, or half a slave,
>   Who slights his country thus;
> But a *true* man, like you, man,
>   Will fill your glass with us.
> We drink the memory of the brave,
>   The faithful and the few.[85]

Prior to the Civil War, few contemporaries would have systematically
parsed out these elements of Irish American masculine identity—drinking,
fighting, firefighting, gangs, militia service, and politics. Instead, they would

have seen them as fluid and indivisible, united in the lives of men who personified for the immigrant community the epitome of Irish American manliness. William McMullen furnishes a remarkable example. Born in Philadelphia, McMullen's immigrant father worked on the docks delivering cargo before eventually opening a grocery store (which in all likelihood sold liquor, too) in the poorest suburb, Moyamensing. From an early age William identified strongly with Irish Catholic interests. Legend has it that he performed his first community action at age twelve when he held candles at night while workers finished constructing the firehouse for the Moyamensing Hose Company. McMullen also quickly developed a reputation for his brute strength and ferocious street-fighting in ethnic gangs and fire companies, earning him the lifelong nickname "Bull." In 1844, he traveled the two and a half miles from his home to Kensington to defend fellow Catholics during the May nativist riots and reportedly was among the crowd that shot George Shiffler. "Bull" McMullen drank hard and fought often, but along with his fellow firefighters, he developed his own ethic of abstinence, choosing to drink only after a fire and never to fight a fire while drunk. McMullen's prestige as a firefighter and his renowned strength as a brawler meant he found himself enlisted in another of the manly arts—politics. During the 1844 elections, when nativist candidates first appeared, he was chosen by the Democratic Party to be his ward's election-day bookman, the official charged with settling disputes over eligible voters and getting out the party vote. By 1846, after continual run-ins with the police for street fighting, McMullen decided to enlist as a volunteer in the Mexican War, along with most of the Killers gang, where they were cited for "the extremest of bravery" in General Winfield Scott's battle for Mexico City. By 1850 McMullen had risen to prominence in local Democratic Party politics. He opened a tavern in 1854, symbolizing an important shift in his political base from fire companies to saloons, was elected alderman in 1856, and thereafter was returned to political office in every election until his death in 1901. McMullen's life typified the hard-edged, working-class masculinity of Irish men in the city, an archetype of manhood that provoked great anxiety among the middle classes, but aroused respect and adulation among Irish Catholic immigrants and other white working men.[86]

Irish Americans also became notorious for their intense animosity and violence directed toward African Americans in northern cities. Hostile relations between Irish immigrants and free blacks grew out of specific efforts by Irish men to assert their claims to whiteness in the northern labor market of a solidifying racial democracy. Conflict between Irish immigrants and free blacks did not derive from some innate Irish race consciousness; rather, it grew out of the historical circumstances by which the Irish in America deliberately distanced themselves from any association with African Americans and the racial category of blackness. When the nineteenth century began, poor Irish and free black men and women often lived in close proximity, working together on the docks or on board ships, socializing and drinking, sharing music, dances, love, and sex without violent confrontations. Both groups shared a similar place among the laboring poor struggling to survive in an urban wage economy. By the time Irish Catholics began arriving in greater numbers in the 1830s, both Irish and black workers faced similar disdain from native-born white Americans. Irish immigrants frequently found themselves associated with African Americans, taunted by whites and blacks alike with labels like "white negroes" and "smoked Irish," leading some Irish Catholics to confess that being called an Irishman was the equivalent to being called a "nigger." In a popular joke at the time, a black man is heard jesting, "My master is a great tyrant, he treats me as badly as if I was a *common Irishman*." In fact, cartoons in newspapers and magazines in England and America often represented black and Irish men with similar ape-like features, as bestial, low-brow, sensual, violent, and thereby less than fully men (figure 12).[87] Irish Americans responded not by championing the plight of the downtrodden regardless of color, but instead by striving to distinguish themselves as free white laboring men, wholly distinct from African Americans. By the 1840s, observers frequently noted that the Irish in America outpaced all other Euro-Americans in their racial antipathy toward northern free blacks.[88]

As David Roediger and Noel Ignatiev have shown, Irish American racism cannot be reduced simply to job competition with African Americans. Free blacks rarely proved to be significant competitors for unskilled jobs with Irish immigrants. With rapidly escalating Irish immigration and a static free black population in Philadelphia, African Americans were quite easily elbowed out of most unskilled labor markets. Irish men in turn secured their identity as white workers by their ability (either through violence or intimidation) to drive all black workers from the work they themselves performed. The ability to be one's own master or to chose freely one's employer or vocation became the defining feature of the mythical "free white laborer." In the words of an Irish immigrant song, "They say I'm now in freedom's land / Where all men masters be." "White man's work," then, became by definition that work from which African Americans were excluded. The institution of slavery ensured the importance of a white identity for northern white workers, and Irish immigrant men understood slavery not as restraint on the release of job competitors but as an institution whose very existence helped define them as both white and men.[89] Out of these same sentiments developed an Irish American hostility to abolitionism. Of course, Irish Catholics had other reasons as well for despising abolitionists; in their minds, Garrison and his fellow reformers were, in the words of one Catholic paper, "bigotted and

OUR EDUCATORS.

THE READING OF THE BIBLE IN THE SCHOOLS.

AMERICAN SCHOOL COMMISSIONER. "But, my good Sir, we have always read the Bible in our American Schools ever since the first settlement of the country."
IRISH SCHOOL COMMISSIONER. "Worse luck, thin; ye'll rade it no more! Father O'Flaherty says it interfares wid our holy religion, an' by the Vargin it won't and it shan't be read!"

FIGURE 12. The hotly contested issue of Bible reading in the public schools was central to the controversy over Catholic immigration. Like African Americans, Irish immigrants were commonly pictured with simian features. "Our Educators," *Harper's Weekly* (October 1, 1859). Courtesy of Swarthmore College Library.

persecuting religionists" who desired "the extermination of Catholics by fire and sword." This developing racial ideology constituted perhaps the logical conclusion of Irish men's efforts to make themselves part of a white republic.[90]

Irish immigrant men developed a simultaneous attraction and repulsion toward black men, displayed most clearly in the popular entertainment that captivated their leisure-time attentions. Irish immigrant men became both the principal performers and audience for a myriad of blackface entertainment that anchored a burgeoning show business industry in mid-century America. Minstrels shows, where performers blackened their faces with burnt cork and assumed grossly stereotypical caricatures of black personas and dialects in song-and-dance routines, had just begun at the time of the nativist riots. Minstrelsy soon developed into the most widely popular form of entertainment for working-class white males, and particularly for Irish laboring men.[91] It was a sex-segregated activity, where men alone assumed the roles of performers and audience alike. Blackface performances allowed northern white men to produce a white fantasy of blackness, characterizing African Americans in ways that promoted a racial politics of white supremacy. Minstrels represented African Americans as animalistic and closely tied to a primitive Africa, lampooned the absurdity of black aspirations of wealth and equality through the urban dandy character Zip Coon, and depicted southern slaves as contented. As one historian has noted, Irish men could join with other northern working-class men and experience through blackface performances "the collective exaltation of their whiteness and their maleness." Minstrelsy helped mediate the ethnic and class conflicts between northern white men, and gave them a shared image of those who were defined as less than fully men. But underneath this racial stereotyping lay an undeniable attraction for performers and audiences alike to the rituals of "acting black" that minstrel shows offered. Defining black as deviant, subversive, and sexual provided a homoerotic attraction both to expropriated cultural forms of black leisure and dance and to white male fantasies about a mythical black manhood. In northern cities, blackface entertainment also frequently spilled over into street violence, as young white men assumed blackface disguises when they preyed on free black neighborhoods and churches. Thus, at a time when nativists tried to represent Irish men as the relative equals of African Americans, Irish men could demonstrate their whiteness through the popular rituals of "acting black."[92]

In the face of the violence they experienced at the hands of Irish immigrants, northern free blacks maintained a complicated relationship with nativism. Black activists generally eschewed the virulent anti-Catholicism that was so prevalent among white native-born Protestants. And yet black newspapers in the North were filled with references to negative Irish stereotypes and jokes about Irish simplemindedness or heavy drinking. Even then, Irish-directed jokes had a double-edged character to them; they could as easily emphasize an Irish person's ignorance as depict a simple Irishman outwitting his wealthy superior. All the same, northern free blacks kept a healthy distance from nativist movements and their supporters, remaining skeptical of nativists' sympathy for their concerns. They were certainly aware of statements like those of nativist minister Joseph Berg, who asserted that southern slaves were free compared to enslaved Catholics. And they wondered whether nativists ever assisted blacks unless it was in their own interests. Two days before the nativist rally in Kensington, for instance, Lewis Levin got into a street brawl in the heart of Philadelphia's black neighborhood when he overheard several men joshing a black man for being a disfranchised "Native American." Levin's violent response to the taunting indicated his fierce defense of a slander against the nativist cause rather than a defense of a threatened African American. Levin apparently attacked the jeering man (described as "quite advanced in years") by fiercely beating him over the head and face, leaving him with a black eye and a cut lip, and then had the temerity to go to the mayor's office and file an assault and battery complaint against his victim. By the late 1840s, black spokesmen were regularly attacking the "bigotry" and "folly" of nativist politics, despite their personal frustration that European immigrants were accorded citizenship rights so easily while those same rights were so ardently denied to native-born African Americans.[93]

Convent Tales

Working-class Irish Catholic masculinity certainly disrupted ideals of middle-class manliness in the antebellum North. Irish immigrant men's civic responsibilities, electoral power, and their appropriation of whiteness gave them a respected masculine identity that counteracted the rough and unrestrained working-class masculinity that bourgeois men derided when asserting their own superior manliness. Yet this disparity pales in comparison with nativists' sensational imaginings about Catholic immigrants and gender. In the antebellum Protestant imagination, Catholics appeared as threats to a solidifying Victorian gender system that had harmoniously married the passionless, dependent, and domestic woman to the sexually restrained, entrepreneurial, and independent man. Beginning in the 1830s, lurid fantasies of lascivious priests and imprisoned nuns transformed the theological treatises of Protestant anti-Catholicism into a popular literature that left its readers with disturbing images of sexual disorder. These fantasies continued to inform nativist perceptions of Catholic men and women for the remainder of the antebellum era.

At the center of these nativist imaginings was the teeming literature of convent tales that flowed from northern presses. Capitalizing on a print revolution that created a market for cheaply published goods, anti-Catholic writers released a stream of exposés recounting the horrors of imprisonment, torture, coerced sex, and murder behind the walls of Catholic convents, and describing the daring escapes of former nuns. Anticonvent literature produced three of the best-selling books before the Civil War—George Bourne's *Lorette* (1833), Rebecca Reed's *Six Months in a Convent* (1835), and Maria Monk's *Awful Disclosures* (1836). Reed's tale sold ten thousand copies in its first week and more than two hundred thousand in all, and Monk's *Awful Disclosures* sold over three hundred thousand copies, outsold only by Harriet Beecher Stowe's *Uncle Tom's Cabin.*[94] The plot is essentially the same in all of these narratives. An unprotected young woman becomes effectively imprisoned in a convent, where she must submit to the controlling will of her superiors or to the carnal desires of licentious priests. Maria Monk spins the most salacious of such tales, describing how her Mother Superior instructs her "to obey the priests in all things," which to her "utter astonishment and horror" she soon discovers means living "in the practice of criminal intercourse with them." Priests roam the convent at all hours, and, as Maria confesses, "often they were in our beds before us." Children that are produced by these liaisons "were always baptized and immediately strangled!" and nuns who refused to submit were murdered as well. In the end, Maria escapes in order to save her own child fathered by a priest with a distinctly Irish surname, Father Phelan. It did not matter to the thousands of readers who believed these tales that Maria Monk was exposed as a fraud soon after the publication of her book; that she had never been a nun, only a mentally disturbed prostitute; or that her story like many other nuns' tales had been ghostwritten by anti-Catholic urban ministers. The powerful appeal of convent narratives grew out of their exploitation of the dominant forms of popular fiction in the early republic. Maria Monk's fable was at once a seduction story, a captivity narrative, and a parable of sentimental domesticity.[95]

Missing from nearly every analysis of Maria Monk's tale, however, are the close parallels between this sensational convent narrative and the central issues that provoked Protestant-Catholic conflict in antebellum cities. By emphasizing the titillating plots of sex, secrecy, captivity, and infanticide, scholars have neglected to note that these tales also spoke directly to the Bible controversy that defined the nativist dispute. *Awful Disclosures* is filled with references to Catholic efforts to keep the Bible out of the hands of the people: Maria never sees a Bible in the convent, and when she stumbles upon a page from the New Testament, she conceals it as a secret treasure, only to be forced to perform penance when she is discovered reading it. This is, in fact, part of the captivity theme. Nuns, and by implication all Catholics, are kept from full access to the Scriptures, much like slaves on Southern plantations. Priests read selected passages only on a few occasions each year, reminding them that common folk's minds are "too limited and weak to understand what God has written." Maria frequently hears priests speak of the evil of the Protestant Bible, and their "great dislike" for the book: "I often heard the Protestant Bible spoken of, in bitter terms, as a most dangerous book, and one which never ought to be in the hands of common people." Of course, when she escapes from the convent, her Protestant benefactors immediately provide her with a Bible, and, in good evangelical fashion, she has an instant epiphany. "I soon began to believe," says Maria, "that God might have intended that his creatures should learn his will by reading his word, and taking upon them the free exercise of their reason, and acting under responsibility to him." The free agency of evangelical Protestant conversion was thus contrasted against the imagined mental captivity and dependence of Catholicism. For bourgeois Protestant men, being denied "the free exercise of their reason," or the freedom to act responsibly toward God, involved the essence of being stripped of one's manhood. Popular anti-Catholic texts introduced Protestants to this gendered threat even before the Bible controversy erupted in city schools.[96]

In nativist imaginations, then, Catholicism produced a cast of dangerous rivals to Protestant middle-class gender conventions. As in all discourses of gender, contradictions abounded in these anti-Catholic fantasies. Convent tales contributed to perceptions of Catholics as all-controlling, powerful, hypersexualized men who dominated others, and at the same time as powerless, effeminate, dependents lacking in rational agency. If these images were readily translated into Catholic men and women, respectively, the danger might have seemed less acute; but such coexisting images were associated with men and women alike. After the publication of convent tales in the 1830s, religious and political nativists continued to rely on these images as they constructed their justifications for denying immigrants equal inclusion in the polity of the republic.

Protestant visions of Catholics were indebted to the gendered ideas embedded in the notion of influence. Indeed, it was the menacing figure of male influence, the corruption associated with the confidence man, that provided the framework for Protestant fears of Catholics in their midst. Maria Monk, for one, portrays lying and deception as inherent features of Catholicism. The nuns and priests in the Montreal convent develop forms of deception into an art. "All the holiness of their lives," Monk discovers, "was merely pretended. The appearance of sanctity and heavenly mindedness . . . was only a disguise to conceal such practices as would not be tolerated in any decent society in the world." Rebecca Reed likewise depicts convent schools as a deceptive scheme for proselytizing Protestant girls. Not surprisingly, nativist attacks during Philadelphia's ethnic-religious conflict in the 1840s resorted to this same language of confidence and deception. The American Protestant Association attributed its origins to the successes of Catholic schools and charities that "were constantly gaining upon the confidence of unsuspecting and benevolent Protestants." Appearances, they feared, were not always what they seemed. Thus, the similarities between Protestant and Catholic benevolence were interpreted not as a shared culture of voluntarism, but as the deceiving designs of Catholic priests to gain, in the words of Rebecca Reed's narrative, "a controlling influence over the minds of our youth."[97]

The mysteries and secrecy that fascinated Protestants about Catholicism became personified in the imagined figures of a prowling and seducing confidence man (the Jesuit priest) and the deceptive painted woman (the cloistered nun). Anti-Catholic polemics were littered with references to "Popery" as a temptress, Jezebel, harlot, or licentious rake. Lewd Protestant fantasies focused on the confessional, where intimacies between priest and confessing young women could be conjured out of the imagined eroticism and feminized piety prevalent in American Protestantism. As nativist Nicholas Murray explained, "like sin and death, confession and seduction follow each other in Rome." Maria Monk describes priests reclining in the confessional, intimately close, whispering indecent and shameful questions into her ear. They "put questions to me," she recalls, "which were often of the most improper and even revolting nature, naming crimes both unthought of, and inhuman." As literary scholar Jenny Franchot has argued, Protestants saw confessions, where beguiled girls disclosed the secret contents of their heart, "as tantamount to illicit sexual intercourse." In this overlap between fiction and fantasy, the sexual had become conversational, closely connecting the act of speaking and telling to sex itself, as Michel Foucault has suggested. Religious emotionalism, the piety of the heart, never strayed too far in American Protestant minds from the disorder of illicit sex. Moreover, the confessional offered the additional danger of freeing the confessor from restraints of conscience—all guilt could be canceled by confessing to a priest.[98]

Underneath this sexual imagery lay fears that Catholicism would strip a man of the independence and self-control that was so essential to entrepreneurial manliness, and thereby leave him a dependent unfit for the public sphere. According to nativist writer David Reese, all Roman Catholics were compelled to render a feminine-like "absolute submission" and obedience to the priesthood and hierarchy. It became the centerpiece of nativist political rhetoric that Irish Catholic men were incapable of thinking and acting for themselves, and therefore needed to be excluded from making judgments on political matters or casting votes in elections. This state of dependence was a product of the all-controlling influence that the Catholic hierarchy allegedly exerted over its constituents. As one nativist declared, "the Bishops and Archbishops held absolute control over the minds of their spiritual subjects" and by this power, they could make a large body of men cast their votes in whichever direction will advance the interests of the Church. For this reason, an anti-Catholic contributor to the *Public Ledger* was convinced in the summer of 1844 that "Irish Catholicism *does not* fit men the best for citizenship under *our* institutions." And by the 1850s, a Philadelphia "Know-Nothing" could bluntly voice the claim that Catholic men had lost the requisite masculine agency to be citizens:

> If men are so destitute of reason and understanding as not to be able to think and act for themselves on matters of a religious nature, but to have some one learned in the arts of chicanery and imposition to lead them by the nose, and direct all their movements, how can it be possible that such ignoramuses can be capable of judging properly on political matters? They cannot; and the voices of the whole of such are but the reechoes of the voice of the priest! Who is himself directed by a higher and foreign power, to do whatsoever he can to destroy republican institutions!!! Will it not then become us to do something to prevent such men either from holding office or polluting our ballot-box by their anti-republican votes?

Nativists thus broached two different but related images of Catholic masculinity—the unrestrained and all-controlling priest and the dependent or mentally enslaved layman—both of which confirmed their predisposition to see Irish Catholic men as unworthy of citizenship in the republic.[99]

Popular anti-Catholic literature also presented Catholicism as a threat to the established gender arrangements of the bourgeois Protestant family. Why else were anti-Catholic writers so obsessed with nunneries? Convents represented spaces for independent working women, women who could live successfully outside the boundaries of male authority and the legal and social constraints of patriarchy. It is not surprising, then, that convent riots in Boston and Baltimore during the 1830s, and sporadic attacks on the homes of Catholic sisters in other cities, resembled brothel riots, where working men combined a chivalric defense of womanhood with an animosity toward independently successful women. Convent tales, however, allowed anti-Catholic fiction writers to evoke these male fantasies of sexually active women while keeping those women under a measure of patriarchal dominance by presenting those stories as narratives of captivity. In the process, they did imagine (perhaps with envy and hatred) the unbridled sexual appetites of Catholics priests that threatened the white masculine sexual privileges that were presumed to be reserved for married men. Like utopian projects during the antebellum era, the celibate priest and the independent nun raised the specter of a different gender and sexual order.[100]

The irony behind this anti-Catholic literature was that in an effort to expose the supposed sexual iniquities of Catholics, nativists produced a form of popular pornography for a broad antebellum reading public. As one historian has suggested, countersubversive movements in the antebellum North commonly resorted to behavior identical to that they wished to condemn in their imaginary enemies. Indeed, paradoxes and ironies were rampant in this literature. The imaginings of powerless Catholic men, deprived of their rational agency by designing priests, bishops, and popes, led to a nativist fear of their own impotence in the face of the growing economic and political presence of Catholic immigrants and the all-powerful secret designs of the pope and his associates. Catholic foreign influence implied the powerlessness of white native-born men, who were rendered politically impotent by the allegedly conspiring political power of the Democratic Party machinery and new immigrant men.[101]

This irony that anti-Catholic visions of a menacing, all-controlling, and unbridled Catholic priesthood actually mirrored nativists' projected fantasies became frighteningly clear in the most popular work of fiction produced during the era of nativist riots. George Lippard's *The Quaker City; or, The Monks of Monk Hall* was serialized beginning in 1844 and was released in its entirety in 1845. A mysterious Gothic tale of lecherous men, sexually captive women, and the secret deceptions behind romance, finance, and religion, Lippard's novel successfully exploited the devices of anti-Catholic narratives. Monk Hall, the gambling den and house of assignation at the center of the story, is implied to have been once occupied by a Catholic priest or used as a nunnery or monastery. Strange rumors spread "about midnight orgies held by the godless proprietor in his subterranean apartments" and about "pretty damsels" who pass through the entry gates clad in "dark robes and sweeping veils." At other times, Lippard alludes to the "secrecy" of the institution, to hidden passages and trap doors, and to a cellar where bodies are buried. And when Lippard asks, "Who were the Monks of Monk Hall?" his answer must have sent shivers down the backs of anti-Catholic readers because the men whom he describes resemble Protestant reformers themselves. They "were lawyers from the court, doctors from the school, and judges from the bench." They "were solemn-faced merchants, whose names were wont to figure largely in the records of 'Bible Societies,' 'Tract Societies,' and 'Send Flannel-to-the-South-Sea-Islanders Societies.'"[102]

The hostile reaction of Philadelphia nativists to the publication of George Lippard's *Monks of Monk Hall* reveals the subversive quality of anti-Catholic narratives. Lippard's "monks," and the sexual captivity and violence of his story, intentionally exposed not the corrupt dangers of Catholicism but the depravity of an aggressive male sexuality that knew no ethnic or religious bounds. The *American Woman* responded with vitriolic hostility to the release of Lippard's novel and, without a hint of irony, issued a criticism that could just as easily have applied to Maria Monk's tale, charging that every page revealed "the *presence* of a grovelling, vitious [sic] taste, of a foul imagination and of a low gross sensualism." The nativist women concluded by warning men not to expose themselves to such imaginings: "Men! American-men! waste not your time, corrupt not your hearts, pollute not your imagination, dissipate not your strength either in the perusal or by the *manufacture* of such publications."[103]

Catholic priests and Irish immigrant men provided nativists with abundant fodder for their imaginings of gender disorder, and their own uncertainties about the stability of a new bourgeois manliness in the nineteenth century. These two masculine figures, at different times, either challenged or mirrored the entrepreneurial masculinity that seemed so troubling to middle-class moralists. Both represented a masculinity without the rigorous self-control that bourgeois men hoped would restrain the assertive traits of self-interest and passionate pleasures. If the priest were a rake, then what were the thousands of "sporting men" who walked the streets of antebellum cities?

Just as the nativist movement burst on the scene of reform politics in the 1840s, Americans also became captivated by their own expanding "empire of liberty." By 1846, the United States was on the verge of a war of conquest with Mexico, and a newspaper editor from New York had just coined the jingoistic phrase "manifest destiny" to justify an aggressive expansionism across the continent. Railroads, telegraphs, and steamboats made millennialist visions of American exceptionalism spill over into imperial aggrandizement, not only on the North American continent, but in the "opening" of China and Japan to U. S. interests as well. Nativism rode the ebbs and flows of these waves of American nationalism. Shortly after the Philadelphia riots, westward expansionism and war with Mexico created new problems of how to incorporate nonwhite peoples from those newly conquered lands, while Irish American men displayed their citizenship, patriotism, and white manliness in fighting that war. The Mexican War and the schemes of empire were built as well on American conceptions of womanhood and the domestic ideal, a discourse that nativist women helped perpetuate at a moment of expansionist and nationalist fervor.

Epilogue

On March 24, 1870, seventy-seven-year-old Lucretia Mott took up the gavel and opened the final meeting of the Philadelphia Female Anti-Slavery Society. In one of the rare moments in her public life, she admitted, her emotions were too overwhelming for her to deliver an address to those assembled. This gathering was an extraordinary event in the history of antebellum reform societies. Antislavery organizations, like this one in Philadelphia, were the only benevolent and reform associations since the founding of the republic to claim that the problem they were created to address had been resolved. For these women abolitionists, the society's work had been accomplished: "Its life is lived; its work is done; its memorial is sealed. It assembles, to-day, to take one parting look across the years; to breathe in silence unutterable thanksgiving; to disband its membership, and cease to be." No other antebellum reformers could make such a claim. Poor-relief organizations knew what Jesus meant when he said that "you will always have the poor with you." Missionary, Bible, tract, and Sunday school societies could never rest while there was another soul left to save. Temperance reformers had saloons to remind them that men continued to drink, and they found renewed life in the goal of eliminating all alcohol consumption through prohibition. Sex and health reformers never achieved that perfect stasis of spirit and body to which they aspired. And new immigrants continued to fuel nativists' fears of a foreign threat to the republic. But these antislavery women declared in the society's final report, "The goal is won, our faith is justified." Lucretia Mott's only words came from the New

Testament, signaling the denouement of a reforming life and career: "Now lettest thou thy servant depart in peace, for mine eyes have seen thy Salvation."[1]

Abolitionist associations such as the female antislavery society considered the passage of the Thirteenth, Fourteenth, and Fifteenth Amendments to the United States Constitution as signs that their work was completed: "today the black man and the white man are equal citizens," the female society declared. And here lies perhaps the deepest irony; while other reformers knew their work continued, antislavery activists felt their work was complete at the moment that the United States stood on the brink of its worst phase of racial violence and white-on-black terror in its history. The radical vision of new racial and gender relationships that inspired these women reformers in the 1830s remained unfulfilled. They knew that race prejudice continued to reign in the hearts of Americans, North and South; and they recognized that the act of granting suffrage to black men still left black and white women excluded from full participation in the public arenas of power. A new generation of black women reformers, including Charlotte Forten Grimké, Hattie Purvis, and Frances Ellen Watkins Harper, knew they needed to take up the sword tirelessly for equal rights for black and white women alike. Indeed, Mary Grew's final words to close the society's last meeting pointed to those battles that still remained: "If we put off our armor here to-day, it is but for a moment's breathing-space, to be resumed for other conflicts. However much we may feel to-day, as we close this meeting and disband our Society, that we should like to depart in peace, our eyes having seen *this* salvation, we are all willing to remain and work elsewhere, as we may be called to work, till we shall hear our Father's summons, 'Come up higher!'"[2]

At that moment, in the first years of Reconstruction, when antebellum abolitionists wondered whether it was time for them to fade into the postbellum night or whether they must steel themselves for a continued struggle for racial and gender equality, we can see the culmination of the forces of nationalism, citizenship, wage labor, and industrial capitalism that had transformed the United States before the Civil War. That bloody war that settled the issue of slavery also ushered in a period of even more aggressive expansionism marked by the rise of large-scale corporations, the conquest of American Indians in the trans-Mississippi West, and the pursuit of foreign markets and missions throughout Asia and Latin America. The unsettled questions of who constituted the nation, and what guaranteed a person's claim to citizenship, became even more acute. African American men had to fight to hold on to the rights guaranteed by the new amendments, while women's suffrage became the central focus of white women's demands to be included as full citizens. As long as both black men and white women were powerless together, white feminists could work alongside black women and black men for universal suffrage. But a year before the Philadelphia Female Anti-Slavery Society disbanded, women suffrage activists divided over whether to support black men's voting rights without a guarantee of women's votes. An abolitionist with no less a pedigree than Elizabeth Cady Stanton conjured the spirit of colonizationists and nativists when she refused to accept the notion of black male citizenship before women's citizenship. Stanton declared it a disgrace that "Patrick and Sambo and Hans and Yung Tung" should legislate for educated women like herself; she was incensed that politicians could "make their wives and mothers the political inferiors of unlettered and unwashed ditch-diggers, bootblacks, butchers, and barbers, fresh from the slave plantations of the South, and the effete civilizations of the Old World." The dream of racial and gender equality vanished amid the political realities of Reconstruction, and native-born reformers again scorned immigrant men for their relatively easy access to male privilege.[3]

The purpose of this study has been to demonstrate the profound impact of gender on the social issues that affected men's and women's lives in the urban North before the Civil War. All Americans in the nineteenth-century city, black and white, men and women, immigrants and native-born, working-class and middle-class, spoke the language of gender in their words and actions. Just as deeply as religion, republicanism, and the economics of market capitalism framed people's understandings of their public and private lives, gender provided men and women with a powerful set of meanings by which to interpret their daily relationships; their personal identities; their ideas about race, politics, citizenship, and nationality; and, most important for this story, the various crises they perceived in their cities. Because gender symbolized what individuals and groups assumed to be natural, it carried the ability to reinforce relationships of inequality and yet also had the potential to offer forceful challenges to those unequal relationships. What it meant to be a man or a woman in that society remained a dynamic and contested process.

This book joins a transformative project already in motion, one that seeks to change the way we think and write about history, so that the invisible might become visible, and the silent and powerless might have their say. For too long, men, and white men in particular, have benefited from a gender system that situated them in positions of naturalized power, and yet, until recently, they have remained largely invisible in general discussions of gender and its history. This study has presented men as gendered beings, and manhood, along with womanhood, as a crucial category of analysis in the study of the history of the United States. Indeed, there is a politics behind the endeavor to treat men as gendered beings. As I frequently tell my students, "We don't need more history exclusively about men." Yet at the same time, I research and write about the categories of masculinity and manhood, and the ways real-life men in the past constituted and employed those categories for their own specific agendas (and encourage my students to do so as well). In this way, our eyes will be opened to the gendering of power and inequality in our own lives, and in our own time.

Abbreviations

Archives and Manuscripts

BAP	Black Abolitionist Papers, Microfilm collection
FHL	Friends Historical Library, Swarthmore College
HSP	Historical Society of Pennsylvania, Philadelphia
LCP	Library Company of Philadelphia
QC	Quaker Collection, Haverford College
PCA	Philadelphia City Archives
PHS	Presbyterian Historical Society, Philadelphia
PPAS	Papers of the Pennsylvania Abolition Society, Historical Society of Pennsylvania

Journals

AHR	*American Historical Review*
AQ	*American Quarterly*
JAH	*Journal of American History*
JATU	*Journal of the American Temperance Union*
JER	*Journal of the Early Republic*
JSH	*Journal of Social History*
PH	*Pennsylvania History*
PMHB	*Pennsylvania Magazine of History and Biography*
WMQ	*William and Mary Quarterly*

Notes

Prologue

1. Lewis Ashhurst is listed without any occupation in the 1833 city directory, but by 1841 he is listed as a merchant on High (Market) Street with a new home on Walnut Street. *DeSilver's Philadelphia Directory and Stranger's Guide, for 1833* (Philadelphia, 1833); *M'Elroy's Philadelphia Directory, for 1841* (Philadelphia, 1841); J. Thomas Scharf and Thompson Westcott, *History of Philadelphia, 1609–1884*, vol. 2 (Philadelphia, 1884), 1348.

2. Lewis R. Ashhurst, Journal, 4 vols., 1834–1874, Feb. 5, 1834, HSP; Mary Ashhurst, Journal, 12 vols., 1834–1887, Feb. 5, 1834, HSP.

3. Mary Ashhurst, Journal, Mar. 4, 7, 1834; Apr. 6, 1834; Jan. 13, 1835.

4. As Caroline Walker Bynum has noted, even when gender symbols have an accepted meaning, those symbols "may be experienced differently by the different genders." Bynum et al., ed., *Gender and Religion: On the Complexity of Symbols* (Boston, 1986), 13. For a similar example, see Susan Juster, *Disorderly Women: Sexual Politics and Evangelicalism in Revolutionary New England* (Ithaca, 1994), chaps. 2, 6. See also Linda K. Kerber, "Separate Spheres, Female Worlds, Woman's Place: The Rhetoric of Women's History," *JAH* 75 (1988): 9–39; Kerber et al., "Beyond Roles, Beyond Spheres: Thinking about Gender in the Early Republic," *WMQ* 46 (1989): 565–85.

5. Clifford S. Griffin, *Their Brothers' Keepers: Moral Stewardship in the United States, 1800–1835* (New Brunswick, 1960); Charles I. Foster, *An Errand of Mercy: The Evangelical United Front, 1790–1837* (Chapel Hill, 1960). Other similar works include John R. Bodo, *The Protestant Clergy and Public Issues, 1812–1848* (Princeton, 1954); Charles C. Cole, Jr., *The Social Ideas of the Northern Evangelists, 1826–1860* (New York, 1954). For alternatives to this perspective, see Timothy L. Smith, *Revivalism and Social Reform in Mid-Nineteenth-Century America* (New York, 1957); Lois W. Banner, "Religious Benevolence as Social Control: A Critique of an Interpretation," *JAH* 60 (1973): 23–41.

6. The two best examples are Paul E. Johnson, *A Shopkeeper's Millennium: Society and Revivals in Rochester, New York, 1815–1837* (New York, 1978); Paul Boyer, *Urban Masses and Moral Order in America, 1820–1920* (Cambridge, Mass., 1978).

7. Nancy F. Cott, *The Bonds of Womanhood: "Woman's Sphere" in New England, 1780–1835*

(New Haven, 1977); Carroll Smith-Rosenberg, *Religion and the Rise of the American City* (Ithaca, 1971); Mary P. Ryan, *Cradle of the Middle Class: The Family in Oneida County, New York, 1790–1865* (New York, 1981), 105–44; Nancy A. Hewitt, *Women's Activism and Social Change: Rochester, New York, 1822–1872* (Ithaca, 1984); Suzanne Lebsock, *The Free Women of Petersburg: Status and Culture in a Southern Town, 1784–1860* (New York, 1984), 195–236; Christine Stansell, *City of Women: Sex and Class in New York, 1789–1860* (New York, 1986); Anne M. Boylan, "Women in Groups: An Analysis of Women's Benevolent Organizations in New York and Boston, 1797–1840," *JAH* 71 (1984): 497–523; Lori D. Ginzberg, *Women and the Work of Benevolence: Morality, Politics, and Class in the Nineteenth-Century United States* (New Haven, 1990); Anne Firor Scott, *Natural Allies: Women's Associations in American History* (Urbana, 1991).

8. Natalie Zemon Davis, "'Women's History' in Transition: The European Case," *Feminist Studies* 3 (1975–76): 90; Gerda Lerner, *The Majority Finds Its Past: Placing Women in History* (New York, 1979), 177–80.

9. Joan W. Scott, *Gender and the Politics of History* (New York, 1988); Denise Riley, *"Am I That Name?" Feminism and the Category of "Women" in History* (Minneapolis, 1988); Judith Butler and Joan W. Scott, eds., *Feminists Theorize the Political* (New York, 1992); Judith Butler, *Gender Trouble: Feminism and the Subversion of Identity* (New York, 1990).

10. Bynum, *Gender and Religion*, 2. For a discussion of the multiple "others" on which manhood has been constructed in America, see E. Anthony Rotundo, *American Manhood: Transformations in Masculinity from the Revolution to the Modern Era* (New York, 1993); Bruce Dorsey, "History of Manhood in America, 1750–1920," *Radical History Review* 64 (1996): 19–30.

11. David R. Roediger, *The Wages of Whiteness: Race and the Making of the American Working Class* (New York, 1991); Gail Bederman, *Manliness & Civilization: A Cultural History of Gender and Race in the United States, 1880–1917* (Chicago, 1995); Louise Michele Newman, *White Women's Rights: The Racial Origins of Feminism in the United States* (New York, 1999).

12. Jürgen Habermas, *The Structural Transformation of the Public Sphere: An Inquiry into a Category of Bourgeois Society*, trans. Thomas Burger (Cambridge, Mass., 1989); Nancy Fraser, *Unruly Practices: Power, Discourse, and Gender in Contemporary Social Theory* (Minneapolis, 1989), 113–43; Nancy Fraser, "Rethinking the Public Sphere: A Contribution to the Critique of Actually Existing Democracy," in *Habermas and the Public Sphere*, ed. Craig Calhoun (Cambridge, Mass., 1992), 109–42; Mary P. Ryan, "Gender and Public Access: Women's Politics in Nineteenth-Century America," in Calhoun, *Habermas and the Public Sphere*, 259–88; Mary P. Ryan, *Women in Public: Between Banners and Ballots, 1825–1880* (Baltimore, 1990), 10–17; Joan B. Landes, *Women and the Public Sphere in the Age of the French Revolution* (Ithaca, 1988); Carol Pateman, *The Disorder of Women* (Cambridge, 1989), 33–57; Lawrence E. Klein, "Gender and the Public/Private Distinction in the Eighteenth Century: Some Questions about Evidence and Analytic Procedure," *Eighteenth-Century Studies* 29 (1995): 97–109; Catherine Hall, "Private Persons versus Public Someones: Class, Gender and Politics in England, 1780–1850," in *Language, Gender and Childhood*, ed. Carol Steedman et al. (London, 1985), 10–33; Dorothy O. Helly and Susan M. Reverby, eds., *Gendered Domains: Rethinking Public and Private in Women's History* (Ithaca, 1992).

13. Joan W. Scott, "Gender: A Useful Category of Analysis," *AHR* 91 (1986): 1074. As Judith Butler has stated, gender is "a construction that regularly conceals its genesis." "Performative Acts and Gender Constitution: An Essay in Phenomenology and Feminist Theory," *Theatre Journal* 40 (1988): 522; see also Victor J. Seidler, *Rediscovering Masculinity: Reason, Language and Sexuality* (London, 1989), 1–13; Riley, *"Am I That Name?,"* 4.

14. Jean Bethke Elshtain, *Public Man, Private Woman: Women in Social and Political Thought* (Princeton, 1981), 4–5; see also Bynum, *Gender and Religion*, 1–19.

15. Ryan, *Cradle of the Middle Class*, 105–44; Lebsock, *Free Women of Petersburg*, 195–236; Boylan, "Women in Groups," 497–523; Anne M. Boylan, "Women and Politics in the Era Before Seneca Falls," *JER* 10 (1990): 363–82; Ginzberg, *Women and the Work of Benevolence*, 36–66; Scott, *Natural Allies*, 11–57.

16. Gary B. Nash, *Red, White, and Black: The Peoples of Early North America*, 4th ed. (Upper Saddle River, N.J., 2000), 153, 177; Sharon V. Salinger, "Colonial Labor in Transition: The Decline of Indentured Servitude in Late Eighteenth-Century Philadelphia," *Labor History* 22 (1981):

165–91; Gary B. Nash and Jean R. Soderlund, *Freedom by Degrees: Emancipation in Pennsylvania and Its Aftermath* (New York, 1991), 16, 74–193; Joanne Pope Melish, *Disowning Slavery: Gradual Emancipation and "Race" in New England, 1780–1860* (Ithaca, 1998).

17. Roediger, *Wages of Whiteness*, 43–92; on northern free black communites, see Gary B. Nash, *Forging Freedom: The Formation of Philadelphia's Black Community, 1720–1840* (Cambridge, Mass., 1988); Shane White, *Somewhat More Independent: The End of Slavery in New York City, 1770–1810* (Athens, Ga., 1991); James Oliver Horton and Lois E. Horton, *In Hope of Liberty: Culture, Community, and Protest among Northern Free Blacks, 1700–1860* (New York, 1997).

18. Paul E. Johnson, "The Market Revolution," in *The Encyclopedia of American Social History*, ed. Mary Kupiec Cayton et al., vol. 1 (New York, 1993), 545–60; Charles Sellers, *The Market Revolution: Jacksonian America, 1815–1846* (New York, 1991), 3–33.

19. Stuart M. Blumin, *The Emergence of the Middle Class: Social Experience in the American City, 1760–1900* (New York, 1989); Leonore Davidoff and Catherine Hall, *Family Fortunes: Men and Women of the English Middle Class, 1780–1850* (London, 1987); Jonathan A. Glickstein, "The World's 'Dirty Work' and the Wages That 'Sweeten' It: Labor's 'Extrinsic Rewards' in Antebellum Society," in *Moral Problems in American Life: New Perspectives on Cultural History*, ed. Karen Halttunen and Lewis Perry (Ithaca, 1998), 59–79.

20. On nationalism in the early republic and antebellum eras, see David Waldstreicher, *In the Midst of Perpetual Fetes: The Making of American Nationalism, 1776–1820* (Chapel Hill, 1997); Reginald Horsman, *Race and Manifest Destiny: The Origins of American Racial Anglo-Saxonism* (Cambridge, Mass., 1981); Alexander Saxton, *The Rise and Fall of the White Republic: Class Politics and Mass Culture in Nineteenth-Century America* (London, 1990); see also Etienne Balibar, "Racism and Nationalism," in *Race, Nation, Class: Ambiguous Identities*, ed. Etienne Balibar and Immanuel Wallerstein (London, 1991), 37–67.

21. Catharine E. Beecher, *A Treatise on Domestic Economy, for the Use of Young Ladies at Home and at School* (Boston, 1841; reprint, New York, 1970), 1–14. See also Amy Kaplan, "Manifest Domesticity," *American Literature* 70 (1998): 581–606.

22. It is important to recognize here that the term "problem" is not without difficulties. I use it because a significant number of antebellum reformers considered these social developments as problems that needed reforming. More accurately, each of these is a response by Northerners to significant social changes.

23. Ralph Waldo Emerson, *Essays and Lectures* (New York, 1983), 591.

1. Gender and Reformers in the New Republic

1. Female Society for the Relief of the Distressed [hereafter FS], Minutes, vol. 1, 1795–98, Dec. 7, 1795, QC (italics in original).

2. Keith Melder, "Ladies Bountiful: Organized Women's Benevolence in Early 19th-Century America," *New York History* 48 (1967): 231–54; Anne M. Boylan, "Women in Groups: An Analysis of Women's Benevolent Organizations in New York and Boston, 1797–1840," *JAH* 71 (1984): 497–523; Suzanne Lebsock, *The Free Women of Petersburg: Status and Culture in a Southern Town, 1784–1860* (New York, 1984); Lori D. Ginzberg, *Women and the Work of Benevolence: Morality, Politics, and Class in the Nineteenth-Century United States* (New Haven, 1990); Anne Firor Scott, *Natural Allies: Women's Associations in American History* (Urbana, 1991).

3. Isabella Graham noted that the first female society she founded in New York City, the Society for the Relief of Poor Widows (1797), also encountered immediate opposition from men. Isabella Graham, "Address to the Society for the Relief of Poor Widows with Small Children, in April, 1806," in *The Power of Faith, Exemplified in the Life and Writings of the Late Mrs. Isabella Graham, of New-York* (New York, 1816), 404–5.

4. This analysis was influenced by Jürgen Habermas, *The Structural Transformation of the Public Sphere: An Inquiry into a Category of Bourgeois Society*, trans. Thomas Burger (Cambridge, Mass., 1989); Dena Goodman, "Public Sphere and Private Life: Toward a Synthesis of Current Historiographical Approaches to the Old Regime," *History and Theory* 31 (1992): 1–20; Jan Lewis, "Politics and the Ambivalence of the Private Sphere: Women in Early Washington, D.C.," in *A Repub-*

lic for the Ages: The United States Capitol and the Political Culture of the Early Republic, ed. Donald R. Kennon (Charlottesville, Va., 1999), 122–51.

5. Thomas Paine, "The American Crisis III (1777)," in *The Complete Writings of Thomas Paine*, ed. Philip S. Foner, vol. 1 (New York, 1945), 79.

6. [Royall Tyler], *The Contrast: A Comedy in Five Acts* (Philadelphia, 1790; reprint, New York, 1970).

7. Analytical books on masculinity and the gendering of men's lives during the revolutionary era are still rare. My analysis draws on Toby L. Ditz, "Shipwrecked; or, Masculinity Imperiled: Mercantile Representations of Failure and the Gendered Self in Eighteenth-Century Philadelphia," *JAH* 81 (1994): 51–80; Carroll Smith-Rosenberg, "Dis-Covering the Subject of the 'Great Constitutional Discussion,' 1786–1789," *JAH* 79 (1992): 841–73; Ruth H. Bloch, "The Gendered Meanings of Virtue in Revolutionary America," *Signs* 13 (1987): 37–58.

8. Tyler, *Contrast*, 112.

9. J. Hector St. John de Crèvecoeur, *Letters from an American Farmer* (1782; reprint, New York, 1997), 42–44.

10. On the English gentry and the social structure of the Anglo-American world, see Peter Laslett, *The World We Have Lost*, 2nd ed. (New York, 1971), 23–54; Keith Wrightson, *English Society, 1580–1680* (New Brunswick, N.J., 1982), 17–118; David Hancock, *Citizens of the World: London Merchants and the Integration of the British Atlantic Community, 1735–1785* (Cambridge, 1995); Gordon S. Wood, "Interests and Disinterestness in the Making of the Constitution," in *Beyond Confederation: Origins of the Constitution and American National Identity*, ed. Richard Beeman et al. (Chapel Hill, 1987), 85–93.

11. J. G. A. Pocock, *The Machiavellian Moment: Florentine Political Thought and the Atlantic Republican Tradition* (Princeton, 1975); Hanna F. Pitkin, *Fortune Is a Woman* (Berkeley, 1984).

12. Frederick B. Tolles, *Meeting House and Counting House: The Quaker Merchants of Colonial Philadelphia, 1682–1763* (Chapel Hill, 1948), 112–23; Thomas M. Doerflinger, *A Vigorous Spirit of Enterprise: Merchants and Economic Development in Revolutionary Philadelphia* (Chapel Hill, 1986), 40–57.

13. Hancock, *Citizens of the World*, 280; Tyler, *Contrast*, 46–47; Garry Wills, *Cincinnatus: George Washington and the Enlightenment* (Garden City, N.Y., 1984); David S. Shields, *Civil Tongues & Polite Letters in British America* (Chapel Hill, 1997), 37–40, 141–45. On the performative nature of gender, see Judith Butler, *Gender Trouble: Feminism and the Subversion of Identity* (New York, 1990), 24–25, 128–41; on the performative nature of gentility, see Richard L. Bushman, *The Refinement of America: Persons, Houses, Cities* (New York, 1992), xiv, 52–58.

14. Ellis Paxson Oberholtzer, *Robert Morris, Patriot and Financier* (New York, 1903); Wood, "Interests and Disinterestness," 98–99.

15. Ditz, "Shipwrecked," 51–80.

16. Benjamin Franklin, *The Autobiography of Benjamin Franklin*, ed. L. Jesse Lemisch (New York, 1961), 78–79. See also Christopher Looby, "'The Affairs of the Revolution Occasion'd the Interruption': Writing, Revolution, Deferral, and Conciliation in Franklin's Autobiography," *AQ* 38 (1986): 72–96; Michael Warner, *The Letters of the Republic: Publication and the Public Sphere in Eighteenth-Century America* (Cambridge, Mass., 1990), 73–96.

17. Leonard W. Labaree et al., eds., *The Papers of Benjamin Franklin*, vol. 7 (New Haven, 1959–2000), 326–55; Franklin, *Autobiography*, 131; Michael Zuckerman, "The Selling of the Self: From Franklin to Barnum," in *Benjamin Franklin, Jonathan Edwards, and the Representation of American Culture*, ed. Barbara B. Oberg and Harry S. Stout (New York, 1993), 157.

18. Ruth H. Bloch, "Women, Love, and Virtue in the Thought of Edwards and Franklin," in Oberg and Stout, *Franklin, Edwards*, 145; Franklin, *Autobiography*, 92–93; Gary E. Baker, "He That Would Thrive Must Ask His Wife: Franklin's Anthony Afterwit Letter," *PMHB* 109 (1985): 27–41.

19. Jay Fliegelman, *Prodigals and Pilgrims: The American Revolution against Patriarchal Authority, 1750–1800* (Cambridge, 1982); Fliegelman, *Declaring Independence: Jefferson, Natural Language & the Culture of Performance* (Stanford, 1993); Gordon S. Wood, *The Radicalism of the American Revolution* (New York, 1992), 14, 23–24, 33; Edwin G. Burrows and Michael Wallace, "The American Revolution: The Ideology and Psychology of National Liberation," *Perspectives in American History* 6 (1972): 190–214; Ditz, "Shipwrecked," 57–58, 70–71.

20. Susanna Parrish Wharton, ed., *The Parrish Family* (Philadelphia, 1925), 44, 51; Samuel Jackson, *Memoir of Isaac Parrish, M.D.* (Philadelphia, 1853), 3; George B. Wood, *A Memoir of the Life and Character of the Late Joseph Parrish, M.D.* (Philadelphia, 1840), 7–8.

21. Benjamin Rush observed in 1769 that few urban artisans were employed "the whole year round." Quoted in Charles S. Olton, *Artisans for Independence: Philadelphia Mechanics and the American Revolution* (Syracuse, 1975), 31. See also Daniel Vickers, "Competency and Competition: Economic Culture in Early America," *WMQ* 47 (1990): 3–29; Billy G. Smith, "Poverty and Economic Marginality in Eighteenth-Century America," *Proceedings of the American Philosophical Society* 132 (1988): 85–118; Billy G. Smith, *The "Lower Sort": Philadelphia's Laboring People, 1750–1800* (Ithaca, 1990), 92–125.

22. *Pennsylvania Gazette*, 8 Aug. 1787; see also 9 June 1785; 2 Sept. 1795; 9 Aug. 1786; 18 Dec. 1793; Steven Rosswurm, *Arms, Country, and Class: The Philadelphia Militia and "Lower Sort" during the American Revolution* (New Brunswick, N.J., 1987), 34–38; Michael Meranze, *Laboratories of Virtue: Punishment, Revolution, and Authority in Philadelphia, 1760–1835* (Chapel Hill, 1996), 98–107; G. S. Rowe, "Black Offenders, Criminal Courts, and Philadelphia Society in the Late Eighteenth Century," *JSH* 22 (1989): 685–712; Shane White, *Somewhat More Independent: The End of Slavery in New York City, 1770–1810* (Athens, Ga., 1991), 185–206.

23. Richard Alan Ryerson, *The Revolution Is Now Begun: The Radical Committees of Philadelphia, 1765–1776* (Philadelphia, 1978); Eric Foner, *Tom Paine and Revolutionary America* (New York, 1976), 56–66; Gary B. Nash, *The Urban Crucible: Social Change, Political Consciousness, and the Origins of the American Revolution* (Cambridge, Mass., 1979), 374–82.

24. Sharon V. Salinger, *"To Serve Well and Faithfully": Labor and Indentured Servants in Pennsylvania, 1682–1800* (Cambridge, 1987), 178–80.

25. Tyler, *Contrast*, 54.

26. For similar frequent responses in the early-nineteenth-century North, see David R. Roediger, *The Wages of Whiteness: Race and the Making of the American Working Class* (New York, 1991), 47; James Forten, *Letters from a Man of Colour on a Late Bill Before the Senate of Pennsylvania* (Philadelphia, 1813), 3–8; Gary B. Nash, *Forging Freedom: The Formation of Philadelphia's Black Community, 1720–1840* (Cambridge, Mass., 1988), 177; Susan G. Davis, *Parades and Power: Street Theatre in Nineteenth-Century Philadelphia* (Philadelphia, 1986), 38–48. American Indians also served as a negative counterpoint to manliness; see Tyler's use of the civilized and savage imagery in Tyler, *Contrast*, 33, 71; Smith-Rosenberg, "Dis-Covering the Subject," 865–69.

27. Smith-Rosenberg, "Dis-Covering the Subject," 850–61; Jan Lewis, "The Republican Wife: Virtue and Seduction in the Early Republic," *WMQ* 44 (1987): 694–702. The words "citizeness" or "citoyenne" never appear in the *Pennsylvania Gazette* from 1784 to 1800 (based on a search of the Accessible Archives CD-ROM of the *Pennsylvania Gazette*). On the meaning of women and citizenship in the new nation, see Linda K. Kerber, "The Paradox of Women's Citizenship in the Early Republic: The Case of *Martin vs. Massachusetts*, 1805," *AHR* 97 (1992): 349–78.

28. Tyler, *Contrast*, 42, 88; Ditz, "Shipwrecked," 54, 58.

29. G. J. Barker-Benfield, *The Culture of Sensibility: Sex and Society in Eighteenth-Century Britain* (Chicago, 1992), chaps. 2–5; Paul Langford, *A Polite and Commercial People: England, 1727–1783* (Oxford, 1989), 59–121, 461–518; John Mullan, *Sentiment and Sociability: The Language of Feeling in the Eighteenth Century* (Oxford, 1988), 1–56; Ruth H. Bloch, "Religion, Literary Sentimentalism, and Popular Revolutionary Ideology," in *Religion in a Revolutionary Age*, ed. Ronald Hoffman and Peter J. Albert (Charlottesville, Va., 1994), 308–30.

30. Norman S. Fiering, "Irresistible Compassion: An Aspect of Eighteenth-Century Sympathy and Humanitarianism," *Journal of the History of Ideas* 37 (1976): 195–218.

31. Adam Smith, quoted in Barker-Benfield, *Culture of Sensibility*, 139. For associations of men with rationality and women with passions, see Natalie Zemon Davis, *Society and Culture in Early Modern France* (Stanford, 1975), 124–51; Linda K. Kerber, *Women of the Republic: Intellect and Ideology in Revolutionary America* (Chapel Hill, 1980), 198–99; Kenneth A. Lockridge, *On the Sources of Patriarchal Rage: The Commonplace Books of William Byrd and Thomas Jefferson and the Gendering of Power in the Eighteenth Century* (New York, 1992), 29–45. This analysis follows Gail Bederman's contention that an historian should expect a discourse to be "multiple, inconsistent,

and contradictory." *Manliness & Civilization: A Cultural History of Gender and Race in the United States, 1880–1917* (Chicago, 1995), 24.

32. Tench Coxe to Benjamin Yard, Dec. 28, 1786; James Pemberton to William Courtney, Feb. 4, 1790, Pennsylvania Abolition Society, Loose Correspondence, PPAS, reel 15. Description of Perot is quoted in Robert C. Moon, *The Morris Family of Philadelphia*, vol. 2 (Philadelphia, 1898), 675–76. See also Dr. Richard Bond's obituary describing him as a "benevolent" man who "felt, with nice Sensibility, all the gentlest Emotions of the human heart." *Pennsylvania Gazette*, 23 Dec. 1772. I thank Sarah Knott for this reference.

33. Benjamin Rush, *An Enquiry into the Effects of Public Punishments Upon Criminals, and Upon Society* (Philadelphia, 1787), 7; Philadelphia Society for Alleviating the Miseries of Public Prisons, Minutes, 1787–88, HSP; Michael Meranze, "The Penitential Ideal in Late Eighteenth-Century Philadelphia," *PMHB* 108 (1984): 435–40; Meranze, *Laboratories of Virtue*, 120–27.

34. *Constitution of the Philadelphia Society for Alleviating the Miseries of Public Prisons* (Philadelphia, 1806), 3–4. Meranze, "Penitential Ideal," 445–50; David J. Rothman, *The Discovery of the Asylum: Social Order and Disorder in the New Republic* (Boston, 1971), 79–108; Negley K. Teeters, *They Were in Prison: A History of the Pennsylvania Prison Society, 1787–1937* (Philadelphia, 1937), 177–217.

35. Shields, *Civil Tongues & Polite Letters*; Kathleen M. Brown, *Good Wives, Nasty Wenches, and Anxious Patriarchs: Gender, Race, and Power in Colonial Virginia* (Chapel Hill, 1996); Scott, *Natural Allies*.

36. Society for the Relief of Negroes Unlawfully Held in Bondage, Minute Book, Apr. 14, 1775; May 29, 1775; Aug. 23, 1775; PPAS, reel 1. On taverns, see chapter 3.

37. Ibid., Apr. 14, 1775; May 29, 1775; May 31, 1784. See also Acting Committee, Minute Book, vol. 1, 1784–88, Apr. 6, 1784; May 20, 1784; PPAS, reel 4; Gary B. Nash and Jean R. Soderlund, *Freedom By Degrees: Emancipation in Pennsylvania and Its Aftermath* (New York, 1991), 80.

38. The society in 1775 was composed primarily of Quakers (70 percent), but the influx of new members in the 1780s reduced Quakers to a bare majority; Nash and Soderlund, *Freedom By Degrees*, 115–19, 130–31.

39. Ibid., 124–36.

40. White, *Somewhat More Independent*, 153; Nash, *Forging Freedom*, 38, 72, 137. Other excellent studies of northern free blacks include Leon F. Litwack, *North of Slavery: The Negro in the Free States, 1790–1860* (Chicago, 1961); Julie Winch, *Philadelphia's Black Elite: Activism, Accommodation, and the Struggle for Autonomy, 1787–1848* (Philadelphia, 1988); James Oliver Horton and Lois E. Horton, *In Hope of Liberty: Culture, Community, and Protest among Northern Free Blacks, 1700–1860* (New York, 1997).

41. Dorothy Sterling, ed., *Speak Out in Thunder Tones: Letters and Other Writings by Black Northerners, 1787–1865* (Garden City, N.Y., 1973), 53–54; William Douglass, *Annals of the First African Church in the United States of America, Now Styled the African Episcopal Church of St. Thomas* (Philadelphia, 1862), 20, 32; Pennsylvania Abolition Society, Treasurer's Accounts, 1792–1800, PPAS, reel 16; FS, Treasurer's Books, vol. 1, 1795–1810, QC.

42. Nash, *Forging Freedom*, 70; 144–71.

43. Ibid., 188, 210–11; Douglass, *Annals*, 15–17. For the importance of mutual benefit societies in the early republic, see Conrad Edick Wright, *The Transformation of Charity in Postrevolutionary New England* (Boston, 1992).

44. Nash, *Forging Freedom*, 202–11, 267–73; Douglass, *Annals*, 110–11; John K. Alexander, *Render Them Submissive: Responses to Poverty in Philadelphia, 1760–1800* (Amherst, 1980), 146–48.

45. Although both black men and women created mutual benefit societies, in the eighteenth century such public service, in the free black community, too, often carried associations with masculine civic virtue; see the section "'Tis Virtue's Work."

46. Douglass, *Annals*, 31–32, 25.

47. Linda K. Kerber originally coined the phrase in "The Republican Mother: Women and the Enlightenment—An American Perspective," *AQ* 28 (1976): 187–205; Kerber, *Women of the Republic*, 200, 228–31, 269–88. Historians have relied on this paradigm so frequently, it would be impossible to cite all instances. Jan Lewis and Margaret Nash have shown how republican

motherhood was not the principal discourse on womanhood in this era in Lewis, "Republican Wife"; Margaret A. Nash, "Rethinking Republican Motherhood: Benjamin Rush and the Young Ladies' Academy of Philadelphia," *JER* 17 (1997): 171–91.

48. Dorothy Sterling, ed., *We Are Your Sisters: Black Women in the Nineteenth Century* (New York, 1984), 105; Wharton, *Parrish Family*, 45–47.

49. Jean R. Soderlund, "Women's Authority in Pennsylvania and New Jersey Quaker Meetings, 1680–1760," *WMQ* 44 (1987): 722–49. Susan Juster, *Disorderly Women: Sexual Politics and Evangelicalism in Revolutionary New England* (Ithaca, 1994).

50. Jürgen Habermas, "The Public Sphere: An Encyclopedia Article (1964)," *New German Critique* 3 (1974): 49. See also Habermas, *Structural Transformation of the Public Sphere*.

51. Craig Calhoun, ed., *Habermas and the Public Sphere* (Cambridge, Mass., 1992), 1. See also Habermas, *Structural Transformation of the Public Sphere*, 42–43.

52. Nancy Fraser, *Unruly Practices: Power, Discourse, and Gender in Contemporary Social Theory* (Minneapolis, 1989), 113–43; Fraser, "Rethinking the Public Sphere: A Contribution to the Critique of Actually Existing Democracy," in Calhoun, *Habermas and the Public Sphere*, 109–42; Mary P. Ryan, "Gender and Public Access: Women's Politics in Nineteenth-Century America," in Calhoun, *Habermas and the Public Sphere*, 259–88; Mary P. Ryan, *Women in Public: Between Banners and Ballots, 1825–1880* (Baltimore, 1990), 10–17. See also Joan B. Landes, *Women and the Public Sphere in the Age of the French Revolution* (Ithaca, 1988).

53. Carol Pateman, *The Disorder of Women* (Cambridge, 1989), 33–57; Lawrence E. Klein, "Gender and the Public/Private Distinction in the Eighteenth Century: Some Questions about Evidence and Analytic Procedure," *Eighteenth-Century Studies* 29 (1995): 97–109; Catherine Hall, "Private Persons versus Public Someones: Class, Gender and Politics in England, 1780–1850," in *Language, Gender and Childhood*, ed. Carol Steedman et al. (London, 1985), 10–33; Dorothy O. Helly and Susan M. Reverby, eds., *Gendered Domains: Rethinking Public and Private in Women's History* (Ithaca, 1992).

54. Jemima Wilkinson is an example of a religious woman and prophet who assumed a masculine persona in the early republic. When Wilkinson preached in Philadelphia in 1784, Jacob Hiltzheimer commented, "She looks more like a man than a woman." Jacob Cox Parsons, ed., *Extracts from the Diary of Jacob Hiltzheimer, of Philadelphia, 1765–1798* (Philadelphia, 1893), 66; Susan Juster, "To Slay the Beast: Visionary Women in the Early Republic," in *A Mighty Baptism: Race, Gender, and the Creation of American Protestantism*, ed. Susan Juster and Lisa MacFarlane (Ithaca, 1996), 19–37.

55. Kerber, *Women of the Republic*, 35–67; Mary Beth Norton, *Liberty's Daughters: The Revolutionary Experience of American Women, 1750–1800* (Boston, 1980), 195–227; Alfred F. Young, "The Women of Boston: 'Persons of Consequence' in the Making of the American Revolution, 1765–76," in *Women and Politics in the Age of the Democratic Revolution*, ed. Harriet B. Applewhite and Darline G. Levy (Ann Arbor, 1990), 194–209; Barbara Clark Smith, "Food Rioters and the American Revolution," *WMQ* 51 (1994): 3–38. Boston loyalist Peter Oliver's contempt for women's role in the rebellion attests to their significance; Douglass Adair and John A. Schutz, eds., *Peter Oliver's Origin & Progress of the American Revolution: A Tory View* (San Marino, Calif., 1961), 61–65, 73, 97.

56. Young, "Women of Boston," 195–97; Milton Halsey Thomas, ed., *Elias Boudinot's Journey to Boston in 1809* (Princeton, 1955), x; Laurel Thatcher Ulrich, "'Daughters of Liberty': Religious Women in Revolutionary New England," in *Women in the Age of the American Revolution*, ed. Ronald Hoffman and Peter J. Albert (Charlottesville, Va., 1989), 211–43; *Pennsylvania Gazette*, 1, 29 Dec. 1773; 16 Aug. 1775; William B. Reed, ed., *Life and Correspondence of Joseph Reed*, vol. 1 (Philadelphia, 1847), 51–56; Benjamin Woods Labaree, *The Boston Tea Party* (New York, 1964), 158–59. Patriot women also organized spinning meetings to manufacture at home the important products they chose to boycott; but, as Jeanne Boydston has argued, this revolutionary-era preoccupation with women's production marked neither a substantive expansion nor a long-lasting celebration of women's productive labor; Jeanne Boydston, *Home and Work: Housework, Wages, and the Ideology of Labor in the Early Republic* (New York, 1990), 30–35.

57. "Patriotic Poesy: The Female Patriots, Address'd to the Daughters of Liberty in America, 1768," *WMQ* 34 (1977): 307–308. See also Hannah Griffits, "Beware the Ides of March," Feb.

28, 1775, Hannah Griffits Papers, LCP; *Pennsylvania Gazette*, 16 Oct. 1775, cited in Kerber, *Women of the Republic*, 39; Benjamin Rush to John Adams, July 13, 1780, in *The Letters of Benjamin Rush*, ed. L. H. Butterfield, vol. 1 (Princeton, 1951), 253.

58. Stephanie McCurry, "The Two Faces of Republicanism: Gender and Proslavery Politics in Antebellum South Carolina," *JAH* 78 (1992): 1245–64; Edmund S. Morgan, *American Slavery, American Freedom* (New York, 1975); Juster, "To Slay the Beast," 23–24; Juster, *Disorderly Women*, chaps. 4–5.

59. *The Female Patriot, No. I. Addressed to the Tea-Drinking Ladies of New-York* ([New York, 1770]), Broadside, LCP, reprinted in *A Rising People: The Founding of the United States, 1765 to 1789* (Philadelphia, 1976), 18. See also Richard Walsh, ed., *The Writings of Christopher Gadsden, 1746–1805* (Columbia, S.C., 1966), 83–84.

60. *Columbian Centinel* (Boston), 16 Mar. 1793, cited in Kerber, "Paradox of Women's Citizenship," 349; Benjamin Rush, "Thoughts upon Female Education (1787)," in *Essays on Education in the Early Republic*, ed. Frederick Rudolph (Cambridge, Mass., 1965), 25–40; *Sketches of the History, Genius, . . . of the Fair Sex in All Parts of the World* (Philadelphia, [1796]); Juster, *Disorderly Women;* Linda K. Kerber, "'I Have Don . . . much to Carrey on the Warr': Women and the Shaping of Republican Ideology after the American Revolution," in Applewhite and Levy, *Women and Politics*, 227–57; Christine Stansell, *City of Women: Sex and Class in New York, 1789–1860* (New York, 1986), 20–30.

61. Benjamin Rush to John Witherspoon, Apr. 30, 1768, in Butterfield, *Letters of Benjamin Rush*, vol. 1, 58; Thomas Branagan, *The Charms of Benevolence, . . . ,* 5th ed. (Philadelphia, 1814), 3.

62. "To the Benevolent Band," Feb. 7, 1797, reprinted in "Sketch of Friends: The Original 'House of Industry' and Its Founder," from *Friend's Intelligencer* [date unknown], in Quaker Scrapbook, vol. 2, 247, HSP.

63. Graham, *Power of Faith*, 406.

64. [Thomas Branagan,] *The Beauties of Philanthropy . . . ,* 2nd ed. (Philadelphia, 1808), 59.

65. Jacob J. Janeway, *The Blessedness of the Charitable* (Philadelphia, 1812), 25. Janeway's last phrase, "the luxury of doing good," is suggestive in numerous ways, perhaps implying that "doing good" had become a discretionary leisure activity for women of a certain class. I thank Leigh Schmidt for this interpretation.

66. William White, *Sermon on the Drawing of Moses Out of the Waters* (Philadelphia, 1815), 24. See also Ashbel Green, *The Christian Duty of Christian Women* (Princeton, 1825), 28; Branagan, *Beauties of Philanthropy*, 29–30; Branagan, *Charms of Benevolence*, 197–98.

67. *The Constitution of the Providence Female Society, for the Relief of Indigent Women and Children* (Providence, R.I., 1801), 3.

68. Female Association for the Relief of Women and Children in Reduced Circumstances [hereafter FA], FA Records, QC; *The Constitution of the Female Association of Philadelphia for the Relief of Women and Children in Reduced Circumstances* (Philadelphia, 1801, 1803).

69. Jacob Brodhead, *A Plea for the Poor* (Philadelphia, 1815), 37. See also Ezra Stiles Ely, "To the Ladies of the Presbyterian Congregation at —— ." in *Religious Remembrancer*, 1 Apr. 1820; Philadelphia Auxiliary Bible Society, Minutes, Jan. 1, 1820, Jan. 1, 1823, PHS; William M. Engles, *Appeal* [On Behalf of the Philadelphia Auxiliary Bible Society] (n.p., [1822]), 9; *The Seventh Report of the Female Bible Society of Philadelphia* (Philadelphia, 1821), 16–17; Ginzberg, *Women and the Work of Benevolence*, 42.

70. "History of the Female Association," typescript history, FA Records, QC; John R. C. Smith to Miss [Rebecca] Gratz, Aug. 1, 1807; Female Association to James Ogilvie, Nov. 15, 1808, FA Correspondence, QC; Anne Farnam, "A Society of Societies: Associations and Voluntarism in Early Nineteenth-Century Salem," *Essex Institute Historical Collections* 113 (1977): 189; Boydston, *Home and Work*, 47–55.

71. Neil McKendrick et al., *The Birth of a Consumer Society: The Commericalization of Eighteenth-Century England* (Bloomington, Ind., 1982); T. H. Breen, "'Baubles of Britain': The American and Consumer Revolutions of the Eighteenth Century," *Past and Present* 119 (1988): 73–104; Lorna Weatherill, *Consumer Behaviour and Material Culture in Britain, 1660–1760* (London, 1988); John Brewer and Roy Porter, eds., *Consumption and the World of Goods* (London, 1993);

Cary Carson, et al., eds., *Of Consuming Interests: The Style of Life in the Eighteenth Century* (Charlottesville, Va., 1994); Carole Shammas, *The Pre-industrial Consumer in England and America* (Oxford, 1990); Bushman, *Refinement of America.*

72. Boydston, *Home and Work,* 83–84, 102–3, 124. See also Weatherill, *Consumer Behaviour,* 138; Barker-Benfield, *Culture of Sensibility,* 173–87; David Jaffee, "Peddlers of Progress and the Transformation of the Rural North, 1760–1860," *JAH* 78 (1991): 511–35; Patricia Cleary, "'She Will Be in the Shop': Women's Sphere of Trade in Eighteenth-Century Philadelphia and New York," *PMHB* 119 (1995): 188–89; Elizabeth Kowaleski-Wallace, *Consuming Subjects: Women, Shopping, and Business in the Eighteenth Century* (New York, 1997), 73–98. Carole Shammas has argued, based on a study of wills, that the revolutionary era produced no great improvement in women's control of wealth or capital; Carole Shammas, "Early American Women and Control over Capital," in Hoffman and Albert, *Women in the Age of the American Revolution,* 134–54.

73. Green, *Christian Duty of Christian Women,* 11–12.

74. Leonore Davidoff and Catherine Hall, *Family Fortunes: Men and Women of the English Middle Class, 1780–1850* (Chicago, 1987); Stuart M. Blumin, *The Emergence of the Middle Class: Social Experience in the American City, 1760–1900* (Cambridge, 1989), 66–107, 138–91.

75. Rosswurm, *Arms, Country, and Class,* 37–39; Nash, *Forging Freedom,* 219–22; White, *Somewhat More Independent,* 185–206; Shane White, "'It was a Proud Day': African Americans, Festivals, and Parades in the North, 1741–1834," *JAH* 81 (1994): 13–50; Shane White and Graham White, *Stylin': African American Expressive Culture from Its Beginnings to the Zoot Suit* (Ithaca, 1998).

76. Joan R. Gundersen, "Independence, Citizenship, and the American Revolution," *Signs* 13 (1987): 59–77; Elaine F. Crane, "Dependence in the Era of Independence: The Role of Women in a Republican Society," in *The American Revolution: Its Character and Limits,* ed. Jack P. Greene (New York, 1987), 253–75.

77. Jeanne Boydston, "The Woman Who Wasn't There: Women's Market Labor and the Transition to Capitalism in the United States," *JER* 16 (1996): 183–206, quotation on p. 192; Claudia Goldin, "The Economic Status of Women in the Early Republic: Quantitative Evidence," *Journal of Interdisciplinary History* 16 (1986): 385–91; Lisa Wilson Waciega, "A 'Man of Business': The Widow of Means in Southeastern Pennsylvania, 1750–1850," *WMQ* 44 (1987): 40–64; Susan Branson, "Women and the Family Economy in the Early Republic: The Case of Elizabeth Meredith," *JER* 16 (1996): 47–71; Cleary, "'She Will Be in the Shop,'" 181–202.

78. Elaine Forman Crane, ed., *The Diary of Elizabeth Drinker,* vol. 2,(Boston, 1991), 795; Lee Virginia Chambers-Schiller, *Liberty, A Better Husband: Single Women in America: The Generations of 1780–1840* (New Haven, 1984), 27; Karin A. Wulf, "'My Dear Liberty': Quaker Spinsterhood and Female Autonomy in Eighteenth-Century Pennsylvania," in *Women and Freedom in Early America,* ed. Larry D. Eldridge (New York, 1997), 83–108; Nancy F. Cott, "Divorce and the Changing Status of Women in Eighteenth-Century Massachusetts," *WMQ* 33 (1976): 586–614; Judith Apter Klinghoffer and Lois Elkis, "'The Petticoat Electors': Women's Suffrage in New Jersey, 1776–1807," *JER* 12 (1992): 159–93; Susan V. Bradford to Samuel Bayard, Feb. 4, 1818, in *The Life, Public Services, Addresses and Letters of Elias Boudinot,* ed. J. J. Boudinot, vol. 2 (Boston, 1896), 171. For a fascinating conflation of the "unlimited liberty" exercised by young women in Philadelphia and illicit sexuality, including "unnatural pleasures with persons of their own sex," see Kenneth Roberts and Anna M. Roberts, eds., *Moreau de St. Méry's American Journey [1793–1798]* (Garden City, N.Y., 1947), 285–86.

79. FS, Minutes, Nov. 16, 1795; James Vanuxem to Mrs. Stocker, Jan. 14, 1814, FA Correspondence. See also Robert Ritchie to the President and Directors of the Female Association, Jan. 9, 1813; James Vanuxem to Mrs. Stocker, Jan. 17, 1814; Feb. 12, 1814; Jan. 9, 1815; James Vanuxem to Mrs. Rush, Jan. 13, 1815; Feb. 3, 1815, FA Correspondence, QC; FS, Minutes, vol. 2, 1798–1813, Dec. 29, 1800, QC; FS, Treasurer Books, vol. 1, 1795–1810, QC; *Pennsylvania Gazette,* 27 Nov. 1797. The earliest women's organizations in New York also received city and state government funds; Raymond A. Mohl, *Poverty in New York, 1783–1825* (New York, 1971), 148–49, 151.

80. Lebsock, *Free Women of Petersburg,* 195–236; Ginzberg, *Women and the Work of Benevolence,* 36–66; Anne M. Boylan, "Women and Politics in the Era Before Seneca Falls," *JER* 10 (1990): 363–82; Boylan, "Timid Girls, Venerable Widows and Dignified Matrons: Life Cycle Patterns

Among Organized Women in New York and Boston, 1797–1840," *AQ* 38 (1986): 782–83. On married women's legal rights, see Norma Basch, *In the Eyes of the Law: Women, Marriage, and Property in Nineteenth-Century New York* (Ithaca, 1982).

81. William Cobbett [William Playfair], *The History of Jacobinism, Its Crimes, Cruelties and Perfidies . . .* (Philadelphia, 1796), 25, quoted in Susan Branson, "Politics and Gender: The Political Consciousness of Philadelphia Women in the 1790s," (Ph.D. diss., Northern Illinois University, 1992), 37–39, 55, 98; Mary Wollstonecraft, *A Vindication of the Rights of Woman* (1792; reprint, New York, 1992), 324, 327; Simon P. Newman, *Parades and the Politics of the Street: Festive Culture in the Early American Republic* (Philadelphia, 1997), 47–49, 66–70, 87–107; David Waldstreicher, *In the Midst of Perpetual Fetes: The Making of American Nationalism, 1776–1820* (Chapel Hill, 1997), 169–72; Rosemarie Zagarri, "Gender and the First Party System," in *Federalists Reconsidered,* ed. Doron Ben-Atar and Barbara B. Oberg (Charlottesville, Va., 1998), 118–34; Zagarri, "Morals, Manners, and the Republican Mother," *AQ* 44 (1992): 192–215.

82. Bloch, "Gendered Meanings of Virtue"; Ian Watt, *The Rise of the Novel: Studies in Defoe, Richardson and Fielding* (Berkeley, 1957); Barker-Benfield, *Culture of Sensibility.*

83. This transition from virtue to influence is discussed further in chap. 2.

84. Ginzberg, *Women and the Work of Benevolence,* 36–66; Boylan, "Women and Politics," 372.

85. Margaret Haviland's social analysis of Quaker women societies supplements my own data. Margaret Morris Haviland, "In the World, But Not of the World: The Humanitarian Activities of Philadelphia Quakers, 1790–1820," (Ph.D. diss., University of Pennsylvania, 1992); Haviland, "Beyond Women's Sphere: Young Quaker Women and the Veil of Charity in Philadelphia, 1790–1810," *WMQ* 51 (1994): 419–46. Two other studies that expose the ways single women challenged male dominance are Chambers-Schiller, *Liberty, a Better Husband;* Karin Wulf, *Not All Wives: Women of Colonial Philadelphia* (Ithaca, 2000).

86. Hugh Barbour, "Quaker Prophetesses and Mothers in Israel," in *Seeking the Light,* ed. J. William Frost and John M. Moore (Wallingford, Pa., 1986), 41–60; Phyllis Mack, *Visionary Women: Ecstatic Prophecy in Seventeenth-Century England* (Berkeley, 1992), 9–10, 215–35.

87. Barry Levy, *Quakers and the American Family: British Settlement in the Delaware Valley* (New York, 1988), 140–44; 193–213. As Levy shows, wealth did, however, assure greater success in keeping children within the Quaker marriage market.

88. Philadelphia Monthly Meeting, Women's Minutes, 1686–1792, FHL; Soderlund, "Women's Authority," 737; Sydney V. James, *A People among Peoples: Quaker Benevolence in Eighteenth-Century America* (Cambridge, Mass., 1963), 50–51.

89. Jack D. Marietta, *The Reformation of American Quakerism, 1748–1783* (Philadelphia, 1984); Tolles, *Meeting House and Counting House,* 234–43.

90. The two most influential histories of eighteenth-century Quaker benevolence (James, *People among Peoples* and Marietta, *Reformation of American Quakerism*) both ignore the gender dimension of this activism, as if the activities of Quaker men were the entire story of Quaker history.

91. Catherine A. Brekus, *Strangers and Pilgrims: Female Preaching in America, 1740–1845* (Chapel Hill, 1998) offers a comprehensive look at the various visionary women (white and black) who became preachers and prophets in early America.

92. Rebecca Larson, *Daughters of Light: Quaker Women Preaching and Prophesying in the Colonies and Abroad, 1700–1775* (New York, 1999), 19–28, 43–63; Elbert Russell, *The History of Quakerism* (New York, 1942), 30–45; Barbour, "Quaker Prophetesses and Mothers in Israel"; Mary Maples Dunn, "Women of Light," in *Women of America: A History,* ed. Carol Ruth Berkin and Mary Beth Norton (Boston, 1979), 120; Margaret Hope Bacon, *Mothers of Feminism: The Story of Quaker Women in America* (San Francisco, 1986), 29. Thirty-seven percent of the ministers from the Philadelphia Yearly Meeting between 1682 and 1800 were women (based on a list of biographies in *The Friend*); Willard Heiss, ed., *Quaker Biographical Sketches of Ministers and Elders . . . of the Yearly Meeting of Philadelphia, 1682–1800* (Indianapolis, 1972).

93. Mack, *Visionary Women,* 1. See also Phyllis Mack, "Women as Prophets during the English Civil War," *Feminist Studies* 8 (1982): 19–45.

94. Larson, *Daughters of Light,* 10–12, 62. According to Barbour and Frost, eighteenth-century Friends's authorities cast a suspicious eye on visionary experiences and censored them from Quaker writings, yet they "remained a part of Quaker lay people's world-view." Hugh Barbour

and J. William Frost, *The Quakers* (Westport, Conn., 1988), 101. Some historians have played down the significance of these phenomena, emphasizing instead the staid quietism of eighteenth-century Quakers. Tolles, *Meeting House and Counting House*; Frederick B. Tolles, "Quietism versus Enthusiasm: The Philadelphia Quakers and the Great Awakening," *PMHB* 69 (1945): 26–49; Jon Butler, *Awash in a Sea of Faith: Christianizing the American People* (Cambridge, Mass., 1990), 27, 118–20. On evangelicals' ecstatic and visionary experiences during eighteenth-century revivals in Scotland and America, see Leigh Eric Schmidt, *Holy Fairs: Scottish Communions and American Revivals in the Early Modern Period* (Princeton, 1989), 145–53; Dee E. Andrews, *The Methodists and Revolutionary America, 1760–1800* (Princeton, 2000), 76–92.

95. "The Journal of Ann Moore," in *Wilt Thou Go on My Errand?: Journals of Three 18th Century Quaker Women Ministers*, ed. Margaret Hope Bacon (Wallingford, Pa., 1994), 371–72.

96. William J. Allinson, ed., *Memorials of Rebecca Jones* (Philadelphia, 1849), 12–13; Levy, *Quakers and the American Family*, 215–21; Bacon, *Mothers of Feminism*, 35–38; "The Journal of Elizabeth Hudson," in Bacon, *Wilt Thou Go on My Errand?* 123, 127, 132.

97. Algie I. Newlin, "Charity Cook," in *The Influence of Quaker Women on American History: Biographical Studies*, ed. Carol and John Stoneburner (Lewiston, N.Y, 1986), 151–89; Bacon, *Mothers of Feminism*, 35–36.

98. "Journal of Ann Moore," 335–41, 345–51, (quotations on 335, 337, 320); Larson, *Daughters of Light*, 172–231.

99. Soderlund, "Women's Authority," 733; "Memoirs of the Life and Travels of Sarah Harrison," in *Friends Miscellany*, ed. John and Isaac Comly, vol. 11 (Philadelphia, 1831–1838), 100–120; Bacon, *Mothers of Feminism*, 35–36.

100. *Elizabeth, A Colored Minister of the Gospel, Born in Slavery* (Philadelphia, 1889), reprinted in Bert James Loewenberg and Ruth Bogin, eds., *Black Women in Nineteenth-Century American Life* (University Park, Pa., 1976), 133, 129; Zilpha Elaw, *Memoirs of the Life, Religious Experience, Ministerial Travels and Labours of Mrs. Zilpha Elaw, . . .* (London, 1846), reprinted in William L. Andrews, ed., *Sisters of the Spirit: Three Black Women's Autobiographies of the Nineteenth Century* (Bloomington, Ind., 1986), 82. See also Nell Irvin Painter, *Sojourner Truth: A Life, A Symbol* (New York, 1996).

101. Jarena Lee, *The Life and Religious Experience of Jarena Lee . . .* (Philadelphia, 1836), reprinted in Andrews, *Sisters of the Spirit*, 27–34.

102. Ibid., 35, 42.

103. *Elizabeth*, 132; Brekus, *Strangers and Pilgrims*, 54, 143–45. "Why should it be thought impossible, heterodox, or improper," Jarena Lee asked, "for a woman to preach? seeing the Saviour died for the woman as well as the man." Lee, *Life and Religious Experience*, 36. Rebecca Cox Jackson received the gift of reading to circumvent a reliance on the men in her life; Jean M. Humez, ed., *Gifts of Power: The Writings of Rebecca Cox Jackson, Black Visionary, Shaker Eldress* (Amherst, 1981), 107–8.

104. Brekus, *Strangers and Pilgrims*, 59, 80–97, 201–6; Christine Leigh Heyrman, *Southern Cross: The Beginnings of the Bible Belt* (New York, 1997), 181–84; Juster, "To Slay the Beast," 25–37; Andrews, *Methodists and Revolutionary America*, 77–80; Catharine Williams, *Fall River: An Authentic Narrative* (Providence, 1833; reprint, New York, 1993), 143–67.

105. Painter, *Sojourner Truth*, 26–31.

106. "An Account of Ann Parrish," in Catharine W. Morris, Notebook, 1802, QC. See also "Ann Parrish," Dictionary of Quaker Biography, QC; Wharton, *Parrish Family*, 47, 73; FS, Minutes, vol. 1, 1795–98, QC; Thompson Westcott, A History of Philadelphia, vol. 3, chap. 380 (originally published in the *Sunday Dispatch*, beginning in 1837), American Philosophical Society; *Some Account of the Aimwell School* (Philadelphia, 1861), 3–4; *Aimwell School: Historical Sketch and the First Printed Report . . .* (n.p., [1916]), 1–3.

107. "Sketch of Friends," 240; Mack, *Visionary Women*, 34.

108. Bruce Dorsey, "Friends Becoming Enemies: Philadelphia Benevolence and the Neglected Period of American Quaker History," *JER* 18 (1998): 399–400; James, *People among Peoples*, 315.

109. "Preamble to the Constitution," FS, Minutes, vol. 1, 1795–98, QC.

110. From letters quoted in "Sketch of Friends," 240, 242–43.

111. Dorothy Ripley, *The Extraordinary Conversion, and Religious Experience of Dorothy Ripley, . . .*

(New York, 1810); Eliza Cope Harrison, ed., *Philadelphia Merchant: The Diary of Thomas P. Cope, 1800–1851* (South Bend, Ind., 1978), 105–7; Crane, *Diary of Elizabeth Drinker*, vol. 2, 1515–16.

112. Ripley, *Extraordinary Conversion*, 132–36; "Some Letters of Richard Allen and Absalom Jones to Dorothy Ripley," *Journal of Negro History* 1 (1916): 436–43.

113. Ripley, *Extraordinary Conversion*, 68, 77, 78, 84; Heyrman, *Southern Cross*, 182; Brekus, *Strangers and Pilgrims*, 18, 204.

114. Nancy Tomes, "The Quaker Connection: Visiting Patterns among Women in the Philadelphia Society of Friends, 1750–1800," in *Friends and Neighbors: Group Life in America's First Plural Society*, ed. Michael Zuckerman (Philadelphia, 1982), 174–95.

115. The women's meeting spent $309 "for our Particular Poor" in 1795, $116 more than its average annual poor expenditures during the previous five years. The Female Society, however, raised over $2,000 during its first year (1795–96), and over $1,200 and nearly $850 during the next two consecutive years. Philadelphia Monthly Meeting, Women's Minutes, 1781–92; 1793–1805, FHL; FS, Treasurer's Books, vol. 1, 1795–1810, QC.

116. FS, Minutes, vol. 1, 1795–98, passim; vol. 2, 1798–1813, Jan. 10, 1801; "Sketch of Friends," 242.

117. Edwin Bronner, "Village into Town, 1701–1746," in *Philadelphia, A 300–Year History*, ed. Russell F. Weigley (New York, 1982), 47; Dorsey, "Friends Becoming Enemies," 395–428.

2. Poverty

1. Guardians of the Poor, Almshouse Daily Occurrence Docket, October 7, 1800, PCA, reprinted in Billy G. Smith, ed., *Life in Early Philadelphia: Documents from the Revolutionary and Early National Periods* (University Park, Pa., 1995), 49. The composite of the perils of poverty has been gleaned from the almshouse daily occurrences dockets, prisoners for trial dockets, newspapers, charitable society reports, and hospital and city dispensary records; see also Billy G. Smith, *The "Lower Sort": Philadelphia's Laboring People, 1750–1800* (Ithaca, 1990), 21–37, 92–125.

2. A partial list of the significant charity and reform societies organized in Philadelphia between 1780 and 1820 includes Pennsylvania Abolition Society (1784), Philadelphia Prison Society (1787), Philadelphia Dispensary (1786), First Day School Society (1790), Female Society for the Relief of the Distressed (1795), Society for the Free Instruction of Female Children (Aimwell School) (1796), Society for the Free Instruction of African Females (1795), Philadelphia Society for the Establishment and Support of Charity Schools (1799), Magdalen Society of Philadelphia (1800), Female Association for the Relief of Women and Children in Reduced Circumstances (1800), Philadelphia Hospitable Society (1802), Female Hospitable Society (1808), Philadelphia Association of Friends for the Instruction of Poor Children (1810), Philadelphia Orphan Society (1814), Dorcas Society of Philadelphia (1816), and Indigent Widows and Single Women's Society (1817).

3. R. J. Morris, "Voluntary Societies and British Urban Elites, 1780–1850: An Analysis," *Historical Journal* 26 (1983): 101.

4. Prominent evangelistic societies in Philadephia before 1820 included Bible Society of Philadelphia (1808), Evangelical Society of Philadelphia (1808), Philadelphia Missionary Society (1813), Auxiliary Bible Society (1813), Female Bible Society (1814), Philadelphia Tract Society (1815), Female Tract Society (1816), Female Domestic Missionary Society (1816), Female Episcopal Tract Society (1816), and the Philadelphia Sunday and Adult School Union (1817).

5. Presbyterian minister John Rodgers in New York City saw no conflict in serving as president of the City Dispensary, Humane Society, Society for Promoting Christian Knowledge, and the New York Missionary Society; Raymond A. Mohl, *Poverty in New York, 1783–1825* (New York, 1971), 121–36, 153–60.

6. Ralston's life and benevolent activities can be traced in Abraham Ritter, *Philadelphia and Her Merchants* (Philadelphia, 1860), 183; Henry Simpson, *The Lives of Eminent Philadelphians, Now Deceased* (Philadelphia, 1859), 825–26; Ashbel Green, *Address at the Interment of Robert Ralston,*

Esq. (Philadelphia, 1836); Robert Ralston correspondence, Simon Gratz Collection, HSP; Gary B. Nash, *Forging Freedom: The Formation of Philadelphia's Black Community, 1720–1840* (Cambridge, Mass., 1988), 116, 236; and the records of the many societies in which he served.

7. Mathew Carey, *Annals of the Social Virtues, No. III* (Philadelphia, 1823), 10–11. Sarah Ralston's life can be traced in Frank Willing Leach, *Old Philadelphia Families* [Clarkson] in *The North American* (1907–1912), HSP; Second Presbyterian Church, Baptisms, Marriages, Burials, 1745–1833, HSP; and the annual reports of the societies in which she worked.

8. Barbara J. Berg, *The Remembered Gate: Origins of American Feminism: The Woman and the City, 1800–1860* (New York, 1978), 160–66; Clifford S. Griffin, *Their Brothers' Keepers: Moral Stewardship in the United States, 1800–1865* (New Brunswick, N.J., 1960), 7–8, 26–33; Charles I. Foster, *An Errand of Mercy: The Evangelical United Front, 1790–1837* (Chapel Hill, 1960), 159–62.

9. Based on a database of over two thousand female benevolent supporters and activists in Philadelphia; see Bruce Dorsey, "City of Brotherly Love: Religious Benevolence, Gender, and Reform in Philadelphia, 1780–1844" (Ph.D. diss., Brown University, 1993), app.

10. Jacob Brodhead, *A Plea for the Poor* (Philadelphia, 1815), 10–11; Jacob Janeway, *The Blessedness of the Charitable* (Philadelphia, 1812), 13. Brodhead was a Dutch Reformed minister, Janeway a Presbyterian minister. See also William White, *Sermon on the Drawing of Moses out of the Waters* (Philadelphia, 1815), 24; Thomas Branagan, *The Beauties of Philanthropy* (Philadelphia, 1808), 21–34; Branagan, *The Charms of Benevolence* (Philadelphia, 1814), 197–98, 203; Branagan, *The Excellency of the Female Character Vindicated* (Philadelphia, 1808), 17; Ashbel Green, *The Christian Duty of Christian Women* (Princeton, 1825), 12, 28; Philip M. Whelpley, *A Sermon Delivered . . . for the Benefit of a Society of Ladies Instituted for the Relief of Poor Widows with Small Children* (New York, 1816), 15.

11. Branagan, *Charms of Benevolence,* 184–85; William Staughton, *Compassion for the Poor Recommended* (Philadelphia, 1810), 8; *Pennsylvania Gazette,* 17 Feb. 1790; 27 July 1796.

12. *Pennsylvania Gazette,* 21 Feb. 1787; 18 July 1787; 5 Nov. 1788; 25 Nov. 1789; 10 Mar. 1790; 18 May 1791; 17 July 1793; 28 Dec. 1796; 27 Sept. 1797; 29 Nov. 1797; 12, 27 Dec. 1798; 13 Mar. 1799; John K. Alexander, *Render Them Submissive: Responses to Poverty in Philadelphia, 1760–1800* (Amherst, 1980), 123; Margaret Morris Haviland, "Beyond Women's Sphere: Young Quaker Women and the Veil of Charity in Philadelphia, 1790–1810," *WMQ* 51 (1994): 423–24.

13. Norman J. Johnston, "Caste and Class of the Urban Form of Historic Philadelphia," *Journal of the American Institute of Planners* 32 (1966): 334–50; Smith, *The "Lower Sort,"* 163–65; Sam Bass Warner, Jr., *The Private City: Philadelphia in Three Periods of Its Growth* (Philadelphia, 1968), 14–18, 49–62; Priscilla Ferguson Clement, *Welfare and the Poor in the Nineteenth-Century City: Philadelphia, 1800–1854* (Rutherford, N.J., 1985), 25; Emma Jones Lapsansky, *Neighborhoods in Transition: William Penn's Dream and Urban Reality* (New York, 1994), 74.

14. Department of Commerce and Labor, Bureau of the Census, *Heads of Families at the First Census of the United States Taken in the Year 1790, Pennsylvania* (Washington, D.C., 1908), 231, 238; Nash, *Forging Freedom,* 68.

15. "Sketch of Friends: The Original 'House of Industry' and Its Founder," from *Friend's Intelligencer* [date unknown], in Quaker Scrapbook, vol. 2, 260, HSP.

16. *Niles Weekly Register,* 2 Sept. 1815; 13 Apr. 1816; 16 Aug. 1816; 26 Oct. 1816; 9, 23 Nov. 1816; 15 Mar. 1817; 23, 29 Nov. 1817; Robert Ralston to Ashbel Green, Aug. 28, 1815, Simon Gratz Collection, HSP. See also Jonathan Roberts to Elizabeth Roberts, Feb. 14, 18, 1815, Jonathan Roberts Papers, HSP; *The Second Crisis of America, or A Cursory View of the Peace . . .* (New York, 1815), 13–29; J. David Lehman, "Explaining Hard Times: Political Economy and the Panic of 1819 in Philadelphia" (Ph.D. diss., University of California, Los Angeles, 1992), chap. 2.

17. Ralston to Green, Aug. 28, 1815; Diane Lindstrom, *Economic Development in the Philadelphia Region, 1810–1850* (New York, 1978), 42; Lehman, "Explaining Hard Times," 138–203, 320–21.

18. *Report of the Library Committee of the Pennsylvania Society for the Promotion of Public Economy* (Philadelphia, 1817), 3.

19. Groups that reported to the committee gave differing estimates for the proportions of women, blacks, and immigrants among the dependent poor; the proportion of women ranged

from as little as one-tenth to as much as three-fourths, African Americans ranged from one-sixth to three-fourths, and nonnatives were estimated at 40 percent of the poor. Ibid., 13–17.

20. Ibid., 12, 17–18.

21. Ibid., 12; *Poulson's American Daily Advertiser* [hereafter *Poulson's*], 15 Nov. 1817, quoted in Lehman, "Explaining Hard Times," 324–25; Mohl, *Poverty in New York*, 116–18, 164, 244–45; David J. Rothman, *The Discovery of the Asylum: Social Order and Disorder in the New Republic* (Boston, 1971), 3–14, 155–61. The best contemporary statement concerning economic liberalism and poverty can be found in Thomas Cooper, *Lectures on the Elements of Political Economy* (Columbia, S.C., 1826). See also Paul K. Conkin, *Prophets of Prosperity: America's First Political Economists* (Bloomington, Ind., 1980), 141–52, 203–7.

22. *Report of the Library Committee*, 7.

23. Murray N. Rothbard, *The Panic of 1819: Reactions and Policies* (New York, 1962), 3–23; Samuel Rezneck, "The Depression of 1819–1822, A Social History," *AHR* 39 (1933): 28–47.

24. Robert Ralston to Ashbel Green, Dec. 13, 1818, Simon Gratz Collection, HSP. *Niles' Weekly Register*, 7 Aug. 1819; 23 Oct. 1819; 24 Feb. 1821; Niles estimated as many as fifty thousand unemployed in New York, Baltimore, and Philadelphia alone. Rezneck, "Depression of 1819–1822," 30–31; over two thousand cotton textile workers were dismissed in Philadelphia, *Hazard's Register of Pennsylvania* 4 (1829): 168–69; Philip Scranton, *Proprietary Capitalism: The Textile Manufacture at Philadelphia, 1800–1885* (Cambridge, 1983), 76, 121; Mathew Carey, *The New Olive Branch . . .* (1821) in Mathew Carey, *Essays on Political Economy* (Philadelphia, 1822), 319–21.

25. *Report of the Joint Committee of Councils Relative to the Malignant or Pestilential Disease . . .* (Philadelphia, 1821); *Niles' Weekly Register*, 2, 9, 16 Sept. 1820; Gouverneur Emerson, "Medical Statistics, Being a Series of Tables Showing Mortality in Philadelphia and Its Immediate Causes," *American Journal of the Medical Sciences* 1 (1827): 116–55; Gouverneur Emerson, "Medical Statistics, Consisting of Estimates Relating to the Population of Philadelphia . . . ," *American Journal of the Medical Sciences* 9 (1831–32): 17–46; Rebecca Gratz to Maria Gist Gratz, Nov. 11, 1820, in *Letters of Rebecca Gratz*, ed. David Philipson (Philadelphia, 1929), 38; Charles Peirce, *A Meteorological Account of the Weather in Philadelphia from January 1, 1790 to January 1, 1847* (Philadelphia, 1847), 20; *Poulson's*, 29, 30 Jan. 1821.

26. Whereas only 2 percent of Philadelphia's population was dependent on public poor relief in 1800, the proportion had increased to nearly 5 percent by 1820; Clement, *Welfare and the Poor*, app. 2, 178–80, 31, 49; Lehman, "Explaining Hard Times," 306, 310, 346–47. New York's Society for the Prevention of Pauperism estimated that the number of poor residents in New York had mushroomed to 8,000 in 1819 and then to nearly 13,000 in 1820, which was more than 10 percent of New York's population. Rezneck, "Depression of 1819–1822," 31.

27. Benjamin J. Klebaner, "The Home Relief Controversy in Philadelphia, 1782–1861," *PMHB* 78 (1954): 415; Clement, *Welfare and the Poor*, app. 1, 174–77. On the evolution of Philadelphia's poor-relief system, see Gary B. Nash, "Poverty and Poor Relief in Pre-Revolutionary Philadelphia," *WMQ* 33 (1976): 3–30; Nash, *The Urban Crucible* (Cambridge, Mass., 1979); William C. Heffner, *History of Poor Relief Legislation in Pennsylvania, 1682–1913* (Cleona, Pa., 1913); Alexander, *Render Them Submissive*.

28. Clement, *Welfare and the Poor*, 51–52; Klebaner, "Home Relief Controversy," 414–15.

29. *First Report of the Provident Society for the Employment of the Poor* (Philadelphia, 1825), 8; Lehman, "Explaining Hard Times," 305–10, 340–42, 346.

30. *Report of the Library Committee*, 16–17. Institutional solutions to free-black poverty became more common after 1820, as the percentages of free blacks in the almshouse and prison outstripped their proportion of the population. Nash *Forging Freedom*, 143, 156, 214, 226; *Niles' Weekly Register*, 10 Jan. 1818; 1 Aug. 1818; Adam Seybert, *Statistical Annals* (Philadelphia, 1818), 29; John Palmer, *Journal of Travels in the United States . . .* (London, 1818), 291; *Poulson's*, 7 Aug. 1817; *Philadelphia Aurora*, 24 July 1819; William F. Adams, *Ireland and Irish Emigration to the New World from 1815 to the Famine* (New Haven, 1932), 97–98; Mohl, *Poverty in New York*, 115–16.

31. Mathew Carey, *Address to the Farmers of the United States* (1821), in Carey, *Essays on Political Economy*, 431. On wage labor and its relationship to the spread of poverty, see Michael B. Katz,

Poverty and Policy in American History (New York, 1983), 10–14, 200–201; Joan Underhill Hannon, "Poverty in the Antebellum Northeast: The View from New York State's Poor Relief Rolls," *Journal of Economic History* 44 (1984): 1007–32; Michael B. Katz et al., *The Social Organization of Early Industrial Capitalism* (Cambridge, Mass., 1982), chap. 1; Michael Reich, "The Development of the Wage-Labor Force," in *The Capitalist System: A Radical Analysis of American Society*, 2nd ed., ed. Richard C. Edwards et al. (Englewood Cliffs, N.J., 1978), 180; Cynthia J. Shelton, *The Mills of Manayunk: Industrialization and Social Conflict in the Philadelphia Region, 1787–1837* (Baltimore, 1986).

32. Clement, *Welfare and the Poor*, 70–71, 76, 110–11; Shelton, *Mills of Manayunk*, 59–62. Before 1820, more women (52–66 percent) than men were admitted to the New York almshouse, but those percentages began declining after 1820; Christine Stansell, *City of Women: Sex and Class in New York, 1789–1860* (New York, 1986), 236. By contrast, women made up approximately one-third of the Philadelphia almshouse residents throughout the first half of the nineteenth century. On female poverty in eighteenth-century Pennsylvania, see Smith, *The "Lower Sort,"* 170–71; Joan M. Jensen, *Loosening the Bonds: Mid-Atlantic Farm Women, 1750–1850* (New Haven, 1986), 58, 67.

33. Stansell, *City of Women*, 3–37; Hannon, "Poverty in the Antebellum Northeast," 1013–15; Barbara L. Bellows, *Benevolence among Slaveholders: Assisting the Poor in Charleston, 1670–1860* (Baton Rouge, 1993), 88–97; Suzanne Lebsock, *The Free Women of Petersburg: Status and Culture in a Southern Town, 1784–1860* (New York, 1984), 202–3.

34. Minutes of the Guardians of the Poor, Mar. 3, 1820, quoted in Lehman, "Explaining Hard Times," 318. See also Shelton, *Mills of Manayunk*, 28, 60–61, 64–65; Stansell, *City of Women*, 105–29; Mathew Carey, *Essays on the Public Charities of Philadelphia* (1828), in Mathew Carey, *Miscellaneous Essays* (Philadelphia, 1830), 154–69 [hereafter all page references will be to this edition]; Cooper, *Lectures on the Elements of Political Economy*, 110–11; Nash, *Forging Freedom*, 162.

35. Clement, *Welfare and the Poor*, app. 1, 174–77, 52; Samuel Emlen to Roberts Vaux, July 10, 1821, Vaux Papers, HSP.

36. *Report of the Committee Appointed by the Board of Guardians of the Poor of the City and Districts of Philadelphia, to Visit the Cities of Baltimore, New-York, Providence, Boston, and Salem* (Philadelphia, 1827), 21–22, 23–27; [Mathew Carey], *Pauperism: To the Citizens of Philadelphia, Paying Poor Taxes, No. I*, (Philadelphia, 1827), 1–3; Blanche D. Coll, "The Baltimore Society for the Prevention of Pauperism, 1820–1822," *AHR* 61 (1955): 77–87; M. J. Heale, "The New York Society for the Prevention of Pauperism, 1817–1823," *New York Historical Society Quarterly* 55 (1971): 133–76; Mohl, *Poverty in New York*, 241–58; Joan Underhill Hannon, "The Generosity of Antebellum Poor Relief," *Journal of Economic History* 44 (1984): 810–21; Clement, *Welfare and the Poor*, 52.

37. *Report of the Committee Appointed at a Town Meeting of the Citizens of the City and County of Philadelphia, on the 23d of July, 1827, . . .* (Philadelphia, 1827), 3–4, 17, 25; Pennsylvania, *Laws of the Commonwealth* (1828), 10:71–79; Klebaner, "Home Relief Controversy," 417–18; Clement, *Welfare and the Poor*, 55–57.

38. Rothman, *Discovery of the Asylum*, 161–65; Michael B. Katz, *In the Shadow of the Poorhouse: A Social History of Welfare in America* (New York, 1986), 16–21.

39. Carey, *Essays on Public Charities*, 155, 170, 192. See also Carey, *Pauperism, No. I*, 1; Lehman, "Explaining Hard Times," 329–31. For examples of critics blaming private charities for increasing pauperism, see *Poulson's*, 24 Dec. 1821; *Philadelphia Gazette*, 15 May 1828.

40. Ironically, Philadelphia had spent a decade scrutinizing its poor-relief system, but was still fertile ground for misinformation and inflammatory rumors. Carey squelched a rumor circulating in 1828 that total city and private poor-relief expenditures exceeded $600,000, a fourfold exaggeration of actual expenditures. Carey estimated that private societies spent less than $60,000. Carey, *Essays on Public Charities*, 155; *Poulson's*, 24 Feb. 1817; *Philadelphia Aurora*, 30 Apr. 1817, cited in Lehman, "Explaining Hard Times," 334–35.

41. Female Hospitable Society, Thirteenth Annual Report (1821), in *Articles of Association. Act of Incorporation and Reports of the Transactions of the Female Hospitable Society of Philadelphia, since Its Commencement in 1808* (Philadelphia, 1831), 23 [hereafter *Reports of FHS*]; *Poulson's*, 12 Nov.

1822; 20 Apr. 1820; 9 Apr. 1821; *American Sentinel,* 25 Dec. 1822; 7 Jan. 1823; *Constitution of the Union Benevolent Association* (Philadelphia, 1831), 6.

42. Carey, *Report on Female Wages* (1829) in *Miscellaneous Essays,* 269. See also, Carey, *Essays on Public Charities,* 155, 189; Carey, *Address to the Liberal and Humane* (Philadelphia, [1828]), 3; Carey, *Benevolent Institutions* (Philadelphia, 1829), 2.

43. Mary A. Snyder and Margaret Silver to Mathew Carey [Nov. 1828], reprinted in Carey, *Essays on Public Charities,* 175; *Poulson's,* 12 Nov. 1822.

44. *Poulson's,* 20 Apr. 1820; 9 Apr. 1821; *First Report of the Provident Society,* 4, 8; *Constitution of the Union Benevolent Association,* 10; *Twenty-Seventh Annual Report of the Female Association* ([Philadelphia], 1828), 2; Abner Kneeland, *A Charity Sermon on the Late Fire at Savannah,* . . . (Philadelphia, 1820), 6, 12.

45. Charles C. Andrews, *The History of the New-York African Free-Schools* (New York, 1830), 132; Richard Allen, *The Life Experience and Gospel Labors of the Rt. Rev. Richard Allen* (Philadelphia, 1887; reprint, Nashville, 1960), 46.

46. "Negro Societies in Philadelphia, 1831," *Hazard's Register,* March 12, 1831, in *A Documentary History of the Negro People in the United States,* ed. Herbert Aptheker, vol. 1 (New York, 1951–1974), 111–14; *The Present State and Condition of the Free People of Color, of the City of Philadelphia* . . . (Philadelphia, 1838), 26–27; Daughters of Africa, Order Book, 1821–1829, HSP; Daughters of Africa, Minutes, 1822–1838, HSP; Nash, *Forging Freedom,* 210–11; Anne Firor Scott, *Natural Allies: Women's Associations in American History* (Urbana, 1991), 13–16, 19.

47. Since the 1760s, public poor-relief institutions in Philadelphia periodically asserted their role as employers of the poor, with limited success, especially in times of economic distress; see Nash, "Poverty and Poor Relief," 16; Alexander, *Render Them Submissive,* 13–14, 86–121; Shelton, *Mills of Manayunk,* 37–46.

48. *Articles of Association of the Female Hospitable Society, Entered into and Agreed on, at One of Their Annual Meetings* (Philadelphia, 1814), 3; Branagan, *Charms of Benevolence,* 213; Carey, *Address to the Liberal and Humane,* 1.

49. Occupations of heads of household are known for 45 percent of the managers from 1814–41 (*N* = 78); 41.3 percent of the women were from families where the head of household was a merchant, shopkeeper, or small-scale retailer; 17 percent were from artisan households.

50. *Articles of Association of the Female Hospitable Society,* 3; *Reports of FHS,* Ninth Annual Report (1817), 17; Tenth Annual Report (1818), 19.

51. *Reports of FHS,* 2; *American Sentinel,* 10 Feb. 1820.

52. John Melish, *The Necessity of Protecting and Encouraging the Manufacturing of the United States* . . . (Philadelphia, 1818), 26; *Poulson's,* 13 Jan. 1821; *Reports of FHS,* 12, 16–25, 32.

53. *Reports of FHS,* 23, 2–3; *Poulson's,* 19 Dec. 1821; Carey, *Address to the Liberal and Humane,* 1; *The Twenty-Eighth Annual Meeting of the Female Hospitable Society* ([Philadelphia, 1836]), 6; *The Thirty-Third Annual Meeting of the Female Hospitable Society* (Philadelphia, 1841), 3.

54. *Reports of FHS,* 1, 4, 5, 35; *The Twenty-Seventh Annual Meeting of the Female Hospitable Society* ([Philadelphia, 1835]), 1, 4.

55. *First Report of the Provident Society,* 3–4, 5–7, 9–10; Clement, *Welfare and the Poor,* app. 1, 174–77; *Reports of FHS,* 30.

56. *Poulson's,* 28 Jan. 1824.

57. *First Report of the Provident Society,* 5, 7; Katz, *Poverty and Policy in American History,* 198.

58. Shelton, *Mills of Manayunk,* 26–53; J. Leander Bishop, *A History of American Manufactures from 1608 to 1860,* vol. 1 (Philadelphia, 1864), 385–88.

59. Edmund S. Morgan, *American Slavery, American Freedom* (New York, 1975), 320–27, 381–87; Vagrancy Docket, 1790–1932, 36 vols., PCA; Prisoners for Trial Docket, 1790–1948, 164 vols., PCA; Mayor's Court Docket, 1759–1837, 16 vols., PCA.

60. Carey, *Report on Female Wages,* 266–72; Matthew Carey, *To the Ladies Who Have Undertaken to Establish a House of Industry in New York* (Philadelphia, 1830); Carey, *A Plea for the Poor, Nos. I-III* (Philadelphia, 1831–32); Carey, *Address to the Wealthy of the Land* . . . (Philadelphia, 1831); Carey, *Case of Seamstresses* (Philadelphia, [1833]); Carey, *Female Wages and Female Oppression, Nos. I-III* (Philadelphia, 1835); Carey, *Letters on the Condition of the Poor* (Philadelphia, 1835); Carey, *Essays on Political Economy;* Carey, *The Crisis* (Philadelphia, 1823).

61. Carey, *Address to the Wealthy*, 10–12; Carey, *Report on Female Wages*, 267–68; Carey, *Essays on Public Charities*, 167–69.

62. Carey, *Essays on Public Charities*, 156–59, 162–63, 182, quotation is on pp. 157–58; Carey, *Benevolent Institutions*, 1. Provident Society receipts declined by nearly $4,000 after the first year; annual subscribers dropped from 1,015 to 300 between 1824 and 1828. *First Report of the Provident Society*, 8; *Second Report of the Provident Society for the Employment of the Poor* (Philadelphia, 1826), 5–7; *Third Annual Report of the Provident Society for Employing the Poor* (Philadelphia, 1827), 5; *Fourth Annual Report of the Provident Society for Employing the Poor* (Philadelphia, 1828), 4; Carey, *Address to the Liberal and Humane*, 1.

63. *Sixth Annual Report of the Provident Society for Employing the Poor* (Philadelphia, 1830), 6–7; Carey, *Address to the Wealthy*, 16; Carey, *Essays on Public Charities*, 163, 183.

64. *Twenty-Seventh Annual Meeting of the Female Hospitable Society*, 1–2; *Historical Sketch of the First Half Century of the Union Benevolent Association . . .* (Philadelphia, 1881), 11; William C. Brownlee, *For Christian Missions . . .* (Philadelphia, 1825), 21–22; *Democratic Press*, 6 Oct. 1827. On the ideology of women and benevolence, see Dorsey, "City of Brotherly Love," chap. 5; Lori D. Ginzberg, *Women and the Work of Benevolence: Morality, Politics, and Class in the Nineteenth-Century United States* (New Haven, 1990), 11–35.

65. *Poulson's*, 22, 24 Dec. 1821; Cooper, *Lectures on the Elements of Political Economy*, 258.

66. *Report of the Library Committee*, 13–14, 18.

67. *Philadelphia Aurora*, 29 Feb., 1820, quoted in Lehman, "Explaining Hard Times," 310; Alice Kessler-Harris, *Out to Work: A History of Wage-Earning Women in the United States* (New York, 1982), 20–72; W. J. Rorabaugh, *The Alcoholic Republic* (New York, 1979), 11–13.

68. E. Anthony Rotundo, *American Manhood: Transformations in Masculinity from the Revolution to the Modern Era* (New York, 1993), 10–25; Charles E. Rosenberg, "Sexuality, Class and Role in Nineteenth-Century America," *AQ* 25 (1973): 131–53. In light of these new ideals of manhood, middle-class men probably adopted liberalism's critique of poverty much earlier than middle-class women; after all, conventions of womanhood were not predicated on an acceptance of the values of market capitalism; see Linda K. Kerber et al., "Beyond Roles, Beyond Spheres: Thinking about Gender in the Early Republic," *WMQ* 46 (1989): 565–85.

69. Rev. William Staughton, as quoted in *The Fourth Report of the Philadelphia Sunday and Adult School Union* (Philadelphia, 1821), 87. Seven new Presbyterian churches were established, and both Methodists and Presbyterians nearly doubled their communicants over the course of the 1820s. By the early 1830s, the Presbyterians and Methodists together could claim more than ten thousand adherents, one in every ten adults in the city and suburbs. William M. Rice, "Introduction," in *The Presbyterian Church in Philadelphia*, ed. William P. White and William H. Scott (Philadelphia, 1894), xix; *Minutes Taken at the Several Annual Conferences of the Methodist Episcopal Church for the Year 1832* (New York, 1832). These population figures have been derived from tables in David T. Gilchrist, ed., *The Growth of the Seaport Cities, 1790–1825* (Charlottesville, Va., 1967), 34–36, 39.

70. First Day Society, Board of Managers, Minutes, 2 vols, 1790–1857, PHS; First Day Society, Board of Visitors, Minutes, 1791–1835, PHS; Edwin Wilbur Rice, *The Sunday-School Movement and the American Sunday-School Union, 1780–1917* (Philadelphia, 1917), 44–48; Alexander, *Render Them Submissive*, 145–57; Anne M. Boylan, *Sunday School: The Formation of an American Institution, 1790–1880* (New Haven, 1988), 6–11; *The First Report of the Philadelphia Sunday and Adult School Union* (Philadelphia, 1818), 11–12; *The Third Report of the Philadelphia Sunday and Adult School Union* (Philadelphia, 1820), 59; Philadelphia Sunday and Adult School Union, Minutes, May 22, 1817, American Sunday School Union Papers, PHS.

71. Anne M. Boylan, "Women in Groups: An Analysis of Women's Benevolent Organizations in New York and Boston, 1797–1840," *JAH* 71 (1984): 500–501.

72. Carey, *Address to the Liberal and the Humane*, 1–4; "History of the Female Association" (typescript history), 15, Female Association Records, QC; Carey, *Essays on Public Charities*, 166–67; Carey, *Benevolent Institutions*. (Catholic and Jewish voluntary societies are discussed in chap. 5.)

73. *Poulson's*, 20 May 1820; J. Orin Oliphant, "The American Missionary Spirit, 1828–1835,"

Church History 7 (1938): 125–37; Foster, *Errand of Mercy*, 121; Carey, *Essays on Public Charities*, 189. For comparison, the Female Hospitable Society's annual donations declined from more than $1,200 in 1820 to approximately $300 in 1831, whereas the Female Bible Society's annual funds remained between $900 and $1300 during the same period.

74. Carey, *Address to the Liberal and Humane*, 3; Carey, *Address to the Wealthy*, viii; Carey, *Essays on Public Charities*, 165. See also Carey, *Annals of Liberality, Generosity, Public Spirit, &c.*, third ser., no. 5 (Philadelphia, 1834), 1; Carey, *To the Public* [on the Cause of the Greeks] (Philadelphia, 1826), 1.

75. *Poulson's*, 14 Dec. 1821. Comparison is based on the annual reports of both societies from 1814 through 1831 (*N* = 39; for the first three years *N* = 24).

76. Evangelicals attributed tremendous power to the written word. Bible and tract societies filled their publications with narratives of miraculous conversions once a Bible or tract was introduced into a family or community. *Poulson's*, 16 Jan. 1822; *Religious Remembrancer*, 19 Aug. 1820; William M. Engles, *Appeal* [on Behalf of the Philadelphia Auxiliary Bible Society] ([Philadelphia, ca., 1821]), 11; Stansell, *City of Women*, 63–75; William G. McLoughlin, *Revivals, Awakenings, and Reform* (Chicago, 1978), 98–131; Nathan O. Hatch, *The Democratization of American Christianity* (New Haven, 1989), 170–79.

77. Henry E. Dwight, *Fifty Years' Work in the "Spread of the Gospel, Relief of the Poor, and Care of Destitute Children" by the Home Missionary Society of the City of Philadelphia* (Philadelphia, 1885), 18.

78. *The Christian Principle in Relation to Pauperism* (Philadelphia, 1826), 9, 14, 26; the biblical reference is 2 Thess. 3:10. Fred J. Hood, *Reformed America: The Middle and Southern States, 1783–1837* (University, Ala., 1980), 147, 156, 158.

79. [Ezra Stiles Ely], *The Journal of the Stated Preacher to the Hospital and Almshouse, in the City of New–York* (New York, 1812), 21; also, 28, 30, 33–34, 91–92, 188–89.

80. E. S. Ely, "Prevention of Pauperism," *Presbyterian Magazine* 2 (Mar. 1822): 230–32. For an extended discussion of Ely's call for a "Christian party" in American politics, see Dorsey, "City of Brotherly Love," chap. 7; Joseph L. Blau, "'The Christian Party in Politics,'" *Review of Religion* 11 (1946): 18–35; Bertram Wyatt-Brown, "Prelude to Abolitionism: Sabbatarian Politics and the Rise of the Second Party System," *JAH* 58 (1971): 316–41.

81. *The Third Annual Report of the Managers of the Female Domestic Missionary Society of Philadelphia* (Philadelphia, 1820), 4. See also *The First Annual Report of the Managers of the Female Domestic Missionary Society of Philadelphia* (Philadelphia, 1817), 3–4; *The Second Annual Report of the Managers of the Female Domestic Missionary Society of Philadelphia* (Philadelphia, 1818), 7; Louis F. Benson, *A Hundred Years' Ministry in the Philadelphia Almshouse* (Philadelphia, 1916), 5.

82. *First Annual Report of Female Domestic Missionary Society*, 12; for an example of a poorhouse resident who excitedly sought the society's spiritual guidance, see p. 14.

83. *Second Annual Report of Female Domestic Missionary Society*, 5–6, 18; *First Annual Report of Female Domestic Missionary Society*, 4–5, 9–12; *The Ninth Annual Report of the Female Domestic Missionary Society of Philadelphia* (Philadelphia, 1825), 4–5; *The Twelfth Annual Report of the Female Domestic Missionary Society of Philadelphia* (Philadelphia, 1828), 6.

84. The best accounts of this gendered language of women's benevolence can be found in Ginzberg, *Women and the Work of Benevolence*, 1–35; and Ann Douglas, *The Feminization of American Culture* (New York, 1977), chap. 2. See also Ruth H. Bloch, "The Gendered Meanings of Virtue in Revolutionary America," *Signs* 13 (1987): 37–58.

85. George Washington Doane, *Woman's Mission*, 2nd ed. (New York, 1840), 13; also 3–53, 65. For examples elsewhere in the North, see also Green, *Christian Duty of Christian Women*, 3–12; Matthew La Rue Perrine, *Women Have a Work to Do in the House of God* (New York, 1817); Gardiner Spring, *The Excellence and Influence of the Female Character* (New York, 1825); Sarah Lewis, *Woman's Mission* (Boston, 1840); Sarah Tuttle, *Female Influence; or, the Temperance Girl . . .*, 2nd ed. (Boston, 1837). For northern black reformers' use of this language, see *Weekly Advocate*, 11 Feb. 1837; 22 Dec. 1860; *Colored American*, 7 Dec. 1839, cited in Shirley J. Yee, *Black Women Abolitionists: A Study in Activism, 1828–1860* (Knoxville, Tenn., 1992), 44–46, 54–56; Maria W. Stewart, *Productions of Mrs. Maria W. Stewart* (Boston, 1835).

86. J. F. Stearns, *Female Influence, and the True Christian Mode of Its Exercise* (Newburyport,

Mass., 1837), 10–11; *Historical Sketch*, 11; *Twenty-Seventh Annual Meeting of the Female Hospitable Society*, 1–2; Branagan, *Beauties of Philanthropy*, 59; White, *Sermon on Moses*, 28; Carey, *Address to the Wealthy*, vii.

87. *Twelfth Annual Report of Female Domestic Missionary Society*, 7; Charles Meigs, *Lectures on Some of the Distinctive Characteristics of the Female* . . . (Philadelphia, 1847), 10–15; James Gardner, *Memoirs of Eminent Christian Females; With an Essay on the Influences of Female Piety* (Philadelphia, 1844), 6, 10; *The Twenty-Third Report of the Female Bible Society of Philadelphia* (Philadelphia, 1837), 4; *The Origination and Constitution of the Sansom Street Baptist Female Missionary Society* (Philadelphia, 1814), 3; "Female Influence," *Ladies Garland* [Philadelphia], 3 June 1837, 55.

88. Mary P. Ryan, "A Women's Awakening: Evangelical Religion and the Families of Utica, New York, 1800–1840," *AQ* 30 (1978): 602–23; Ryan, *Cradle of the Middle Class: The Family in Oneida County, New York, 1790–1865* (New York, 1981), 83–98; Barbara Leslie Epstein, *The Politics of Domesticity: Women, Evangelism and Temperance in Nineteenth-Century America* (Middletown, Conn., 1981), 45–65; Boylan, *Sunday School*, chap. 5.

89. Barbara Welter, "The Feminization of American Religion, 1800–1860," in *Clio's Consciousness Raised: New Perspectives on the History of Women*, ed. Mary S. Hartman and Lois Banner (New York, 1974), 137–57; Douglas, *Feminization of American Culture*; Richard D. Shiels, "The Feminization of American Congregationalism, 1730–1835," *AQ* 33 (1981): 46–62; Nancy F. Cott, "Young Women in the Second Great Awakening in New England," *Feminist Studies* 3 (1975): 15–29. The proportion of women was increasing in many Philadelphia churches throughout the first half of the nineteenth century, with the percentage of women in some evangelical churches reaching as high as 75–80 percent; Dorsey, "City of Brotherly Love," 208–9; Terry D. Bilhartz, *Urban Religion and the Second Great Awakening: Church and Society in Early National Baltimore* (Rutherford, N.J., 1986), 21–22.

90. Over sixty novels were written about the plight of urban workers between 1840 and 1870; see Mari Jo Buhle, "Needlewomen and the Vicissitudes of Modern Life: A Study of Middle-Class Construction in the Antebellum Northeast," in *Visible Women: New Essays on American Activism*, ed. Nancy A. Hewitt and Suzanne Lebsock (Urbana, 1993), 145–65; Adrienne Siegel, *The Image of the American City in Popular Literature, 1820–1870* (Port Washington, N.Y., 1981), 76–99; David S. Reynolds, *Beneath the American Renaissance: The Subversive Imagination in the Age of Emerson and Melville* (New York, 1988), 351–57; Amal M. Amireh, "The Factory Girl and the Seamstress: Imagining Gender and Class in Nineteenth-Century American Fiction," (Ph.D. diss., Boston University, 1997).

91. Maria L. Buckley, *A Sketch of the Working Classes of New York; or, The Sufferings of the Sewing Girls*, published with Maria L. Buckley, *Amanda Willson; or, The Vicissitudes of Life* (New York, 1856), 34–35.

92. Buckley, *Amanda Willson*, 5–6; Buckley, *Sketch of the Working Classes*, 31; T. S. Arthur, *Lizzy Glenn; or, The Trials of a Seamstress* (Philadelphia, 1859), 29–30, 141 (this story first appeared as T. S. Arthur, *The Seamstress: A Tale of the Times* [Philadelphia, 1843]); Charles Burdett, *The Elliott Family; or, The Trials of New-York Seamstresses* (New York, 1850), 13–14. See also William B. English, *Gertrude Howard, The Maid of Humble Life*, . . . (Boston, 1843); Sarah J. Hale, "Sketch from the History of the Poor," *Arthur's Magazine* (January 1845): 10–12; Allen Hampden, *Hartley Norman: A Tale of the Times* (New York, 1859), 13, 26–27.

93. Arthur, *Lizzy Glenn*, 23–24. See also T. S. Arthur, "Ups and Downs," in *The Young Music Teacher, and Other Tales* (Philadelphia, 1847), 77–95.

94. Kathleen Waters Sander, *The Business of Charity: The Woman's Exchange Movement, 1832–1900* (Urbana, 1998), 1–37, quotation on p. 11.

95. Arthur, *Lizzy Glenn*, 29–30.

96. Arthur, *Lizzy Glenn*; Maria Maxwell, *Ernest Grey; or, The Sins of Society. A Story of New York Life* (New York, 1855), 334; Mary Denison, *Edna Etherill, The Boston Seamstress* (New York, 1847); Arthur, "Ups and Downs"; English, *Gertrude Howard*.

97. Burdett, *Elliott Family*, 57–66.

98. Maxwell, *Ernest Grey*, 106, 117, 137; Arthur, *Lizzy Glenn*, 34; Hampden, *Hartley Norman*, 28–29; see also *The Orphan Seamstress: A Narrative of Innocence, Guilt, Mystery and Crime* (New York, 1850), 23–24.

3. Drink

1. John Watson, *Observations on the Customary Use of Distilled Spirituous Liquors* (Philadelphia, 1810), 5–13; William Cobbett, *A Year's Residence in the United States of America* (London, 1818; reprint, Carbondale, Ill., 1964), 197–99; W. J. Rorabaugh, *The Alcoholic Republic: An American Tradition* (New York, 1979), 16–29; Mark Edward Lender and James Kirby Martin, *Drinking in America: A History* (New York, 1982), 9–21.

2. John Fanning Watson, *Annals of Philadelphia and Pennsylvania in the Olden Time*, vol. 1 (Philadelphia, 1844), 238–39; Rorabaugh, *Alcoholic Republic*, 66–67.

3. Rorabaugh, *Alcoholic Republic*, 7–11, 69–100, 232–33; W. J. Rorabaugh, "Estimated U.S. Alcoholic Beverage Consumption, 1790–1860," *Journal of Studies of Alcohol* 37 (1976): 360–61; wholesale price for a gallon of rye whiskey dropped from 67¢ to 18¢ between 1797 and 1841; Anne Bezanson et al., *Wholesale Prices in Philadelphia, 1784–1861*, vol. 2 (Philadelphia, 1936), 249–50; Thomas P. Slaughter, *The Whiskey Rebellion: Frontier Epilogue to the American Revolution* (New York, 1986).

4. Albert Barnes, "Introduction," in *Young Man's Closet Library*, by Robert Philip, 2nd ed. (New York, 1836), 3.

5. I use the plural here to emphasize that there existed many different but overlapping cultures of male drinking.

6. See Stephanie Wolf's insight that separate spheres often meant "an absence of women as a gender, not females as a sex," since women often owned or served food and drink in taverns. Stephanie Grauman Wolf, *As Various as Their Land: The Everyday Lives of Eighteenth-Century Americans* (New York, 1993), 82.

7. William Penn, *Some Fruits of Solitude* (London, 1693), reprinted in Frederick B. Tolles and E. Gordon Alderfer, eds., *The Witness of William Penn* (New York, 1957), 173.

8. For the cultural and moral definitions of middle-class formation, see Karen Halttunen, *Confidence Men and Painted Women: A Study of Middle-Class Culture in America, 1830–1870* (New Haven, 1982), 25–26, 45–50, 195.

9. Jacob Cox Parsons, ed., *Extracts from the Diary of Jacob Hiltzheimer, of Philadelphia, 1765–1798* (Philadelphia, 1893), 10, 17–18, 20, *passim;* Alexander Hamilton, *Gentleman's Progress: The Itinerarium of Dr. Alexander Hamilton, 1744*, ed. Carl Bridenbaugh (Chapel Hill, 1948); Alexander Graydon, *Memoirs of a Life . . .* (Harrisburg, 1811), 70–72, 84–85; Eric Foner, *Tom Paine and Revolutionary America* (New York, 1976), 109–11.

10. Carl Bridenbaugh, *Cities in Revolt: Urban Life in America, 1743–1776* (New York, 1955), 365–66; "The Cock Fighter," *PMHB* 44 (1920): 73–76; Gordon S. Wood, *The Radicalism of the American Revolution* (New York, 1992), 41–42.

11. Peter Thompson, *Rum Punch & Revolution: Taverngoing & Public Life in Eighteenth-Century Philadelphia* (Philadelphia, 1999), 75–82; Robert Earle Graham, "The Taverns of Colonial Philadelphia," in *Historic Philadelphia: From the Founding until the Early Nineteenth Century* (Philadelphia, 1953), 318–25; Kym S. Rice, *Early American Taverns* (New York, 1983).

12. Parsons, *Extracts from the Diary of Jacob Hiltzheimer*, 11; Alfred F. Young, "George Roberts Twelves Hewes (1742–1840): A Boston Shoemaker and the Memory of the American Revolution," *WMQ* 38 (1981): 561–62; David S. Shields, *Civil Tongues & Polite Letters in British America* (Chapel Hill, 1997), 66–67; Peter Thompson, "'The Friendly Glass': Drink and Gentility in Colonial Philadelphia," *PMHB* 113 (1989): 549–73; Richard J. Hooker, "The American Revolution Seen through a Wine Glass," *WMQ* 11 (1954): 52–77; Pauline Maier, *From Resistance to Revolution: Colonial Radicals and the Development of American Opposition to Britain, 1765–1776* (New York, 1972), 163; Simon P. Newman, *Parades and the Politics of the Street: Festive Culture in the Early American Republic* (Philadelphia, 1997), 29–33, 92–94; David Waldstreicher, *In the Midst of Perpetual Fetes: The Making of American Nationalism, 1776–1820* (Chapel Hill, 1997). For a sampling of revolutionary-era toasts, see *Pennsylvania Gazette*, 2 May 1766; 31 Mar. 1768; 23 Mar. 1769; 21 Sept. 1774; 14 July 1778; 25 July 1781; 23 Apr. 1783.

13. Thompson, *Rum Punch & Revolution*, 145–62, 185–87.

14. Parsons, *Extracts from the Diary of Jacob Hiltzheimer*, 128; also 63–64, 76, 78–79, 93, 126–28, 130, 137, 143, 153.

15. Hamilton, *Gentleman's Progress*, 26; Shields, *Civil Tongues & Polite Letters*, 66–67, 88–98; Waldstreicher, *In the Midst of Perpetual Fetes*, 82, 168–70.

16. David W. Conroy, *In Public Houses: Drink and the Revolution of Authority in Colonial Massachusetts* (Chapel Hill, 1995), 177–88, 241–309; Thompson, *Rum Punch & Revolution*, 116–81.

17. Parsons, *Extracts from the Diary of Jacob Hiltzheimer*, 176, 179, 182–83, 184–85.

18. Watson, *Observations*, 11–12; Rorabaugh, *Alcoholic Republic*, 15, 132; Sean Wilentz, *Chants Democratic: New York City & the Rise of the American Working Class, 1788–1850* (New York, 1984), 53–54; Marcus Rediker, *Between the Devil and the Deep Blue Sea: Merchant Seamen, Pirates, and the Anglo-American Maritime World, 1700–1750* (New York, 1987), 166, 186–93; Hamilton, *Gentleman's Progress*, 56.

19. On the symbolic exchange of drink prior to a wage-labor system, see Marianna Adler, "From Symbolic Exchange to Commodity Consumption: Anthropological Notes on Drinking as a Symbolic Practice," in *Drinking: Behavior and Belief in Modern History*, ed. Susanna Barrows and Robin Room (Berkeley, 1991), 376–98; Brian Harrison, *Drink and the Victorians: The Temperance Question in England, 1815–1872* (Pittsburgh, 1971), 43–57.

20. Herbert G. Gutman, *Work, Culture, and Society in Industrializing America* (New York, 1976), 36–39; Alan Dawley and Paul Faler, "Working-Class Culture and Politics in the Industrial Revolution: Sources of Loyalism and Rebellion," *JSH* 9 (1976): 466–80; Bruce Laurie, *Working People of Philadelphia, 1800–1850* (Philadelphia, 1980), 54–57. For a critique of this consensus, see Peter Way, "Evil Humors and Ardent Spirits: The Rough Culture of Canal Construction Laborers," *JAH* 79 (1993): 1397–1428.

21. Prisoners for Trial Docket, 1790–1948, 164 vols., Sept. 24, 1922, Oct. 15, 1822, Oct. 28, 1822, PCA; *Public Ledger*, 17 Feb. 1843; Way, "Evil Humors and Ardent Spirits," 1412–14; Anne Royall, *Mrs. Royall's Pennsylvania, or Travels Continued in the United States*, vol. 1 (Washington, 1829), 126; for a fascinating firsthand account of a working man's drinking, see William Otter, *History of My Own Times*, ed. Richard B. Stott (Ithaca, 1995), 44–53.

22. Thompson, *Rum Punch & Revolution*, 41–46; J. Thomas Scharf and Thompson Westcott, *History of Philadelphia, 1609–1884*, vol. 2 (Philadelphia, 1884), 996–97; Claudia Goldin, "The Economic Status of Women in the Early Republic: Quantitative Evidence," *Journal of Interdisciplinary History* 16 (1986): 375–404; Jeanne Boydston, "The Woman Who Wasn't There: Women's Market Labor and the Transition to Capitalism in the United States," *JER* 16 (1996): 183–206.

23. Hamilton, *Gentleman's Progress*, 90–91, 96, 102; Thompson, *Rum Punch & Revolution*, 89–90; Boydston, "Woman Who Wasn't There," 202.

24. A sampling of the Prisoners for Trial Docket for Sept. 1822, Oct. 1822, Feb. 1823, Jan. 1824, and Feb. 1824 reveals that women made up 47.1 percent of those charged with public intoxication ($n = 51$); Prisoners for Trial Dockets, PCA, Feb. 16, 1824; Oct. 30, 1822. See also Billy G. Smith, ed., *Life in Early Philadelphia: Documents from the Revolutionary and Early National Periods* (University Park, Pa., 1995), 77–86; Christine Stansell, *City of Women: Sex and Class in New York, 1789–1860* (New York, 1986), 80.

25. Othniel A. Pendleton, Jr., "Temperance and the Evangelical Churches," *Journal of Presbyterian History* 25 (1947): 15.

26. Cobbett, *Year's Residence*, 198.

27. Thompson Westcott, "History of Philadelphia" (1833), 72, HSP.

28. White men created a Young Men's Domestic Missionary Society (1824), Temperance Society (1828), Bible Association to Spread the Scriptures in South America (1828), an Association for the Gratuitous Instruction of Male Colored Persons [renamed Clarkson Institute] (1829), Temperance Society of Kensington (1830), Tract Society (1832), Anti-Tobacco Society (1833), Colonization Society (1834), a Second Temperance Society (1835), a Bible Society (1837), Methodist Colonization Society (1838), and Temperance Association (1842). The Young Men's Anti-Slavery Society (1835) was the only biracial society. Black men established a Young Men's Rising Beneficial Society (1833), Colored Young Men Association (1838), Library Association (ca. 1839), Vigilant Society (ca. 1839), Wilberforce Debating Society (ca. 1837), and Bible Association of the Second African Presbyterian Church (ca. 1842).

29. Joseph F. Kett, *Rites of Passage: Adolescence in America, 1790 to the Present* (New York,

1977), 11–14; John Demos, *Past, Present, and Personal: The Family and Life Course in American History* (New York, 1986), 100–101; Howard P. Chudacoff, *How Old Are You?: Age Consciousness in American Culture* (Princeton, 1989), 9–28.

30. Based on an analysis of 291 young men reformers in Philadelphia, 92 of whose birth dates could be ascertained; see Bruce Dorsey, "City of Brotherly Love: Religious Benevolence, Gender, and Reform in Philadelphia, 1780–1844" (Ph.D. diss., Brown University, 1993), 263, 267 (tables 6.4, 6.5, 6.7). These "young men" were also not all recent immigrants from rural areas. Perhaps as many as 25–40 percent were urban natives. Jacksonian young men's societies were not, then, early precursors of the Young Men's Christian Association (YMCA) of the 1850s, which involved an older leadership and an adolescent membership and which was designed to protect rural boys during their earliest encounters with the city.

31. Barnes, "Introduction," 3; Philadelphians were presented with a feast of such publications, including the *Young Man's Sunday Book* (1833), the *Young Man's Own Book* (1833), Stephen Tyng's *The Young Man's Glory and the Duty of a Young Disciple* (1832), and Robert Philip's *Manly Piety in Its Spirit* (1837); see also Kett, *Rites of Passage*, 86–108.

32. Several historians argue unconvincingly for an early nineteenth-century flight of youths from farms to the cities; see Kett, *Rites of Passage*, 93–94; Paul Boyer, *Urban Masses and Moral Order in America, 1820–1920* (Cambridge, Mass., 1978), 109. Census data do not confirm this. The proportion of male youths (ages 16–25) and young adult men (ages 26–44) in Philadelphia's male population remained very consistent for the entire period between 1800 and 1860; see Everett S. Lee and Michael Lalli, "Population," in *The Growth of the Seaport Cities, 1790–1825*, ed. David T. Gilchrist (Charlottesville, Va., 1967), 25–37; *Population of the United States in 1860: Compiled from the Original Returns of the Eighth Census* (Washington, D.C., 1860); Dorsey, "City of Brotherly Love," 255–58.

33. Erik H. Erikson, *Identity: Youth and Crisis* (New York, 1968); Kenneth Keniston, "Youth: A 'New' Stage of Life," *American Scholar* 39 (1970): 631–54; Keniston, "Social Change and Youth in America," *Daedalus* 91 (1962): 145–71; John Demos and Virginia Demos, "Adolescence in Historical Perspective," *Journal of Marriage and Family* 31 (1969): 632–38; Lois W. Banner, "Religion and Reform in the Early Republic: The Role of Youth," *AQ* 23 (1971): 678–79; Kett, *Rites of Passage*.

34. Both turn-of-the-century youth organizations (including the Boys Scouts) that coincided with that era's "crisis" in masculinity and the affinity between youth movements and the sexual and feminist revolutions during the 1960s confirm this; for the former, see David I. Macleod, *Building Character in the American Boy: The Boy Scouts, YMCA, and Their Forerunners, 1870–1920* (Madison, 1983).

35. [Charles Jared Ingersoll], *Inchiquin, The Jesuit's Letters, during a Late Residence in the United States of America . . .* (New York, 1810), 122–23; Joyce Appleby, *Capitalism and a New Social Order: The Republican Vision of the 1790s* (New York, 1984), 79–105; Steven Watts, *The Republic Reborn: War and the Making of Liberal America, 1790–1820* (Baltimore, 1987), 2–16; Wood, *Radicalism of the American Revolution*, 325–47.

36. Thomas C. Haliburton, *The Clockmaker; or, the Sayings and Doings of Samuel Slick of Slickville* (Philadelphia, 1839), 112; Philadelphia *Aurora*, 4 June 1812, quoted in Watts, *Republic Reborn*, 74; Alexis de Tocqueville, *Democracy in America*, ed. J. P. Mayer (Garden City, N.Y., 1969), 526, 536, 621–22; Ruth H. Bloch, "The Gendered Meanings of Virtue in Revolutionary America," *Signs* 13 (1987): 37–58.

37. Charles E. Rosenberg, "Sexuality, Class and Role in Nineteenth-Century America," *AQ* 25 (1973): 150; E. Anthony Rotundo, "Learning about Manhood: Gender Ideals and the Middle-Class Family in Nineteenth-Century America," in *Manliness and Morality: Middle-Class Masculinity in Britain and America, 1800–1940*, ed. J. A. Mangan and James Walvin (Manchester, UK., 1987), 35–51.

38. John Bach McMaster, *The Life and Times of Stephen Girard, Mariner and Merchant*, 2 vols. (Philadelphia, 1918); Harry Emerson Wildes, *Lonely Midas: The Story of Stephen Girard* (New York, 1943).

39. Thomas M. McDade, *The Annals of Murders: A Bibliography of Books and Pamphlets on American Murders from Colonial Times to 1900* (Norman, Okla., 1961); David Brion Davis, *Homicide in*

American Fiction, 1783–1860: A Study in Social Values (Ithaca, 1957); Rorabaugh, *Alcoholic Republic,* 7–11, 16, 18–21; David J. Rothman, *The Discovery of the Asylum: Social Order and Disorder in the New Republic* (Boston, 1971), 111, 115. See also Scott Sandage, *Forgotten Men: Failure in American Culture, 1819–1893* (Cambridge, Mass., forthcoming); Edward J. Balleisen, *Navigating Failure: Bankruptcy and Commercial Society in Antebellum America* (Chapel Hill, 2001).

40. Barnes, "Introduction," 5–6; Henry A. Boardman, *Piety Essential to Man's Temporal Prosperity* (Philadelphia, 1834), 22; William M. Engles, *A Plea for Religion* (Philadelphia, 1833), 22; Engles, *The Wages of Unrighteousness* (Philadelphia, 1834); *Public Ledger,* 15 Apr. 1836; 4 May 1836; 28 Mar. 1837; 3, 4 Apr. 1837.

41. Barnes, "Introduction," 6–7; Albert Barnes, "Revivals of Religion in Cities and Large Towns," *American National Preacher* 15 (1841): 23; Albert Barnes, *The Choice of a Profession* (Amherst, 1838), 11; John Todd, *The Moral Influence, Dangers and Duties, Connected with Great Cities* (Northampton, Mass., 1841), 137–80; Tocqueville, *Democracy in America,* 621; *The Young Man's Sunday Book* (Philadelphia, 1835), 269. Cornelius C. Cuyler, *The Signs of the Times: A Series of Discourses Delivered in the Second Presbyterian Church, Philadelphia* (Philadelphia, 1839), 93.

42. Engles, *Plea for Religion,* 21–27; Joseph R. Ingersoll, *Address Delivered before the National Convention of Young Men's Societies for Moral and Intellectual Improvement* (Philadelphia, 1834), 9, 20; "Influence of Youth," *American Sunday School Magazine* 5 (Apr. 1828): 102–3; Halttunen, *Confidence Men and Painted Women,* 4–11.

43. Allen Steinberg, *The Transformation of Criminal Justice: Philadelphia, 1800–1880* (Chapel Hill, 1989), 16–55, quotation on p. 18.

44. *Public Ledger,* 5, 12 Apr. 1836; 25, 26 Mar. 1836; 19, 23 Apr. 1836; 2, 3 May 1836; see also 4 Apr. 1837; 23 Sept. 1837; 3 Mar. 1842; 3 Apr. 1844.

45. *Public Ledger,* 3 Mar. 1842; 18 Apr. 1842; cited in Steinberg, *Transformation of Criminal Justice,* 19. The Helen Jewett murder in New York City provoked worries that "genteel scoundrels" similar to Richard Robinson (Jewett's paramour and accused murderer) might be "strutting through the streets of Philadelphia," needing to be deterred by "a spirit of manly independence." *Public Ledger,* 3 May 1836; 12, 14, 15, 22 Apr. 1836; Patricia Cline Cohen, "Unregulated Youth: Masculinity and Murder in the 1830s City," *Radical History Review* 52 (1992): 33–52; Patricia Cline Cohen, *The Murder of Helen Jewett* (New York, 1998).

46. *Public Ledger,* 20 Apr. 1836; 30 Mar. 1836; 18 Apr. 1836; Gary B Nash, *Forging Freedom: The Formation of Philadelphia's Black Community, 1720–1840* (Cambridge, Mass., 1988), 135–36, 146.

47. W. Jeffrey Bolster, "'To Feel Like a Man': Black Seamen in the Northern States, 1800–1860," *JAH* 76 (1990): 1173–99; Bolster, "'Every Inch a Man': Gender in the Lives of African American Seamen, 1800–1860," in *Iron Men, Wooden Women: Gender and Seafaring in the Atlantic World, 1700–1920,* ed. Margaret S. Creighton and Lisa Norling (Baltimore, 1996), 138–68; Bolster, *Black Jacks: African American Seamen in the Age of Sail* (Cambridge, Mass., 1997).

48. Nash, *Forging Freedom,* 219–22; Shane White, *Somewhat More Independent: The End of Slavery in New York City, 1770–1810* (Athens, Ga., 1991), 185–206; Shane White, "'It Was a Proud Day': African Americans, Festivals, and Parades in the North, 1741–1834," *JAH* 81 (1994): 13–50; Shane White and Graham White, *Stylin': African American Expressive Culture from Its Beginnings to the Zoot Suit* (Ithaca, 1998).

49. The literature on masculinity in the nineteenth century has become extensive; see E. Anthony Rotundo, *American Manhood* (New York, 1993); Mark C. Carnes, *Secret Ritual and Manhood in Victorian America* (New Haven, 1989); Mark C. Carnes and Clyde Griffen, eds., *Meanings for Manhood: Constructions of Masculinity in Victorian America* (Chicago, 1990); Cohen, "Unregulated Youth,"; Gail Bederman, *Manliness & Civilization: A Cultural History of Gender and Race in the United States, 1880–1917* (Chicago, 1995).

50. I have identified more than sixty young men's reform societies in other northern towns, including fourteen in New York City, twelve in Boston, and four in Baltimore.

51. Dorsey, "City of Brotherly Love," 267; Carnes, *Secret Ritual,* chap. 4.

52. These young male reformers certainly expressed other forms of masculine identity, including, as Anthony Rotundo and Donald Yacovone have suggested, strong loving and intimate relationships with close male friends. Rotundo, *American Manhood,* chap. 4; Donald Yacovone,

"Abolitionists and the 'Language of Fraternal Love'," in Carnes and Griffen, *Meanings for Manhood*, 85–95; Karen V. Hansen, "'Our Eyes Behold Each Other': Masculinity and Intimate Friendship in Antebellum New England," in *Men's Friendships*, ed. Peter M. Nardi (Newbury Park, Calif., 1992), 35–58.

53. Most white young male reformers were professionals, with the exception of the antislavery society, where artisans predominated; see Dorsey, "City of Brotherly Love," 268–70 (tables 6.9 and 6.10).

54. Ingersoll, *Address*, 21–22; Engles, *Plea For Religion*, 22; *Constitution of the Young Men's Colonization Society [of New York]* (New York, 1832), 6; Banner, "Religion and Reform," 677–95.

55. J. R. Tyson, *A Discourse before the Young Men's Colonization Society of Pennsylvania, . . .* (Philadelphia, 1834), 6; *Second Annual Report of the Young Men's Tract Society, of Philadelphia* (Philadelphia, 1833), 19; *The Third Annual Report of the Young Men's Bible Society* (Philadelphia, 1841), 8; *Constitution of the Young Men's Colonization Society*, 6.

56. Lewis R. Ashhurst, Journal, vol. 1, 1834–44, HSP; Gideon Burton, *Reminiscences of Gideon Burton* (Cincinnati, 1895), 66–78.

57. Burton, *Reminiscences of Gideon Burton*, 75.

58. *Colored American*, 16 Oct. 1841, BAP, 4:0263; Howard H. Bell, ed., *Minutes of the Proceedings of the National Negro Conventions, 1830–1864* (New York, 1969); Julie Winch, *Philadelphia's Black Elite: Activism, Accommodation, and the Struggle for Autonomy, 1787–1848* (Philadelphia, 1988), 99–100.

59. Benjamin Quarles, "Antebellum Free Blacks and the 'Spirit of '76'," *Journal of Negro History* 61 (1976), 229–42; Winch, *Philadelphia's Black Elite*, 95.

60. Sam Bass Warner, Jr., *The Private City: Philadelphia in Three Periods of Its Growth* (Philadelphia, 1968), 49–78; Diane Lindstrom, *Economic Development in the Philadelphia Region, 1810–1850* (New York, 1978), 23–40; Cynthia J. Shelton, *The Mills of Manayunk: Industrialization and Social Conflict in the Philadelphia Region, 1787–1837* (Baltimore, 1986); Laurie, *Working People of Philadelphia*, 3–30; Charles Sellers, *The Market Revolution: Jacksonian America, 1815–1846* (New York, 1991), 19–28; Stuart M. Blumin, *The Emergence of the Middle Class: Social Experience in the American City, 1760–1900* (New York, 1989), 83–107.

61. Norman J. Johnston, "Caste and Class of the Urban Form of Historic Philadelphia," *Journal of the American Institute of Planners* 32 (1966): 334–50.

62. George Rogers Taylor, "'Philadelphia in Slices' by George G. Foster," *PMHB* 93 (1969): 35; Scharf and Westcott, *History of Philadelphia*, vol. 1, 466–67, 482, 549. See also Bruce Laurie, "Fire Companies and Gangs in Southwark: The 1840s," in *The Peoples of Philadelphia: A History of Ethnic Groups and Lower-Class Life, 1790–1940*, ed. Allen F. Davis and Mark H. Haller (Philadelphia, 1973), 71–87; Wilentz, *Chants Democratic*, 300–301; Stansell, *City of Women*, 89–101; and Cohen, "Unregulated Youth."

63. Robert Adair, *Memoir of Rev. James Patterson* (Philadelphia, 1840), 45–48, 50–51, 59–74; E. H. Gillett, *History of the Presbyterian Church in the United States of America*, vol. 2 (Philadelphia, 1864), 489–90; "Revivals of Religion," *The Panoplist* 12 (May 1816): 242; Thomas James Shepherd, *History of the First Presbyterian Church, Northern Liberties* ([Philadelphia], 1882), 56–57; Richard Carwardine, "The Second Great Awakening in the Urban Centers: An Examination of Methodism and the 'New Measures'," *JAH* 59 (1972): 327–40.

64. Charles G. Finney to Theodore Weld, Mar. 27, 1828, in *Letters of Theodore Dwight Weld and Angelina Grimké Weld and Sarah Grimké, 1822–1844*, [hereafter *Weld-Grimké Letters*] ed. Gilbert H. Barnes and Dwight L. Dumond, vol. 1 (New York, 1934), 10. Finney remembered these events differently when he penned his autobiography many decades later, emphasizing instead his successes in Philadelphia. Charles G. Finney, *Memoirs of Rev. Charles G. Finney. Written By Himself* (New York, 1876), 238–55.

65. Paul E. Johnson, *A Shopkeeper's Millennium: Society and Revivals in Rochester, New York, 1815–1837* (New York, 1978); Whitney R. Cross, *The Burned-Over District* (Ithaca, 1950), 154–56, 168–69.

66. American Temperance Society (ATS), *Fourth Report of the American Temperance Society* (Boston, 1831), in *Permanent Temperance Documents of the American Temperance Society* (Boston, 1835), 28, 38, 161, 342 [all references to ATS annual reports (1831–36) are from this edition.]; John Allen Krout, *The Origins of Prohibition* (New York, 1925), 128–29; Ian R. Tyrrell, *Sobering Up:*

From Temperance to Prohibition in Antebellum America, 1800–1860 (Westport, Conn., 1979), 87–88; Tyrrell, "Women and Temperance in Antebellum America, 1830–1860," *Civil War History* 28 (1982): 132; Winthrop Hudson, *Religion in America*, 2nd ed. (New York, 1973), 129.

67. Pendleton, "Temperance and the Evangelical Churches," 34, 35.

68. *Constitution of the Pennsylvania Society for Discouraging the Use of Ardent Spirits* (n.p., [1827]), 1–4; *A Warning Voice against Intemperance!* (Philadelphia, 1828), 1–4; *Proceedings of Pennsylvania Society for Discouraging the Use of Ardent Spirits*, in *Reports of Temperance Societies* (n.p., [1828]), 4–5.

69. Despite this emphasis on moral suasion, political activity was always a part of the temperance crusade from its beginning. Examples of legislative efforts by the Pennsylvania Temperance Society to restrict the manufacture and sale of liquor can be seen in *The Third Anniversary Report of the Managers of the Pennsylvania Society for Discouraging the Use of Ardent Spirits* (Philadelphia, 1832), 17–18.

70. Rorabaugh, *Alcoholic Republic*, 7–11, 232–33; *The Anniversary Report of the Managers of the Pennsylvania Society for Discouraging the Use of Ardent Spirits* (Philadelphia, 1831), 8.

71. *Journal of Health* 1 (1829–30): 288; John Bell, *Address to the Medical Students' Temperance Society, of the University of Pennsylvania* ([Philadelphia], 1833); Stephen Nissenbaum, *Sex, Diet, and Debility in Jacksonian America: Sylvester Graham and Health Reform* (Westport, Conn., 1980), 74–79. Although the *Journal of Health* included occasional articles on women's health, its focus was primarily temperance and its effects on the health of male workers; see "Physical Education of Girls," *Journal of Health* 1 (1829–30): 14–15.

72. *Genius of Temperance*, 6 Apr. 1831; 4 May 1831. On mixed reactions to Graham's lectures, see Edith Walters Cole, "Sylvester Graham, Lecturer on the Science of Human Life: The Rhetoric of a Dietary Reformer," (Ph.D. diss., Indiana University, 1975), 66–67.

73. *Genius of Temperance*, 25 May 1831

74. *Genius of Temperance*, 4 May 1831; *Anniversary Report of the Pennsylvania Temperance Society*, 8, 22–23; Pendleton, "Temperance and the Evangelical Churches," 30.

75. *Journal of Health* 2 (1830–31): 113–14; Nissenbaum, *Sex, Diet, and Debility*, 79–82.

76. Richard H. Shryock, "Sylvester Graham and the Popular Health Movement, 1830–1870," *Mississippi Valley Historical Review* 18 (1931): 175; Mildred V. Naylor, "Sylvester Graham, 1794–1851," *Annals of Medical History* [3rd ser.] 4 (1942): 237–39; Cole, "Sylvester Graham," 65–70.

77. Sylvester Graham, *A Lecture to Young Men on Chastity* (Boston, 1837); Naylor, "Sylvester Graham," 239.

78. Graham, *Lecture to Young Men*, 34–43, 44–47, 50–51; G. J. Barker-Benfield, "The Spermatic Economy: A Nineteenth-Century View of Sexuality," in *The American Family in Social-Historical Perspective*, 2nd ed., ed. Michael Gordon (New York, 1978), 374–402.

79. Graham, *Lecture to Young Men*, 51–52, 49, 62–66, 68–73, 77–115, 149–51. Graham's early life, filled with losses, abandonment, and physical and mental breakdowns, reveals a great deal about his obsessions as a lecturer. The seventeenth child of a Connecticut clergyman (the seventh by his second wife), Graham suffered his father's intestate death and his mother being declared "deranged" before he was eight. Like many New England residents forced into a landless, wage-earning status, Graham worked on neighbors' farms and in mills, moved in and out of schools, and was bounced among his older siblings until he was twenty-nine. He had a history of frail physical and emotional health to the point of extreme exhaustion, and he was bitter and angry throughout his life. Graham had difficulty dealing with intense emotional and physical stress, and never found an outlet for his feelings of anger toward those who had failed or abandoned him. He thus conceived the ideal existence as one without stimulation of the passions, whether from food, drink, sexual desire, or emotions. Helen Graham Carpenter, *The Reverend John Graham of Woodbury, Connecticut and His Descendents* (Chicago, 1942), 183–84, 188–89; *Genius of Temperance*, 25 May 1831; Cole, "Sylvester Graham," 8–16; Naylor, "Sylvester Graham," 236–37; Nissenbaum, *Sex, Diet, and Debility*, 10–13; Sylvester Graham to Theodore Weld, Mar. 19, 1839, in *Weld-Grimké Letters*, vol. 2, 753–55.

80. H. B. Stanton et al. to Theodore D. Weld, Aug. 2, 3, 4, 1832, in *Weld-Grimké Letters*, vol. 1, 85.

81. Thomas P. Hunt, *Life and Thoughts of Rev. Thomas P. Hunt: An Autobiography* (Wilkes-Barre, Pa., 1901), 40, 98, 108, 298–302, 169–71; Pendleton, "Temperance and the Evangelical Churches," 38–39; *JATU* (February 1837).

82. Tyrrell, *Sobering Up*, 159–224; Krout, *Origins of Prohibition*, 182–222.

83. Nearly 73 percent of the members of the Southwark temperance beneficial association (*n* = 135) were artisans or unskilled laborers. *Preamble and Resolutions, Temperance Beneficial Association, Southwark Branch, No. 1*, 2–4 (n.p., n.d.), LCP. A Moyamensing association included 85 percent journeymen and unskilled laborers; Laurie, *Working People of Philadelphia*, 121–22.

84. Laurie, *Working People of Philadelphia*, 121.

85. *Address of the Executive Committee of the Young Men's Temperance Society, to the Young Men of Philadelphia* (Philadelphia, 1828), 11–2; *Circular Addressed to Members of the Massachusetts Society for the Suppression of Intemperance* (1814), in Krout, *Origins of Prohibition*, 92–93; Tyrrell, *Sobering Up*, 76.

86. Tyrrell, *Sobering Up*, 159–71; *Charter and By-Laws of the Temperance Beneficial Association, Western Branch No. 2* (Philadelphia, 1837); *Preamble and Resolutions, Temperance Beneficial Association, Southwark Branch, No. 1; First Anniversary of the William Penn Temperance Beneficial Association, Branch No. 19* (Philadelphia, 1842).

87. *Minutes and Proceedings of the Second Annual Convention, for the Improvement of the Free People of Color . . .* (Philadelphia, 1832), 36; *Minutes and Proceedings of the Third Annual Convention, for the Improvement of the Free People of Color . . .* (New York, 1833), 15–19; *National Anti-Slavery Standard*, 11, 18, 25 Aug. 1842; Frederick Douglass, "Intemperance and Slavery: An Address Delivered in Cork, Ireland, on 20 October 1845," in *The Frederick Douglass Papers*, series 1, ed. John W. Blassingame et al., vol. 1 (New Haven, 1979), 55–57; Donald Yacovone, "The Transformation of the Black Temperance Movement, 1827–1854: An Interpretation," *JER* 8 (1988): 296; Benjamin Quarles, *Black Abolitionists* (New York, 1969), 95–96.

88. Lyman Beecher, *Six Sermons on the Nature, Occasions, Signs, Evils, and Remedy of Intemperance*, 6th ed. (Boston, 1828), 64–73; Anthony Benezet, *The Mighty Destroyer Displayed . . .* (Philadelphia, 1774), 8; Albert Barnes, *The Connexion of Temperance with Republican Freedom* (Philadelphia, 1835); Heman Humphrey, *Parallel between Intemperance and the Slave Trade* (Amherst, 1828); David R. Roediger, *The Wages of Whiteness: Race and the Making of the American Working Class* (New York, 1991), 43–87.

89. On the relationship between temperance and nativism, see chapter five below, and Joseph R. Gusfield, *Symbolic Crusade: Status Politics and the American Temperance Movement*, 2nd ed. (Urbana, 1986), 55–57.

90. *Minutes and Proceedings of the Third Annual Convention*, 18. Jacob C. White, an African American and young men's reformer, employed the same rhetoric to support the prohibition of liquor sales, stating that free blacks had the greatest stake in temperance reform, "so that they should have men to fight their battles, and contend with our enemies for our rights." "Essay by Jacob C. White, Jr., 24 March 1854," in *Black Abolitionist Papers*, ed. C. Peter Ripley et al., vol. 4 (Chapel Hill, 1985–92), 210–11.

91. William Whipper, "Address Delivered before the Colored Temperance Society of Philadelphia, January 8, 1834," *The Liberator*, 21 June 1834, reprinted in Ripley et al., *Black Abolitionist Papers*, vol. 3, 126; *Minutes and Proceedings of the First Annual Meeting of the American Moral Reform Society . . .* (Philadelphia, 1837), reprinted in *Early Negro Writing, 1760–1837*, ed. Dorothy Porter (Boston, 1971), 200–248; Richard P. McCormick, "William Whipper: Moral Reformer," *PH* 43 (1976): 23–46. Donald Yacovone has argued that northern black reformers initially saw slavery as a metaphor for intemperance and then eventually viewed intemperance as a metaphor for slavery; "Transformation of the Black Temperance Movement," 285, 290–91. Perhaps those ideas were interchangeable throughout the antebellum era; see *Frederick Douglass Papers*, ser. 1, vol. 1, 55–59, 165–70, 205–9, 264–68, 339–41.

92. Since the revolutionary era, black elites had repeated the refrain that they possessed a legitimate title as true men and citizens because they were not like "the dissolute, intemperate, and ignorant" mass "of the colored population." *Minutes and Proceedings of the First Annual Convention of the People of Color* (Philadelphia, 1831), 4; Melvin H. Buxbaum, "Cyrus Bustill Addresses

the Blacks of Philadelphia," *WMQ* 29 (1972): 99–108; Nash, *Forging Freedom*, 217–23; Winch, *Philadelphia's Black Elite*, 6–7.

93. Yacovone, "Transformation of the Black Temperance Movement," 297.

94. Robert Purvis to Henry Clarke Wright, Aug. 22, 1842, in Ripley et al., *Black Abolitionist Papers*, 389–90; *National Anti-Slavery Standard*, 11, 18, 25 Aug. 1842; 1 Sept. 1842; Winch *Philadelphia's Black Elite*, 148–50; Joseph A. Boromé, "The Vigilant Committee of Philadelphia," *PMHB* 92 (1968): 325–27.

95. John Marsh, *Temperance Hymn Book and Minstrel* (New York, 1842); *The Washington Temperance Song-Book* (Harrisburg, 1842–1843); George W. Ewing, *The Well-Tempered Lyre: Songs and Verse of the Temperance Movement* (Dallas, 1977).

96. Tyrrell, *Sobering Up*, 176–79; Bayard Tuckerman, ed., *The Diary of Philip Hone, 1828–1851*, vol. 2 (New York, 1889), 80. One writer observed that every town seemed to have temperance lectures, "temperance negro operas; temperance theaters; temperance eating houses, and temperance every thing, and our whole population, in places, is soused head-over-heels in temperance." Baynard Rust Hall, *Something for Every Body* (New York, 1846), cited in David S. Reynolds, "Black Cats and Delirium Tremens: Temperance and the American Renaissance," in *The Serpent in the Cup: Temperance in American Literature*, ed. David S. Reynolds and Debra J. Rosenthal (Amherst, 1997), 22.

97. T. S. Arthur, *Six Nights with the Washingtonians: A Series of Original Temperance Tales* (Philadelphia, 1842); Arthur, *Temperance Tales*, (Philadelphia, 1843); Arthur, *The Club Room, and Other Temperance Tales* (Philadelphia, 1845); Arthur, *Illustrated Temperance Tales* (Philadelphia, 1850).

98. Herbert Ross Brown, *The Sentimental Novel in America, 1790–1860* (Durham, 1940), 201–40; Jean R. Kirkpatrick, "The Temperance Movement and Temperance Fiction, 1820–1860," (Ph.D. diss., University of Pennsylvania, 1970); David S. Reynolds, *Beneath the American Renaissance: The Subversive Imagination in the Age of Emerson and Melville* (Cambridge, Mass., 1988), 65–73, 357–59; Reynolds and Rosenthal, *Serpent in the Cup;* Judith N. McArthur, "Demon Rum on the Boards: Temperance Melodrama and the Tradition of Antebellum Reform," *JER* 9 (1989): 517–40.

99. *JATU* (April 1837): 58; Ewing, *Well-Tempered Lyre*, 116.

100. American Temperance Society (ATS), *Fourth Report*, app., 85–86, 7, 39; ATS, *Fifth Report* (1832), app., 92–93; ATS, *Sixth Report* (1833), 20–21; Pennsylvania Temperance Society, *Third Anniversary Report*, 9; "Order of Exercises," First Anniversary of the Juvenile Temperance Society of the Third Presbyterian Church, Nov. 9, 1841, Broadside, PHS; *Genius of Temperance*, 4 May 1831, 19 Dec. 1832; Rorabaugh, *Alcoholic Republic*, 199.

101. *Public Ledger*, 28 Mar. 1837; 30 Jan. 1843; 3 Feb. 1843; Hunt, *Life and Thoughts*, 107. See also Karen Sánchez-Eppler, "Temperance in the Bed of a Child: Incest and Social Order in Nineteenth-Century America," *AQ* 47 (1995): 1–33; Jerome Nadelhaft, "Alcohol and Wife Abuse in Antebellum Male Temperance Literature," *Canadian Review of American Studies* 25 (1995): 15–43.

102. Arthur, *Temperance Tales*, 9–56. For other examples see Arthur, "The Drunkard's Wife," in *Six Nights with the Washingtonians;* Thomas P. Hunt, *It Will Never Injure Me: Or, Those Who Never Drink Often Suffer Most* (Philadelphia, 1846). The most sensational story of parental abuse from intemperance is Maria Lamas, *The Glass; or, The Trials of Helen More, A Thrilling Temperance Tale* (Philadelphia, 1849), 22, in which a drunken mother locks her child in a closet while she goes on a drinking spree. When the boy is discovered, he had been so starved that he had eaten the flesh off his own arm before dying.

103. T. S. Arthur, *Ten Nights in a Bar-Room, and What I Saw There* (Philadelphia, 1854; reprint, 1864), quotations from pp. 209, 139, 123–24.

104. Ibid., 126, 46, 38, 113, 205; Halttunen, *Confidence Men and Painted Women*, 46–50, 66–67, 188; Carnes, *Secret Ritual, 17–36*.

105. George Stuart, among Philadelphia's young reformers, recalled how an older friend responded to news of his new temperance convictions: "If I were as young as you I would do the same." Robert Ellis Thompson, ed., *The Life of George H. Stuart, Written Mainly By Himself*

(Philadelphia, 1890), 36–37; Bell, *Address to the Medical Students' Temperance Society*, 4–7; *Christian Examiner* 18 (March 1835): 30–31.

106. *Address of the Executive Committee of the Young Men's Temperance Society*, 15; Irvin G. Wyllie, *The Self-Made Man in America: The Myth of Rags to Riches* (New Brunswick, N.J., 1954), 45–49.

107. *JATU* (January 1837): 4–5; *Public Ledger*, 20 May, 1843; ATS, *Fourth Report*, 55; William Breitenbach, "Sons of the Fathers: Temperance Reformers and the Legacy of the American Revolution," *JER* 3 (1983): 69–82.

108. See order of exercises and temperance hymns interspersed throughout *JATU*, February 1837 to March 1838, LCP; William B. Tappan, "Temperance Jubilee Hymn," in *The Sunday School and Other Poems* (Boston, 1847), 231; Tappan, "Ode for the Fourth of July: Who are the Brave?," in Marsh, *Temperance Hymn Book and Minstrel*, 90; Tappan, "The Drunkard's Death," in *Sacred and Miscellaneous Poems* (Boston, 1847), 143–45.

109. *Address of the Executive Committee of the Young Men's Temperance Society*, 7. See also *Life and Death of King Alcohol* (Philadelphia, 1846); *Public Ledger*, 20 May 1843; *American Woman*, 21 Sept. 1844. On the relationship between patriotic citizenship and manhood in America, see Paula Baker, "The Domestication of Politics: Women and American Political Society, 1780–1920," *AHR* 89 (1984): 620–47; Roediger, *Wages of Whiteness;* Nick Salvatore, *Eugene V. Debs: Citizen and Socialist* (Urbana, 1982); Mark E. Kann, *On the Man Question: Gender and Civic Virtue in America* (Philadelphia, 1991).

110. *Constitution of the Pennsylvania Temperance Society*, 3; Tyrrell, "Women and Temperance in Antebellum America"; Krout, *Origins of Prohibition* 148–50; Jed Dannenbaum, "The Origins of Temperance Activism and Militancy among American Women," *JSH* 15 (1981): 235–52.

111. *JATU* (January 1837): 5.

112. Albert Barnes, "Are You a Mother?" *JATU* (August 1837): 115.

113. *JATU* (March 1838): 35.

114. *Temperance Recorder* (Albany, N.Y.), 5 June 1832, quoted in Tyrrell, "Women and Temperance in Antebellum America," 133; Justin Edwards, *Letter to the Friends of Temperance in Massachusetts* (Boston, 1836), 5.

115. *Colored American*, 1 Apr. 1837; 25 Dec. 1841; *Provincial Freeman*, 2, 16 Sept. 1854; 9 June 1855.

116. *The Second Annual Report of the Female Total Abstinence Society of Philadelphia* (Philadelphia, 1838), 7; Ruth M. Alexander, "'We Are Engaged as a Band of Sisters': Class and Domesticity in the Washingtonian Temperance Movement, 1840–1850," *JAH* 75 (1988): 763–85, quotation on p. 770; *American Woman*, 15 Mar. 1845, 19 Oct. 1845; Philadelphia *Sun*, 14 Sept. 1844; *Graham's Magazine* 33 (Nov. 1848): 253–56. On late-nineteenth-century women's temperance activism, see Ruth Bordin, *Woman and Temperance: The Quest for Power and Liberty, 1873–1900* (Philadelphia, 1981); Glenda Elizabeth Gilmore, *Gender and Jim Crow: Women and the Politics of White Supremacy in North Carolina, 1896–1920* (Chapel Hill, 1996), 45–59.

117. Victor J. Seidler, *Rediscovering Masculinity: Reason, Language and Sexuality* (London, 1989), 1–13. As Judith Butler has stated, gender is "a construction that regularly conceals its genesis." "Performative Acts and Gender Constitution: An Essay in Phenomenology and Feminist Theory," *Theatre Journal* 40 (1988): 522.

4. Slavery

1. Michael A. Gomez, *Exchanging Our Country Marks: The Transformation of African Identities in the Colonial and Antebellum South* (Chapel Hill, 1998), 164–67.

2. Henry Box Brown, *Narrative of Henry Box Brown, Who Escaped from Slavery, Enclosed in a Box Three Feet Long, Two Wide, and Two and a Half High* (Boston, 1849), 60, 20, 63. For other instances of slaves being sent to freedom in a box, see William Still, *The Underground Railroad* (Philadelphia, 1872), 46–48, 281–84, 608–10.

3. Albert J. Raboteau, *Slave Religion: The "Invisible Institution" in the Antebellum South* (New York, 1978), 311–12; Raboteau, *A Fire in the Bones: Reflections on African-American Religious History* (Boston, 1995), 28–36.

4. Joseph Blake to R. R. Gurley, A.C.S., Mar. 9, May 13, 1835, American Colonization Society Papers, Library of Congress, Reel 153. Blake never received the redress he petitioned for and left Liberia for Sierra Leone in 1837. "Roll of Emigrants That Have Been Sent to the Colony of Liberia, Western Africa, by the American Colonization Society and Its Auxiliaries, to September 1843," U.S. Congress, *Senate Documents*, 28th Congress, 2nd Sess., 1844, IX, pp. 152, 156; Tom W. Shick, *Behold the Promised Land: A History of Afro-American Settler Society in Nineteenth-Century Liberia* (Baltimore, 1980), 38; James Wesley Smith, *Sojourners in Search of Freedom: The Settlement of Liberia by Black Americans* (Lanham, Md., 1987), chap. 7.

5. On white women abolitionists and women's rights, see Blanche Glassman Hersh, *The Slavery of Sex: Feminist-Abolitionists in America* (Urbana, 1978); Aileen S. Kraditor, *Means and Ends in American Abolitionism* (New York, 1967); Gerda Lerner, *The Grimké Sisters from South Carolina* (New York, 1967); Nancy A. Hewitt, *Women's Activism and Social Change* (Ithaca, 1984); Jean Fagan Yellin, *Women and Sisters: The Antislavery Feminists in American Culture* (New Haven, 1989); Karen Sánchez-Eppler, *Touching Liberty: Abolitionism, Feminism, and the Politics of the Body* (Berkeley, 1993); Debra Gold Hansen, *Strained Sisterhood: Gender and Class in the Boston Female Anti-Slavery Society* (Amherst, 1993); Julie Roy Jeffrey, *The Great Silent Army of Abolitionism: Ordinary Women in the Antislavery Movement* (Chapel Hill, 1998); Jean Fagan Yellin and John Van Horne, eds., *The Abolitionist Sisterhood: Women's Political Culture in Antebellum America* (Ithaca, 1994), especially Nancy A. Hewitt, "On Their Own Terms: A Historiographical Essay," 23–30, which informed the analysis in this paragraph.

6. With one exception, Herbert Aptheker, *Abolitionism: A Revolutionary Movement* (Boston, 1989), none of the general histories of abolitionism since 1984 (all written by men) engages the issues of women or gender aside from passing references to woman's rights. One of the most recent surveys of antebellum reform, Robert H. Abzug, *Cosmos Crumbling: American Reform and the Religious Imagination* (New York, 1994) frames his final two chapters around the twin issues of the "Woman Question" and the struggle for woman's rights.

7. Benjamin Quarles, *Black Abolitionists* (New York, 1969); Shirley J. Yee, *Black Women Abolitionists: A Study in Activism, 1828–1860* (Knoxville, Tenn., 1992); Nell Irvin Painter, *Sojourner Truth: A Life, A Symbol* (New York, 1996); Rosalyn Terborg-Penn, *African American Women in the Struggle for the Vote, 1850–1920* (Bloomington, Ind., 1998). Jeffrey, *Great Silent Army* is a refreshing exception that integrates the history of black and white women abolitionists. By contrast, histories of antebellum reform published in the 1990s—Lori D. Ginzberg, *Women and the Work of Benevolence* (New Haven, 1990); Abzug, *Cosmos Crumbling;* Steven Mintz, *Moralists and Modernizers: America's Pre-Civil War Reformers* (Baltimore, 1995)—write about the antislavery movement as if African Americans are either nonexistent or can be relegated to a few pages on black abolitionists.

8. I use the term "colonization" when referring to white-sponsored plans to expatriate former slaves and free blacks to Africa, modeled on or auxiliary to the American Colonization Society, and "emigration" to refer to plans initiated by African Americans to create black communities outside the borders of the United States, whether in the western hemisphere or on the African continent. Lawrence J. Friedman, *Gregarious Saints: Self and Community in American Abolitionism, 1830–1870* (Cambridge, 1982); Paul Goodman, *Of One Blood: Abolitionism and the Origins of Racial Equality* (Berkeley, 1998), incorporate colonization into their histories of abolitionism, but do not address black emigrationist movements.

9. *Minutes of the Fourth Annual Convention, for the Improvement of the Free People of Colour, in the United States, . . . 1834* (New York, 1834), 5, reprinted in Howard H. Bell, ed., *Minutes of the Proceedings of the National Negro Conventions, 1830–1864* (New York, 1969); American Colonization Society (ACS), *Third Annual Report* (Washington, D.C., 1820), 3, in *Annual Reports of the American Society for the Colonizing of Free People of Colour of the United States*, vol. 1–33 (Washington, D.C., 1818–50; reprint, New York, 1969) [hereafter all ACS annual report citations are from this edition]; *African Repository* 9 (July 1833): 150; P. J. Staudenraus, *The African Colonization Movement, 1816–1865* (New York, 1961), 1–11; 120–21; ACS, *First Annual Report* (1818), 1–3; *African Repository* 12 (July 1836): 207; 9 (May 1833): 95; 9 (July 1833): 159; 16 (Apr. 1840): 112; 16 (July 1840): 207; 13 (Jan. 1837): 33, 38; 12 (June 1836): 186; Mathew Carey, *Letters on the Colonization Society . . . ,* 5th ed. (Philadelphia, 1832), 18–19.

10. Frederick Freeman, *Yaradee; A Plea for Africa, in Familiar Conversations on the Subject of Slavery and Colonization* (Philadelphia, 1836), 175–76; Sarah Forten to Angelina Grimké, Apr. 15, 1837, in *Letters of Theodore Dwight Weld and Angelina Grimké Weld and Sarah Grimké, 1822–1844* [hereafter *Weld-Grimké Letters*], ed. Gilbert H. Barnes and Dwight L. Dumond, vol. 1 (New York, 1934), 380; George M. Fredrickson, *The Black Image in the White Mind: The Debate on Afro-American Character and Destiny, 1817–1914* (New York, 1971), 16–19.

11. *Resolutions and Remonstrances of the People of Colour against Colonization to the Coast of Africa* (Philadelphia, 1818), 3–8; Louis R. Mehlinger, "The Attitude of the Free Negro toward African Colonization," *Journal of Negro History* 1 (1916): 277–79; ACS, *First Annual Report*, 14–16; *Constitution of the Young Men's Colonization Society [of New York]* (New York, 1832), 5, 10; Augustus Washington, "Thoughts on the American Colonization Society," *African Repository* 27 (1851), reprinted in Wilson Jeremiah Moses, ed., *Liberian Dreams: Back-to-Africa Narratives from the 1850s* (University Park, Pa., 1998), 195; *Liberator*, 22 Jan. 1831, 12 Mar. 1831, 19 Mar. 1831; William Lloyd Garrison, *Thoughts on African Colonization* (Boston, 1832), pt. 2, 9–13; *Anti-Slavery Reporter* 1 (June 1833): 7–9; Edwin P. Atlee, "What Are the Respective Merits of the Anti-Slavery and Colonization Societies" [1832], PPAS, reel 25; Julie Winch, *Philadelphia's Black Elite: Activism, Accommodation, and the Struggle for Autonomy, 1787–1848* (Philadelphia, 1988), 27–47; Gary B. Nash, *Forging Freedom: The Formation of Philadelphia's Black Community, 1720–1840* (Cambridge, Mass., 1988), 233–41.

12. Based on an analysis of the American Colonization Society's annual reports 1817–40 and these colonization newspapers: the *African Repository* (Washington, D.C.), 1825–40; the *Colonization Herald* (Philadelphia), 1835–40, and *The Colonizationist* (Boston), 1833–34. I have identified another nineteen women's societies between 1832 and 1840, but they were still heavily outnumbered by men's groups—by nearly six to one (33 to 6), in the *African Repository* in 1833–34, for example. For southern white women's activism as colonizationists, see Elizabeth R. Varon, "Evangelical Womanhood and the Politics of the African Colonization Movement in Virginia," in *Religion and the Antebellum Debate over Slavery*, ed. John R. McKivigan and Mitchell Snay (Athens, Ga., 1998), 169–95.

13. Friedman, *Gregarious Saints*, 14–16.

14. ACS, *Annual Reports;* Philip S. Foner, ed., *The Life and Writings of Frederick Douglass*, vol. 1 (New York, 1950), 390.

15. Staudenraus, *African Colonization Movement*, 19–22, 34–36, 48–58, 169–87; *National Intelligencer*, 16 Jan. 1817; *Colonization Herald*, 16 Apr. 1836; 4 Apr. 1835; 21 Jan. 1837; 4 Feb. 1837; n.s. 1 (Mar. 1839): 120–25; *African Repository* 12 (May 1836): 152; ACS, *Second Annual Report* (1819), 10–17; ACS, *Third Annual Report*, 11–14, 33, 37; Carey, *Letters on the Colonization Society*, 15, 17.

16. *African Repository* 9 (May 1833): 95; 9 (June 1833): 99; 9 (July 1833): 159–60; 9 (Dec. 1833): 315; 12 (May 1836): 140; 14 (May 1838): 160; John H. Kennedy, *Sympathy, Its Foundation and Legitimate Exercise Considered* . . . (Philadelphia, 1828), 10; Foner, *Life and Writings of Frederick Douglass*, vol. 2, 189; Susan G. Davis, *Parades and Power: Street Theatre in Nineteenth-Century Philadelphia* (Philadelphia, 1986), 38–48.

17. For contrasting views that suggest that the political arena was not exclusively male, see Elizabeth R. Varon, *We Mean to Be Counted: White Women and Politics in Antebellum Virginia* (Chapel Hill, 1998); Mary P. Ryan, *Women in Public: Between Banners and Ballots, 1825–1880* (Baltimore, 1990); Paula Baker, "The Domesticiation of Politics: Women and American Political Society, 1780–1920," *AHR* 89 (1984): 620–47; Linda K. Kerber, "The Paradox of Women's Citizenship in the Early Republic: The Case of *Martin vs. Massachusetts*, 1805," *AHR* 97 (1992): 349–78. For the shift from moral suasion to political action, see Lori D. Ginzberg, "'Moral Suasion Is Moral Balderdash': Women, Politics, and Social Activism in the 1850s," *JAH* 73 (1986): 601–22.

18. J. R. Tyson, *A Discourse before the Young Men's Colonization Society of Pennsylvania* . . . (Philadelphia, 1834), 8; *Colonization Herald*, 18 Apr. 1835; Kurt Lee Kocher, "A Duty to America and Africa: A History of the Independent African Colonization Movement in Pennsylvania," *PH* 51 (1984): 128–41; Eli Seifman, "The United Colonization Societies of New-York and Pennsylvania and the Establishment of the African Colony of Bassa Cove," *PH* 35 (1968): 37–44.

19. "Cresson," in Frank Willing Leach, *Old Philadelphia Families* in *The North American* (Philadelphia, 1907–1912), HSP; Joseph S. Hepburn, "The Life and Works of Elliott Cresson," *Journal of the Franklin Institute* 281 (1966); Kocher, "Duty to America and Africa," 123–28; R. J. M. Blackett, *Building an Antislavery Wall: Black Americans in the Atlantic Abolitionist Movement, 1830–1860* (Baton Rouge, 1983), 51–70; Walter M. Merrill, ed., *The Letters of William Lloyd Garrison*, vol. 1 (Cambridge, Mass., 1971–1981), 235–71.

20. ACS, *Twelfth Annual Report* (1829), vi; *Constitution of the Young Men's Colonization Society,* 9.

21. For an example later in the century, see Gail Bederman, *Manliness & Civilization: A Cultural History of Gender and Race in the United States, 1880–1917* (Chicago, 1995).

22. *Colonization Herald,* 4 Apr. 1835; *African Repository* 12 (June 1836): 185–86; 14 (Sept. 1838): 261; *Colonization Herald* n.s. 1 (Mar. 1839): 120–25.

23. ACS, *First Annual Report,* 10; *Colonization Herald,* 5 Mar. 1836; 17 Dec. 1836; 4 Apr. 1835; James Oakes, *The Ruling Race: A History of American Slaveholders* (New York, 1982), 76–95; Joan E. Cashin, *A Family Venture: Men and Women on the Southern Frontier* (New York, 1991), chaps. 2, 5.

24. "Roll of Emigrants," 152–299. African American women made up 43.5 percent of the 508 adult emigrants sent on the American Colonization Society's first fifteen voyages between 1820 and 1828.

25. The literature on empire and domesticity has burgeoned, most prominently in the fields of literature and cultural studies; see Karen Sánchez-Eppler, "Raising Empires like Children: Race, Nation, and Religious Education," *American Literary History* 8 (1996): 399–425; Amy Kaplan, "Manifest Domesticity," *American Literature* 70 (1998): 581–606; Vicente L. Rafael, "Colonial Domesticity: White Women and United States Rule in the Philippines," *American Literature* 67 (1995): 639–66; Rosemary Marangoly George, "Homes in the Empire, Empires in the Home," *Cultural Critique* 26 (1993–94): 95–127; Anna Davin, "Imperialism and Mortherhood," *History Workshop* 5 (1978): 9–65; Anne McClintock, *Imperial Leather: Race, Gender, and Sexuality in the Colonial Contest* (New York, 1995); Karen Tranberg Hansen, ed., *African Encounters with Domesticity* (New Brunswick, 1992).

26. *African Repository* 12 (June 1836): 185; ACS, *First Annual Report,* 15; *African Repository* 9 (Sept. 1833): 196–99; *Minutes of the Fourth Annual Convention, for the Improvement of the Free People of Colour,* 5; *African Repository* 14 (Sept. 1838): 255–62; *Colonization Herald* n.s. 1 (Jan. 1839): 27–28; *The Colonizationist,* Aug. 1833, 107; Charles Stuart, *Remarks on the Colony of Liberia and the American Colonization Society* . . . (London, 1832), 7, cited in Blackett, *Building an Antislavery Wall,* 57. For other criticisms of the missionary objectives of the colonization society, see Lydia Maria Child, *Anti-Slavery Catechism* (Newburyport, Mass., 1836), 28; William Lloyd Garrison, *An Address Delivered before the Free People of Color, in Philadelphia, New-York, and Other Cities,* . . . (Boston, 1831), 22; Lott Cary to Rev. Dr. [William] Staughton, Mar. 13, 1821, cited in *Apropos of Africa,* ed. Adelaide Cromwell Hill and Martin Kilson (London, 1969), 81.

27. *Freemen Awake!* . . . (Philadelphia, 1832), 17.

28. *Maryland Colonization Journal,* reprinted in the *Colonization Herald* n.s. 1 (Jan. 1839): 15–16; *Colonization Herald,* 4 Apr. 1835.

29. Roy Harvey Pearce, *Savagism and Civilization: A Study of the Indian and the American Mind* (Berkeley, 1988); George W. Stocking, Jr., *Victorian Anthropology* (New York, 1987); Bederman, *Manliness & Civilization.*

30. Isaac V. Brown, *Memoirs of the Rev. Robert Finley, D. D.* . . . , 2nd ed. (New Brunswick, N.J., 1819), 39, 83–96, quoted in Staudenraus, *African Colonization Movement,* 21; Alexander T. McGill, *The Hand of God with the Black Race. A Discourse Delivered before the Pennsylvania Colonization Society* (Philadelphia, 1862), 11–12; ACS, *First Annual Report,* 21; *Colonization Herald* n.s. 1 (Apr. 1839): 159–60; n.s. 1 (June 1839): 266; *The Colonizationist,* May 1833, 42–43; *Constitution of the Young Men's Colonization Society,* 7; Deborah Gray White, *Ar'n't I a Woman?: Female Slaves in the Plantation South* (New York, 1985), chap. 1.

31. Rebecca Stott, "The Dark Continent: Africa as Female Body in Haggard's Adventure Fiction," *Feminist Review* 32 (1989): 69–89; Patrick Brantlinger, *Rule of Darkness: British Literature and Imperialism, 1830–1914* (Ithaca, 1988), 190; Ann Laura Stoler, "Carnal Knowledge and Imperial

Power: Gender, Race, and Morality in Colonial Asia," in *Gender at the Crossroads of Knowledge: Feminist Anthropology in the Postmodern Era*, ed. Micaela di Leonardo (Berkeley, 1991), 51–101. See also Sander L. Gilman, *Difference and Pathology: Stereotypes of Sexuality, Race, and Madness* (Ithaca, 1985), 76–108; Edward W. Said, *Orientalism* (New York, 1978), 207; Richard C. Trexler, *Sex and Conquest: Gendered Violence, Political Order, and the European Conquest of the Americas* (Ithaca, 1995).

32. David Brion Davis, "Some Themes of Counter-Subversion: An Analysis of Anti-Masonic, Anti-Catholic, and Anti-Mormon Literature," *Mississippi Valley Historical Review* 47 (1960): 205–24; Charles E. Rosenberg, "Sexuality, Class and Role in Nineteenth-Century America," *AQ* 25 (1973): 131–53; Carroll Smith-Rosenberg, "Sex as Symbol in Victorian Purity: An Ethnohistorical Analysis of Jacksonian America," *American Journal of Sociology* 84 (1978): supplement, 212–47; Norma Basch, "Marriage, Morals, and Politics in the Election of 1828," *JAH* 80 (1993): 890–913.

33. Phrases such as "social intercourse," "intimate union," and "social equality" became euphemisms for "amalgamation." The term "miscegenation" was not coined until the Civil War years, when Democrats invented it as a political attack on Lincoln to raise fears of the Emancipation Proclamation during the election of 1864; see Martha Hodes, "Miscegenation," *Encyclopedia of African-American Culture and History*, ed. Jack Salzman et al., vol. 4 (New York, 1996), 813–15.

34. *Freemen Awake!*, 21; Carey, *Letters on the Colonization Society*, 12; Oliver Bolokitten, Esq. [pseud.], *A Sojourn in the City of Amalgamation, in the Year of Our Lord 19—* (New York, 1835); Lorman Ratner, *Powder Keg: Northern Opposition to the Antislavery Movement* (New York, 1968), 14, 24. William H. Burleigh remarked that colonization in Pennsylvania "is simply anti-abolitionism." *Pennsylvania Freeman*, 5 Apr. 1838.

35. *Minutes and Proceedings of the First Annual Convention of the People of Color* (Philadelphia, 1831), 15, reprinted in Bell, *Minutes of the Proceedings of the National Negro Conventions;* Peter Williams, *A Discourse Delivered in St. Philip's Church . . .* (New York, 1830), 7–8; *Liberator*, 2 July 1831.

36. [Robert Purvis], *Appeal of Forty Thousand Citizens, Threatened with Disfranchisement, to the People of Pennsylvania* (Philadelphia, 1838), reprinted in Herbert Aptheker ed., *A Documentary History of the Negro People in the United States*, vol. 1 (New York, 1951–74), 176–86; *Colored American*, 27, 30 Jan. 1838; 8 May 1841; *Pennsylvania Freeman*, 22 Mar. 1838; *National Enquirer*, 1 Mar. 1838; *Liberator*, 14 Apr. 1832; Leon F. Litwack, *North of Slavery: The Negro in the Free States, 1790–1860* (Chicago, 1961), 20; Edward Price, "The Black Voting Rights Issue in Pennsylvania, 1780–1900," *PMHB* 100 (1976): 356–73; David McBride, "Black Protest against Racial Politics: Gardiner, Hinton and Their Memorial of 1838," *PH* 46 (1979): 149–62.

37. *Freemen Awake!*, 11, 23. For a parallel development in the Reconstruction South, see Martha Hodes, *White Women, Black Men: Illicit Sex in the Nineteenth-Century South* (New Haven, 1997), chap. 7.

38. Litwack, *North of Slavery*, 69; ACS, *First Annual Report*, 14; *Pennsylvania Freeman*, 15 Mar. 1838.

39. John Runcie, "'Hunting the Nigs' in Philadelphia: The Race Riot of August 1834," *PH* 39 (1972): 187–218; Paul A. Gilje, *The Road to Mobocracy: Popular Disorder in New York City, 1763–1834* (Chapel Hill, 1987), 162–70; Linda K. Kerber, "Abolitionists and Amalgamators: The New York City Race Riots of 1834," *New York History* 48 (1967): 131–43; Leslie M. Harris, "From Abolitionist Amalgamators to 'Rulers of the Five Points': The Discourse of Interracial Sex and Reform in Antebellum New York City," in *Sex, Love, Race: Crossing Boundaries in North American History*, ed. Martha Hodes (New York, 1999), 191–212; *Presbyterian*, 27 Aug. 1835; *Hazard's Register of Pennsylvania*, 29 Aug. 1835.

40. [Calvin Colton], *Colonization and Abolition Contrasted* (Philadelphia, 1839), 2, 5; *Presbyterian*, 13, 27 Aug. 1835; Leonard L. Richards, *"Gentlemen of Property and Standing": Anti-Abolitionist Mobs in Jacksonian America* (New York, 1970), 30–37, 43–46; Litwack, *North of Slavery*, 20–24. See also Tyson, *Discourse;* Jesse Burden, *Remarks . . . in the Senate of Pennsylvania, on the Abolition Question* (Philadelphia, 1838); William W. Sleigh, *Abolitionism Exposed!* (Philadelphia, 1838).

41. *History of Pennsylvania Hall, Which Was Destroyed by a Mob, on the 17th of May, 1838* (Philadelphia, 1838), 3–11, 136–43, quotation on p. 138; Board of Managers, Pennsylvania Hall Association, Minute Book, 1837–1864, HSP; Sam Bass Warner, Jr., *The Private City: Philadelphia in*

Three Periods of Its Growth (Philadelphia, 1968), 131–37; William N. Needles to Wendell P. Garrison, June 23, 1885, Dreer Collection, HSP; *Pennsylvania Freeman*, 5 July 1838.

42. Diary of A. J. Pleasonton, May 17, 1838, HSP; *Public Ledger*, 18 July 1838, quoted in Warner, *Private City*, 136–37; *Pennsylvania Freeman*, 1 Nov. 1838, 6 Dec. 1838.

43. Othniel A. Pendleton, Jr., "Slavery and the Evangelical Churches," *Journal of Presbyterian History* 25 (1947): 169, 172; Daniel Neall, Jr., to John Priestley, May 21, 1838, Daniel Neall Papers, FHL.

44. James Forten to Paul Cuffe, Jan. 25, 1817, Paul Cuffe Papers, New Bedford Free Public Library, microfilm ed., reel 2; Sarah Forten to Angelina Grimké, Apr. 15, 1837, *Weld-Grimké Letters*, vol. 1, 380; Winch, *Philadelphia's Black Elite*, 27–61; Raboteau, *Fire in the Bones*, 98–99; Floyd J. Miller, *The Search for a Black Nationality: Black Emigration and Colonization, 1787–1863* (Urbana, 1975), 47–50, 74–82. For Richard Allen's later opposition to colonization, see *Freedom's Journal*, 2 Nov. 1827.

45. Lewis C. Holbert to William McLain, Sept. 7, 1847, in Carter G. Woodson, ed., *The Mind of the Negro, As Reflected in Letters Written During the Crisis, 1800–1860* (Washington, D.C., 1926), 47 [spelling modernized]; "Roll of Emigrants," 152–60.

46. Charles Henry Huberich, *The Political and Legislative History of Liberia*, vol. 1 (New York, 1947), 440; Winch, *Philadelphia's Black Elite, 39–40*.

47. *African Repository* 27 (1851): 259–65; Moses, *Liberian Dreams*, 181–97.

48. *Freedom's Journal*, 7 Mar. 1829; Hill and Kilson, *Apropos of Africa*, 79; Martin R. Delany, *The Condition, Elevation, Emigration, and Destiny of the Colored People of the United States* (Philadelphia, 1852; reprint, New York, 1969), 159–60, 205, 208.

49. See the volumes of letters in the American Colonization Society Papers, Library of Congress; Bell I. Wiley, ed., *Slaves No More: Letters from Liberia, 1833–1869* (Lexington, Ky., 1980); Randall M. Miller, ed., *"Dear Master": Letters of a Slave Family* (Ithaca, 1978).

50. "Roll of Emigrants," 152–60; Carey, *Letters on the Colonization Society*, 25–26; Smith, *Sojourners in Search of Freedom*, 206–8; Kocher, "Duty to America and Africa," 147.

51. Prior to 1844, over 20 percent of the emigrants died within their first twelve months in Liberia; "Roll of Emigrants," 152–60; *Liberator*, 20 Aug. 1831; Shick, *Behold the Promised Land*, 27, 50; Smith, *Sojourners in Search of Freedom*, 206–8; Kocher, "Duty to America and Africa," 147.

52. Joshua Simpson, "Old Liberia Is Not the Place for Me," in *Original Antislavery Songs* (Zanesville, Oh., 1852), 24–27, reprinted in Vicki L. Eaklor, *American Antislavery Songs* (Westport, Conn., 1988), 10–12 (italics in original).

53. Miller, *Search for a Black Nationality*, 74–82; Winch, *Philadelphia's Black Elite*, 49–61; Haytien Emigration Society of Philadelphia, *Information for the Free People of Colour, Who Are Inclined to Emigrate to Hayti* (Philadelphia, 1825).

54. Litwack, *North of Slavery*, 25; *Liberator*, 12 Feb. 1831; 24 Sept. 1831; 27 Aug. 1859; *Colored American*, 11 Apr. 1840; David Walker, *Walker's Appeal, in Four Articles . . .* (Boston, 1830), 21; *Proceedings of the Colored National Convention, Held in Rochester, July 6th, 7th and 8th, 1853* (Rochester, 1853), 55–57, reprinted in Bell, *Minutes of the Proceedings of the National Negro Conventions;* Williams, *Discourse Delivered in St. Philip's Church*, 7–8.

55. *Fifteenth Annual Report of the Pennsylvania Anti-Slavery Society, October 25, 1852* (Philadelphia, 1852); *Liberator*, 4 Apr. 1851, cited in Quarles, *Black Abolitionists*, 219. See also "Negro Societies in Philadelphia, 1831," *Hazard's Register*, Mar. 12, 1831, in Aptheker, *Documentary History*, vol. 1, 111–14; *The Present State and Condition of the Free People of Color, of the City of Philadelphia . . .* (Philadelphia, 1838), 26–27; *Minutes of the Fifth Annual Convention for the Improvement of the Free People of Colour in the United States, . . . 1835* (Philadelphia, 1835), 14–15, reprinted in Bell, *Minutes of the Proceedings of the National Negro Conventions;* Leonard P. Curry, *The Free Black in Urban America, 1800–1850* (Chicago, 1981), 237; Ira Berlin, *Slaves without Masters: The Free Negro in the Antebellum South* (New York, 1974), 168–69.

56. Martin R. Delany, "Political Destiny of the Colored Race on the American Continent" (1854), reprinted in Frank A. Rollin, *Life and Public Services of Martin R. Delany* (Boston, 1883), 358; Harriet Jacobs, *Incidents in the Life of a Slave Girl* (Boston, 1861), reprinted in Henry Louis Gates, Jr., ed., *The Classic Slave Narratives* (New York, 1987), 503; Quarles, *Black Abolitionists*, 197–215.

57. For a recent example of this binary approach to Douglass and Delany, see Tunde Adeleke, *UnAfrican Americans: Nineteenth-Century Black Nationalists and the Civilizing Mission* (Lexington, Ky., 1998). For discussions of the similarities between the two men, see Wilson J. Moses, *The Golden Age of Black Nationalism, 1850–1925* (New York, 1978), 37–41; Robert S. Levine, *Martin Delany, Frederick Douglass, and the Politics of Representative Identity* (Chapel Hill, 1997).

58. Delany, *Condition; North Star,* 26 Jan. 1849, in Foner, *Life and Writings of Frederick Douglass,* vol. 1, 351; *Proceedings of the Colored National Convention,* 3–11; *Proceedings of the National Emigration Convention of Colored People; Held at Cleveland, Ohio . . . 1854* (Pittsburgh, 1854).

59. Delany, "Political Destiny," 349; Delany, *Condition,* 7; Levine, *Martin Delany, Frederick Douglass,* 91; Nicole Etcheson, "Manliness and the Political Culture of the Old Northwest, 1790–1860," *JER* 15 (1995): 59–77.

60. Delany, *Condition,* 10, 182–83, 196, 199; Delany, "Political Destiny," 353.

61. *Speech of H. Ford Douglass, in reply to Mr. J. M. Langston before the Emigration Convention, at Cleveland, Ohio . . .* (Chicago, 1854), reprinted in Aptheker, *Documentary History,* vol. 1, 367–68.

62. *Proceedings of the National Emigration Convention,* 8, 9, 14, 16–18.

63. Jane Rhodes, *Mary Ann Shadd Cary: The Black Press and Protest in the Nineteenth Century* (Bloomington, Ind., 1998), 10–99; Jason H. Silverman, "Mary Ann Shadd and the Search for Equality," in *Black Leaders of the Nineteenth Century,* ed. Leon Litwack and August Meyer (Urbana, 1988), 87–100; *North Star,* 23 Mar. 1849; 8 June 1849.

64. Mary A. Shadd, *A Plea for Emigration; or Notes of Canada West . . .* (Detroit, 1852); Rhodes, *Mary Ann Shadd Cary,* 63; Jim Bearden and Linda Jean Butler, *Shadd: The Life and Times of Mary Shadd Cary* (Toronto, 1977), 139. For the independence experienced by black women fugitives to Canada, see Benjamin Drew, *The Refugee: Or the Narratives of Fugitive Slaves in Canada* (Boston, 1856; reprint, Toronto, 1972), 177, 233.

65. Rhodes, *Mary Ann Shadd Cary,* 77–80, 88–89; Quarles, *Black Abolitionists,* 218; *Frederick Douglass' Paper,* Dec. 2, 1853, in Foner, *Life and Writings of Frederick Douglass,* vol. 5, 300.

66. Bear in mind that white women also became a rare sight in evangelical-dominated antislavery societies after they withdrew from Garrison's American Anti-Slavery Society in 1840.

67. *Third Annual Report of the Ladies Liberia School Association* (Philadelphia, 1835); *Fourth Annual Report* (1836) in the *Colonization Herald,* 28 May 1836; *Ninth Annual Report of the Board of Managers of the Ladies Liberia School Association* (Philadelphia, 1841).

68. Bruce Dorsey, "City of Brotherly Love: Religious Benevolence, Gender, and Reform in Philadelphia, 1780–1844," (Ph.D. diss., Brown University, 1993), chaps. 2, 5.

69. *African Repository* 16 (July 1840): 202–5; Catharine Beecher, *An Essay on Slavery and Abolitionism with Reference to the Duty of American Females* (Philadelphia, 1837), 97–109; Kathryn Kish Sklar, *Catharine Beecher: A Study in American Domesticity* (New Haven, 1973), 132–37. See also *Colonization Herald,* 19 Mar. 1836; 23 July 1836; Varon, "Evangelical Womanhood," 171. On the connections between nineteenth-century politics and prizefighting, see Elliott J. Gorn, *The Manly Art: Bare-Knuckle Prize Fighting in America* (Ithaca, 1986), 125–27, 135.

70. *Thirty-Sixth and Final Annual Report of the Philadelphia Female Anti-Slavery Society* (Philadelphia, 1870), 39; *Proceedings of the Anti-Slavery Convention, Assembled at Philadelphia, December 4, 5, and 6, 1833* (Philadelphia, 1833). Black women were carefully observing this convention; see Margaretta Forten's poem praising the founders of the American Anti-Slavery Society; *Emancipator,* 14 Jan. 1834, BAP, 1:0389; *Liberator,* 21 Dec. 1833.

71. Philadelphia Female Anti-Slavery Society, Minute Book, Dec. 9, 14, 1833, [hereafter, PFASS, Minutes], PPAS, reel 30,; *Address of the Female Anti-Slavery Society of Philadelphia to the Women of Pennsylvania* (Philadelphia, 1836), 3, 8. For a similar encapsulation of the abolitionist philosophy, see the American Anti-Slavery Society's commission to Theodore D. Weld in 1834, in *Weld-Grimké Letters,* vol. 1, 124–28.

72. Martin Delany contended that abolitionism began "among colored men," and that white abolitionists "were converts of the colored men, in behalf of their elevation." Delany, *Condition,* 26.

73. Amy Swerdlow, "Abolition's Conservative Sisters: The Ladies' New York City Anti-Slavery Societies, 1834–1840," in Yellin and Van Horne, *Abolitionist Sisterhood,* 31–44; Lewis Perry, *Radical Abolitionism: Anarchy and the Government of God in Antislavery Thought* (Ithaca, 1973), 92–113;

John R. McKivigan, *The War against Proslavery Religion: Abolitionism and the Northern Churches, 1830–1865* (Ithaca, 1984), 66–68, 93–110.

74. *Proceedings of the American Anti-Slavery Society, at Its Third Decade, . . .* (Philadelphia, 1864), 42–43. Historians who emphasize only the theme of inexperience in Mott's explanation include Otelia Cromwell, *Lucretia Mott* (Cambridge, Mass., 1958), 130–31; Alma Lutz, *Crusade for Freedom: Women of the Antislavery Movement* (Boston, 1968), 52; Carolyn Williams, "The Female Antislavery Movement: Fighting against Racial Prejudice and Promoting Women's Rights in Antebellum America," in Yellin and Van Horne, *Abolitionist Sisterhood*, 162.

75. *Proceedings of the American Anti-Slavery Society, at its Third Decade*, 42–43; clearly, they made a conscious decision to choose a black man, since white abolitionist Samuel J. May was also present; PFASS, Minutes, Dec. 9, 1833.

76. Memorial of Females of Philadelphia against Slavery in the District of Columbia, Dec. 23, 1831; Tabled (HR 22A-H1.5); (NA Box 6 of LC Box 58, 1831–32); 22nd Congress; Records of the House of Representatives, Record Group 233, National Archives, Washington, D.C.; *Address of the Female Anti-Slavery Society*, 2–8; Circular from the Anti-Slavery Convention of American Women, in PFASS, Minutes, July 14, 1837; Gilbert H. Barnes, *The Antislavery Impulse, 1830–1844* (New York, 1933), 109–45, 266; Gerda Lerner, *The Majority Finds Its Past* (New York, 1979), 112–28; Goodman, *Of One Blood*, 228–29.

77. PFASS, Minutes, Feb. 9, May 18, July 14, Sep. 14, 1837; June 14, Sep. 14, Dec. 13, 1838; *A Memorial of Sarah Pugh: A Tribute of Respect from Her Cousins* (Philadelphia, 1888), 22; *Fourth Annual Report of the Philadelphia Female Anti-Slavery Society* (Philadelphia, 1838), 6; *Proceedings of the Anti-Slavery Convention of American Women, Held in Philadelphia, May 15th, 16th, 17th, and 18th, 1838* (Philadelphia, 1838), 5; Lerner, *Majority Finds Its Past*, 124; Jeffrey, *Great Silent Army*, 89–93; Goodman, *Of One Blood*, 230–31; Deborah Bingham Van Broekhoven, "'Let Your Names Be Enrolled': Method and Ideology in Women's Antislavery Petitioning," in Yellin and Van Horne, *Abolitionist Sisterhood*, 189–90.

78. *Proceedings of the Anti-Slavery Convention of American Women, Held in the City of New York, May 9th, 10th, 11th and 12th, 1837* (New York, 1837), reprinted as *Turning the World Upside Down* (New York, 1987), 12; *An Appeal to the Women of the Nominally Free States, Issued by an Anti-Slavery Convention of American Women*, 2nd ed. (Boston, 1838), 5–6; *Proceedings of the Third Anti-Slavery Convention of American Women, Held in Philadelphia, May 1st, 2nd, and 3rd, 1839* (Philadelphia, 1839), 26; Elizabeth Cady Stanton et al., *History of Woman Suffrage*, vol. 1 (New York, 1881–1922), 336; A. E. Grimké, *Letters to Catharine E. Beecher, In Reply to An Essay on Slavery and Abolitionism, Addressed to A. E. Grimké* (Boston, 1838), 112, 115, 118–19.

79. Stanton et al., *History of Woman Suffrage*, vol. 1, 339; *Anti-Slavery Convention of American Women, 1837*, 12–13, 17; *Anti-Slavery Convention of American Women, 1838*, 5–6. For the best account of the simultaneous conservative and radical implications of this ideology of female influence, see Ginzberg, *Women and the Work of Benevolence*. On African American uses of this discourse, see *Freedom's Journal*, 10 Aug. 1827, in Aptheker, *Documentary History*, vol. 1, 89; *Weekly Advocate*, 7 Jan. 1837, BAP, 1:0888; *Colored American*, 30 Sept. 1837, BAP, 2:0205; *North Star*, 2 June 1848; William Lloyd Garrison to Sarah M. Douglass, Mar. 5, 1832, in Merrill, *Letters of William Lloyd Garrison*, vol. 1, 144; Yee, *Black Women Abolitionists*, 44–46, 54–56, 61–62; Julie Winch, "'You Have Talents—Only Cultivate Them': Philadelphia's Black Female Literary Societies and the Abolitionist Crusade," in Yellin and Van Horne, *Abolitionist Sisterhood*, 106–107; James Oliver Horton, "Freedom's Yoke: Gender Conventions among Antebellum Free Blacks," *Feminist Studies* 12 (1986): 51–76.

80. *Appeal to the Women of the Nominally Free States*, 1, 19–53; "Essay by 'A Colored Woman,'" *Black Abolitionist Papers*, vol. 3, ed. C. Peter Ripley et al. (Chapel Hill, 1985–92), 326–27.

81. PFASS, Minutes, May 19, 1842; Dec. 3, 1835; May 13, 1841; Dec. 8, 1842; *Seventh Annual Report of the Philadelphia Female Anti-Slavery Society* (Philadelphia, 1841), 15–16; *Fourteenth Annual Report of the Philadelphia Female Anti-Slavery Society* (Philadelphia, 1848), 7; Kraditor, *Means and Ends*, 79–90; Perry, *Radical Abolitionism*, 55–59, 88–91.

82. *Liberator*, 19 Sept. 1835; Angelina Grimké, *Appeal to the Christian Women of the South* (New York, 1836); PFASS, Minutes, Nov. 11, 1836; Sept. 14, 1837; Nov. 9, 1837; *Weld-Grimké Letters*, vol. 1, 374–75. The best biographies are Lerner, *Grimké Sisters*; Katharine Du Pre Lumpkin,

The Emancipation of Angelina Grimké (Chapel Hill, 1974). The sisters joined an Orthodox Quaker meeting because of their personal relationships with leading members, without realizing that they shared views more consistent with Hicksite Friends. Quakers had divided into two camps in 1827: Hicksite Friends wished to retain the mystical traditions and separateness of the sect, while Orthodox Friends wished to remain close in doctrine and association with evangelical Protestant groups.

83. Samuel J. May, *Some Recollections of Our Antislavery Conflict* (Boston, 1869), 235; William Lloyd Garrison to Mrs. Sarah T. Benson, May 19, 1838, in Merrill, *Letters of William Lloyd Garrison*, vol. 2, 363. For the Grimké sisters' account of slaveholding cruelties in the South, see *American Slavery as It Is* (New York, 1839), 22–24, 52–57.

84. Stanton et al., *History of Woman Suffrage*, vol. 1, 81–82; Lerner, *Grimké Sisters*, 194.

85. Angelina Grimké to Theodore D. Weld and John Greenleaf Whittier, Aug. 20, 1837, in *Weld-Grimké Letters*, vol. 1, 427–32.

86. *Appeal to the Women of the Nominally Free States*, 13–14; Benjamin Quarles, *Black Abolitionists*, 248; Grimké, *Letters to Catharine Beecher*, 114; Sarah Grimké, *Letters on the Equality of the Sexes, and the Condition of Woman*, ed. Elizabeth Ann Bartlett (Boston, 1838; reprint, New Haven, 1988), 48–49, 72–77; Hersh, *Slavery of Sex*, 128; Yellin, *Women and Sisters*, 29–52.

87. PFASS, Minutes, May 14, 1834; Jan. 17, 1839; Feb. 14, 1839; Mar. 14, 29, 1839; Apr. 12, 1839.

88. Frederick Douglass, *Narrative of the Life of Frederick Douglass, An American Slave* (Boston, 1845; reprint, Boston, 1993), 105; Sarah Douglass to William Basset, Dec. 1837, in *Weld-Grimké Letters*, vol. 2, 830–31; *Liberator*, 4 June 1831; *North Star*, 23 Mar 1849. See also *Colored American*, 8, 15 Apr. 1837; 2 Dec. 1837; 30 June 1838; 24 Oct. 1840; *North Star*, 24, 30 Mar. 1848; *Frederick Douglass' Paper*, 8 Jan. 1852.

89. *Anti-Slavery Convention of American Women, 1837*, 13, 17, 25.

90. Nathan O. Hatch, *The Democratization of American Christianity* (New Haven, 1989), 44–46, 99–100, 170–79; Bruce Dorsey, "Friends Becoming Enemies: Philadelphia Benevolence and the Neglected Period of American Quaker History," *JER* 18 (1998): 407–14.

91. Angelina Grimké to Theodore D. Weld and John Greenleaf Whittier, Aug. 20, 1837, in *Weld-Grimké Letters*, vol. 1, 428; Stanton et al., *History of Woman Suffrage*, vol. 1, 82–83; Lucretia Mott to Nathaniel Barney, Oct. 8, 1842, in *James and Lucretia Mott: Life and Letters*, ed. Anna Davis Hallowell (Boston, 1884), 233.

92. *Sixth Annual Report of the Philadelphia Female Anti-Slavery Society* (Philadelphia, 1840), 17; *Anti-Slavery Convention of American Women*, 1838, 5–7; *Tenth Annual Report of the Philadelphia Female Anti-Slavery Society* (Philadelphia, 1844), 4, 9–10; *Thirteenth Annual Report of the Philadelphia Female Anti-Slavery Society* (Philadelphia, 1847), 7–8; Hallowell, *James and Lucretia Mott*, 122; *Pennsylvania Freeman*, 15 Nov. 1849; Ira V. Brown, *Mary Grew: Abolitionist and Feminist, 1813–1896* (Selinsgrove, Pa., 1991), 40–45, 136–38. Not every abolitionist woman in Philadelphia agreed with Grew's "come-outer" spirit; see the society's tabling of resolutions by Grew in 1844 calling for members to withdraw "from all ecclesiastical organizations which are pro-slavery in their character or conduct." PFASS, Minutes, Sept. 12, 1844, Oct. 10, 1844.

93. John F. McClymer, *This High and Holy Moment: The First National Woman's Rights Convention, Worcester, 1850* (Fort Worth, 1999), 69, 147.

94. Undoubtedly he cited Genesis 3:16 to argue that God selected man to rule over women after the Fall, and he certainly read I Corinthians 14:34–35, in which St. Paul wrote that women should remain silent and not speak in the church.

95. Stanton et al., *History of Woman Suffrage*, vol. 1, 379–83; Brown, *Mary Grew*, 23–27, 55–56; Frederick B. Tolles, ed., "Slavery and the 'Woman Question': Lucretia Mott's Diary of Her Visit to Great Britain to Attend the World's Anti-Slavery Convention of 1840," *Journal of the Friends' Historical Society*, supplement 23 (1952): 31; *Proceedings of the General Anti-Slavery Convention: . . . Held in London, from Friday, June 12th, to Tuesday, June 23rd, 1840* (London, 1841), 27. See also Kathryn Kish Sklar, "'Women Who Speak for an Entire Nation': American and British Women at the World Anti-Slavery Convention, London, 1840," in Yellin and Van Horne, *Abolitionist Sisterhood*, 301–33.

96. Lucretia Mott to J. M. McKim, Jan. 1, 1834, in Hallowell, *James and Lucretia Mott*,

117–18; Stanton et al, *History of Woman Suffrage*, vol. 1, 380; Lucretia Mott, *Discourse on Woman, Delivered at the Assembly Buildings,* . . . (Philadelphia, 1850); Cromwell, *Lucretia Mott,* 107–110.

97. Although antebellum abolitionists never used the term "racism," I use the term interchangeably with their term "prejudice" because in common parlance they have roughly the same meaning.

98. James Forten, Jr., *An Address Delivered before the Ladies' Anti-Slavery Society of Philadelphia* (Philadelphia, 1836), 8; *Anti-Slavery Convention of American Women, 1837,* 18–19; *Anti-Slavery Convention of American Women, 1839,* 8–9, 22–23; *Sixth Annual Report of the Philadelphia Female Anti-Slavery Society,* 13; *Appeal to the Women of the Nominally Free States,* 60–61.

99. *Anti-Slavery Convention of American Women, 1838,* 8; *Sixth Annual Report of the Philadelphia Female Anti-Slavery Society,* 11, 13; Goodman, *Of One Blood.*

100. Elias Hicks, *A Series of Extemporaneous Discourses* . . . (Philadelphia, 1825), 79; Swerdlow, "Abolition's Conservative Sisters," 40.

101. *Anti-Slavery Convention of American Women, 1837,* 19; *Anti-Slavery Convention of American Women, 1838,* 8; "An Appeal to American Women, on Prejudice against Color," in *Anti-Slavery Convention of American Women, 1839,* 21–24; *Appeal to the Women of the Nominally Free States,* 62–63.

102. Jean R. Soderlund, "Priorities and Power: The Philadelphia Female Anti-Slavery Society," in Yellin and Van Horne, *Abolitionist Sisterhood,* 70, 74; PFASS, Minutes, Mar. 14, 1839.

103. PFASS, Minutes, Dec. 14, 1833, June 9, 1834; Sept. 10, 1835; Feb. 11, 1836; Mar. 8, 1838; Jan. 9, 1840; Apr. 9, 1840; Feb. 8, 1849; Mar. 8, 1849; Philadelphia Female Anti-Slavery Society, Board of Managers, Minute Book, June 2, 1834, Jan. 28, 1835; Apr. 3, 1835; Feb. 7, 1839; PPAS, reel 30; *Fifth Annual Report of the Philadelphia Female Anti-Slavery Society* (Philadelphia, 1839), 3–4; *Seventh Annual Report of the Philadelphia Female Anti-Slavery Society,* 7–8; Soderlund "Priorities and Power," 76–77.

104. By the mid-1970s, the literature on abolitionists and racism had reached its completion: Litwack, *North of Slavery,* 224–30; William H. Pease and Jane H. Pease, "Antislavery Ambivalence: Immediatism, Expediency, Race," *AQ* 17 (1965): 682–95; Pease and Pease, *They Who Would Be Free: Blacks' Search for Freedom, 1830–1861* (New York, 1974), 82–93; Merton L. Dillon, *The Abolitionists: The Growth of a Dissenting Minority* (DeKalb, Ill., 1974), 49–77.

105. *Colored American,* 4 Nov. 1837; Sarah Forten to Angelina Grimké, Apr. 15, 1837, in *Weld-Grimké Letters,* vol. 1, 380–81; Dillon, *Abolitionists,* 59; Delany, *Condition,* 26–30.

106. *Eighth Annual Report of the Philadelphia Female Anti-Slavery Society* ([Philadelphia, 1842]), 2; *Fifteenth Annual Report of the Philadelphia Female Anti-Slavery Society* (Philadelphia, 1849), 9; PFASS Minutes, Mar. 14, 1839–Jan. 12, 1843; Oct. 8, 1846; *Pennsylvania Freeman,* 26 July 1838; Joseph A. Boromé, "The Vigilant Committee of Philadelphia," *PMHB* 92 (1968): 320–51 (includes the Minute Book of the Vigilant Committee of Philadelphia, 1839–1844, HSP); Still, *Underground Railroad,* 610–16; Quarles, *Black Abolitionists,* 154–61; Hallowell, *James and Lucretia Mott,* 265.

107. See Kraditor, *Means and Ends,* for the best account of this schism.

108. The relationship between white women abolitionists and the woman's rights movement is a familiar one and need not be repeated here. See Hersh, *Slavery of Sex;* Kraditor, *Means and Ends;* Lerner, *Grimké Sisters from South Carolina;* Hewitt, *Women's Activism and Social Change;* Yellin, *Women and Sisters;* Sánchez-Eppler, *Touching Liberty;* Hansen, *Strained Sisterhood;* Jeffrey, *Great Silent Army;* Yellin and Van Horne, *Abolitionist Sisterhood;* Ellen DuBois, "Women's Rights and Abolition: The Nature of the Connection," in *Antislavery Reconsidered: New Perspectives on Abolitionists,* ed. Lewis Perry and Michael Fellman (Baton Rouge, 1979), 238–51. On the role of black women abolitionists, including Philadelphia black women, see Terborg-Penn, *African American Women,* 13–35.

109. Like white women, few African American women (with the exception of Maria W. Stewart) became public speakers before Sojourner Truth in 1845 and Frances Ellen Watkins (Harper) in 1857. But given the potential for violence and the indifference of white abolitionist leaders in choosing black men as their agents, this might be less surprising than the reticence of white women.

110. Forten, *Address,* 14; Robert B. Forten's address, printed in the *Liberator,* 7 Mar. 1835;

"Speech by Sarah M. Douglass, Delivered before the Female Literary Society of Philadelphia, June 1832," *Liberator*, 21 July 1832, reprinted in Ripley et al., *Black Abolitionist Papers*, vol. 3, 116. See also *Liberator*, 1 Mar. 1834; *National Enquirer*, 11, 25 Jan. 1838; Jeffrey Steele, "The Gender and Racial Politics of Mourning in Antebellum America," in *An Emotional History of the United States*, ed. Peter N. Stearns and Jan Lewis (New York, 1998), 91–106.

111. See chapter one above; Elizabeth B. Clark, "'The Sacred Rights of the Weak': Pain, Sympathy, and the Culture of Individual Rights in Antebellum America," *JAH* 82 (1995): 463–93; Cathy N. Davidson, *Revolution and the Word: The Rise of the Novel in America* (New York, 1986); Jane P. Tompkins, *Sensational Designs: The Cultural Work of American Fiction, 1790–1860* (New York, 1985); Nina Baym, *Woman's Fiction: A Guide to Novels by and about Women in America, 1820–1870* (Ithaca, 1978).

112. Ada [pseud.], "A Mother's Grief," *Liberator*, 7 July 1832; Ella [pseud.], "The Mother and Her Captive Boy," *National Enquirer*, 8 Oct. 1836. See also Ada, "Past Joys," *Liberator*, 19 Mar. 1831; "Reflections on Slavery," *Liberator*, 9 Apr. 1831; *Anti-Slavery Record* 1 (May 1835): 51–52. For the identity of the various pseudonyms under which black women wrote, including Sarah Forten as "Ada" and Sarah Douglass as "Ella," see Winch, "You Have Talents," 101–18.

113. "The Slave Mother," in *Complete Poems of Frances E. W. Harper*, ed. Maryemma Graham (New York, 1988), 4–5; also 10, 19.

114. *Liberator*, 11 Feb. 1837, quoted in Ronald G. Walters, *The Antislavery Appeal: American Abolitionism after 1830* (Baltimore, 1978), 61; *North Star*, 29 Sept. 1848, in Foner, *Life and Writings of Frederick Douglass*, vol. 1, 333; *Anti-Slavery Record* 1 (Sept. 1835): 104; 2 (Jan. 1836): 11.

115. Fredrickson, *Black Image in the White Mind*, 109; Pease and Pease, "Antislavery Ambivalence," 683; Walters, *Antislavery Appeal*, 59. The analysis in this section has been influenced by Kristin Hoganson, "Garrisonian Abolitionists and the Rhetoric of Gender, 1850–1860," *AQ* 45 (1993): 558–95.

116. *Anti-Slavery Convention of American Women, 1838*, 6; Angelina Grimké to Jane Smith, 1837, quoted in Yellin, *Women and Sisters*, 40. The best summary of sentimentalism can be found in Philip Fisher, *Hard Facts: Setting and Form in the American Novel* (New York, 1985), 91–104.

117. Forten, *Address*, 12; Clark, "'Sacred Rights of the Weak'," 480; *Quarterly Anti-Slavery Review* 1 (July 1836): 317.

118. Douglass, *Narrative*, 41–42, 45, 51–52, 65, 69, 82; Magawisca [pseud.], "Abuse of Liberty," *Liberator*, 26 Mar. 1831.

119. *Liberator*, 5 Feb., 1831, quoted in Walters, *Antislavery Appeal*, 73; *Anti-Slavery Record* 1 (Jan. 1835): 7.

120. Theodore D. Weld to Angelina Grimké, Mar. 12, 1838, in *Weld-Grimké Letters*, vol. 2, 602. On Weld and Grahamism, see Robert H. Abzug, *Passionate Liberator: Theodore Dwight Weld and the Dilemma of Reform* (New York, 1980), 157–60, 206–10; Weld to Sarah Grimké, Feb. 8, 1838, and Sylvester Graham to Weld, Mar. 19, 1839, in *Weld-Grimké Letters*, vol. 2, 531, 753–55. For Weld's earlier ideas on manliness and reform, see *First Annual Report of the Society for Promoting Manual Labor in Literary Institutions, Including the Report of Their General Agent, Theodore D. Weld* (New York, 1833), 65–120.

121. Brown, *Narrative of Henry Box Brown*, 42.

122. Donald Yacovone, "Abolitionists and the 'Language of Fraternal Love'," in *Meanings for Manhood*, ed. Mark Carnes and Clyde Griffen (Chicago, 1990), 85–95; Yacovone, *Samuel Joseph May and the Dilemmas of the Liberal Persuasion, 1787–1871* (Philadelphia, 1991), 95–128; Stacey M. Robertson, *Parker Pillsbury: Radical Abolitionist, Male Feminist* (Ithaca, 2000); Chris Dixon, *Perfecting the Family: Antislavery Marriages in Nineteenth-Century America* (Amherst, 1997), 161.

123. Lydia Maria Child, *An Appeal in Favor of That Class of Americans Called Africans* (Boston, 1833; reprint, Amherst, 1996), 168–85; William Ellery Channing, "Emancipation," in *The Works of William E. Channing*, vol. 6 (Boston, 1873), 51–52; Fredrickson, *Black Image in the White Mind*, 105–07, 123; Walters, *Antislavery Appeal*, 58–59.

124. Lydia Maria Child, "The African Race," *National Anti-Slavery Standard*, 27 Apr. 1843; Alexander Kinmont, *Twelve Lectures on the Natural History of Man* (Cincinnati, 1839), 218; Theodore Tilton, *The Negro; A Speech at Cooper Institute . . .* (New York, 1863), quoted in

Fredrickson, *Black Image in the White Mind*, 114–15. This imagery continued to be employed after the Civil War; sociologist Robert Park wrote in 1919, "The Negro is, so to speak, the lady among the races." "The Conflict and Fusion of Cultures with Special Reference to the Negro," *Journal of Negro History* 4 (1919): 129–30.

125. Harriet Beecher Stowe, *Uncle Tom's Cabin* (1852; reprint, New York, 1981), 200, 623–24, 46–49, 82–84, 133; Harriet Beecher Stowe, *The Key to Uncle Tom's Cabin* (Boston, 1854; reprint, New York, 1968), 257. The recent scholarship by literary scholars on *Uncle Tom's Cabin* includes Fisher, *Hard Facts*, 127; Tompkins, *Sensational Designs*, 122–46; Gillian Brown, "Getting in the Kitchen with Dinah: Domestic Politics in *Uncle Tom's Cabin*," *AQ* 36 (1984): 503–23; Thomas F. Gossett, *Uncle Tom's Cabin and American Culture* (Dallas, 1985); Eric J. Sunguist, ed., *New Essays on Uncle Tom's Cabin* (Cambridge, 1986); Arthur Riss, "Racial Essentialism and Family Values in *Uncle Tom's Cabin*," *AQ* 46 (1994): 513–44; Cynthia Griffin Wolff, "'Masculinity' in *Uncle Tom's Cabin*," *AQ* 47 (1995), 595–618.

126. Stowe, *Uncle Tom's Cabin*, 42, 282, 342, 164–65, 68, 79, 111, 165, 231, 555, 611; Fredrickson, *Black Image in the White Mind*, 108.

127. Douglass, *Narrative*, 79, 75.

128. Frederick Douglass, "The Heroic Slave" (1853), in Foner, *Life and Writings of Frederick Douglass*, vol. 5, 475, 503. See also Richard Yarborough, "Race, Violence, and Manhood: The Masculine Ideal in Frederick Douglass's 'The Heroic Slave,'" in *Frederick Douglass: New Literary and Historical Analysis*, ed. Eric J. Sundquist (Cambridge, 1990), 166–88; Levine, *Martin Delany, Frederick Douglass*, 81–85.

5. Immigration

1. The best historical accounts of the 1844 riots are Michael Feldberg, *The Philadelphia Riots of 1844* (Westport, Conn., 1975); Vincent P. Lannie and Bernard C. Diethorn, "For the Honor and Glory of God: The Philadelphia Bible Riots of 1840," *History of Education Quarterly* 8 (1968): 44–106; Ray Allen Billington, *The Protestant Crusade, 1800–1860* (New York, 1938), 220–37; Sam Bass Warner, Jr., *The Private City: Philadelphia in Three Periods of Its Growth* (Philadelphia, 1968), 143–52; David Montgomery, "The Shuttle and the Cross: Weavers and Artisans in the Kensington Riots of 1844," *JSH* 5 (1972): 411–46; Elizabeth M. Geffen, "Violence in Philadelphia in the 1840's and 1850's," *PH* 36 (1969): 381–410.

2. *The Protestant Banner* 2 (Feb. 16, 1843): 45.

3. Kerby A. Miller, *Emigrants and Exiles: Ireland and the Irish Exodus to North America* (New York, 1985), 197; Warner, *Private City*, 137–38; United States Immigration Commission, *Reports of the Immigration Commission*, vol. 3 (Washington, D.C., 1911), 19–25.

4. Miller, *Emigrants and Exiles*, 26–54, 201–23; L. M. Cullen, *An Economic History of Ireland since 1660*, 2nd ed. (London, 1987), 100–133.

5. Miller, *Emigrants and Exiles*, 89–101, 228–49; Lawrence J. McCaffrey, *The Irish Catholic Diaspora in America* (Washington, D.C., 1997), 33–60.

6. William E. Gienapp, "'Politics Seem to Enter into Everything': Political Culture in the North, 1840–1860," in *Essays on American Antebellum Politics, 1840–1860*, ed. Stephen E. Maizlish and John J. Kushma (College Station, Tex., 1982), 14–69; Harry L. Watson, *Liberty and Power: The Politics of Jacksonian America* (New York, 1990), 66–70, 216–26; Elizabeth R. Varon, *We Mean to Be Counted: White Women and Politics in Antebellum Virginia* (Chapel Hill, 1998), 71–102. For the argument that antebellum Americans remained detached from popular politics, see Glenn C. Altschuler and Stuart M. Blumin, *Rude Republic: Americans and Their Politics in the Nineteenth Century* (Princeton, 2000).

7. William O. Bourne, *History of the Public School Society of the City of New York* (New York, 1870); James P. Wickersham, *A History of Education in Pennsylvania* (Lancaster, Pa., 1886); Carl F. Kaestle, *Pillars of the Republic: Common Schools and American Society, 1780–1860* (New York, 1983), 58–59.

8. Lori D. Ginzberg, *Women and the Work of Benevolence* (New Haven, 1990), 98–118; Aileen S. Kraditor, *Means and Ends in American Abolitionism: Garrison and His Critics on Strategy and Tactics,*

1834–1850 (New York, 1969), 118–77; Jed Dannenbaum, *Drink and Disorder: Temperance Reform in Cincinnati from the Washingtonian Revival to the WCTU* (Urbana, 1984), 69–155.

9. George Lippard, *The Nazarene; or, The Last of the Washingtons* (Philadelphia, 1846), 168; Montgomery, "Shuttle and the Cross," 411–16; Bruce Laurie, *Working People of Philadelphia, 1800–1850* (Philadelphia, 1980), 24–25, 124–26; John R. Commons, ed., *A Documentary History of American Industrial Society*, vol. 8 (New York, 1958), 236–40; Edwin T. Freedley, *Philadelphia and Its Manufactures* (Philadelphia, 1858), 250–56.

10. Montgomery, "Shuttle and the Cross," 415–16, 439; Leonard Tabachnik, "Origins of the Know-Nothing Party: A Study of the Native American Party in Philadelphia, 1844–1852" (Ph.D. diss., Columbia University, 1973), 30.

11. Laurie, *Working People of Philadelphia*, 126–27; Feldberg, *Philadelphia Riots of 1844*, 35–38; *Native American*, 16 July 1844; Tabachnik, "Origins of the Know-Nothing Party," 108–9; John Bach McMaster, *A History of the People of the United States*, vol. 7 (New York, 1886–1913), 374.

12. Based on a comparison of the leaders of Philadelphia's principal religious and political nativist groups (the American Protestant Association (APA) and the Native American Party). Only two of the 107 founders of the APA (both were laymen, not ministers) helped found the political party, while only 5 percent of the party's over six hundred founding members were active in any religious benevolent societies. *Address of the Board of Managers of the American Protestant Association; with the Constitution and Organization of the Association* (Philadelphia, 1843), 5–11; John Hancock Lee, *The Origin and Progress of the American Party in Politics* (Philadelphia, 1855), 255–64.

13. *Address of the Board of Managers of the American Protestant Association; First Annual Report of the American Protestant Association* (Philadelphia, 1844); Billington, *Protestant Crusade*, 96–98, 166–68, 183–85, 192, 243–49.

14. Lee, *Origin and Progress*, 13–44; Billington, *Protestant Crusade*, 193–219.

15. On Philadelphia Jewish societies, including the Hebrew Sunday School Society (1838), see Evelyn Bodek, "'Making Do': Jewish Women and Philanthropy," in *Jewish Life in Philadelphia, 1830–1940*, ed. Murray Friedman (Philadelphia, 1983), 143–62; Dianne Ashton, *Rebecca Gratz: Women and Judaism in Antebellum America* (Detroit, 1997), 93–169.

16. Edith Jeffrey, "Reform, Renewal, and Vindication: Irish Immigrants and the Catholic Total Abstinence Movement in Antebellum Philadelphia," *PMHB* 112 (1988): 407–31; Dale B. Light, *Rome and the New Republic: Conflict and Community in Philadelphia Catholicism between the Revolution and the Civil War* (Notre Dame, Ind., 1996), 285–94; Francis E. Tourscher, ed., *Diary and Visitation Record of the Rt. Rev. Francis Patrick Kenrick, 1830–1851* (Lancaster, Pa., 1916), 191; Marc Antony Frenaye to Francis Patrick Kenrick, July 24, 1840, in *The Kenrick-Frenaye Correspondence*, ed. Francis E. Tourscher (Philadelphia, 1920), 28–29; John Francis Maguire, *Father Mathew: A Biography* (New York, 1864); J. Thomas Scharf and Thompson Westcott, *History of Philadelphia, 1609–1884*, vol. 2 (Philadelphia, 1884), 1375–81; *Catholic Herald*, 25 June 1840; 2 July 1840; 29 Oct. 1840; 5 Nov. 1840; 11 Mar. 1841; 12 Aug. 1841; 10 Feb. 1842.

17. *Episcopal Recorder*, 28 Apr. 1843, quoted in Lannie and Diethorn, "For the Honor and Glory," 60, 99; *Catholic Herald*, 30 Dec. 1841; Anne M. Boylan, *Sunday School: The Formation of an American Institution, 1790–1880* (New Haven, 1988), 52–59; *Second Annual Report of the American Sunday School Union* (Philadelphia, 1826), 15–16.

18. *Rome's Policy towards the Bible; or, Papal Efforts to Suppress the Scriptures in the Last Five Centuries Exposed* (Philadelphia, 1844), 88–89, 92, 98; *The Pope and the Presbyterians* (Philadelphia, 1845), 53; *The American Protestant Magazine* 1 (June 1845): 26; David M. Reese, "Romanism and Liberty," *Quarterly Review of the American Protestant Association* 2 (April 1845): 128–29; *Catholic Herald*, 23 Nov. 1843.

19. Billington, *Protestant Crusade*, 157–58; *American Woman*, 7, 21 Sept. 1844; 10 May 1845; John Dowling, *The Burning of the Bibles* (Philadelphia, 1843); *The Burning of the Bibles: Being a Defense of the Protestant Version of the Scriptures against the Attacks of Popish Apologists for the Champlain Bible Burners* (New York, 1845).

20. Billington, *Protestant Crusade*, 142–65; Vincent P. Lannie, *Public Money and Parochial Education: Bishop Hughes, Governor Seward, and the New York School Controversy* (Cleveland, 1968).

21. Lannie and Diethorn, "For the Honor and Glory," 49–52, 56–57; *Catholic Herald*, 5, 12 Apr. 1838; 24 June 1841; 25 Nov. 1841; 14 Mar. 1844; Hugh J. Nolan, *The Most Reverend Francis Patrick Kenrick, Third Bishop of Philadelphia, 1830–1851* (Philadelphia, 1948), 293–95.

22. *First Annual Report of the American Protestant Association*, 25.

23. *Presbyterian*, 21 Jan. 1843; *Christian Observer*, 27 Jan. 1843.

24. Walter Colton, *The Bible in Public Schools* (Philadelphia, 1844), 7, 9, 11, 15–16.

25. *Catholic Herald*, 15 Feb. 1844.

26. Bruce Dorsey, "Friends Becoming Enemies: Philadelphia Benevolence and the Neglected Era of American Quaker History," *JER* 18 (1998): 407–14. On national schools in Ireland, see Donald H. Akenson, *The Irish Education Experiment: The National System of Education in the Nineteenth Century* (London, 1970). On schools as training sites for American nationalism, see Jean H. Baker, *Affairs of Party: The Political Culture of Northern Democrats in the Mid-Nineteenth Century* (Ithaca, 1983), 71–107.

27. *The Truth Unveiled; or A Calm and Impartial Exposition of . . . the Terrible Riots and Rebellion in Philadelphia . . .* (Baltimore, 1844), 30–32; Lannie and Diethorn, "For the Honor and Glory," 65–68.

28. Contemporary accounts of the riots were undeniably partisan, yet I have gleaned the basic events from the following: *A Full and Complete Account of the Late Awful Riots in Philadelphia* (Philadelphia, 1844); *Truth Unveiled;* "The Philadelphia Riots," *New Englander* 2 (July 1844): 470–84; *Public Ledger*, 7–9 May 1844; *Catholic Herald*, 16, 23, 30 May 1844; *Christian Observer*, 10, 17 May 1844; *Native American*, 7 May 1844; Raymond H. Schmandt, comp., "A Selection of Sources Dealing with the Nativist Riots of 1844," *Records of the American Catholic Historical Society of Philadelphia* 80 (1969): 68–113.

29. *Native American*, 7 May 1844; *Christian Observer*, 17 May 1844; Feldberg, *Philadelphia Riots of 1844*, 102, 108.

30. Nicholas B. Wainwright, ed., *A Philadelphia Perspective; The Diary of Sidney George Fisher, Covering the Years 1834–1871* (Philadelphia, 1967), 167–68; Lee, *Origin and Progress*, 57; *Public Ledger*, 7, 13, 27 May 1844; 20 July 1844. For a discussion of the culture of Irish women's fighting in New York and Ireland, see Christine Stansell, *City of Women: Sex and Class in New York, 1789–1860* (New York, 1986), 59; see also George Rudé, *The Crowd in History: A Study of Popular Disturbances in France and England, 1730–1848* (New York, 1964); Paul A. Gilje, *The Road to Mobocracy: Popular Disorder in New York City, 1763–1834* (Chapel Hill, 1987).

31. *Freeman's Journal* (New York), 25 May 1844, reprinted in *The American Protestant*, 29 May 1844; Tourscher, *Diary of Kenrick*, 223–24; Tourscher, *Kenrick-Frenaye Correspondence*, 192; Nolan, *Kenrick*, 316, 328; Lannie and Diethorn, "For the Honor and Glory," 77–80.

32. *Public Ledger*, 7, 8 June 1844; Presentment of the Grand Jury, *Catholic Herald*, 20 June 1844, reprinted in Schmandt, "Selection of Sources," 90. Caroline Sweeney might well have been defending herself against domestic violence or have been a victim in the past, but witnesses testified that she was the one intoxicated, and Dominick certainly did not fall on his knife seven times.

33. Laurie, *Working People of Philadelphia*, 123; *American Woman*, 14 Sept. 1844.

34. Nativist riots and the Independence Day parade in 1844 ostensibly ended Fourth of July temperance celebrations in Philadelphia. Protestant celebrations had already begun to wane, and public displays by Catholics were unthinkable in the aftermath of the rioting. *Public Ledger*, 6, 7 July 1840; 7 July 1841; 6 July 1842; *Catholic Herald*, 30 June 1842; Bishop M. O'Connor to Dr. Cullen, Jan. 10, 1842, in "Papers Relating to the Church in America," *Records of the American Catholic Historical Society of Philadelphia* 7 (1896): 348–49; Jeffrey, "Reform, Renewal, and Vindication," 424–29.

35. Lee, *Origin and Progress*, 136–61; *American Woman*, 7 Sept. 1844; Lannie and Diethorn, "For the Honor and Glory," 82–83.

36. "The Philadelphia Riots," *New Englander* 2 (October 1844): 624.

37. The economic appeal of nativism derived not from direct job competition, but from the way new immigrants contributed to the restructuring of wage work in an industrial society; see Amy Bridges, *A City in the Republic: Antebellum New York and the Origins of Machine Politics* (Ithaca, 1987), 94–96.

38. On the Southwark riots in July, see *Tremendous Riots in Southwark* (Philadelphia, 1844), reprinted in *Records of the American Catholic Historical Society of Philadelphia* 80 (1969): 176–95; Feldberg, *Philadelphia Riots of 1844*, 143–61; *Public Ledger*, 6–24 July 1844.

39. Why Cadwalader chose to defend the church with an Irish militia company remains a mystery. Perhaps he assumed that they were more determined to prevent its destruction, yet their presence obviously aggravated nativist hostilities; see the letters between Capt. John Colohan and Cadwalader, July 7, 11, 1844 in George Cadwalader Military Papers, Cadwalader Collection, HSP. George S. Roberts, Statement to the Grand Jury, July 22, 1844, in Schmandt, "Selection of Sources," 86.

40. Roberts, Statement to the Grand Jury, 86, 89; Alexander McClure, *Old Time Notes of Pennsylvania* (Philadelphia, 1905), cited in Geffen, "Violence in Philadelphia," 400.

41. Lee, *Origin and Progress*, 195–98; Billington, *Protestant Crusade*, 201–203; Tabachnik, "Origins of the Know-Nothing Party," 13, 27, 40, 124; Elizabeth M. Geffen, "Industrial Development and Social Crisis, 1841–1854," in *Philadelphia: A 300–Year History*, ed. Russell F. Weigley (New York, 1982), 358; John A. Forman, "Lewis Charles Levin: Portrait of an American Demagogue," *American Jewish Archives* 12 (1960): 150–94.

42. On nativist women, see Jean Gould Hales, "'Co-Laborers in the Cause': Women in the Ante-bellum Nativist Movement," *Civil War History* 25 (1979): 119–38; Judith A. Hunter, "Before Pluralism: The Political Culture of Nativism in Antebellum Philadelphia" (Ph.D. diss., Yale University, 1991), chap. 5.

43. *American Woman*, 7 Sept. 1844; 23 Nov. 1844; 12 Oct. 1844; Hunter, "Before Pluralism," 195.

44. *American Woman*, 23 Nov. 1844; 28 Dec. 1844.

45. *American Woman*, 28, 14 Sept. 1844; 2 Nov. 1844; *Public Ledger*, 22 June 1844. See also *American Woman*, 12, 26 Oct. 1844; 28 Dec. 1844; 10 May 1845; *Public Ledger*, 6 July 1844; *American Banner*, 5 May 1853; John Brougham, *The Irish Yankee* (New York, 1856).

46. *American Woman*, 7, 21 Sept. 1844; 2, 30 Nov. 1844; 10 May 1845; 22 Feb. 1845; Hales, "Co-Laborers in the Cause," 129; Hunter, "Before Pluralism," 31, 215–17.

47. *American Woman*, 7, 21 Sept. 1844; 9, 23, 30 Nov. 1844.

48. *Public Ledger*, 28 June 1844, 2, 3, 6 July 1844; *American Woman*, 7 Sept. 1844; Mary P. Ryan, *Women in Public: Between Banners and Ballots, 1825–1880* (Baltimore, 1990), 30–57; Varon, *We Mean to Be Counted*, 74–84.

49. *American Woman*, 4 Jan. 1845; 28 Dec. 1844; 22 Mar. 1845; 5 July 1845; Hales, "Co-Laborers in the Cause," 122–24.

50. *American Woman*, 14, 21, 28 Sept. 1844; 12 Oct. 1844; 9, 16 Nov. 1844; 4 Jan. 1845; 1 Feb. 1845; Nancy F. Cott, *The Bonds of Womanhood: "Woman's Sphere" in New England, 1780–1835* (New Haven, 1977); Cott, "Passionlessness: An Interpretation of Victorian Sexual Ideology, 1790–1850," *Signs* 4 (1978): 219–36; Barbara Welter, "The Cult of True Womanhood: 1820–1860," *AQ* 18 (1966): 151–74.

51. *American Woman*, 28 Sept. 1844; 23 Nov. 1844; Chris Dixon, *Perfecting the Family: Antislavery Marriages in Nineteenth-Century America* (Amherst, 1997).

52. Hales, "Co-Laborers in the Cause," 130.

53. *American Woman*, 7 Sept. 1844; Boylan, *Sunday School*, 115; Kaestle, *Pillars of the Republic*, 125.

54. *American Woman*, 7, 28 Sept. 1844; 5 Oct. 1844; 16, 23, 30 Nov. 1844; 7, 14 Dec. 1844; 18 Jan. 1845; 10 May 1845. For additional references by nativists to female influence, see Philadelphia *Sun*, 25, 31 Jan. 1845; *American Banner*, 10, 24 May 1851; Jacob Broom, *An Address Pronounced before the Order of the United Sons of America at Philadelphia, . . .* (Philadelphia, 1850), 17.

55. *American Woman*, 7 Sept. 1844; 14 Dec. 1844.

56. Amy Kaplan, "Manifest Domesticity," *American Literature* 70 (1998): 581–606; Karen Sánchez-Eppler, "Raising Empires like Children: Race, Nation, and Religious Education," *American Literary History* 8 (1996): 399–425; Jenine Abboushi Dallal, "The Beauty of Imperialism: Emerson, Melville, Flaubert, and Al-Shidyac" (Ph.D. diss., Harvard University, 1996), chap. 2; Rosemary Marangoly George, "Homes in the Empire, Empires in the Home," *Cultural Critique* 26

(1993–94): 95–127; Anna Davin, "Imperialism and Motherhood," *History Workshop* 5 (1978): 9–65.

57. *American Woman*, 14 Sept. 1844.

58. *American Woman*, 21 Sept. 1844; 7 Dec. 1844. This prefigured the Progressive era discourse on race and civilization; see Gail Bederman, *Manliness & Civilization: A Cultural History of Gender and Race in the United States, 1880–1917* (Chicago, 1995); Louise Michele Newman, *White Women's Rights: The Racial Origins of Feminism in the United States* (New York, 1999); Peggy Pascoe, *Relations of Rescue: The Search for Female Moral Authority in the American West, 1874–1939* (New York, 1990).

59. See Etienne Balibar, "Racism and Nationalism," in *Race, Nation, Class: Ambiguous Identities*, ed. Etienne Balibar and Immanuel Wallerstein (London, 1991), 37–67.

60. Peter Way, *Common Labour: Workers and the Digging of North American Canals, 1780–1860* (Cambridge, 1993); Hasia R. Diner, *Erin's Daughters: Irish Immigrant Women in the Nineteenth Century* (Baltimore, 1983), 41; Matthew E. Mason, "'The Hands Here Are Disposed to be Turbulent': Unrest among the Irish Trackmen of the Baltimore and Ohio Railroad, 1829–1851," *Labor History* 39 (1998): 253–72.

61. Elizabeth Malcolm, "The Rise of the Pub: A Study in the Disciplining of Popular Culture," in *Irish Popular Culture, 1650–1850*, ed. James S. Donnelly and Kerby A. Miller (Dublin, 1998), 55–64; Elizabeth Malcolm, *"Ireland Sober, Ireland Free": Drink and Temperance in Nineteenth-Century Ireland* (Syracuse, N.Y., 1986), 1–55; K. H. Connell, *Irish Peasant Society* (Oxford, 1968), 1–50; James R. Barrett, "Why Paddy Drank: The Social Importance of Whiskey in Pre-Famine Ireland," *Journal of Popular Culture* 11 (1977): 155–66; "The Story of an Irish Cook," *Independent* 58 (March 30, 1905): 715–17, reprinted in Hamilton Holt, ed., *The Life Stories of Undistinguished Americans as Told by Themselves* (New York, 1906; reprint, New York, 2000), 89.

62. Malcolm, "Rise of the Pub," 51; Valerie Hey, *Patriarchy and Pub Culture* (London, 1986), 30; Lawrence J. McCaffrey, *Textures of Irish America* (Syracuse, N.Y., 1992), 58; Hugh Brody, *Inishkillane: Change and Decline in the West of Ireland* (New York, 1974), 157–83.

63. Way, *Common Labour*, 181–87; William V. Shannon, *The American Irish* (New York, 1963), 40; Geffen, "Industrial Development and Social Crisis," 335.

64. John Brougham, *O'Flannigan and the Fairies* (New York, 1856), 4–5; "thrate" is supposed to be Irish dialect for "treat," as in treating other men to a drink. See also G. C. Duggan, *The Stage Irishman: A History of the Irish Play and Stage Characters from the Earliest Times* (Dublin, 1937), 230–31.

65. Mr. and Mrs. S. C. Hall, *Ireland: Its Scenery, Character, &c.*, vol. 1 (London, 1841–1843), 256–58. See also Patrick F. McDevitt, "Muscular Catholicism: Nationalism, Masculinity and Gaelic Team Sports, 1884–1916," *Gender and History* 9 (1997): 262–84.

66. Miller, *Emigrants and Exiles*, 60–61; Patrick O'Donnell, *The Irish Faction Fighters of the Nineteenth Century* (Dublin, 1975); Samuel Clark, *Social Origins of the Irish Land War* (Princeton, 1979), 74–86; Paul E. W. Roberts, "Caravats and Shanavest: Whiteboyism and Faction Fighting in East Munster, 1802–11," in *Irish Peasants: Violence and Political Unrest, 1780–1914*, ed. Samuel Clark and James S. Donnelly, Jr. (Madison, Wis., 1983), 64–101; Elizabeth Malcolm, "Popular Recreation in Nineteenth-Century Ireland," in *Irish Culture and Nationalism, 1750–1950*, ed. Oliver MacDonagh et al. (New York, 1983), 40–45; Carolyn Conley, "The Agreeable Recreation of Fighting," *JSH* 33 (1999): 57–95. This masculine desire for fighting was expressed with the support and participation of Irish women; Hall and Hall, *Ireland*, 426; Diarmaid O'Muirthe, *A Seat behind the Coachman: Travellers in Ireland, 1800–1900* (London, 1972), 56–58.

67. William Carleton, *Traits and Stories of the Irish Peasantry* (1830–33; reprint, New York, n.d.), 194–95; Maurice Harmon, "Cobwebs before the Wind: Aspects of the Peasantry in Irish Literature from 1800 to 1916," in *Views of the Irish Peasantry, 1800–1916*, ed. Daniel Casey and Robert E. Rhodes (Hamden, Conn., 1977), 129–59; S. J. Connolly, *Priests and People in Pre-famine Ireland, 1780–1845* (Dublin, 1982), 122–23, 230–31, 264–71.

68. Miller, *Emigrants and Exiles*, 258; Way, *Common Labour*, 193–204, 246–49, 287–95; Mason, "'Hands Here Are Disposed'," 260–68, 271–72.

69. David R. Johnson, *Policing the Urban Underworld: The Impact of Crime on the Development of the American Police, 1800–1887* (Philadelphia, 1979), 79–89, 189–91; George Rogers Taylor,

" 'Philadelphia in Slices' by George Foster," *PMHB* 93 (1969): 34–38; *Life and Adventures of Charles Anderson Chester, the Notorious Leader of the Philadelphia "Killers"* (Philadelphia, 1850); George Lippard, *The Killers: A Narrative of Real Life in Philadelphia . . .* (Philadelphia, 1850); Herbert Asbury, *The Gangs of New York* (Garden City, N.Y., 1927), 1–62; Gilje, *Road to Mobocracy*, 262–64.

70. On boy culture, see E. Anthony Rotundo, *American Manhood: Transformations in Masculinity from the Revolution to the Modern Era* (New York, 1993), 31–55.

71. Bishop Kenrick to Dr. Kirby, Aug. 21, 1845, in "Papers Relating to the Church in America," 320.

72. Laurie, *Working People of Philadelphia*, 58–61, 151–58; Bruce Laurie, "Fire Companies and Gangs in Southwark: The 1840s," in *The Peoples of Philadelphia: A History of Ethnic Groups and Lower-Class Life, 1790–1940*, ed. Allen F. Davis and Mark H. Haller (Philadelphia, 1973), 75, 78–82; Johnson, *Policing the Urban Underworld*, 86–88; Andrew H. Neilly, "The Violent Volunteers: A History of the Volunteer Fire Department of Philadelphia, 1736–1871" (Ph.D. diss., University of Pennsylvania, 1959), 70–84.

73. Amy S. Greenberg, *Cause for Alarm: The Volunteer Fire Department in the Nineteenth-Century City* (Princeton, 1998), 21–27; Scharf and Westcott, *History of Philadelphia*, vol. 3, 1883–912; Matthew Arrison, Record of Fires in Philadelphia from November 1837, HSP, as quoted in Emma Jones Lapsansky, *Neighborhoods in Transition: William Penn's Dream and Urban Reality* (New York, 1994), 126.

74. Scharf and Westcott, *History of Philadelphia*, vol. 3, 1906–7.

75. *Public Ledger*, 14 Jan. 1853; Taylor, " 'Philadelphia in Slices' by George Foster," 35–36; Johnson, *Policing the Urban Underworld*, 84–5; Laurie, *Working People of Philadelphia*, 58–59; Charles Godfrey Leland, *Memoirs* (New York, 1893), 216–20; Wainwright, *Diary of Sidney George Fisher*, Aug. 8, 1841, 122; Greenberg, *Cause for Alarm*, 3. Greenberg has shown that volunteer fire companies in other cities had greater class and ethnic diversity than those in Philadelphia and New York. Firemen embraced a shared masculinity rather than competing class interests, identifying themselves first and foremost, she writes, "as manly men," who viewed fire companies as "a masculine brotherhood." "Gender, and not class, is the key to understanding the internal order of the volunteer fire department" (9).

76. Elliott J. Gorn, *The Manly Art: Bare-Knuckle Prize Fighting in America* (Ithaca, 1986), 81–97, 129–47.

77. David R. Roediger, *The Wages of Whiteness: Race and the Making of the American Working Class* (London, 1991), 136.

78. Philadelphia had "a semi-private, semi-public militia system," with the majority of poor laboring white men forced to muster in public units twice a year, whereas men who joined volunteer companies resembling private clubs (usually the wealthy and aspiring middle class) accrued prestige by displaying their uniforms at public ceremonies and drilling more frequently. African Americans were excluded from both parts of the militia system. Susan G. Davis, *Parades and Power: Street Theatre in Nineteenth-Century Philadelphia* (Philadelphia, 1986), 51–58.

79. Dennis Clark, *The Irish in Philadelphia: Ten Generations of Urban Experience* (Philadelphia, 1973), 35; Michael H. Kane, "The Irish Lineage of the 69th Pennsylvania Volunteers," *Irish Sword* 18 (1991): 185–87; Kenneth Moss, "St. Patrick's Day Celebrations and the Formation of Irish-American Identity, 1845–1875," *JSH* 29 (1995): 125–48; Davis, *Parades and Power*, 61, 65–72; Noel Ignatiev, *How the Irish Became White* (New York, 1995), 23, 74, 141–43.

80. George Potter, *To the Golden Door: The Story of the Irish in Ireland and America* (Boston, 1960), 473–98; Robert Ryal Miller, *Shamrock and Sword: The Saint Patrick's Battalion in the U.S.-Mexican War* (Norman, Okla., 1989), 9.

81. Lee Benson, *The Concept of Jacksonian Democracy* (Princeton, 1961), 321–24.

82. Oliver MacDonagh, *The Emancipist: Daniel O'Connell, 1830–47* (New York, 1989); Potter, *To the Golden Door*, 387–404; McCaffrey, *Irish Catholic Diaspora in America*, 138–44; Miller, *Emigrants and Exiles*, 3–8, 240–49.

83. Gilbert Osofsky, "Abolitionists, Irish Immigrants, and the Dilemmas of Romantic Nationalism," *AHR* 80 (1975): 889–912; Ignatiev, *How the Irish Became White*, 6–31; Roediger, *Wages of Whiteness*, 134–37, 140–44; Baker, *Affairs of Party*, 212–58; John Binns et al. to Daniel O'Con-

nell, Feb. 2, 1838, in *The Correspondence of Daniel O'Connell* ed. Maurice R. O'Connell, vol. 6 (Dublin, 1973–1980), 128–30; the text of the Address can be found in the *Liberator*, 10 Sept. 1841.

84. Baker, *Affairs of Party*, 177–80, 243–49.

85. "The Memory of the Dead: A Repeal Song," *Public Ledger*, 14 June 1843.

86. Harry C. Silcox, *Philadelphia Politics from the Bottom Up: The Life of Irishman William Mc-Mullen, 1824–1901* (Philadelphia, 1989), 35–49.

87. *Irish American*, 6 Jan. 1850; Ignatiev, *How the Irish Became White*, 41–42; Dennis Clark, "Urban Blacks and Irishmen: Brothers in Prejudice," in *Black Politics in Philadelphia*, ed. Miriam Ershkowitz and Joseph Zikmund II (New York, 1973), 15–30; Carl Wittke, *The Irish in America* (Baton Rouge, 1956), 125–26; Max Berger, "The Irish Emigrant and American Nativism as Seen by British Visitors, 1836–1860," *PMHB* 70 (1946): 148; L. Perry Curtis, Jr., *Apes and Angels: The Irishman in Victorian Caricature* (Washington, D.C., 1971); Leon F. Litwack, *North of Slavery: The Negro in the Free States, 1790–1860* (Chicago, 1961), 164.

88. Frederick Douglass wondered on several occasions "why a people who so nobly loved and cherished the thought of liberty at home in Ireland could become, willingly, the oppressors of another race here." Quoted in Albon P. Man, Jr., "The Irish in New York in the Early Eighteen-Sixties," *Irish Historical Studies* 7 (1950): 97–98.

89. Roediger, *Wages of Whiteness*, 147–49; Ignatiev, *How the Irish Became White*, 110–19; "The Irish Emigrant's Lament," in *Irish Emigrant Ballads and Songs*, ed. Robert L. Wright (Bowling Green, Oh., 1975), 505.

90. Madeleine Hooke Rice, *American Catholic Opinion in the Slavery Controversy* (New York, 1944), 79.

91. Alexander Saxton, "Blackface Minstrelsy and Jacksonian Ideology," *AQ* 27 (1975): 3–28; Roediger, *Wages of Whiteness*, 147–49; Baker, *Affairs of Party*, 212–58; Eric Lott, *Love and Theft: Blackface Minstrelsy and the American Working Class* (New York, 1995); William J. Mahar, *Behind the Burnt Cork Mask: Early Blackface Minstrelsy and Antebellum American Popular Culture* (Urbana, 1999); W. T. Lhamon, Jr., *Raising Cain: Blackface Performance from Jim Crow to Hip Hop* (Cambridge, Mass., 1998). In the summer of 1844, between the violent riots in Kensington and Southwark, blackfaced performers known as the Congo Minstrels played out skits entitled "Negro Dandies of the North" and "Slaves of the South" at the Summer Theatre on Arch Street in Philadelphia; *Public Ledger*, 22 June 1844.

92. Lott, *Love and Theft*, 52–54, 71; Davis, *Parades and Power*, 103–09; Roediger, *Wages of Whiteness*, 104–10.

93. Jay Rubin, "Black Nativism: The European Immigrant in Negro Thought, 1830–1860," *Phylon* 39 (1978): 193–202; *Public Ledger*, 3 May 1844; Hunter, "Before Pluralism," 19; *National Era*, 21 Oct. 1847. Frederick Douglass's newspaper declared that there was never "a meaner, more profligate or despicable faction" than Pennsylvania's nativist party. *North Star*, 30 Nov. 1849. Tyler Anbinder, *Nativism and Slavery: The Northern Know Nothings and the Politics of the 1850s* (New York, 1992) is a terrific study of white nativist politics, arguing that the Know Nothings presented themselves as an antislavery party; yet African Americans are completely absent from Anbinder's book.

94. Billington, *Protestant Crusade*, 90–117; Jenny Franchot, *Roads to Rome: The Antebellum Protestant Encounter with Catholicism* (Berkeley, 1994), 112–61; Susan M. Griffin, "Awful Discourses: Women's Evidence in the Escaped Nun's Tale," *PMLA* 111 (1996): 93–107.

95. Early in the tale, Maria is led astray by a man she hardly knows, who seduces and marries her before she can learn of his true character. Concealing her marriage and returning to the nunnery, she finds herself, like the fallen women in many seduction novels, in the equivalent of a brothel, where she no longer has control over her own body. Readers could also easily consider Catholicism itself, or the priests, to be her real seducers. And like all seduction narratives, Maria concludes with a moral lesson to protect other young women from falling into the seducer's snares. A summary of the typical plot of a seduction novel can be found in Cathy N. Davidson, *Revolution and the Word: The Rise of the Novel in America* (New York, 1986), 89–109, 136–50; Elizabeth Barnes, *States of Sympathy: Seduction and Democracy in the American Novel* (New York, 1997), 40–73. For imprisonment and captivity themes in Monk's narrative, see Franchot, *Roads to Rome*, pt 2. Fi-

nally, Maria also depicts her escape as the work of a protective mother, as a work of virtuous sentimental domesticity. On this domestic fiction and women readers, see Jane Tompkins, *Sensational Designs: The Cultural Work of American Fiction, 1790–1860* (New York, 1985); Mary Kelley, *Private Woman, Public Stage: Literary Domesticity in Nineteenth-Century America* (New York, 1984); Nina Baym, *Woman's Fiction: A Guide to Novels by and about Women in America, 1820–1870* (Ithaca, 1978).

96. *Awful Disclosures of Maria Monk* (New York, 1836; facsimile ed., Hamden, Conn., 1962), 25–26, 49, 99, 230–31.

97. *Awful Disclosures of Maria Monk*, 82–83, 164–66, 170; *Six Months in a Convent; or, The Narrative of Rebecca Theresa Reed* (Boston, 1836), 8–11; *Address of the Board of Managers of the American Protestant Association*, 37–38; Reese, "Romanism and Liberty," 140; Franchot, *Roads to Rome*, 119.

98. *The Protestant Banner*, 17 June 1842; 15 Dec. 1842; 4 May 1843; *Awful Disclosures of Maria Monk*, 27, 29, 41–42, 124–25; Franchot, *Roads to Rome*, 121–26; Karen Halttunen, *Confidence Men and Painted Women: A Study of Middle-Class Culture in America, 1830–1870* (New Haven, 1982); Michel Foucault, *The History of Sexuality: An Introduction*, vol. 1 (New York, 1978), 17–21, 58–64.

99. Reese, "Romanism and Liberty," 132; *The Sons of the Sires: A History of the Rise, Progress, and Destiny of the American Party* (Philadelphia, 1855), 30; *Public Ledger*, 11 June 1844; *An Alarm to Heretics* (Philadelphia, 1854), quoted in Hunter, "Before Pluralism," 30.

100. Nancy Lusignan Schultz, *Fire and Roses: The Burning of the Charlestown Convent, 1834* (New York, 2000); Joseph G. Mannard, "The 1839 Baltimore Nunnery Riot: An Episode in Jacksonian Nativism and Violence," *Maryland Historian* 11 (1980): 13–23; Mary Ewens, *The Role of the Nun in Nineteenth-Century America* (New York, 1978), 145–61. On brothel riots, see Timothy J. Gilfoyle, *City of Eros: New York City, Prostitution, and the Commercialization of Sex, 1790–1920* (New York, 1992), 76–88.

101. David Brion Davis, "Some Themes of Counter-Subversion: An Analysis of Anti-Masonic, Anti-Catholic, and Anti-Mormon Literature," *Mississippi Valley Historical Review* 47 (1960): 205–24; Elliott J. Gorn, "'Good-Bye Boys, I Die a True American': Homicide, Nativism, and Working-Class Culture in Antebellum New York City," *JAH* 74 (1987): 397; Franchot, *Roads to Rome*, 100.

102. George Lippard, *The Quaker City; or, The Monks of Monk Hall: A Romance of Philadelphia Life, Mystery, and Crime* (Philadelphia, 1845; reprint, Amherst, 1995), 46–49, 53, 55–56, 111, 115–16, 121, 227. Lippard had also been a Democratic Party newspaperman, critical of reform and Whig politics.

103. *American Woman*, 12 Oct. 1844.

Epilogue

1. *Thirty-Sixth and Final Annual Report of the Philadelphia Female Anti-Slavery Society* (Philadelphia, 1870), 28–29, 4, 33.

2. *Thirty-Sixth and Final Annual Report of the Philadelphia Female Anti-Slavery Society*, 22, 37; *A Memorial of Sarah Pugh: A Tribute of Respect from Her Cousins* (Philadelphia, 1888), 115, 118; Rosalyn Terborg-Penn, *African American Women in the Struggle for the Vote, 1850–1920* (Bloomington, Ind., 1998), 24–35, 47–48, 62–64. On abolitionists during and after the Civil War, see James M. McPherson, *The Abolitionists Legacy: From Reconstruction to the NAACP* (Princeton, 1975); Lyde Cullen Sizer, *The Political Work of Northern Women Writers and the Civil War, 1850–1872* (Chapel Hill, 2000).

3. Elizabeth Cady Stanton et al., *History of Woman Suffrage*, vol. 2 (New York, 1881–1922), 353–55; Nell Irvin Painter, *Sojourner Truth: A Life, A Symbol* (New York, 1996), 220–33.

Index

293